# STORYTIME *in* INDIA

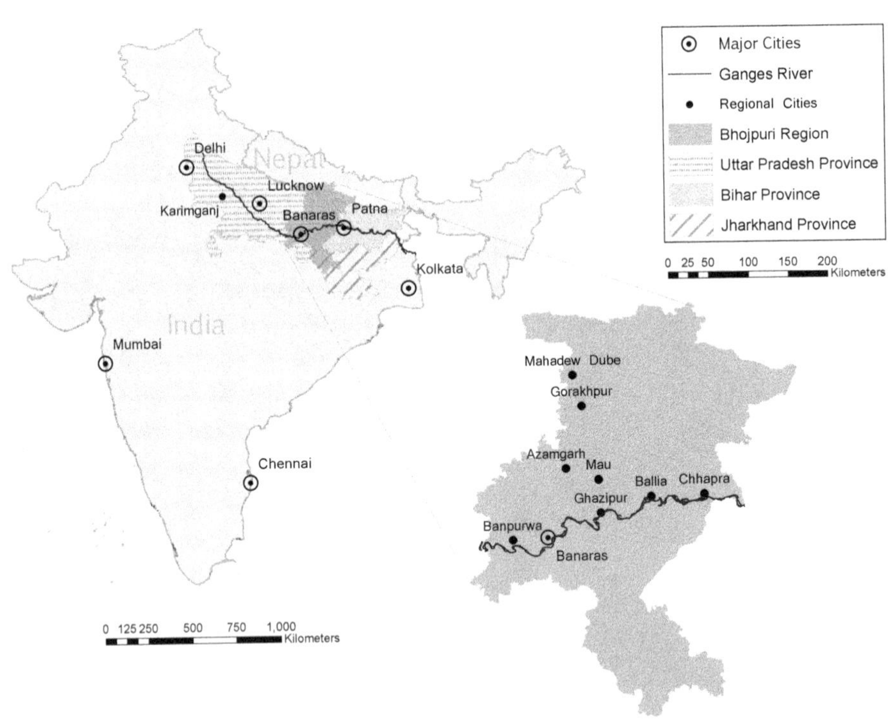


Map of India and Nepal, showing the Bhojpuri Region. *By Jordan Blekking.*

# STORYTIME *in* INDIA

*Wedding Songs, Victorian Tales, and the Ethnographic Experience*

HELEN PRISCILLA MYERS
*and* UMESH CHANDRA PANDEY

INDIANA UNIVERSITY PRESS

*This book is a publication of*

Indiana University Press
Office of Scholarly Publishing
Herman B Wells Library 350
1320 East 10th Street
Bloomington, Indiana 47405 USA

iupress.indiana.edu



*Manufactured in the United States of America*

Cataloging information is available from the Library of Congress.

ISBN 978-0-253-04162-3 (hardback)
ISBN 978-0-253-04163-0 (paperback)
ISBN 978-0-253-04165-4 (ebook)

1 2 3 4 5 24 23 22 21 20 19

*To the memory of our mothers,*
*Elsie Phillips Myers Stainton*
*Atarpyari Pandey*

# CONTENTS

## ACKNOWLEDGMENTS

MANY PEOPLE HELPED US ALONG THE JOURNEY TO CREATE THIS BOOK. First of all, we would like to thank all the women of villages across eastern Uttar Pradesh and western Bihar who gave freely of their time, their singing, and their art and who hosted us and prepared feasts for us as we visited their villages. How many cups of tea were offered with such kindness? A special thank-you goes to the many brides and bridegrooms and their parents who kindly allowed us to enter their homes to document the most intimate moments of their family weddings and to record on audio and video tape their family women singing wedding songs. In this age of Trump, I reflect on their essential decency and courtesy and generosity with longing.

This book would not have been possible without the gracious help of Gangajali, the extraordinary singer from Ballia in eastern Uttar Pradesh. Herein her story is told. There, tucked in a villagelike corner of a most humble Ballia neighborhood, we found her with ease as everybody in the district town seemed to have heard of her great talent. She sat with us for endless hours in the exhausting heat of Indian summertime, singing the songs she loved. Mostly, to accommodate the sensitive Schoeps condenser stereo microphone, we turned the overhead fan off during each song. Together we endured the sweat and oppressive heat that often enough nearly overcame us as we recorded song after song. Umesh and I promised Gangajali that her songs would be preserved in important archives in India and in the United States. And we promised to write a book about her, her songs, and her rather amazing courage in facing life's challenges, a story told below.

Many thanks go out to our very first host in an Indian village, Ram Sagar Singh of Banpurwa village, Banaras. A professor of chemistry at Banaras Hindu University, he helped us to record both men's and women's songs in Banpurwa. It was an exciting start to our research work together. Over the years, Ram Sagar has become a fast friend. His family graciously allowed us to live with him, and they prepared feast after feast of wonderful food for us and endless cups of *deshi chai*.

A special thanks goes out to Dr. Shubha Chaudhuri, graduate of Jawaharlal Nehru University, New Delhi, who introduced me to Umesh in 1986 and who has supported our work for thirty-three years now. Shubha is head of the Archives and Research Centre for Ethnomusicology, Gurgaon, India. This unique archive is part of the American Institute of Indian Studies and is designed especially to copy the recordings of visiting scholars, ethnomusicologists, as they depart from India at the end of their fieldwork. Shubha and her helpers at ARCE have achieved amazing feats of archival work, often in an incredible rush, as donors wait for their homebound flights. Profound thanks to you, Shubha, for your friendship, for all those lunches, and for the "Remembered Rhythms" tour, which took me with my Trinidadian East Indian group, d'Bhuyaa Saaj, back to their motherland to play and dance chutney in the major cities of India. You and the Archive have always been there for me. Shubha, you are an amazing lady of action, and you do make the impossible happen.

Alan Burdett, Director of the Archives of Traditional Music, Indiana University, has faithfully helped me to preserve digitally the hundreds of recordings I made in India and islands beyond over the last forty-five years. This great archive holds the original tapes from this research as well as the documentation.

I would like to thank my sons for their generous support of my work over the past three decades. They understand what makes me happy, so when I announce out of the blue that I am going to India next week, my twins, Sean and Adam Woolford, take it in stride as life as normal. They arrange rides for me at ungodly hours from Bristol, CT, to JFK, and they bring me back home on the return. My oldest son, Ian Woolford, who teaches Hindi language and literature at La Trobe University, Melbourne, has been an immense resource in helping me understand the political scene in present-day India. Ian has also been faithfully keeping me up to date about the developing scene on the ground in India—from Dadri to JNUSU and the recent arrests for "sedition."

Their father, recording engineer Bob Woolford, has organized a kit of the best hi-fi equipment on earth for every trip, beginning in 1977—helping me transition from open reel and cassette to DAT to wav. This book would have not been possible without his continuous help. I am particularly grateful to him for allowing me to record with his Schoeps condenser microphones and for teaching me their proper use. He also reengineered the cassette recording that Umesh made of Ram Sarup so that we were able to translate it. At proof stage, Bob read the entire proof aloud so that I could check it against copy—every word, every period, every italic, every open or close parentheses. Most of all, he patiently edited the audio files for the 111 songs for the website that accompanies this book, removing the sounds of clattering teacups, rickshaw bells, and slamming doors. For this and all the other, I thank him.

Umesh and I have dedicated this book to our mothers. My mother, the late Elsie Phillips Myers Stainton (1911–2007), was an amazing woman who raised my brother, the author Jim Myers, and me single-handedly after the untimely death of our father, aged forty-nine, in 1955. She poured love on us and supported us on every journey that life took us on. She instilled in us the love of knowledge, of writing, of discovery, and of adventure. She introduced me to the East Indians of Trinidad and joined me in Trinidad and also on an Indian tour in the late 1960s, when we spent lovely weeks together in Srinigar. Managing editor of the Cornell University Press, she and I had the pleasure of sharing our work as she taught me how to edit. Together we forged ahead in our respective fields, always reading and editing each other's work. The immense grief that I experienced in August 2007 is discussed in the pages that follow. Hey, Mom, this storybook is for you.

"My mother was very simple," Umesh explains. "She never went to school. But she could write her name. She could write the alphabet. She learned that at home. Her mother died when she was six months old. And she was raised by her older sisters, who lived in her mother's home with her husband. She married my father when she was eleven years old. Her father died soon after her wedding.

"My mother used to work morning to night—cooking, cleaning, whatever jobs are carried out Behind Mud Walls in northern India. My oldest sister died at an early age, so it was important to celebrate the birthday of the next child, which happened to be me. My nose was punched on the right-hand side (as with women of India). My birthday used to be celebrated according to the lunar calendar. It was carried out until I was married. My mother had a needle and a string in it so every year she tied another knot in it. But the string was lost over the years. But we kept celebrating my birthday up to my marriage. It was impossible to tell my real birthday. I am six months older than one of my uncles, and the school certificate shows me six months younger than him.

"My mother loved me very much. She loved me so much that she used to say, 'Oh, Umesh, what will you do if I die now?' and I didn't know what to say. And she was smiling to hear my answer. She never knew the effect of these words on my brain. When she was about to die, I reminded her twice, 'Mother, when I was a child, you used to say these words to me.' When I said this the second time, she replied, 'I never knew, Umesh, that you were so hurt.'"

Funding for this project was generously supplied by the National Endowment for the Humanities and the Fulbright Foundation. Additional academic and financial support was provided by the American Institute of Indian Studies, the Wenner Gren Foundation, the British Academy, and the American Philosophical Society. We would like to offer our profound gratitude to these organizations for believing in our work.

Many, many thanks are due to the anthropologist Professor Don Brenneis of the University of California, Santa Cruz, to the ethnomusicologist and tabla player Professor James Kippen, University of Toronto, and to Dr. Jay Pillay, himself an "overseas Indian immigrant," now US citizen, who hails from South Africa. This book depended on the encouragement of these top scholars. They have supported this work from its very inception and have supported our new and different approaches to studies in ethnomusicology.

Many scholars over the years have supported our mission to place Umesh in the role of author. These include Professor Charlotte Frisbie (Southern Illinois University), Professor Anthony Seeger (UCLA), Professor Krister Malm

(Stockholm), the late Professor John Blacking (Queen's University, Belfast), my mentor, Dr. Peter R. Cooke (Edinburgh), and the late Professor Nazir Jairazbhoy (UCLA). The work of these visionary scholars, in addition to their personal support, provided an inspiration for Umesh and me from year to year. And these individuals lifted up our spirits throughout the decades as we ventured forth to make a transition from "the village informant" and "the research assistant" to "the village author."

Janice Frisch was our champion at Indiana University Press, helping smoothly guide the book to production with professional attention to the tiniest details and also protecting the grand sweep of the entire story. She expressed interest after having had the proposal for only twelve hours, giving Umesh and me the courage to press on to completion. It was a true meeting of the minds. Darja Malcolm-Clarke and Jamie Armstrong, project managers, saw the book through production. Darja supported me through production, and we exchanged lively letters that kept me pressing on. And she read the proofs, a true friend of the author. Kate Schramm dealt with so many necessary forms and checked everything. Rhonda E. Vander Dussen and the entire marketing department helped with the book blurb. Jordan Blekking kindly engineered the map. Jennifer Witzke designed the cover and created the design, using those very few colors and swirls in Gangajali's sari to make something lovely. Jennifer went on to lend those feminine graces to the design of the text, with elegant curls and flourishes. I am touched that she could create the very beautiful section ornament from an inexpensive polyester sari. Gangajali would have been so pleased. Compositor Tony Brewer made it all happen on the pages, one after another.

My deep thanks go to my mentor, Dr. Peter R. Cooke, at the University of Edinburgh, Scotland. He has never failed to remind me of the joy of music, especially as understood through deep listening. His transcriptions from sound to Western notation (often supported by unconventional notation) are unmatched in our field. The hours he devoted to me while I was writing my doctoral dissertation and his lessons about music and about life itself have enriched all aspects of my experience.

I have reserved my deepest and warmest thanks for my brother, Jim Myers, who over the years never failed to ask, "How's that book of yours coming along." We tread together along the footprints of our parents, Elsie Phillips Myers Stainton and Henry Alonzo Myers, and Jim always aims our focus on True North.

## LIST OF SONGS AND ACCESSING THE AUDIO FILES

Audio materials are available for this volume and can be viewed online at **https://purl.dlib.indiana.edu/iudl/media/296w925k2c.**

Information and links for each individual entry follow.

# STORYTIME
# *in* INDIA

# PROLOGUE

THIS IS A BOOK OF STORIES. TRADITIONAL INDIAN VILLAGE STORYtelling typically takes the form of a story within a story (and even within another story and another), told over several nights as village farmers guard their crops. This format guides the structure of this book. Some of these stories are very short but very meaningful. Others are longer narratives and set the scene for some of the other stories. So let's begin.

Once upon a time, *ek samay ki baat hai*, there was an Indian farmer named Umesh Pandey. And once upon a time, there was an American scholar named Helen Myers. Despite their many differences, they were a perfect match. This is the story of their relationship and their research together.

The Indian farmer and elder brought stories from his village. And the American scholar brought her stories from the West. For thirty-three years, they shared these stories as they traveled all around Uttar Pradesh and Bihar, India, collecting songs and stories.

During their research, Helen had the idea of reading another story, *The Eustace Diamonds*, by Anthony Trollope, to Umesh. A deceptively lighthearted tale from the era of British colonialism in India, it is Helen's favorite book, and she thought he would like it. Umesh loved *The Eustace Diamonds*. Soon, he took over the job of reading, and Helen listened. They loved storytime. She wondered how he would interpret this classic novel. By the end, he said that it was the most wonderful book and that Anthony Trollope was a noble author.

Trollope has an important role in this story. Umesh's comments on the chapters of *The Eustace Diamonds* force us to confront the white colonial and postcolonial presence in India. For Western scholars, this presence is always the elephant in the room. Umesh and Helen decided to put the colonialist front and center in *Storytime in India*. Colonialism and postcolonialism are not a subtext here. They are the text.

Umesh's commentary on the passages of *The Eustace Diamonds* violently interrupts the ethnographic flow of the story with thoughts of the colonial hold over India. Although *The Eustace Diamonds* is an engaging story of a vain young woman, of pairs of lovers, of greed and jewels (and an absurd subplot about the "Sawab of Mygawb"), it has been included here not only because it is a pleasant story but also to bring forth our collective memories of Thomas Babington Macaulay's "Minute on Indian Education" (1835), the Indian Rebellion of 1857, the Jallianwala Bagh massacre of 1919, and more—much, much more.

Throughout the book, the reader will notice how Umesh helped Helen in every situation she faced in India. He would arrange a big bed for her and a little bed for himself. He ordered the best sponge mattress for her and had a simple cotton mattress for himself. Try as she might, there was very little she could do to change or reverse this situation. She believes in a fair world for all, yet there she was, in India, where she was constantly confronted with the legacy of the colonial past. Was it fair?

At the heart of this storybook, there is another story—told in song—by a dear friend, Gangajali, who lived in Ballia in eastern Uttar Pradesh. We spent much time with her from 1989 to 1990. As she was a great singer, dancer, and dramatist, she agreed to participate with us in documenting the Bhojpuri Indian wedding in Ballia. She understood that these recordings would be preserved in great archives. Every song that she sang told a story. She was unique in our experience in that she was able to sing all the songs of the Indian wedding, from start to finish, boy's side and girl's side both, without losing her place or getting distracted. And she could explain her songs.

We all loved those afternoons together. Gangajali would finish her cleaning job at the clothes store and gladly join us for tea and snacks in the Hotel Sarang, Ballia. We would laugh and talk. But when we got down to the business of singing, she would be very serious. She was a Meistersinger. Song was her devotion and her profession. Now these tape recordings have been copied by the Archives and Research Centre for Ethnomusicology (ARCE) in Gurgaon, India. The Indiana University Archives of Traditional Music (ATM), Bloomington, Indiana, which also holds the original quarter-inch open-reel tapes in climate-controlled vaults, has digitized them. The four thousand pages of documentation of the Gangajali tapes are also housed in the Indiana ATM. It is our sincerest hope that young scholars of the future may enjoy delving further into this marvelous collection, which extends around the Bhojpuri diaspora—to Trinidad, Guyana, Mauritius, and Fiji—as well as throughout eastern Uttar Pradesh and western Bihar.

We have included Gangajali's entire repertory of 111 Bhojpuri wedding songs that she sang in 1989, translated into English. We have included Gangajali's explanations of these songs as well as Umesh's interpretations of them. The recordings of these songs, in Bhojpuri, have been posted online for those readers who are interested—for pleasure, to hear the tunes, and to feel close to Gangajali (see List of Songs and Accessing the Audio Files). Quotations from Gangajali have been translated from Bhojpuri to English. Umesh's remarks are in his original English as are those of Helen.

Toward the end of our work on this book, Umesh told Helen the story of Nal and Motini from his village, Karimganj. In fact, it is *Dhola*, a sung epic. He rushed to tell her this story because, after listening to the final lines of *The Eustace Diamonds*, he discovered a connection of his story of Motini with Lady Eustace and with Gangajali.

Why so many stories? Because humans are storytelling animals. We turn our own lives into stories. Stories connect us as a human family through all time. As the novelist Cormac McCarthy says, "Things separate from their stories have no meaning. They are only shapes. Of a certain size and color. A certain weight. When their meaning has become lost to us they no longer even have a name. The story on the other hand can never be lost from its place in the world for it is that place" (*The Crossing*, 84).

This is a book to enjoy. We hope it suggests new approaches in ethnomusicology, for we firmly believe that our first goal as scholars—in India or elsewhere—is to seek out local authors who wish for an audience for their thoughts. Colonialism must end in all its manifestations. Our new job now is to listen carefully as people explain their own lives.

So please sit back and enjoy a little journey through time and space.

It's a journey to India.

It's storytime.

INTRODUCTION

# UMESH EXPLAINS STORYTIME

*In our New Delhi apartment after packing my bags, March 31, 2014, the morning of my flight back to the United States*

"Storytime in India is at night when people go to bed," Umesh explained. "They are in their beds, and one person tells a story. So many people are sleeping just around and around. It is wintertime. At night we cannot see each other, so the listener makes the sound *hun, hun*. It tells the storyteller that the person is awake and listening to him. These stories are usually told by men. Stories are both long and short. They sometimes go for two hours, sometimes for only one hour. It depends on the length of the story.

"In olden times farmers used to be at the threshing place for their wheat or barley, and they slept far away from their houses. There were several men who could tell the story, but one of them was the best, and he was asked to tell the story. The big saying was 'tell the story so we can pass the night' (*Ek baat kaho jisase raat katie*). This saying is very very nice. Inside the story, two persons like to sleep, they want to be remain awake, so they say, *Ek baat kaho jisase raat katie*. The sky is dark, but dense stars are shining.

"So, a story might begin from here. In this story, suppose two people went far away by horse. They had to stay somewhere that was not a safe place, so they had to stay awake. So to keep their horses, or whatever they had, what keeps them awake? Only a nice story. Then one person begins to tell another story. It is a story within a story. Somebody is telling about a king and his friend. The king's son is going far away, and at night they had to stay somewhere, so someone had to tell a story. In the story, they are suffering so many things along the way. It is evening, so in the story they have to rest. So the stories have already begun—going somewhere to do some business or something. Another story could begin from there, and finally, in fact, the farmers fall asleep. This story is not finished yet. The first story begins again as soon as they get up. As the new day begins, the first story begins again.

"In the summertime, we are in the threshing yard. It is summer, and it is so nice outside without mosquitoes. We sleep on the threshed chap with the seed inside it, and it is just like a mattress. So it is cool, without mosquitoes. A nice place to sleep. So people love it. This is also the time when a story begins.

"So there are two or three times when the stories are told. In the wintertime when people are sleeping in the house or in the summer in the threshing yard or also in winter when there is a big bonfire and people warm themselves, sit around the fire, and tell stories.

"Women tell stories at night. Kids ask their mother or grandmother to tell them a story. And also when children don't want to sleep, the mother or grandmother gathers them by saying, 'Oh, come on. I will tell you a story.' And they tell them funny stories to make them laugh—children's stories so they can enjoy and they can understand.

"So the reader of our book should imagine that they are story listeners, perhaps in an Indian village, and enjoy the charm of these stories."

ONE

# A FULBRIGHT GRANT TO BANARAS, INDIA

> It was admitted by all her friends, and also by her enemies—who were in truth the more numerous and active body of the two—that Lizzie Greystock had done very well with herself. We will tell the story of Lizzie Greystock from the beginning, but we will not dwell over it at great length, as we might do if we loved her. She was the only child of old Admiral Greystock, who in the latter years of his life was much perplexed by the possession of a daughter. . . . He had no particular fortune, and yet his daughter, when she was little more than a child, went about everywhere with jewels on her fingers, and red gems hanging round her neck, and yellow gems pendent from her ears, and white gems shining in her black hair.
>
> —Anthony Trollope, *The Eustace Diamonds* (1873)

### *At our apartment in Banaras, September 14, 2007*

My mother died on August 31, 2007—smack in the middle of my Fulbright grant to Banaras, India. I did manage to reach her Maryland bedside a couple of times to attend to her care, and then in time to say a long sad farewell before she faded. We buried her on September 11, 2007, in the East Lawn Cemetery, next to my father, and overlooking Cornell University, where they had both worked. On September 12, I left Ithaca and my family, and I flew back to India. Umesh met me in New Delhi at the Indira Gandhi International Airport.

Here, on this particular September afternoon, having just flown from New York to Delhi and then taken the twenty-four-hour train ride to Banaras, I was soothed by the opening words of *The Eustace Diamonds*, by Anthony Trollope. The book was on my bookshelf in our Banaras apartment. I had pulled it off the shelf to get my mind off my personal grief.

I loved Trollope, and I loved India. After thirty-three years of wonderful experiences and a few adventures, I had come to feel that India was a second home and that India was the most amazing country in the world. And I also had come to feel a personal responsibility for the violence that Western peoples, mainly white, had inflicted on Indians for centuries. But on this particular afternoon, I was just feeling lonely and lost.

But reading Trollope was comforting and familiar. And he was a big help to me in sorting out my feelings. *The Eustace Diamonds* is, indeed, wonderfully and delightfully told. Anyhow, there was solace for me in these several well-written familiar sentences. The flow, the detail, the humor, the sharp beginning. I dwelled on each phrase. These well-crafted lines were engaging. In my dark hour, I held on to this classic novel.

I have loved the writings of Anthony Trollope since my teenage years. I loved those well-formed sentences, seemingly written without effort. He wrote so fast, by the word and to the clock. Did he ever go back and revise them? His autobiography tells how this flow of prose was his gift. Contrapuntal lines twist and turn, weaving seamlessly from one thought to the next. The words flow and flow, and often they lead to absurd conclusions about the human condition. He is not Jane Austen. He is not the Brontë sisters, much though I love these earlier authors. His stories have real action plots—burglary, suicide, murder—and he is a comedian. The more carefully you read Trollope, the more you notice how carefully he builds to an ironic conclusion.

And then there is the exotic Victorian punctuation that I so love;—semi, dash, semi, dash. To me it looked like musical notation;—semi, dash. It brought comfort to the mind and reminded me of all the happy hours of escaping into another world with a copy of Trollope in my hand.

The Fulbright Committee paid for each award recipient to ship four boxes of books to their research site. This was just before the age of the Kindle. My boxes were sent to India, where I had been awarded a nine-month senior fellowship to join Umesh and study Indian village women's wedding songs. Our destination was Banaras, the holiest city of India, on the Ganges, the most sacred river of India;—the city and its river, where the faithful go to die. The four boxes included some light reading, but the bulk was classics by Trollope.

The mocking of India and India's nobility stands out in *The Eustace Diamonds*. That a contest between the Lords and the Commons should break out over such an insignificant matter as a "Sawab of Mygawb" is an absurdity. Trollope is making fun of British India. But he had traveled the world, first as an agent of the British General Post Office, and, later, on his own.

In fact, Mom and I had read Trollope out loud together many times. She, with her keen eye and ear, noticed details of style. Her favorite example was how Trollope inserted a proper name in reference to a "he" or a "she" when it was not entirely clear which "he" or "she" he was referring to. He simply put in a comma, and added the name, followed by a second comma.

TWO

# TOAST

*In our apartment, Banaras, September 14, 2007, evening*

Although I felt alone with my grief, Umesh was just across the way in his room, settling down after having escorted me home to Banaras, or, more properly, Varanasi, or, more historically, Kashi. When we finally reached our apartment, we were both exhausted from travel, and we were very grubby. Our little apartment had an Indian bathroom en suite off his room and a Western-style bathroom en suite for me. I mean to make it sound elegant. Well, it was, and it was not.

We both cleaned up and then had a light dinner. Toast and butter. That was our special treat. In kitting out our place, we had splurged on a bright red Western toaster that we discovered in Banaras in a tiny corner electronics shop, the kind that you had to pop up yourself when you figured the toast was done. Umesh liked making toast.

I had known Umesh since my first research trip to India in 1986. We met in the Archives and Research Centre for Ethnomusicology (ARCE) of the American Institute of Indian Studies (AIIS) in New Delhi. I was looking for somebody to aid me with my Hindi and to assist me in documenting women's songs in the village setting. Then, with the generous support of numerous grants, we had traveled for months and months to the remote and impoverished villages of eastern

Uttar Pradesh and western Bihar, searching for women's songs, especially songs for the Hindu wedding. And we found and recorded and documented many—so many—weddings.

A fast friendship formed between Umesh and me. He had just arrived on the steam train from Damoh, and, naturally, he was filthy. ARCE is the type of archive that really understands the needs of fieldworkers. Scholars arrive directly from rural areas and are offered a fresh clean towel and shower, then tea and biscuits, and, for the night, a clean and comfortable guesthouse with delicious home cooking. So Umesh went off to take a shower and change clothes.

This man soon became one of the very best friends of my life and a steady, trustworthy research colleague with uncanny village wisdom and powerful village emotions. He is a village elder and a farmer, a Brahman (Pandey), and he is impoverished despite his lovely village home and his beautiful fields. During our decades together, I've been pretty broke myself, so we were true equals.

His physical constitution is weak, and we spent many hours seeing doctors, local in the villages, in small towns, and in important hospitals—in fact, everywhere we went. He was usually sick, and his complaint was serious: breathing. Sometimes he just couldn't breathe. It was asthma and then more than asthma. For all the doctoring, we never really got a proper diagnosis. In Banaras in 2007, doctors at Heritage Hospital determined, through a battery of tests, that it was allergies—allergies to the most common substances found in an Indian village: dust, straw and hay, cow dung, mold, plus common foods such as water buffalo milk, cane sugar, wheat flour, ghee. The list went on and on. They made up special serums for him to inject daily to boost his immune system. It all made sense to me. And he and I had hope, really for the first time, that we might have found a cure.

But we had no refrigeration, which was essential for maintaining the serums. And then his reaction taking the very first dose was so violent that I had to rush him immediately back to Heritage Hospital, with his rescue inhaler in hand. He was incapacitated for several weeks, resulting from this single injection of the wonder cure. The serums expired, and we spoke of more tests and a new set of serums, milder ones that he could tolerate. But the months flew by. And he fell sick with malaria, which took a tremendous toll.

There were other problems—I would like to say too many to enumerate, but it was more a case of too many to treat. But the asthma was a daily problem. He suffered, and I expended a great deal of effort to ease his ills, given that we were in India—village India. When I brought him to the United States, some five times, he was upset about the cost of American doctors and drugs. In Mauritius, in 1996 and again in 1999, we found wonderful doctors. When we got together for the Festival of India in Stockholm in 1987, the top Swedish hospital treated him for free and cured him of hookworm.

In January 2016, Umesh had an acute heart attack at home in his village of Karimganj. I was at home in the USA. The family phoned me on Skype. And I could see that there he lay on his string cot in unendurable pain as the thick fog of January in North India had closed in for the night. It seemed that he might die before we could get him to a private cardiologist.

My son, Ian Woolford, who lives in Melbourne, sent out an appeal on Twitter for help. Thanks to the generosity and kindheartedness of Indian folk, Indian people from all over the world answered Ian's plea. The story was taken up by ETV in Lucknow and also by the editor of *The Hindu* newspaper in New Delhi. Before long, Ian received a message from the chief minister of Uttar Pradesh, the Honorable Akhilesh Yadav, who offered his good offices to help. With the assistance provided by so many private individuals, the press, the CM, and ETV television, it was possible to rush Umesh to the Heart Center, a first-class private hospital in Agra. After some months of tests and treatments, Umesh was released from the hospital. It was found that his blood pressure was a bit high, so Umesh bought a blood pressure machine to check this for himself.

Umesh recovered but remained weak for many months. The doctors had said that he suffered from a lack of oxygen in his body. During my November 2016 visit, India was wrapped in a cloud of pollution following the Diwali festival of lights. I could hardly believe the sounds coming from his lungs, a horrible, suffocating wheeze that I had never, ever heard before. When we reached Delhi, I bought a Philips air purifier for him and a nebulizer. After he took his first dose from the nebulizer, he suddenly sat up and announced, "My eyes are open!"

So Umesh and I sat in my room, munching on buttered toast. When the electricity was on, we hung out in my room because I had had an air conditioner installed. In fact, they had broken down the entire wall to install it—surprising to me. But that was the way it is done in India. It was locked carefully inside a metal cage, too high to reach (and steal) from the ground. I ran it with a remote control. I loved my air conditioner, but Umesh was suspicious of it out of the local fear of mixing hot and cold. It is considered dangerous to go from outside and the summer heat straight into an air-conditioned room. It is dangerous to drink hot coffee and eat yogurt for breakfast. Don't bathe before going to bed! These are basic beliefs of Indian villagers and city folk alike.

So, toast. He took on the task of buttering. He cut the slices into triangles, and we both ate. There was butter on our fingers and crumbs in my bed. I didn't mind. That was daily business as we didn't have a dining room table—or a dining room for that matter.

*In our Banaras apartment, September 15, 2007, morning*

In the morning, the milk arrived early. It was water buffalo milk, extremely rich and creamy—delicious and addictive. The milkman delivered it fresh every day. Umesh's milk-boiling ritual took about five minutes. Boiling and skimming and never letting it boil over onto our two-burner gas stove in our tiny kitchen—that was the job. Then he made *desi chai*—black Indian tea, spiced with ginger in the winter and cardamom in the summer. As it was September with the monsoon rains winding down, but not yet cold, we had cardamom on the morning of September 15. And toast. More buttered toast. We never tired of it. The bright red toaster.

You wouldn't think that they sold cheap Western-style sliced white bread in India, would you? But they do, and Indians love it. At the end of our lane, there was a small shop that sold white bread for ₹10 (15 cents) a loaf, along with some other simple treats that we had come to enjoy like Cadbury Dairy Milk chocolate bars and various flavors of spicy hot potato chips. The shopkeeper became our friend, and he would order extra bread for us. Umesh could also buy a Hindi newspaper there and keep us in touch with the outside world. No television, no radio, no Internet, no *Newsweek* or *Time*—the local paper was our contact with the outside world.

We lingered over breakfast, me in my pajamas, Umesh in his full-length saronglike *lungi* and T-shirt. Umesh would read to me from the newspaper. Some of the stories were so strange, they challenged the imagination. Of the most spectacular was one, purportedly from Germany, of doctors who were keeping alive a severed human head. There was a drawing showing the head with an expression of desperation. The head rested on a large plate, with electrodes attached to a machine—a box with dials. They were keeping him alive, even though he begged them (with his eyes, for he couldn't speak) to let him die. Oh my. The local news.

## INTERLUDE ONE

# LIZZIE GREYSTOCK

AFTER BREAKFAST, AND AFTER A LONG CHAT WITH UMESH, I WENT back to my Trollope. Chapter 1 was a whirlwind of action, a complete surprise. We are introduced to Lizzie, told of the demise of her father, the Admiral, and her moving in with her aunt, Lady Linlithgow. In the presence of her many cousins, Lizzie was in the habit of calling Lady Linlithgow a "termagant," "a vulturess," yet she was happy to take advantage of an offer of free room and board from her. Lady Linlithgow's objective, which she took as a duty, was to arrange a suitable marriage for Lizzie.

Lizzie was a liar, was vain, and was keen to marry for money. She had caught the eye of Sir Florian Eustace. But her jewels had been pawned, and she had a plan, laced with falsehood, to recover them. Before the engagement had been formalized, she went to Messrs. Harter and Benjamin to take out a loan to recover her jewels, claiming that she was of age (she was not) and that an engagement had been formalized (it had not). Knowing that Sir Florian Eustace was rich, Messrs. Harter and Benjamin agreed to the loan.

*"Those two little blemishes in her statement must be admitted. But it was true that Sir Florian Eustace was at her feet; and that by a proper use of her various charms—the pawned jewels included—she might bring him to an offer."*

And the jewels came back, as Lady Linlithgow observed—the ornaments, one by one.

Trollope's introduction of Sir Florian to the reader is abrupt and harsh:

*"The match with Sir Florian Eustace—for a match it came to be—was certainly very splendid. Sir Florian was a young man about eight-and-twenty, very handsome, of immense wealth, quite unencumbered, moving in the best circles, popular, so*

*far prudent that he never risked his fortune on the turf or in gambling-houses, with the reputation of a gallant soldier, and a most devoted lover. There were two facts concerning him which might, or might not, be taken as objections. He was vicious, and—he was dying."*

Jet lag slowly hit me, and I fell asleep.

Evening fell, and as I woke, I decided to read *The Eustace Diamonds*, at least a few pages, to Umesh. It seemed to me that these human qualities were possibly universal and that this great novel could just as well have been written about India.

I started again, right from the beginning, but Umesh grabbed the book and read it back to me.

"A girl, a beautiful girl who has jewelry she likes. She wants to show she is rich," Umesh explained. "She is rich because of jewelry. Otherwise she is poor. Her aunt is good in one way to perform her duties to take care of her niece in so many ways. But Lizzie doesn't like her and calls her 'vulturess'—who eats the flesh—and she tells her friends and cousins that she is a vulturess.

"She, Lizzie, loves tricking people," Umesh went on. "So she lies in several ways. She is tricking the lawyer, and the lawyer knows it. But anyhow she made him loan her money, and she got her jewelry back. And vulturess aunt couldn't know how she did it. The aunt searched everywhere, but she did not succeed to find the jewels. Lizzie's father had died, and Lizzie thinks she doesn't care about her father. It was just like some animal had died—only this was Lizzie's father!—so she keeps little little jewelry on, even though she was in mourning.

"For marriage she is eager to get some husband—like rich. But the author says her choice for a husband, well, he is vicious, and he is dying." Umesh laughed and said, "Better go for this very quick."

"Tell me about ornaments and India," I asked, thinking of Lizzie's gems.

"It is not only the girls who want these, it is men on the Earth. There are also exceptions on the Earth. In India, people have ornaments for several reasons. Village people don't understand that ornaments are worth currency. But they know that you can keep gold, and it will remain forever. You can spend money for small things, but if you buy gold, you are not selling this every day. But in emergency—illness, wedding, education—you can sell it for emergency, real emergency. It is a wise thing to have.

"Yes, there is a reason for these ornaments in India. In olden days, we had no banks. The gold, precious things were like banks. Villagers used to dig holes in the ground and hide them. They would put the gold and ornaments inside a metal pot and bury it. Sometimes lucky people in the village find these pots and find the gold of some man who died with his secret hiding place.

"Ornaments have many purposes. They let a person know how wealthy your family is. So this is the reason that ornaments are important in India.

“Also the ornaments, especially gold, make the Indian complexion beautiful. But Indian people must not put gold on their feet,” he cautioned. “It is bad luck. Only queens can do this. For simple people it is bad luck. Around the waist and above is good. The waist is the most precious place.” Umesh placed his hands around his waist as if he were protecting an unborn child.

THREE

# SETTING UP OUR APARTMENT IN BANARAS, 2007

*Looking back to the first day we arrived at our apartment in Banaras, 2007*

"When we arrived, the apartment was empty except two old *chauki*s," Umesh explained. "A *chauki* is a wooden cot. Most Indian cots are made of strings, made out of a kind of grass that is very thick, called *munj* grass. In the village, people take it and beat it to make it thin and take it and make very thick strings out of it. And some people weave these strings to the frame of the cot. But in Banaras, we didn't buy a string cot. In Banaras, I felt we needed two *chauki*s for nine months.

"String might break in a few months," Umesh advised. "I did not buy plastic ones because they are very uncomfortable. *Chauki* was the best choice. Easy to move from one place to another place, comfortable, and we also laid our things on the *chauki* instead of the ground—so many books and papers. The owner left two *chauki*s inside the house because he had no place to put them except outside of his house, where the climate could quickly ruin them. And we happily accepted to keep them and to use them.

"If he had told me this in advance, at least we would have not have bought two *chauki*s," Umesh said. "So we went to the carpenter where they make *chauki*s, and we saw and chose *chauki*s. For you, one biggish one and one smaller for me. For that time they were expensive, I thought. The wood was not good. We did not know what kind of wood that was. But we needed them for only nine to ten months, and we knew they would last that long.

"And we had two bicycle rickshaws to bring them back to our place—it was a house, but we tried to make it a home," Helen said. "Mine went ahead, and Umesh came behind. Umesh's *chauki* fell on the ground. In going, we looked like two giant turtles moving one after the other down the street. Somehow we arrived, with much difficulty."

"There was so much crowd on the street it was hard to pass," Umesh recalled in a bit of a huff. "Sometimes rickshaw, sometimes three-wheeler, bicycle, people walking on the road, crossing the streets. It was to cross the junction near Banaras Hindu University Road. You were laughing because you thought it would be great in a book."

"But your turtle broke in half, and I couldn't stop laughing."

"I believe Narayan (our friend and three-wheeler driver) was with us, because he led us to the *chauki* place, and he helped me to put the *chauki*s inside. Helen, you were doing nothing. You were just walking and laughing.

"I recall now that I was saying, I was telling to the rickshaw puller shift the *chauki* this way," Umesh said. "He said, 'Yes yes,' but he was not doing anything. He put his hand, but he did not do it. I said, 'No! It will fall down.' He said, 'No, no, it will not, it will not.' He held the rickshaw by the handles. I was holding the *chauki* by the back. But it was slipping, and I could not control it. And it fell.

"And Helen was having fun. And I was shouting at the rickshaw puller, 'I told you so! I told you so!' Narayan ran back to help me and the rickshaw puller, and Narayan got the *chauki* back on the rickshaw.

"The day we shifted *chauki*s into the apartment, Helen got the bigger one, and I got the smaller," Umesh said. "You needed that for your computer, books, and so forth, on the cot. Both were comfortable.

"We then went to the mattress shop," Umesh continued. "We saw, we checked, we saw, we checked several types of sponge. This sponge was for Helen's bed. We used Narayan to get it. We bought the best sponge. We paid and ordered it. We got it in the evening (we were still living in the Sandhya Guesthouse). And I am now resting on it as we talk in 2014." (We were in Karimganj at Umesh's home, enjoying these memories.) "The next day, after we bought this mattress, I believe we moved into our house."

"And when we got to our home, I wanted an Indian mattress too," I said. "So we went to the place where they have cotton, bed sheets, and puffed cotton."

"We bought fabric," Umesh said. "The fabric for one Indian mattress for me, and then you decided that you wanted an Indian mattress too—to go on top of your sponge. So we had one big one and one small one. We got them in the evening. We bought cotton for the mattresses and gave them to be puffed, stuffed, and stitched. We went to buy sheets and curtain cloth and had the curtains stitched for windows and doors because the windows were completely open.

"The next morning we went to the Bread of Life restaurant, had our tea and breakfast—croissants. And we bought some bread and butter there too. We bought mineral water and went back home.

"Then Narayan took us to the right shop to buy light bulbs. The three ceiling fans we bought a few days later. And soon we needed a battery because we were not getting enough electricity. There was a daily midday power cut from ten to two. Then we bought quite a big battery and stabilizer for charging the battery. The battery alone cost ₹10,000 ($147.00), so it was expensive. We wanted a stove and gas *chula*, gas cylinder for cooking. I chose for you a special cup for ₹175 ($2.50), but there was only one. It was yours. We didn't buy *thali* (large stainless-steel plates). We bought one big *tassla* (large bowl) to make dough—it is a stainless-steel pot. We had three glasses to take tea, *tasa* to cook chapattis, pots and pans for vegetables. We had one *karahai* for cooking vegetables. We still use it here at my home. My wife is glad to have it. Our cook wanted a pressure cooker. But we didn't buy that. We bought two plastic buckets and two or three plastic cups for morning showers. We bought three plastic wastebaskets because you insisted.

"And then we bought bookcases made out of bamboo. I had never seen this type before. They were cheap. The university was very close by, so students needed them and came and bought them from these vendors. You spotted them from the rickshaw and wanted them for your many books.

"There were cupboards in this house, so we used his cupboards," Umesh continued. "While we were buying mattresses, we bought four plastic chairs and one folding table that I used for transcription work. And we bought the red toaster. Also a rolling pin and *chakala* and *belan* (wooden cutting board and rolling pin) to make chapattis. And what else did we buy?"

"We bought spoons, forks, and knives—not too many, just enough," I said. "And I had the idea of buying god posters to decorate the walls. In front of the Diamond Hotel they were selling bright Technicolor posters of the Indian gods. I thought it would be good to have something holy to look at."

"Then we bought two clocks," Umesh said. "I was sent to buy them, and I bought one that had white plate outside and one was golden. Two days later, Helen said it jumps ten minutes ahead. Helen wanted me to change it. I didn't believe it! But finally you took my one and gave me your one. I set it to the right time, but suddenly next day it was ten minutes ahead. So I kept it, and finally it is here in Karimganj and hidden in some back room where it will not trouble anyone."

FOUR

# THE DAILY ROUTINE

*The next morning, Banaras, September 2007, after toast*

Neither Umesh nor I wanted to get to work the next day, the day after I had arrived home following my mother's funeral. I had serious jet lag, and Umesh was still exhausted from the two long train rides, Banaras–Delhi–Banaras, and the long wait in Indira Gandhi International Airport to meet my midnight flight. I had been gone for over a month to attend to my mother in her final hours. We had missed each other very much.

"Gangajali. It's time we did Gangajali," Umesh said.

Umesh loved these songs and this story, the story of the Hindu wedding, and he went straight to the cupboard on the floor by my bed. There were the twelve four-inch aging and dusty files that contained his Devanagari transcriptions of the Gangajali recordings. Approximately four thousand pages of transcriptions into Bhojpuri. This collection comprised the songs of the complete Bhojpuri wedding cycle and the explanation of the complete Bhojpuri wedding by Gangajali of Ballia.

An opera omnia.

These songs were an entire musical world and constituted a story, a long story that you will read in this book. Umesh hauled them out for me, and we looked through them. Dust flew everywhere. It was an immense task, and I suppose he was wondering, as was I, how we could ever translate four thousand pages of Bhojpuri songs.

INTERLUDE TWO

# SIR FLORIAN

THE NEXT DAY—EPISODE TWO. UMESH READ TO ME OF THE ENGAGEment of Lizzie to Sir Florian, their marriage, their travels, and his sudden death in Naples. As Sir Florian died, he knew what a woman he had married—that she only wanted his money and not his love. So, as Umesh was reading aloud, we escaped back into the story.

*"Lizzie read poetry well, and she read verses for him—sitting very near to him, almost in the dark, with a shaded lamp throwing its light on her book. He was astonished to find how sweet a thing was poetry. By himself he could never read a line, but as it came from her lips it seemed to charm him."*

And then he proposed marriage to Lizzie. The jewels, the pretty little face, the dimly lit room, the poetry. Sir Florian had been captured. Lizzie had prevailed. That she did not love him, there was no question. But to be Lady Eustace—that was a prize that came with many riches.

They married in haste due to his ill health, honeymooned at his castle in Scotland, and then made their way to Italy. It was on this trip that the bills from Mr. Benjamin began to arrive, big bills, little bills. Lizzie lied about the transactions with Mr. Benjamin, but Sir Florian knew the truth. Halfway through the winter, in Naples, brokenhearted and knowing well what a woman he had married, he died.

*"But, even in these early days, friends and enemies did not hesitate to say that Lizzie Greystock had done very well with herself; for it was known by all concerned that in the settlements made she had been treated with unwonted generosity."* So it was that Umesh learned about the "beautiful" people of England, back during the Raj, when the British ruled his country.

Umesh read slowly, lingering over the structure of each sentence. The ordering of the words was not quite what one might expect. It was difficult to read aloud, and the sound was musical. Likewise, the ordering of the words in Gangajali's Bhojpuri songs were not what an English speaker would expect. Verbs and nouns seemed to fall in all the wrong places, for that is the structure of the language. As with Trollope, it was intensely musical. I pondered. It was good to read great prose while doing translations and especially while writing. It opens the heart and mind to new thoughts. Maratha Nussbaum, in *Upheavals of Thought* (2001), describes how reading fiction enhances the human capacity for empathy. The sound of music flowed through the Trollope, informing the decisions involved in the Gangajali translations.

Umesh read Trollope's tale carefully. Then he spoke.

"First of all, we have arranged marriages, not love marriages in India. We do have some love marriages. But who would like to marry someone who is going to die so soon, because in India people don't like to marry the widower or divorced woman. It is very deep in them. I don't know why. People like to say that is a 'used up' woman, and they don't want their son to marry her. Sometimes people arrange marriages of their daughters or their sisters if the man is a widower and if he does not have a child and if the man is in a good position financially, or if he has a good business or a good job he gets married easily.

"But sometimes he has a daughter, and his wife died. Even then prospective brides' parents compromise to marry their daughter to the man because his daughter will get married, and she will go to her husband's home. If the woman died leaving a son behind, a daughter's parents think hundreds of times to arrange marriage to such a person. This boy, this child, is going to be a part of the family. There will always be enmity between the first wife's child and the children of the second wife. These are rival children. The second wife cannot give the kind of love to the first wife's son as she gives to her own. All mothers are not like the stepmother of Abraham Lincoln. She helped him to study. Although she was the stepmother, she gave him books.

"Here, in this story, this man is ill. He is explaining that he has a serious illness. First of all, the family of the groom will not like him to get married. Some girl will come soon and take the family property. Maybe some greedy people can make a decision to arrange this marriage to make themselves wealthy. So the control is from the girl's side over the boy's side family.

"The culture of India now is changing slowly. If any widow girl gets married without having children, her parents will arrange her marriage elsewhere. But things have changed in so many ways. If some man doesn't get married, they do get married with a widow woman. If the widow woman is qualified or rich, she also easily gets remarried. It happens now. Women were not working before. It was not so before. Indian village culture is slowly changing."

FIVE

# ARRANGING AN INDIAN WEDDING

*We are in Banaras at the Sandhya Guesthouse, 2006*

On a visit to India in 2006, Umesh and I had the opportunity to discuss the wedding practices of eastern India. We had attended and documented dozens of Bhojpuri weddings together. But I was so curious to learn how an arranged marriage was actually—well—arranged. Umesh had arranged the marriages of his two sisters and then of his younger brothers. In fact, I never met Umesh at a time when he *wasn't* arranging a marriage. When we first met in 1986, he was arranging the marriage of his younger sister, Rajini. In 2006, he had been searching for a bridegroom for his daughter Alka. Thus, he was a genuine expert on this topic. Basically, the arrangement has to do with negotiations between the father of the girl and the father of the boy. Each side makes demands. Through middlemen, both families conduct careful investigations of the other family. Reputation and social status are paramount. And money is the deciding factor. The father of the boy knows the worth of his son, and he will expect that amount of money to be "donated" by the father of the girl.

"To explain the Indian wedding, it is better to start from the girl's side," Umesh said. "Because the bride's side is the most important to talk about. There is so much work for her family to do. The boy's side begins only when the wedding begins, but the girl's side begins when she is born.

"These days it is considered very easy to know whether a girl is in the womb or a boy. And sometimes people have an opportunity to find out whether it is a girl or a boy. The government of India has made a law that pregnant women cannot have an ultrasound to learn about the gender of the child. So, as the girl appears in the world, the parents get worried that someday she has to leave their home to serve in her husband's home. So they begin to think to accumulate money to arrange her wedding in a proper, nice family. They don't do it. They begin to think about it. If it is their first child, and it is a girl, people are happy—they are not sad. Some people do get sadness, but usually they are happy. But one after another, if they keep getting girls, they get very concerned to raise them, then collect money to arrange their weddings.

"So it is also quite a big change from old traditions to the new traditions. I remember around thirty years ago, people used to say, well, 'Why educate a girl? She will belong to another family.' And girls had the least education or no education. But the boy was considered a family name carrier, so the parents gave him the best education they could. Also in olden times the groom's side never asked about the education of the girl who was going to be a bride in their family. They always asked, 'How much have you made up your mind to donate for your daughter?' They always say 'donation,' never 'dowry.' The bridegroom's family never says this word *dahej* (dowry), but it is always understood. So it was the first question. 'How much have you thought to donate?' It used to be the first question from the bridegroom's side to the girl's side. Thereafter the boy's side said, 'I shall bring so many people in the *barat* (party of groomsmen). The *barat* will be such and such big, and how many people can you take care of?' So the decision is made about the *barat* from both sides, the girl's side and the boy's side. The girl's side always asks for the least number of people in the *barat*, and the boy's side always asks for more people in the *barat*. If sometimes the bride's side is rich or proud, they say, 'Never mind, bring as many as you want to show off.'

"These days if a girl's father goes to search for a groom, the groom's parents ask first what is the education of the girl, the bride. There was no place for education thirty or forty years ago. Now, these days, what is the height of your daughter, what is her complexion, what subjects is she studying? If she has mathematics, science, biology, English—they are considered good subjects. The arts are not considered great subjects. So this is the priority people give to the girl's side. Thereafter the boy's family also considers what kind of occupation the girl's family has—businessman, serviceman, farmer, or whatever they are. This is for status.

"I had a chance to go with one person who was searching for a groom for his daughter. In a sense, he was a relative to the family where we went to see the boy. And the father was an officer in a government job. He said that he was not a 'dirt-digging family'—*matikor*. 'We are not a *matikor* people.' It means, 'We are not farmers.' But the girl's family didn't understand at all what he meant. But the father said, 'We will be in touch. I will let you know what will happen.'

"So he will invite, he will call. In one case, I explained to a girl's father that this marriage was to going to take place because he is an officer. He will arrange for his son the officer's girl. He is not thinking about the dowry, he is thinking about status, and money will come with the status. My friend visited there once again, and he kept hoping that he would be able to arrange this wedding with the help of money. But it didn't work out. The girl had an MA in sociology, and the boy had an MSC in physics and was working with a very good job at some airport. But the arrangement didn't work out. They wanted the status of the family. They didn't want any businessman or farmer. And this farmer was a businessman as well as a farmer.

"What does the boy's side expect from the girl's side? They want tall girls—not too tall. She should be as tall as the groom. They want a fair complexion, an Indian fair complexion. Ever since the demand has increased to get an educated bride. The mother is the first teacher of the child. If the mother is educated, she can take better care of her children, and also she can give the beginning of the education—alphabetical. She can read some books for the child before they go to school. It is easier for her to go to see the doctor if she is educated. If she is educated enough, she can get a job, so the earning comes from both sides. They can live a better life. On the other hand, suppose a woman is educated and she is a housewife, and her husband has a government job. Unluckily he dies. She can get a job in the same institution according to the law of the government. So she gets a pension and also gets a job. It means that she can raise her children—this helps. I have seen several people who have had this bad luck, and the bride is living a better life because of her good education. They are able to give a better education to their children.

"When we go to search for a groom, the groom's father wants to see the girl—whether she is as has been told. They can ask for her certificates and what percentage of marks she obtained in her schooling. So when all this is done, they say, 'We are agreed. How much will you spend for this wedding? We want such and such things. We want a bed, refrigerator, or we want a washing machine, TV, four-wheeler vehicle or two-wheeler vehicle. And this much cash. And thereafter I shall bring such a big *barat*. We want this and this variation of foods, *pan cobbler* to polish the shoes, *pan wallah*, tea stall, coffee stall, snack stalls, and food stalls.' On one side are the fat food stalls, and on the other side are the real food stalls.

"The girl's side has to decorate their house, arrange a place to take the *barat* and feed them, put up a tent, call a cooker to cook for them, arrange serving people, all this has to be arranged."

SIX

# THE SEARCH FOR A BOY

*Banaras, relaxing at the Sandhya Guesthouse, 2006*

"The girl's father does not find a groom in one picking," Umesh exclaimed. "Some people say no, other people say yes. Then the girl's father makes a search of the 'yes' people. He searches for the groom with height and a fair complexion. The mother wants a handsome groom. She says, 'If the groom is ugly, I'll fall in the well with my daughter. He must be handsome, healthy.' This is the mother's wish. Or she will say, 'I will suicide with my daughter if the groom looks ugly at my door.'

"The father sees it from a different angle. His angle is to see a better future for his daughter—a respectable family, well-off, educated, whether they want a girl or not—or whether they want only money. Are they hungry for money or for a person? Surely the girl's father wants to find a handsome groom. But handsome is the middle part for the father. The priority is the future of his daughter. She will not eat up the handsomeness. She cannot live by licking on it. If he is handsome but if he drinks and gambles, he is useless. If a person is short and well educated and dark, he will give my daughter a better life.

"Certainly, we think if the family is honorable, about their social reputation. If they are a thief, a dacoit, if they drink, if they gamble, if anything bad has happened in the family, if the sisters are married respectably, if the groom's father was married respectably, in all the family if the people were married respectably.

"The boy must have merits, I mean talent. Even though people make mistakes. Sometimes we believe, 'Oh, the family is rich, the family is big. They have a good reputation in society.' If they don't see the groom thoroughly without investigation, people make mistakes. If you don't see the character of the boy, only the family, it is not helpful. We sneak it out. We ask people, and people just tell. Village people—not one person, several people—there are so many ways to refuse. 'Oh, he is okay'—it means something is wrong. '*Tikh hii hai* (he is good enough)'—something is wrong. '*Tikh hai* (he is good)' means he is good. Sometimes a person is so powerful, they keep silent and don't say anything because they are afraid. Sometimes people make too much appreciation—be careful. Every step is difficult. People can make a mistake easily. It becomes like a poll about the boy. Out of ten, if two say no and eight say yes, it means that the boy is a good man.

"The middleman is the most important person in the whole wedding. Nothing is given to him, and he gets sworn at by both sides. Because something goes wrong from the boy's side, the girl's side swears at him. If something goes wrong on girl's side, the boy's side swears at him. He doesn't get paid. Mostly he is some relative or a village relative—a person in their caste.

"Big people may give a dowry like factories, or they establish a factory for their daughter, or a share in the factory—this is for big people. For small people, status is important. For the lower, simple people, they see the boy. We never mind if they are educated or not if they have enough land or if the boy is working somewhere, doing some job. His family can arrange a wedding. As they are not so rich, they cannot afford a vehicle. They give little things, or even they can give nothing. But they have to see what the groom is doing. These days everybody is looking for an employed bridegroom, whether he has money or not. Everybody wants an employed bridegroom. Or we see the situation of the family and imagine, 'Will he be able to get employed?' Especially, people are looking for a groom with a government job. A government job has a good salary and security. The groom can stay with his family, or they can get a house from the government, plus the social standard benefit of status. Nowadays private companies are giving more money than the government jobs, so people are also trying to look in the private sector. Government jobs include policeman, court, agriculture department, railway department, post office department, so many other departments. Everybody wants those jobs, but everybody cannot have it. Similarly, for their social status, all the people want a government job instead of a private job. Suppose my child can get a job in the court. We will get social status. Farmers are always in trouble because of farming court cases. Similarly, there are other jobs that farmers need. Agricultural department, banking department. Those people who are working in the banks get a good salary. I haven't mentioned the big officers such as IAS, SP, DM because village people don't have that kind of money. But if the girl is well qualified, they can look for such type of groom.

"It also depends on the status of the middleman. If you go to a farmer middleman, he will show you a farmer's family. If you have a friend or relative among the businessmen, he will show you the businessmen. If you visit some government employees, he can show you the employees with government jobs. All these are related to each other, they are linked—farmers, government jobs, and businessmen—because living in small towns, we are linked to each other. Even so, the farmer may find the businessman, the businessman may find the farmer. But most of the help comes from the real person—from the employee to the employee.

"As a father searches afar, he may find a different middleman. One person can't be the middleman for everywhere. A middleman can carry you to those people only to whom he knows. We people go and find who can help in the situation and get his help if he agrees. *Manjhya* is the name of the middleman. Why does he do it if he doesn't get paid? Because a marriage cannot be performed without a middleman. We might get in trouble and arrange a wedding with another caste if we don't get a *manjhya*. Some people have the charm to be a *manjhya*. If somebody comes from my *sasural*, the person has to become a *manjhya*.

"Suppose the girl's side says, 'I cannot spend more than two *lakh* rupees (₹200,000, or $3,000).' The *manjhya* asks first how much you can spend for the wedding. So you have to go to the place where the person deserves that amount. If I have five *lakh* rupees ($7,500) and am looking for a boy the worth of ten *lakh* rupees ($14,700), the wedding can't be arranged. The boy doesn't know what he is worth, but the parents know it. If the family is good, suppose the boy is in a good government job and he also has property at home and he has a good house—so whatever he gets in the marriage, the money will stay with the family."

"If people have money, why do they want more money?" I asked.

"This is Laxmi, you know," Umesh said. "People never get satisfied for Laxmi. As much as they have, people want more. Why is she a goddess then? That *is* why she is a goddess. As much as you have, you want more. That is why we said at the time when there were no trains, no cars, the wealth of cows, the wealth of elephants, the wealth of horses, the wealth of gems, all these kinds of wealth. When you get the wealth of satisfaction, all the other types of wealth are just like dust on the earth. The greatest wealth is satisfaction."

"So how do we get satisfaction?" I asked.

"Satisfaction is not in a school to teach. It comes in the mind from the experiences, sufferings, I believe. This is how people get it. People teach this. Wealth is unending hunger. Get satisfied. You mentioned Bill Gates—he got satisfaction. Now he is putting his money into charities—this is great. Not to gain money out of that but to give money. That is deep satisfaction, I believe. Until you keep accumulating money, it is not satisfaction. Making a pile, a deep deep pile, and when you die, you see such a big pile. But it is useless. And nobody knows what will happen to this wealth, who is going to use this after he dies. But the person who is accumulating this wealth and he knows how it will be used, then he feels he has done a great job in his life, and he can see the use of his wealth.

"When a person does not have food, he says, 'Oh God, I don't want anything, but give me enough food so we can live.' Then he works hard, or God provides him food. Then he says, 'Oh Lord, I wish I could have a good house.' The time comes, and he gets a good house, and then he says, 'Oh Lord, I want a good business, a good job.' And he gets it. Then he thinks, and he prays, 'Oh Lord, I must have four-wheeled vehicles.' As soon as he begins to gain these things, his status goes up, his friendship spreads, and his mind goes wide. Now he has known so many people who were doing different jobs, businesses, he demands from God to be more rich. This is a kind of human thinking. He is working and also praying to God. Unending hunger. Unending hunger. Greed is also necessary for our children. It is natural that everybody wants to improve too. When giving begins, when that kind of satisfaction comes, he begins to give away for good reasons, and it does not stop. Satisfaction means satisfaction. He gives because whatever he has, he wants to see other people happy. Is that also a weakness? It is a kind of weakness too. So don't destroy your everything in donation so you can't live.

"So that is why we need a nice person, a powerful person as the middleman. I will see if they need a girl in their family or not. Or only money. What about if there are already other *bahu*s (daughters-in-law)? Yeah, this is also a way to know. I will also be seeing the *bahu*s. I will be seeing them, or my son can go in the house to touch feet of these *bahu*s. If the *bahu* is in trouble in the family, we can learn by her talking, behaving. She might say something against the family if she is in trouble. This is also a way to learn if the family is good or not."

I asked, "Would you want Alka to be the big *bahu* or the little *bahu*?" Alka is Umesh's daughter.

"I don't know. She should be the older *bahu*, I believe, because she is the oldest daughter of mine. There is a rule for that. The older child should be married to the older child. They go well together. It is very complicated. But slowly it can be easily understood if you work on it, to find out everything clearly. Searching for a boy is a job for old people, not young people with black hair. Who is the master of the family, he must do it. You must be talking to the gray-headed people, not the black-headed people. Gray hair is considered responsible. Who is to spend money—gray hair or black hair? Usually gray hair.

"So you are investigating several boys at the same time. If I almost like the boy, I give some money to the family. First, it used to be one rupee. When you go to buy a bullock, you give the farmer one rupee (two cents), and then the talk begins. Similarly, when searching for a boy, when you think we might have this groom, you give ₹100 ($1.50), ₹500 ($7.50). Touch their feet, and if he takes the money, it means he has almost agreed to the wedding. If he doesn't take it, he may say, 'Never mind, come back later.' If he takes that money, it forms a kind of agreement up to a certain amount of time—until I come after one month or two months. If the groom's side is ready to arrange a marriage and then he takes the money, he will not take money from other people. Suppose I say I will come back within a month. How long can he wait? If he can get another girl, he won't wait. Or if another family approaches him, he can say, 'Come after one month.' Then we have made an agreement. And this works only with the dignified person. If he is a dignified person, he will keep his promise. Mostly people are dignified.

"So what happens next? You give ₹500 and say you will come back in one month or a little before. Then I'll take my brothers, my relatives, my son and uncles to have a look. I have seen with two eyes. So many people see the boy for the family. They have their own points of view. They will go and meet this family, brothers, son, uncles, friends. I have to pay them for their fare. We will all go to see this family within a month. Suppose we go with five or six people. Everybody has his own point of view, his own views that will bring the facts, whether we want to arrange a wedding here or not. That is the second meeting. Then we can also arrange the *tilak* (engagement ceremony) at the same time, or we can put them on hold."

"How do you know on the spot what to do?" I asked.

"We go back to the house of the middleman and talk to each other and to the middleman. The middleman will be arranging food. We are going to outside now, to find a private place to have a talk. In the city, we just go for a walk, or we go upstairs and talk without the middleman. If we don't want the boy, we tell the middleman, 'Please find another boy for me.' If we do want the boy, we say we do and tell the middleman to make an arrangement how can we have this boy. And the talk begins."

SEVEN

# HELEN AND UMESH MEET

*At the Archives and Research Centre for Ethnomusicology (ARCE), October 31, 1986*

It just took one glance.

The year was 1986, and Umesh and I began our song journey, deep into the remote interior towns and villages of eastern India. Little did we know that in 2019, thirty-three years later, we would come to realize that a great voyage had been made and that amazing songs had been found here and there—in fact, everywhere—in Bhojpur.

Back in those years, travel in this part of eastern Uttar Pradesh, considered "backward" by most Indians, was so difficult. The steam trains were slow and dirty, the roads barely paved. Sometimes we just walked. It did seem that we found ourselves in a region that was remote. At the time of writing, 2019, this journey is much easier. New roads, new railway lines, better trains, great hotels have been built. There is no longer such thing as an isolated Indian village in 2019.

### *Shubha's office in Delhi, Archives and Research Centre for Ethnomusicology, Halloween 1986*

"It was my first visit to the archive. I came to Shubha's office, and you were in the shower," I recalled. "And I began to think, *What kind of archive is this?*"

"Actually, I didn't know who was coming," Umesh replied. "Some kind of scholar was coming. So I requested Shubha where was the bathroom. After a long train ride, I wanted to present myself clean. I think you had some kind of pink or red clothes on, and you were full of energy, smiling and talking. We met each other in the dining room, and Shubha took us into her office to talk this over. And then Shubha saw us, and all of the sudden—she didn't tell me anything in front of you—she told me later that I had a good job there in Damoh at the Diamond Cement Company. She told me that she was not forcing me for this job with you, and it was only a six-months job. She believed that the Damoh job would be good for me. She had a kind of fear that I would be jobless and the burden would be on her."

"I said to you, 'Would you like to fly on an airplane to Banaras? I bought two tickets.'"

"'Yes, I will be in heaven,'" Umesh replied. "Heaven is on top, you know."

"I was thinking you looked like a movie star. And you were wearing your 'police officer' outfit. You had a pair of tan pants and a tan shirt that made you look like a police officer, and you liked that."

"So we decided to go to Banaras. I, Umesh, was staying with Dr. Scott Marcus in Connaught Place."

"And I, Helen, was staying in the American Institute of Indian Studies (AIIS) guesthouse in Defence Colony, New Delhi.

"So we arranged to meet the next evening to go to the airport and fly to Banaras. We got a taxi. You, Umesh, had one small suitcase. And I had so many big suitcases and also several small bags. When the taxi driver started to throw my suitcases full of delicate recording equipment on the luggage rack on top of the car, I began to shout, 'Not on top.'"

"And I, Umesh, said something very different. 'What is wrong with that? If it is placed on top of the car, what is wrong with that? It is safe there.' But your face was telling me—it was the very first time that I saw your strict face—and the smiling and laughing was completely vanished from your face. I saw the eyeballs coming out of your face. So I was shut up. And I told the driver, 'Do as she likes because there must be some important things in those bags.' But deep inside I was annoyed. 'She is just like other Americans, and I've got to be ready for that,' I thought. I learned it later when we were going to Banpurwa, I think, that the most important thing was the Stellavox tape recorder and the reels of tape. It they are not kept safe, the visit is completely wasted. And the mics, Schoeps mics from Switzerland. Your equipment was the most important, not anything else. And then when the work is over, when you were leaving, only the recorded tapes were the most important thing. What else?"

"So we made our way to the Delhi airport domestic terminal. And along the way, I, Helen, was explaining to you about how to take a trip by plane."

"We flew in the evening from Delhi for Banaras," Umesh said. "And it was dark. Helen wanted me to have the window seat because it was my first plane ride. I was not scared. (I learned that fear later. After very many flights, fear began slowly, especially after Mr. Mehinderatta's flight was hijacked in Karachi.) And then we got on the plane, touching everyone from side by side in the narrow way between the seats. For me it was like a cage. Because a very narrow way. Seats were good enough. I didn't even know where to place our hand baggage."

Helen said, "I had carefully explained to you about the assigned seating on the plane. But when we found our seats, two fat gentlemen were already sitting in them. And you laughed and laughed and said, 'Oh, it's just like an Indian bus.' Fortunately, the plane was empty enough, so there was no problem."

"And I, Umesh, was sitting on the left side of the plane, and I was looking out the left window. I shouted, 'Oh, look, the stars on the earth!'"

"And I said, 'Umesh, today is Diwali.'

"We arrived in Banaras in about an hour, and we didn't know where we were going. Shubha had given me instructions to go to the Diamond Hotel, and the original plan was to send Umesh out to find a simple place to stay. But when we arrived at the hotel, I immediately decided to book two rooms, one for me and one for Umesh. I certainly didn't want you to be running around a strange city in the night, looking for some bed to sleep on. Oh, it was great to be in Kashi.

"That night I played Bhojpuri songs from Trinidad for you."

"First thing was that I had never heard the Bhojpuri dialect of songs yet," Umesh recalled. "When I heard these songs from Trinidad, I could understand quite a few words. Later I could understand these old wedding songs quite easily. I didn't really know where Trinidad was, and I really didn't know that Indian people lived there. I did know, when I entered college, that Kalicharan was a famous cricketer from the West Indies. I used to hear the cricket commentary from small transistors. But until I met you, I didn't know that the British had taken these peoples from Bhojpur and scattered them around—West Indies, Mauritius, Fiji, East Indies—and that they are carrying out their culture until today."

# EIGHT

# VIEWING THE BRIDE

*Banaras, Sandhya Guesthouse, 2006*

Twenty years after we met, in 2006, Umesh and I found ourselves in the Sandhya Guesthouse in Banaras once again. We were, as usual, working on our song journey into eastern Uttar Pradesh. It was December, and it was damn cold. We were planning to spend Christmas there.

On Christmas Eve, we decided to go to the Bread of Life bakery down the road for a special meal. I took this opportunity to have some non-veg food. I ordered the chicken potpie. Umesh ordered a vegetarian meal.

When we arrived back at the guesthouse, we played Christmas carols on my iPod, using split leads so we both could hear the same music at the same time. The real treat was Benjamin Britten's *A Ceremony of Carols*. We have never forgotten that special Christmas.

We decided to visit an Indian village where our great friend Dr. Ram Sagar Singh lived. In the old days—the 1980s—Umesh and I had slowly made our way there by three-wheeled bicycle rickshaw. The ride took almost two hours. Om Prakash, our rickshaw driver, had loved those visits. Ram Sagar always offered him food and a bed for the night for however many days that we stayed. Om Prakash loved the music that we recorded, and he loved being treated with courtesy.

For this occasion in 2006, we hired a three-wheeled motor scooter to take us to the village. In the 1980s, I had always found the bicycle rickshaw ride to and from Banpurwa so peaceful, so quiet, even religious, with only the sounds of birds to accompany our thoughts. On those rides, I loved to imagine that I was having an adventure in India—an India that actually didn't exist. Those were Orientalist thoughts. The peace, the stillness, the exotic.

For this new venture in 2006, we hired a motor rickshaw, a "three-wheeler." The ride was horrible. It was bumpy . . . Bump! . . . BUMP! . . . BUMP!!! On this last bump, I cut my head on the roof of the scooter, and we had to stop. I was terrified. And by the time we reached Banpurwa, I was drained, emotionally and physically.

Even so, we had a great visit. There was a new *bahu* in the house, as Ram Sagar's son had married. And she was a wonderful cook. We were shown every convenience. And Ram Sagar had installed three private toilet booths. That was so welcome. We had a wonderful day. And then we took the scooter back to Banaras . . . bump . . . Bump!

After Christmas, we had a bit of a letdown. I was missing my family. Umesh knew the cure for me. He didn't hesitate. He immediately suggested that he would tell, and I would type. He would tell all the details about the arranged Hindu wedding in North India. He really understood me well at that point, so I was comforted by us launching ourselves into intensive work. Below are the comments that Umesh made on that occasion. I had to type very fast.

"Before the *tilak* (engagement), the custom is changed," Umesh explained. "The groom's side wants to see the bride, the girl. When they agree to arrange the wedding, then they want to see the girl before the *tilak*.

"Usually they meet at a temple or some dharmshala or some relative's house—or whatever place is chosen. The parents go, or sometimes the brother and father go, and there must be one woman with the girl. If we arrange this with some family—the middleman—the family women make her comfortable. This is a test. She has to pass a test. It is quite discouraging. She meets her mother-in-law, *nanad* (bridegroom's sister), maybe the bridegroom's brothers' wives—his *bhabi*s—and most probably the bridegroom. It is quite scary for her because she is seeing those people whom she has never seen and with whom she will live forever. So it is quite scary. Will she pass this test or not?"

"What does she have to do?" I asked.

"They make her move around. Walk around so they can see if she is lame. They look into her eyes, whether she can see properly. There are so many ways to ask—to show her hands and feet."

"Anything else?" I asked.

"So that they can see if her hands are good, if she can walk well, this is a physical test. Can she hear or not? Is she deaf? They make her talk to see whether she will be able to talk or not—or stutter. So they try to search in this way. If the *nanad* (boy's sister) is educated or the *bahu*s (the other daughters-in-law of the home) are educated, they ask some questions either in English or in some other subjects. Any kind of questions to test if she has knowledge of her subject. Maybe they talk about general knowledge. Yeah, a big test. The boy also talks to the girl. They put them in one room with some women so they can talk. They are not alone. The door is closed but not locked. Her face is not covered. Her forehead is covered. She can't look up because she is so shy. She cannot look into the eyes to face the situation. The women are around. He asks questions, and she answers. Nothing more.

"This is very new. It was not when I was married—not at all. Thirty or forty years ago, the groom had no chance to see the bride. Even the family people did not see the bride. Even the lame woman or the one-eyed woman was married to the man. A deformed woman could get married in a good house in those days. And that family's responsibility was to take care of the deformed girl.

"If the girl is seen at the temple, her mother will be there. The temple is the best place to show the girl because there is no room, just an open area, and you can talk at the place of the Lord. So I think this is the best place. Usually we consider the temple the best place.

"Suppose the girl fails. People will know it. Once a girl is failed, if you arrange a wedding elsewhere, there they will like to know why she was failed. It becomes a kind of question mark. Why was she failed? What could cause the failure?

"She can fail in so many ways. Suppose they don't like the height of the girl, complexion, features, and they think she is not intelligent enough when she talks to these people. If they like her, they all of the sudden give a ring to the girl. If they don't, they don't. They may have something to offer. Mostly a ring. A ring is one small ornament. They can carry it easily, and easily she can put it on. Even though the agreement is done, sometimes even those agreements fail. It can fail due to money—if something goes wrong with the dowry. In olden days, people would say they could give so much. They lied. These days if you lie, it is trouble. They can kill the girl. So many cases come—we don't know whether they killed the girl or if the girl died herself.

"The government made a law that after marriage, before six years or seven years pass, if the girl dies in the groom's family, if she is not ill accidentally, it is considered murder—dowry murder. I am not sure what the real law is. These cases always get into the newspaper."

NINE

# THE *TILAK* TALK BEGINS

*We are still in Banaras at the Sandhya Guesthouse, 2006*

Umesh was determined to keep my mind on our work. It was like a trick, but I fell for it. Every day, he found new topics to discuss with me, topics about the Hindu arranged marriage. He made me count the words. Each day we had to reach our quota of 750 to 1,000 words. There would be no rest until that had been accomplished. He was quite firm about this. On the previous day, we had only reached 763 words. Although technically it was within our quota, Umesh wasn't satisfied.

On this next day, he wanted to tell me about the *tilak* ceremony.

"For the *tilak*, a party of the girl's side goes to offer presents to the boy's side. The boy's family feeds the *tilak* party. Go and buy some sweets, dishes, fruits, dry fruits, coconut, whatever is considered important. The women in the family of the middleman tell the girl's family what to buy. The custom may be different in their area. The girl's father must do the custom according to the boy's village. And the boy's side has to carry out all our customs when they take the *barat* to my village. If I carry out the same customs for *tilak* as in my area, it is awkward—the groom's side can get very annoyed. 'This is wrong, this is wrong.' So we have to carry out their customs. Sometimes the family has their own customs too. Family traditions. So you take the things for the *tilak* and maybe ₹1,000 ($15.00)—it depends—maybe ₹5,000 ($73.00). If they give ₹5,000 at that time, it will be added with the other amount that has been asked by the groom's side.

"The *tilak* is an agreement. The girl's brother makes a saffron mark on the forehead of the boy. This is also called a *tilak*. It is made of lime and turmeric, and it makes a saffron color, and some rice is in it. The brother puts the *tilak* on the forehead of the prospective groom. He may also give a garland and perhaps a ring. Actually, the very clever families want all the money at the time of *tilak*. We bring sweets to give the boy's side and *thali*s (large plates) these days. We go there and sit down, and the barber's wife makes a *chauk* (altar), and the priest comes. It is done religiously. It takes fifteen minutes to half an hour. Not a big job. There is so much talking. But altogether it takes the whole day. Then the *tilak* is done."

"What kind of commitment is that?" I asked.

"The marriage is settled."

TEN

# GANGAJALI

*The scene shifts forward one year. We are in Banaras again, at our apartment, 2007*

Umesh came into the room, interrupting Trollope's adventures of Lizzie Eustace. I was grieving and upset and didn't want to put the book down.

"Look," Umesh said. "Gangajali begins with songs for the *tilak* ceremony. We could start there, do some translation together." He was gently trying to coax me to work.

"So what do we have here?" I asked, and we both hunched over the file.

*Hotel Sarang, Ballia, July 14, 1989*

Here we have to set the scene. We had set out for Ballia in eastern Uttar Pradesh, arriving on July 11, 1989. We had just arrived from Chapra, Bihar. It had proved really difficult by train as we had to switch lines and cross the Ganges. Once in Ballia, exhausted, we had installed ourselves in the Sarang Hotel. It was really the only hotel in Ballia.

Umesh didn't like the hotel and felt that the food was poor considering the prices they charged. Wherever we went, he was never satisfied with the chapattis, and we had fought about that. I had learned to shut up and just agree. After arriving in Ballia, we recorded some dancing girls outside the hotel. It was a start, and we were able to ask them about good singers. Everybody recommended a woman named Gangajali.

It was not difficult to find her as she lived just behind the VJ Talkies, one of the biggest buildings in Ballia. Her husband had operated the movies there before his untimely death years ago. Everyone we asked knew where she lived. Her singing and dancing were famous throughout the city.

We met together—Gangajali, her friend Sashi, Umesh, and me. And there was no doubt that she was the expert wedding song singer of the town. She said so herself. Umesh explained to her carefully in Bhojpuri about our mission in India—to learn all about the women's role in the Hindu wedding. Although she was kind and sympathetic, I'm not sure that she really believed that our interest was genuine. Then I sang several Bhojpuri wedding songs from Felicity, Trinidad. She was surprised, confused, and enthusiastic. Why was this white lady singing in Bhojpuri? So we made an arrangement to meet with her on the following day.

And here she was, on July 14, 1989, in my hotel room, ready to sing. We had taken hours to set up the equipment to record. The Schoeps stereo mic was set up. The Stellavox was loaded with fresh tape, and all the proper settings had been made. The Walkman Pro backup cassette recorder was loaded with a fresh cassette. The Stellavox and the Walkman were on pause. First we had a little friendly chat. But Gangajali had come to work.

"I am very interested in wedding songs," I explained to her. "All of the wedding songs from Ballia," I continued, "from the beginning of the wedding to the very end. All of the ceremonies and rituals, all of the celebrations."

Gangajali listened intently as Umesh explained in Bhojpuri the meaning of what I was saying. "Songs performed in the bride's home and also songs performed in the home of the bridegroom," I continued. "And I am hoping that you can explain these songs to me so that I can understand them within the context of the wedding. Everything that you people in India do here is very different from what we do in the United States. Certainly, the wedding ceremony is much longer and much more complex here in India than in my country."

Gangajali obviously knew that I was *videshi*, a foreigner. There was no surprise there. Obviously, she saw that I was white, and in India that is a big deal. Certainly, at first, she wondered why a white lady wanted to learn about the wedding songs of Ballia. Indians were always astonished that an American wedding could take less than an hour and that the only pieces of jewelry exchanged were two simple gold bands made of, for them, cheap eighteen-carat gold. Indian jewelry is made of nearly pure twenty-two-carat gold.

"Well, let's start at the beginning," she said. "First, the girl's people come to the door of the bridegroom's home to perform the *tilak* (engagement) ceremony. I will sing for you those songs that are sung before, during, and after *tilak*."

"That is wonderful," I said. "So we can start at the beginning."

For obvious reasons, which nevertheless puzzled me, it was rare to meet a singer who could grasp the concept of singing the songs of the wedding in order, all the songs, outside the context of an actual wedding. The songs were so interwoven with the action of the wedding, the two were so intertwined, that it was difficult to recall these songs out of context. The action cued the songs, and the singers of the village watched the goings on and easily commented with the appropriate song. Over the course of what was once a five-day ritual and is now a three-day ritual or even shorter, hundreds of songs might be sung. We had documented dozens of weddings live—audio, video, still photography. But we were hoping to sit down quietly, away from the hustle and bustle of the wedding—with people everywhere, cooks and their fire pits in the ground, kids running around, animals tethered and feeding, and, especially troublesome, loud, loud Indian filmi music pumping from enormous loudspeakers—to record each old song without the distorted blasting of the loudspeakers and reflect on its meaning together with the singer.

Gangajali said, "By the end I will finish everything to do with weddings that is done here in Ballia, here in India—the customs of the wedding from the beginning to the end."

"Are you afraid of so many recording machines and microphones?" I asked.

"No, no, no. I know how to face the storm from the beginning to the end," she said. "So I am not afraid of anything."

ELEVEN

# THE *TILAK*, EXPLAINED BY UMESH

*Chatting at the Sandhya Guesthouse, Banaras, 2006*

"To move wedding plans ahead, the priest makes a letter, and he writes on it the names of the bride and groom," Umesh explained. "Their respective fathers' names, and, according to astrology, what day is good for the girl's side, what day for the *barat*, when it will come, when it will go, when they have to do the *haldi* (turmeric) ceremony and *tel* (oil) ceremony. Thereafter, this letter is given in the hands of the bridegroom at the altar at the time of the *tilak* ceremony.

"For the *tilak* party, the brother goes, the uncle goes, some relatives, some village people. The boy's side family must give a feast, a party, at the time of *tilak*. There are snacks and tea, Coca-Cola or cold drinks, and so many types of food. People can also judge the food or call it *banigi*—'As you sow, so you will reap. As you feed, so I will feed you the same.'

"This is a jokey time. It is not so serious. But people keep it in their mind. So those people who go in the *tilak* party, when they reach there at the bridegroom's home, they are filled up all the time, some biscuits, some sweets, some fruits, whatever a family can afford, they give that.

"After the bride's party are fed, the time comes to perform the *tilak* ceremony. The girl's side men sit down (the girl is back at home). And the brother or the uncle, they begin to take things out like dried fruits, coconuts, fruits, clothes, also some vehicle. The dowry is given at *tilak*. Yes, also cash. These days they want the dowry at the time of *tilak*. They don't want to wait for the wedding because people tell lies, so they want the dowry in advance. The *tilak* is ten or fifteen days before the wedding, maybe a little bit more. There must be not much time between the *tilak* and the *barat* (wedding procession).

"So cash is given then, but there are still some other dowry items, like TV, washing machine, bed, *almyra* (large closet), fridge, clothes, mattress, sheets, quilts. These are given at the time of the wedding. Or they can say, 'We don't want these things. We want money. I have everything at my home.' Very clever people do it. 'I buy my own.'

"People keep receipts. The girl's side does not pass on the receipts to the groom's family unless it is something important, like if they buy a motorcycle, then it is important. If something goes wrong, the girl's father can claim for that. The receipt is shown so that they can see that we have spent what we agreed—it has been given in cash or in kind. Bed this, sheet this, mattress this—the price of everything is counted. And the boy's side won't like it. They want cash *and* things! They don't want to count the cost of the things with the money. Suppose the marriage was agreed at six *lakh* rupees (around $9,000.00). The boy's side wants all six *lakh*s rupees in cash. The girl's side puts the food, whatever is fed, other things like bed, fridge, ornaments, everything is included because it is out of the pocket. The girl's side father, who spends so much money, wants to give something at his door so that he can show in society that he is giving so many things for the wedding. He doesn't want to give just hard cash. There is no show for that. He wants the respect of the people in his village. And the village people should know how much the family is spending for a daughter's wedding."

"So everybody knows how much is spent for the wedding? Everybody in the village knows that?" I asked.

"Yes. Those who go with the *tilak* know that, and it spreads everywhere. If something goes hidden, nobody will know it, and the girl's family doesn't want that. Sometimes it happens that people have a lump sum of money. The question comes, 'Where did they get the money from?' The question of income tax comes. They cannot give it in a check. Hard cash, no checks."

TWELVE

# SONG JOURNEY

*Meeting Umesh. Morning at the Diamond Hotel, Banaras, November 3, 1986*

We always went downstairs in the morning to have breakfast in the Diamond Hotel restaurant. Certainly we had tea, and probably we had toast and butter. When we got the toast, the crust had been cut off, and we were sorry because we both liked the crust the most. I don't think I learned about the traditional breakfast foods of North India for quite a while—*pakora* (battered and fried vegetables), stuffed *paratha* (fried bread pancakes stuffed with potato or other vegetables), *dahi* (yogurt), and sometimes *kachori* (round flattened dough balls stuffed with lentils). In a Westernized hotel, and the Diamond pretended to be one of these, they offered an "English" menu of scrambled eggs, omelets, boiled eggs, orange juice, coffee, and so forth.

After breakfast, we went exploring in Banaras. I was fascinated by the sounds of the streets, the many tones of the rickshaw bells—*ghanti*—sounds of car horns, motorcycles. There were male bullocks pulling heavy carts, tractors pulling trolleys, mixed with pedestrians and cyclists. To me, it all seemed very dangerous and so exciting and colorful. And there was a special music of the street that I wanted to record. So we circled back to the Diamond Hotel and picked up some recording equipment and set out to record the sounds of Kashi. That was the evening of November 3, 1986.

After breakfast the next day, Umesh had a plan to take me to some village. *Any village.* In front of the Diamond Hotel there was a tea stall made of wood. And so many rickshaw wallahs waited there to take passengers from the hotel around the holy city. So we set out by bicycle rickshaw pulled by our friend Raju, the rickshaw wallah.

On November 4, we began the search for a village. Actually, we had spent a few days just talking, finding friendship, and having lots of laughs. But finally the day came when we began our search. We had no idea where we were going. We went by bicycle rickshaw toward Banaras Hindu University, and we entered into the university through the gate. And we kept asking people, "Where is a village? Where is a village? Where is *any damn village*? India is 70 percent villages, but where the hell are they?"

To whomever we met, we asked these stupid questions. "Where is a village?" Finally, a kind man, taking pity on the fools, advised us, "Go on the left-hand side of the university in the back. There is a little door, and you can get out of it. When you are out of the university, you can find some village." So Raju took us to the back road of the university on the left side, through the little door, and we were out of the university.

There were a few houses on either side of the *kaccha* (unpaved) road. But it did not look like a village at all. So Raju kept moving ahead, and we found a *pakkah* (paved) road made of charcoal. And we kept moving ahead, but we couldn't find a village. It was a long way.

As it turns out, we had passed the real village on the right and unknowingly had kept moving forward. No people were found on the road with whom we could talk. So we kept moving on the road, passed the village, and found a house on the left of the road where an old man was sitting on a cot and a few women were winnowing wheat.

I jumped down immediately, running and singing at the women with a small tape recorder in my hand. When I reached the women, immediately I began to sing a Trinidad Bhojpuri wedding song, "Shankara koriya baharo oh baba." The women were quite amused. And I asked them to sing some songs. But unfortunately, the old master, who was also the *pradhan* (headman) of the village, was the boss, and the women didn't feel free to sing. These women did not know what to sing. I handed Umesh a notebook, and he read several Trinidad Bhojpuri songs from them. Then I began to sing song after song. All of a sudden, the women recognized what to sing, and they sang a couple of Bhojpuri wedding songs. Then I handed the main singer my Walkman Pro so she could hear her own voice. And she was thrilled, as were all the other women. Umesh asked the old man, "How can we meet people? Will you help us? We are searching for wedding songs. How can we record such songs?"

The man gave us the name of Dr. Ram Sagar Singh. He told us that Dr. Ram Sagar Singh worked with the university, but the *pradhan* did not know in which department he worked. It was not easy to find Dr. Singh as Banaras Hindu

University has an enormous and beautiful sprawling campus with many faculties. In fact, Ram Sagar was a lab attendant in the chemistry department. After a long search we found him in the university chemistry lab. We were offered tea made in their test tubes. And Dr. Ram Sagar Singh gave us his address in Banpurwa (Baikunthpuri, where the ashram is located) and told us how to get to his home. We were really excited. We had found the right person.

The next morning, after tea and toast, we called for Raju and set out for Banpurwa. It was a Sunday, and Dr. Ram Sagar Singh had the day off from work. We reached his home, and the family greeted us so nicely. He was there with his wife and his son and five daughters. Little did we know what a fantastic friendship had begun. We were offered tea and some salty snacks.

Umesh said, "We had taken with us all the weapons to fight the battle of music—the Stellavox, mics, mic stands, windscreens, reels of blank tape, backup cassette recorders—bags of weapons."

THIRTEEN

# *TILAK* SONGS

*We remain at the Hotel Sarang, Ballia, July 1989*

As we began, Gangajali explained, "Before the *tilak* ceremony, we sing devotional *baithaki* to Lord Shiva. Here is one of these." What followed was a beautiful song sung with her amazingly clear voice.

## SONG 1

### *Tilak*

Mahadewa, I had the courtyard plastered with cow dung.
Oh Mahadewa, I had the altar made of elephant pearls.
The altar is made, oh the altar is made.
Listen, oh Shiva.
A proclamation in the name of Lord Shiva. Listen, oh Shiva.
Seated at the altar, Mahadewa became sleepy.
Gauradei nudged him with her toe to wake him up.
Oh wake him up, oh wake him up.
Listen, oh Shiva.
A proclamation in the name of Lord Shiva. Listen, oh Shiva.
Mahadewa got annoyed when she nudged him with her toe.
Gauradei appeased him by leaning against him with her arm.
Listen oh Shiva, oh, was appeased.

A proclamation in the name of Lord Shiva. Listen, oh Shiva.
Mahadewa, you will not get anything at the time of the wedding.
Mahadewa, you will get everything at the time of the *gauna*.
Oh, you will get everything. You will get everything.
Listen, oh Shiva.
A proclamation in the name of Lord Shiva. Listen, oh Shiva.
Father will present elephants and horses.
Brother will present a new mother cow.
Mother will present a yellow *dhoti*.
*Bhauji* a ring for the hand,
Oh *bhauji*, a ring for the hand.
Listen, oh Shiva.
A proclamation in the name of Lord Shiva. Listen, oh Shiva.
You will ride on the elephants and horses.
You will drive the new mother cow home.
You will put on the yellow *dhoti*.
You will put on the ring.
Oh, you will put on the ring.
Listen, oh Shiva.
A proclamation in the name of Lord Shiva. Listen, oh Shiva.
Having eaten a meal off the dish, Mahadewa drank water out of the jug.
Oh Mahadewa, you will be given a cot to sleep on and a quilt to cover yourself,
Oh, a quilt to cover yourself. Listen, oh Shiva.
Mahadewa will sleep on the cot and cover himself with the quilt.
Mahadewa will eat a meal off the dish and drink water out of the jug.
Mahadewa will sleep on the cot and cover himself with the quilt.
You will sleep with Gauradei on that cot,
Oh, sleep with her.
A proclamation in the name of Lord Shiva. Listen, oh Shiva.
A proclamation in the name of Lord Shiva. Listen, oh Shiva.

SPOKEN

"The End"

In Delhi, in our apartment in April 2017, I played for Umesh the first song of Gangajali, a song of Mahadewa, who was her personal god. I asked Umesh how the musical sound seemed to him.

"I am not an expert on music," he said. "But slowly it comes up. The singing begins down like a graphical chart. It goes up, then down, then up, then comes more down, then a little up, then down, and it finally slips down the hill. At the last, the hill comes slowly to the plain. It is not like the Rift Valley—*SZOOM*!!—at the end. It comes slipping slowly to the plain. As she comes to move on the plain, she stops. Before she stops singing, she is already off the hill, and the hill comes slowly slowly to the plain. As the end of the plain comes, she stops. The end is different. The last Shiva word goes, and she slows down just a bit. Not too much, not too slow. Just a bit. Well, this sings in the heart. At the end, it is neither happy nor sad. It is very peaceful. It does not hurt me."

"After it ends," I said. "when the slowing word comes and then stops, I feel a bit of grief. It is like saying goodbye. I feel a bit lonely."

Umesh answered, "Now Sushma is here in the kitchen. Now she is cleaning pots—making sound. I am here. Here is absolutely peaceful. How will you feel? Completely peaceful. But if Sushma goes, if I go, it will bring you loneliness in a little while. In outer space, there is no air. There is clean silence. So people are in a spaceship. There are so many people together. There is absolute silence on the spaceship. There may be music, or they may talk to each other. I don't think they are lonely because they talk to each other. And when you are here, although sounds are outside—comes inside—the house is empty and peaceful, and a person gets lonely."

"I don't feel lonely when the song begins," I said.

"Yes," Umesh said. "That is right. You are hearing the song. You are enjoying it. Suppose if you don't enjoy this song, you will turn it off. Then the peace will come, then the next turn in loneliness. I was in Mauritius. I had enough job to do to record the radio songs. This was after you and Ian left and I was left alone for one day—at the seashore. Nobody was around. And the beautiful songs of music began to bite me. There was no life around. And I became really lonely. And this was my first experience of real loneliness. I knew this word, but I did not know the deep meaning. I learned it that very day. Loneliness is just like killing. And I was walking all around such a beautiful bungalow, but nothing helped. And I had forgotten to meditate. Meditation is the best medicine."

I was absolutely stunned—speechless—at the beauty of this song. Gangajali's voice was clear, and the song had a lively rhythm and a catchy tune that turned out to be quite popular. It was a song about the marriage of the gods, of Shiva and Gauri. I could immediately hear that the song was long, that it had a rich text with many lines—"A proclamation in the name of Lord Shiva. Listen, oh Shiva." Some lines were repeated. How could the marriage of the gods in the sky be compared to a peasant wedding in a humble village?

It is not necessary to have any formal musical training to appreciate the sincerity of this song, even though the tonalities, rhythms, and text may be totally unfamiliar. Gangajali was a serious and sincere woman who loved singing and believed that song had great importance in the perpetuation of her culture. It was her fond hope that recording and preserving her songs with us might help people in future generations to understand the culture in which she had lived. She was very clear on this point—that she didn't want her songs to die with her. She was excited to know that they would be deposited in important sound archives, even in the United States, and that this book was to be written.

This particular song, dedicated to the Hindu god Lord Shiva (Mahadewa), has a pure, unaccompanied vocal line. This basic style, called monody, is the most prevalent form of music in the world.

The melodies of this first song are clearly divided into fairly short individual phrases, which can be identified despite the readers' unfamiliarity with the Bhojpuri language. Some of these phrases, or musical sentences, dwell at a lower, or one might say tonic, level, and other phrases are focused around five scale tones (or a fifth higher). This lends a pleasing variety to the melody, and the shift in registers also presents a bit of a challenge for an ordinary singer. This basic structure is repeated many, many times in the Gangajali songs that are presented here.

As she sang, Gangajali moved both of her hands through the air as if drawing the scene and the emotional quality of the scene in an empty space. She was totally focused on the execution of the song, including remembering the many verses and staying in tune. If one listens carefully, you will hear the jingling of her glass bangles as she "conducts" the song while singing. Unfortunately, during the singing, the hotel boy arrived near the end of this recording to collect our cups and plates from the tea we had before the singing started. Although some sound editing has been done, if you listen carefully, you may hear the door open and then hear it close. For me, these misadventures distinguish a real live field recording from something rather artificial that could be produced in a studio.

Gangajali was a devotee of Lord Shiva and worshiped at the tiny Shiva temple in the corner at the end of her lane. Probably this is why she chose this song to be her Song Number One, to launch our new work. You can hear her devotion as she closes out the last phrase of the song, "Listen, oh Shiva." For this was her fondest wish. She slows down a tiny bit. It is touching.

"That's absolutely lovely," I said. "So very beautiful. Can you tell me more about the meaning of that song?"

Gangajali was quick and eager to reply. "Mahadewa sits at the altar to get married," she explained. "He gets dozy. He begins to fall, and his head starts bobbing. Then Gaura Parvati hits him a little bit to wake him up. Then Lord Shiva gets annoyed. Deviji gets puzzled, so she appeases him by leaning her arm on him, and she says, 'Don't get angry. You will get nothing at wedding time. When you will come again to perform the *gauna* ritual (final departure of the bride from her childhood home), then you will get everything—elephants, horses, wealth, a cot to be seated on, a dish to eat on, a small pitcher to drink from—you will get all that. And people will also give me away to you.' That's what it means."

Umesh explained, "It does not happen usually when the wedding takes place under the *marawa* that Mahadewa was seated at the altar (*chauk*) and got sleepy. He could go to sleep. She just woke him with the toe. It does not happen like that. The bride must never touch the bridegroom with her foot. This is a very deep part of Indian culture. That a girl (the bride) would touch him with the toe to wake up. She might do it if by chance he falls on her—for her own dignity. Actually, these marriage priests take too much time. The groom and bride almost always begin to sleep. Usually this song would be sung after midnight. This song could be for *tilak*, but actually it refers to what takes place under the wedding tent while they get married. But the girl is too shy to touch the man with her toe.

"This is an arranged wedding," Umesh said. "She has never seen this man. Actually, this is for Lord Shiva. Gauradei had had visions of Shiva for a long time. She had visions of him again and again. Finally, he blessed her. It is like an arranged marriage. But this song is for the gods, but it is also about the ordinary people. At the same time, it does not happen when Gauradei kicked Shivaji with her toe, Shivaji became angry. The priest is chanting mantras. She leaned on him with her elbow. It does not happen. There is no way it can happen like this. If they like each other, the girl can show with her eyes or show other people that she was touching unknowingly.

"Then she is saying—words put into her mouth by the composer—these words are from the mouth of Gauradei, and she is telling to Shiva, 'You will not get anything at the time of the wedding. You will get everything at the time of *gauna*.' But absolutely this would never happen. I don't think the girl would ever say these words. But this is a song. And tradition is this, that he would not receive dowry at the time of the wedding. He would get dowry at the time of *gauna*, the final departure of the bride. Because in olden days, the girl would get married at a very young age—a child marriage. So whatever was given to the groom was given at the time of *gauna*, which could be after the age of thirteen or fourteen. In the olden days, they donated a *kanya* (child virgin), not a lady. Untouched. She goes to her *sasural* (husband's home) and is under the control of the *sas* (mother-in-law). The *sas* will decide when is the right time for her to go to her husband.

"Now she says that the father will donate elephant and horses, and the brother will offer the new cow. Mother will offer the yellow *dhoti* (dress). *Bhabi* (sister-in-law) will offer the ring. The groom will ride on elephant and horse. The elephant and the horses are to ride, and the cow will go behind, and a man will go behind to encourage the cow to go with a small stick. Put on the yellow *dhoti*. And put a ring on your finger. After having a meal off the dish, Mahadewa drank water out of the jug. And Mahadewa slept on the cot covered with quilt. I think the next words come from the composer. That you will sleep with Gauradei with you on that cot.

"So they are taking so many things to her *sasural* (in-laws' home). This song explains for the dowry, also useful things for a groom to take from his *sasural*. Family people also offer a cot and quilt—they give them to the groom. Before, the family wouldn't let any man touch or even see their daughter. But for the bridegroom, they offer the cot and the quilt."

I was excited. Here was a rare jewel of a wedding singer who had the whole ritual, lasting days and days, clearly worked out in her head. And here was a bridegroom, Mahadewa, who was just as greedy as Lizzie. Were weddings worldwide about the exchange of goods?

I was sincere. "We are very lucky that we met you here in Ballia," I said to her.

"She has a very sweet voice," Umesh said.

"Whatever I sing I will also give you the meaning and explain everything to you," Gangajali said, taking delight in our delight.

After this exchange, the three of us—me and Umesh and Gangajali—seemed to have a meeting of minds. From that moment onward, we grew very close.

*Moving ahead in time, at our apartment, Banaras, 2007*

All this had taken two hours to translate into English. We wondered what elephant pearls were. But we were pleased with our work. Later we had the chance to look up elephant pearls in the Hindi dictionary. They are special round bones that are found in the head of certain elephants. When the elephant dies, people bury the elephant until all the flesh is eaten—which takes months. Then they dig up the bones for ivory. They may find that this elephant has an elephant pearl.

Umesh coaxed me on to translate one more *tilak* song.

We turned back to the heavy file, noting that the number of pages that we had turned over—that we had done—was but small.

*Again, back at the Sarang Hotel with Gangajali, Ballia, 1989*

"Now people arrive with the *tilak* presentations at the door of the bridegroom," Gangajali said. "Then what will the bride's people sing? And what will the bridegroom's people sing?"

**SONG 2**

*Tilak*

Where is the *tilak* party from?
Where are you going with this *tilak*?
You are going with the *tilak*.
Where are the father and son from?
You are going with the *tilak*.
At whose door do the father and son go with the *tilak*?
The *tilak* party is composed of foreigners.
They have arrived at the door of India.
Oh, they stand at the door of India.
I am the father of the daughter.
Oh, I will perform the *tilak*.
I am the father of the daughter.
Oh, I will perform the *tilak*.
The groom's father shouts,
Oh, I will not accept the *tilak*.
I will not accept the *tilak*.
My son is studying Sanskrit.
The *tilak* gifts are not enough.
My son is studying Sanskrit.
Oh, the *tilak* gifts are not enough.
The daughter's father speaks politely.
Oh, I will perform the *tilak*.
Oh, I will perform the *tilak*.
I have a virgin daughter at home.
Oh, I will perform the *tilak*.
I have coconut, flowers, and betel leaves in my hands.
This is my capacity.
This is my capacity.
I will take my daughter and donate her at your feet.
I will take my daughter and donate her at your feet.
Then the bridegroom's father happily said,
Oh, I will accept the *tilak*.
Oh, I will accept the *tilak*.
Laxmi will appear in my home.
I will accept the *tilak*.

The study of such music, a repertory of songs such as that of Gangajali, is known as ethnomusicology, an ever-broadening field that redefines its mission over and over—and takes that job very seriously. Although we may think of ethnomusicology as a new field of study, in fact, basic interest in foreign music has existed for centuries. Western interest in non-Western music dates back to the voyages of discovery, and the philosophical rationale for the study of foreign cultures derives from the Age of Enlightenment.

Jean-Jacques Rousseau (1712–1778) argued that music is cultural, not natural, and that diverse peoples would react differently to "diverse musical accents." His *Dictionnaire de Musique* (1768) includes samples of Swiss, Iranian, Chinese, and Canadian First Nations music.

As early as the seventeenth century, Europeans, including missionaries, explorers, and civil servants, made contributions to music research in the colonies through references in diaries and monographs. Captain James Cook (1728–1779) recorded careful descriptions of the music and dance of Pacific islanders (1784). The Swiss theologian Jean de Léry (1534–1611) wrote about Brazilian music in *Histoire d'un voyage faict en la terre du Brésil* (1578), which includes musical notation and describes antiphonal singing between men and women and dancers in elaborately feathered costumes. Jacques Cartier (1491–1557) observed Canadian First Nations singing and dancing on his New World voyages (1534, 1535–1536), and his crew entertained the Amerindians with "trompettes et aultres instruments de musique."

One of the fathers of ethnomusicology, then known as comparative musicology, was the Austrian scholar Erich M. von Hornbostel (1877–1935). Although Hornbostel's PhD was in chemistry, he moved from Vienna to Berlin, where he was taken under the wing of Carl Stumpf (1848–1936), whose interests lay in music psychology and psychoacoustics. Together they worked at the Berlin Psychological Institute, later the Berliner Phonogramm-Archiv, which remains one of the great sound archives of Europe. Their work, along with that of their students, was the beginning of what is now known as the Berlin School of Ethnomusicology.

What would von Hornbostel make of Gangajali's *tilak* song here? In his pursuit of musical meaning, he searched for performances that were similar, analogous, or equivalent to one another. Hornbostel insisted that transcriptions and analyses of music could never be free of subjectivity and that Western analyses would suffer without the interpretation of the local musician, which he regarded as "essential." I believe he would have been particularly pleased to work with Gangajali as her repertory is vast and her songs long and complex. So much material to compare. Hornbostel would have compared these songs carefully, one with the next, to articulate the generalities of her style. Unfortunately, he was only able to work with wax cylinders with a maximum length of from two to four minutes. And in most cases, he himself had not collected these samples—from here and there around the world. I know he would have been especially delighted to discuss Gangajali's songs with Umesh and with Gangajali herself—local perspectives from the inside that he considered critical.

Umesh said, "In this song, the question is being asked to those people who are coming to perform the *tilak*. 'Where are you from? Where are you going? Where are you from, son and father?' They are moving, and people are asking, 'Where are you from? Where are you going carrying the *tilak*?'

"'Father and son, to whose door are you going with the *tilak*?' The *tilak* people are from a foreign land and arrived at the Gate of India." Umesh laughs. "And stood at the door of India. I am father of the daughter. I will arrange this wedding. I will perform this ritual of the *tilak*. The groom's father shouted in anger, 'I will not let the *tilak* be performed. My son has gone to study near the priest. The dowry of the *tilak* looks little.' The daughter's father requested, 'I will perform the *tilak*. I have a *kanya* at my home.' It looks for us unusual to say 'virgin girl.' *Kanya* is a very auspicious word. Even saying 'pure' looks ugly in front of the word *kanya*. *Kanya* is a goddess.

"This is a very nice song," Umesh continued. "'I have flowers, betel leaf, and coconut. This is my limit. This is all that I have. I will donate my daughter at your feet.' It shows he has the right to be angry whether he gets anything or not. Then, smilingly, the groom's father said, 'I will accept the *tilak*. Laxmi (the goddess of wealth) will appear at my home. I will accept the *tilak*.' We consider the *bahu* (bride) is the Laxmi of the house. She brings blessings to the house. She brings children and also helps in so many ways to run the household."

Gangajali said, "This is sung before the *tilak* ceremony. Now the *tilak* will continue, and several songs will be sung when they come and sit at the altar to perform the ritual. The ritual and the songs concern the *tilak* itself—whatever is given and taken. Let's continue.

"These songs are sung at the house where there is a wedding," Gangajali said. "If anybody knows them, then women sing the entire songs. And if they don't know the song, they will just sing three or four lines. Whenever a wedding takes place in Ballia this song will be sung."

"Now the bride's side people come to the altar to perform the *tilak*," Umesh added. "They get to see the courtyard of the bridegroom's family. People look around and see if the courtyard is big or small. As the bridegroom's family is demanding a dowry, the bride's father is curious. What do they have that they are asking for so much dowry? Then the bridegroom's father says . . ."

Gangajali began to hum. "The *tilak* is little."

"Sing any song," Sashi said.

"No, no," I said.

"Doesn't she want the important songs?" Gangajali asked Sashi.

"Yes, I want all the important songs, all of them," I said.

"What do you mean the main song?" Sashi asked. "She wants all the songs. Then sing the main one for the *tilak*. How about 'The plate is made out of brass'? Sing that one. Sing a *gali* for her. At least sing a little bit. The tape is running."

"She, Sashi, was thinking that you were doing nothing," Umesh said. "She didn't understand your job at all. She thought you wanted to hear a few Indian songs and then just run away after a day or two."

Gangajali knew Sashi well. As with practically all groups of Indian village singers, one woman is the leader, and the others follow. Gangajali was the leader. She had brought Sashi to support her, to reinforce the singing, and to repeat the line if she grew weary. In fact, Sashi didn't sing very much. Mostly, she lay on my bed and just commented with whatever came into her mind. Gangajali also brought Sashi because Sashi was of a high caste. With Sashi's help, Gangajali could keep her dignity and respect, even though they were singing in a hotel.

She ignored Sashi's interruption and continued her repertory of *tilak* songs.

"Then the girl's side people are saying . . ."

### SONG 3

#### *Tilak*

Son, sit down properly.
The people have come for the *tilak*.
Son, sit down properly.
The people have come for the *tilak*.
He has the coconut in its shell in his hand to offer in your hand.
He has the coconut in its shell in his hand to offer in your hand.
Son, sit down properly.
The people have come for the *tilak*.
He has rupees in his hand.
He will give them in your hand.
He has a garland in his hand.
He will give it in your hand.
He has gold in his hand.
He will give it in your hand.
Son, sit down properly.
The people have come for the *tilak*.
He has cloth in his hand.
He will give it in your hand.
He has a pot in his hand.
He will give it in your hand.
Son, sit down properly.
The people have come for the *tilak*.
All the gentlemen have come to see you.
Son, sit down properly.
The people have come for the *tilak*.
He has a watch in his hand.
He will give it in your hand.
He has a golden chain in his hand.
He will give it in your hand.

Son, sit down properly.
The people have come for the *tilak*.
The people have come for the *tilak*.

This song, unlike Song 2, is not a dialogue. It is entirely from the perspective of the girl's father, offering helpful advice to the son. The father's comments explain clearly what is about to happen.

There are two phrases in each verse of the song. We can label them. Phrase A begins around the tonic and rises to the fifth degree during phrase B. Phrase C starts around the fifth degree and descends to the tonic in phrase D. In this simple manner, the song proceeds, with the father telling the son what is about to happen. "Son, sit down properly. It is time for the *tilak* ceremony. They will give you a coconut, rupees, a garland, gold, cloth, a pot, a watch, and a golden chain."

For this song, I believe that von Hornbostel would have been interested in the repeating four-line stanzas and also the melodic structure, which he might have expressed as ABCD. For him, however, most noticeable would have been the melodic contour of the song. Phrase A lingers around the tonic; phrase B rises to the fifth degree; phrase C opens high and begins to descend; and phrase D descends further down right to the tonic. There is symmetry here, and I believe this would have fascinated our pioneering comparative musicologist, Hornbostel. He might have been considering songs from other cultures that had similar melodic contours and puzzling about what such commonalities meant. The goal was to compare all the music of all the world. I suppose it still is.

When the song finished, I asked, "Who is 'he'?"

"The girl's father," Gangajali replied. "He has all these things to offer. This song is explaining all those things of those days that were given at the time of *tilak*."

"She did not mention a TV," Umesh said. "She did not say bicycle. She did not mention motorcycle or car. She could mention so many things of these days. Suppose she were singing of today. She was singing of olden days—what things were given at the time of *tilak*.

"I got a watch at the time of my marriage," Umesh said. "It was golden but not gold. Oh, I used it for a long long time, I did. It was not electronic. My watch cost ₹110 ($2.25) at that time. These days a watch is for ₹3,000, ₹4,000, ₹5,000 ($40.00 to $74.00). We get electronic watches. I got this one I'm wearing for ₹600 ($9.00).

"We still give these things, like pots, coconut, betel leaf to chew, garland, cloth, such things. These are always there. Nobody gives a watch to the groom these days. People do not give a bicycle now. People give motorbikes and cars."

"It gets quite expensive," I said.

"Yeah, this is a part of the dowry. If they say we want these things at the time of *tilak*, then we must do it. Otherwise, a fight begins. Sometimes gifts are not given. Sometimes the requirement comes at the beginning from the groom's side—what they want at the *tilak*. So sometimes we make the settlement when these things will be given. Sometimes the girl's side does not agree to give at the time of *tilak*. Then the groom's side can say, 'We do not accept the *tilak*.' This is very serious business. They can reject the wedding because of lack of dowry at the time of *tilak* or before the *tilak*," Umesh said.

"Is this the *tilak* one?" Sashi asked. "He didn't give the golden dish. He didn't bring the brass jug. Sing this one."

"Sashi said something wrong," Umesh said. "Sashi speaks and interrupts in the song. Interrupts her if she sings something wrong."

Gangajali ignored Sashi and said, "This song is from the boy's side, at his house, where the *tilak* is performed. The men from the bride's party have arrived with their presents for the bridegroom. The bridegroom sits at the altar. Then the bride's side people say, 'Son, sit down properly. All have come with the *tilak*. And he has the coconut in the shell in his hand. He will give it. He has gold, he has a watch. And they have come with clothes, pots, and everything to give in your hand. And you sit down properly. He will give everything in your hand.' So the boy got seated."

*At our apartment, Banaras, September 17, 2007, evening*

By the time we had translated these three songs, many hours had passed, and night had fallen. It was slow work that had to be done very carefully. Umesh left my room to let me rest.

There was solace in work, I reflected. It was time consuming and intellectually challenging—for us to decide on the exact word in English, the exact phrases that would convey the Bhojpuri meaning in a beautiful way. It was a goal that we could never reach. But we could try—try hard. The English-speaking reader should catch on to something of the grace of these songs and the complexity of the poetry and the complexity of the wedding.

It is not easy to create a translation, a poem to be read in English based on a sung text in Bhojpuri. And all the while, we had been communicating in Hindi, a third language. And why would the *tilak* begin with songs of Shiva, the almighty Lord Mahadewa, and his consort, Gauri? Is the marriage in this simple village to be compared with the marriages of the gods in the sky? Might this Shiva song appease the gods? These were big questions.

FOURTEEN

# "DRESS HIM IN A BRA AND BODICE": *GALI* FOR THE *TILAK*

*At our apartment, Banaras, September 18, 2007*

The next morning, when Umesh came in with the day's quota of work, it was appropriate enough that these were *gali*s, loving songs of insult and abuse. Trollope could have made great use of these in his work. When women sing *gali*s for you, you could be sure that they love you. You had to have become a great friend as they contained obscenity and swearing. For these, Umesh was rarely asked to leave the room, despite the common notion that *gali* are not sung before men—at least in a hotel room. But Gangajali was happy to sing them for Umesh. She had come to trust us both.

We turned again to the big file. More pages had been turned over, a little progress made.

"So here we have *gali*," Umesh explained. He was pleased.

*Continuation of our first session, back at Hotel Sarang, Ballia, July 1989*

Once again, the year is 1989, and Gangajali's friend Sashi is speaking.

"Now when the party from the bride's side arrives in the groom's village, then the groom's side women will sing *gali* for them."

"Yes," Gangajali said. "There are so many more songs for *tilak*. Here is a *gali*."

### SONG 4

#### *Tilak*

Show me some light so I can inspect the *tilak*.
Show me some light so I can inspect the *tilak*.
Show me some light so I can inspect the *tilak*.
Show me some light so I can inspect the *tilak*.
If he has brought the old gold, we will swear at him a thousand times.
If he will bring the old gold, we will swear at him a thousand times.
We will tie up the *tilak* people in the courtyard.
We will tie up the *tilak* people with the pole.
Show me some light so I can inspect the *tilak*.
Show me some light so I can inspect the *tilak*.
If they will bring the old watch, we will swear at them a thousand times.
If they will bring the old clothes, we will swear at them a thousand times.
We will tie up the *tilak* people in the courtyard.
We will tie up the *tilak* people with the pole.
Show me some light so I can inspect the *tilak*.
Show me some light so I can inspect the *tilak*.
If they will bring the rotten fruit, we will swear at them a thousand times.
If they will bring the rotten fruit, we will swear at them a thousand times.
We will tie up the *tilak* people in the courtyard.
We will tie up the damn *samdhi* (bride's father) in the courtyard.
Show me some light so I can inspect the *tilak*.
Show me some light so I can inspect the *tilak*.
If he will bring the old golden chain, we will swear at them a thousand times.
If he will bring the old golden chain, we will swear at them a thousand times.
We will tie up the *tilak* people in the courtyard.
We will tie up the damn *samdhi* with the pole.
Show me some light so I can inspect the *tilak*.
Show me some light so I can inspect the *tilak*.
If he will bring the old clothes, we will swear at him a thousand times.
If he will bring the rotten coconut, we will swear at him a thousand times.
We will tie up the *tilak* people in the courtyard.
We will tie up the damn *samdhi* in the courtyard.
We will tie up the damn *samdhi* in the courtyard.
Show me some light so I can inspect the *tilak*.
Show me some light so I can inspect the *tilak*.

### SPOKEN

"This is sung after the *tilak*."

This song has an awkward start as the ladies try to decide which song to sing next. The first two lines are sung tentatively until Gangajali swings into full voice on line three. The melodic structure of this song is quite basic. Phrase A is used for all the verses and moves around the lower pitches of the octave. The melody switches to phrase B when the singer declares, "If he will bring the old clothes, we will swear at him a thousand times" and similar lines. The pitch for phrase B is at a higher level than that for phrase A.

In the mid-nineteenth century, scholars believed that such songs belonged to the body of so-called "primitive" music, with its monophonic style, and that such songs might hearken back to the music of prehistory—Paleolithic cavemen and -women. A theory developed called the contemporary ancestor, whereby anthropologists believed that they might learn of prehistoric peoples by studying isolated peoples in modern times, in particular those that had not yet been "discovered." Contemporary with the publication of Charles Darwin's *On the Origin of Species* (1859) were anthropologists arriving at similar conclusions about evolutionary theories—social Darwinism—as applied to human culture. Edward Taylor's *Researches into the Early History of Mankind* (1865) drew on a vast array of increasingly available ethnographic sources to argue that modern Europeans had evolved from so-named "savages," an idea that appeared to be confirmed by the simultaneous arise of archaeology, which provided great resources and examples.

For comparative musicologists, this notion in the field of cultural study had the most unfortunate effect of dividing so-called simple songs, and in these they would include the songs of Gangajali, from later so-called evolved forms, such as, I suppose, a Haydn symphony—a polyphonic composition played by many different instruments all tuned to the same tonality and all following the same (rather simple) rhythmic patterns according to an agreed-upon set of fixed rules. Although all modern ethnomusicologists have rejected this idea, for scholars in the mid-nineteenth century, the notion proved to be fascinating. Was it really that contemporary thinkers supposed that as Gangajali and her descendants and her tribe and in particular the "population" to which she belonged evolved, their descendants would compose symphonies?

From my perspective, Gangajali's body of songs presented here is as great a human artistic achievement as Wagner's *Ring*. She illustrates every stage of a long and complex ceremony, protecting all participants with magical incantations against the ancestors, natural forces such as dust storms and floods, destructive creatures such as cobras and scorpions, and even basic kitchen equipment, which can also turn against you without warning. She warns the women to tie up the winnowing basket. Bundling up these evil spirits together for the duration of the wedding, she then leads the women singers through the complex and essential songs for the rituals held at the home of the bride and the home of the bridegroom. All this leads up to the climax—the actual donation by the father of the bride, his virgin daughter, to the bridegroom. At this very moment, an almighty eclipse violently shakes the entire world, both the Earth and the Moon. It shakes the universe. At this critical point, the bride cries out for help to all her kinfolk by name, one by one, to save her from her fate. But no one steps forward.

Her lineage is lost, her face covered, and she is shortly to be whisked off to the home of strangers to live for the rest of her life. Is this power any less than that of Wotan?

The mood in the hotel room grew lighthearted as Gangajali explained this *tilak* song. "This song is sung while the *tilak* is being performed," she explained. At the beginning of this first session, I had been completely anxious and tense. Now, I too was laughing with everybody else.

Gangajali continued her explanation. "As it happened, the light was out while they were inspecting the *tilak*. 'Oh brother, show the light a bit so I can inspect the *tilak* in case these people have brought the inferior things for the *tilak*. In case there are old things, if the clothes are inferior, if the coconut is rotten, or if these people have brought brass in place of gold. If they have offered these things, then these people will remain tied up in the courtyard. We will not let them go.'"

"Actually, they are not swearing," Umesh said. "But this is the way they will swear. This *gali* is really a very good *gali*. If they had not done it, then we would have sworn. They will not bring old gold. They will bring new gold. They will not bring a rotten coconut. They will bring a new one. So, similarly, she is singing that 'we will do, we will do. We will swear at you if the things are old, if the things are rotten.' But they are not swearing. Even then, whatever comes, women will sing these songs. They can make a talk. Women might whisper inside but not in front of the groom and his father. In front they will sing *gali*."

"They bring the golden chain, the watch, all these things," Sashi said. "The golden locket. We people have the silver one, but that locket is of gold. At this ceremony three or four women sing together. Then the sound is louder. She is singing alone here."

"Yes," Gangajali added. "We normally have three or four in a group. We sing with musical instruments. Then it sounds sweet."

"Don't they play with *dholak-olak* and other instruments?" asked Sashi.

"Yes," said Gangajali. "Each throat gets support from each other. Even if I have to sing alone, there will be a harmonium, and that will help. But with the harmonium the words are difficult to understand. You would not understand it. The voice will get drowned out by the sound of the harmonium."

"I understand," I said. "I know. Still, your sound is very sweet."

"Next the women of the bridegroom's side sing *gali* to the men of the *tilak* party," Gangajali said.

### SONG 5

*Tilak Gali*

Oh dishonest *samdhi*, you cheated my boy.
Oh dishonest *samdhi*, you cheated my boy.
We were promised silver coins.
We were promised silver coins.
Oh dishonest *samdhi*, you offered the paper money.
Oh dishonest *samdhi*, you offered the paper money.
Oh dishonest *samdhi*, you cheated my boy.
Oh dishonest *samdhi*, you cheated my boy.
You promised gold earrings.
You promised gold.
Oh dishonest *samdhi*, you brought fake gold.
Oh dishonest *samdhi*, you brought brass instead of gold.
Oh dishonest *samdhi*, you cheated my boy.
You promised a bundle of silk cloth.
You promised a bundle of silk cloth.
Oh dishonest *samdhi*, you gave thick *markin* cloth.
Oh dishonest *samdhi*, you gave thick *markin* cloth.
Oh dishonest *samdhi*, you gave thick *markin* cloth.
Oh dishonest *samdhi*, you cheated my boy.
Oh dishonest *samdhi*, you cheated my boy.
You promised four or five types of fruit.
You promised four or five types of fruit.
Oh dishonest *samdhi*, you brought rotten fruit.
Oh dishonest *samdhi*, you brought rotten fruit.
Oh dishonest *samdhi*, you cheated my boy.
You promised a ring and a watch.
You promised a ring and a watch.
Oh dishonest damn *samdhi*, you didn't give anything.
Oh dishonest damn *samdhi*, you didn't give anything.
Oh dishonest *samdhi*, you cheated my boy.
Oh dishonest *samdhi*, you cheated my boy.
You promised to come with five or ten men.
You promised to come with five or ten men.
Oh dishonest *samdhi*, you have brought hundreds and hundreds of men.
Oh dishonest *samdhi*, you brought one hundred men.
Oh dishonest *samdhi*, you cheated my boy.

This straightforward *gali* has two main melodies. Phrase A at the lower level is the most frequently sung. By contrast, phrase B at a higher pitch level is sung at every verse when the singer is enumerating the broken promises: "You promised a bundle of silk cloth," "You promised gold earrings," "You promised four or five types of fruit," or, "You promised a ring and a watch." These broken promises stand out musically in this little narrative due to the change in the melody and the higher pitch level.

"She is singing you promised to bring gold coins and you brought the paper money," Umesh said. "Silver is silver. Song is song. They might have never said that they would bring silver money. These *tilak gali* are from the boy's side women because the girl's side people brought the *tilak*. Here the song says that the song is sung from boy's side people swearing to the girl's side people. But when it promised earrings, it is from girl's side. So these women are mixed up with this song. Boys don't put on golden earrings. So all this is from the girl's side song. It begins as a boy's side song and suddenly comes as a girl's side song. 'You promised to bring the silky cloth (unstitched cloth—*than*). Now you brought the thick *markin*—real simple cloth.' It looks real ugly. It is just swearing. Nobody will do it. Everything that comes—the boy's side is singing to the girl's side.

"Here it is once again," Umesh continued. "These days sometimes people go in a bus. In those days, five or six people used to go. Now a full bus goes for the *tilak*. This is costly for the boy's family because they have to feed them. And it can be hell. If the boy's side doesn't have food, you can be starving. They said bring forty to fifty people in the *barat*. So they must have cooked for seventy-five people. But people were two hundred. This was in the old days.

"I remember one *barat* I joined long ago. We went by bullock carts. We needed food to feed the bullocks. We had stopped with family people for a nice lunch. Then we reached the *barat*. In the evening, after arrival, we were fed stomach-full food. But the next day we got up and ran to take a bath. I was beginning to wait for breakfast. And it didn't arrive at all. We were waiting for lunch. And at the same time, we had pouring rain. It was summer, and we stayed in the mango grove. And everybody got wet. They took off their clothes and were drying their clothes. In two or three hours, everybody got their clothes dried. But there was no food. And at almost five o'clock, the bride's side people sent two *puri*s (small fried bread pancakes) for each person. For farmers, that is nothing. But at least they could drink water. And the shop of the village was ordered to close, so even we could not even get *gur* (raw sugar). But at night, they gave a really good feast around nine o'clock in the evening—a good feast with sweets, yogurt, several types of vegetables. The wedding took place at midnight, and the departure from there was very soon. But those people who had their cycles, they left before the sun rose—very soon. They feared they would not get breakfast. The bullock carts must have left at eight o'clock in the morning. I think in summer we used to travel in bullock carts because we moved before sunrise, but it took the entire day to get home. It was hell. Nothing to eat from morning to night. I have had this happen to me, and it was just horrible."

"This is another *tilak* song," Gangajali said. "All these items are in Bhojpuri, not Hindi. This is the groom's side people saying that you cheated my son. My son is so educated. And whatever we asked for, we were promised, they did not bring. Instead of gold they brought fake gold. And we asked for Terry cotton or silk, and they brought thick *markin* cloth. They have come with all these things. And they have come with rotten fruit. And we asked for silver rupees, and they brought paper money. Now these people have cheated our boy. This is the meaning of it.

"Now the performance of *tilak* is done," Gangajali explained. "But the *tilak* people are still seated in the courtyard. All the women friends who are seated in the courtyard, now they all together sing *gali*s to these people to have them listen.

"Whatever thing there is, I am singing," Gangajali said.

"Oh, yes," Sashi said. "Those people who are Indian will understand that all these songs are from the Indian side. Now let's sing the *gali* of welcome. We welcome the *tilak* people with *gali*."

### SONG 6

*Gali*

Girlfriends, have them listen to these *gali*s of welcome.
Girlfriends, have them listen to these *gali*s of welcome.
This *tilak* person does not have glasses.
This *tilak* person does not have glasses.
Oh, put *kajal* (charcoal makeup) in his eyes.
Girlfriends, put a little bit.
Put the *kajal* in his eyes.
Girlfriends, put a little bit.
Have them listen to the *gali*s of welcome.
This damn *samdhi* does not have a *kurta* (shirt) on.
This damn *samdhi* does not have a *kurta* on.
Oh, dress him in a bra and bodice.
Girlfriends, dress him up.
Dress him in a bra and bodice.
Girlfriends, dress him a bit.
Have them listen to the *gali*s of welcome.
Girlfriends, have them listen to these *gali*s of welcome.
This damn *samdhi* does not have a watch on.
This damn *samdhi* does not have a watch on.

Dress up the *samdhi* with bangles.
Girlfriends, dress him a bit.
Dress up the *samdhi* with bangles.
Dress up the *samdhi* with bangles.
Girlfriends, have them listen to these *gali*s of welcome.
Girlfriends, have them listen to these *gali*s of welcome.
Girlfriends, have them listen to these *gali*s of welcome.
This damn *samdhi* does not have a *dhoti* (traditional white Indian trousers) on.
This damn *samdhi* does not have trousers on.
Dress him up in a sari and a skirt.
Girlfriends, dress him a bit.
Dress him up in a sari and a skirt.
Girlfriends, dress him a bit.
Have them listen to the *gali*s of welcome.
Girlfriends, have them listen to these *gali*s of welcome.
Girlfriends, have them listen to these *gali*s of welcome.
This damn *samdhi* does not have shoes on.
This damn *samdhi* does not have shoes on.
Dress him up in ladies' sandals and slippers.
Girlfriends, dress him a bit.

Sashi burst in with great enthusiasm, interrupting the song, adding some new words here and there. These *gali* were the songs that she had wanted Gangajali to sing from the very beginning.

"Dress him with sandals, anklets, and toe rings," Sashi sang. "Girlfriends, dress him a bit."

Gangajali joined in.

Have them listen to the *gali*s of welcome.
Girlfriends, have them listen.
This damn *samdhi* does not have a cap on.
These *tilak* people do not have caps on.
Oh, dress them in braid and ribbons.
Girlfriends, dress them a bit with braids and ribbons.
Girlfriends, dress them a bit.
Have them listen to the *gali*s of welcome.
Girlfriends, have them listen to these *gali*s of welcome.
Girlfriends, have them listen to these *gali*s of welcome.

Even through the entire drama of the wedding, climaxing in the frightful eclipse that shakes the world, the solar system, the universe, women singers entertain the wedding guests, regularly and often, with jokes and joking songs called *gali*. Most of these jokes are sexy jokes. Some are very mild or even composed entirely in metaphor and somewhat incomprehensible to observers unfamiliar with Indian village culture. However, others are downright straight and filthy dirty. This particular funny and delightful *gali* is mild, abusing the father-in-law of the bride (*samdhi*). The song begins with the chorus, sung at the lower pitch, descending from the fourth degree above the tonic. "Girlfriends, have them listen to these *gali*s of welcome. Girlfriends, have them listen to these *gali*s of welcome."

Then the verse lines of total abuse follow. "This *tilak* person does not have sunglasses. / This *tilak* person does not have sunglasses. / Oh, put *kajal* (charcoal makeup) in his eyes. / Girlfriends, put a little bit. / Put the *kajal* in his eyes. / Girlfriends, put a little bit." These abusive accusations lead to laughter and are easy to hear since they are sung at a higher pitch level, descending from the sixth degree above the tonic. The total effect is that of a question–answer form.

The cross dressing that is suggested here happens often enough at Indian weddings, for between the many solemn Sanskrit mantras, there is jolly chasing around among the children, with the women hurling these insults, together with funny dramas. This counterdistinction between mirth and the inevitability of life's ofttimes painful journey is an insight that Gangajali understands and of which she sings.

"Here is not just a *gali*," Umesh said. "Sometimes they *really do* put *kajal* onto the eyes of the *samdhi*. Never mind if he has a *kurta* or not, the women do dress the *samdhi*s in saris, or they put bangles on them. Really they do! It depends what kind of culture people have. Also the culture of the other side—they accept it. It is fun. Actually, they do not put sandals. But they put *bindi* here, they put lipstick there.

"Recently I participated in a wedding from the boy's side," Umesh continued. "I was in the *barat*, and they were nice. It was good food. Because in these days the *barat* goes in the evening after taking lunch there at the house of the bride, and they return in the night. But important people of the family, the relatives, stay with the bridegroom. So we people, *barat* people, return in the morning around six o'clock. And we were at home when the family people—there were four or five *samdhi*s there (uncles are all *samdhi* to the girl's side)—they were all dressed in expensive, beautiful saris—nevermind petticoats. They had lipstick, *kajal*, toe rings, and *bindi* on. Even *sindur*. The boy's father brought two saris. I don't know if all of them got two saris or not. It was Holi (the springtime festival of colors), and they all played Holi on them. And they were so courageous. They didn't mind. They may have taken an oath to go home in the same costume and show themselves to their wives. And they did. And they got out of the car and ran into the house."

Cross-dressing does take place in Indian villages. In days past, in dramas, men dressed up as women and played the women's roles. Fortunately, or unfortunately, the importance of village dramas has waned. Most homes have a television set (these days even flat-screen sets), and there are TV dramas available every hour of the day. TV series are especially popular these days.

"All the women are seated in the courtyard," Gangajali explained. "All the people are dressed up. But after all, I have to swear at them, so *gali*s have to be sung for all of them. That he does not have a watch on so he should be dressed up with bangles, and he does not have a cap on, then make a braid for him, and tie a ribbon on it. He does not have shoes on. He should be dressed in women's sandals, and he does not have a *kurta* on, so he should be dressed up with a blouse. He does not have a *choti* or a suit on, so cover him with a *lahanga* (long dress of olden days) and scarf. All the women swear at him like this. Do you understand it?" Gangajali asked.

"Are you liking it?" Sashi asked.

"Yes! I'm having a great time. I like it very, very much. It is amusing, and it helps me to understand the *tilak* ceremony better, the importance of the meeting of the bride's people with the bridegroom's people and the importance of exchanging gifts."

Gangajali continued her explanation. I wondered if this demure lady would sing some really rough *gali*. I suspected that she would not.

"While this song is sung, the bridegroom is seated at the altar," she said. "All these songs are sung at the altar in the courtyard. They did not get up yet. And the women are seated in the courtyard to one side on a sheet or mat laid on the ground. And they are singing, and the men are listening with pleasure. Later, as the people are eating, the women are seated behind them to sing. This too is still part of the *tilak* celebration. And after singing some more *gali*s, what do the women sing? Here is another type of *gali* song."

### SONG 7

#### *Gali*

Look at the *samdhi*. Oh, look at the *samdhi*. He is unusually brave.
Look at the *samdhi*.
Oh, look at the *samdhi*. He is unusually brave.
Oh, look at the *samdhi*. He is unusually brave.
The *samdhi*'s face shines brightly (twinkling).
The *samdhi*'s face shines brightly.
The *samdhi*'s face shines brightly.
Untie his *dhoti*. He has no balls or dick.
Look at the *samdhi*. Untie his *dhoti*. Look, he is a eunuch.
The damn *samdhi*.
Oh, look at the *samdhi*. He is unusually brave.

Look at the *samdhi*.
Look at the *samdhi*. He is unusually brave.
Look at the *samdhi*.
This *samdhi* comes on a donkey.
This *samdhi* comes driving an elephant.
Oh, people say he is a coachman.
Look at the *samdhi*.
People say he is an elephant driver.
Look at the *samdhi*.
Oh, look at the *samdhi*. He is unusually brave.
Look at the *samdhi*.
This *samdhi* comes on a donkey.
This *samdhi* comes on a donkey.
Oh, people say he is the damn washerman.
Look at the *samdhi*.
Oh, look at the *samdhi*. He is unusually brave.
Look at the *samdhi*.
Oh, this *samdhi* juggles with monkeys.
Oh, this *samdhi* juggles with monkeys.
Oh, people say he is a damn juggler.
Look at the *samdhi*.
Look at the *samdhi*. He is unusually brave.
Look at the *samdhi*.
This *samdhi* comes with his sister and has her dance.
This *samdhi* comes with his sister and has her dance.
Oh, people call him a damn panderer.
Oh look, the *samdhi* is a damn panderer.
Look at the *samdhi*. He is unusually brave.
Look at the *samdhi*.
This *samdhi* comes with his *bhauji* and has her dance.
This *samdhi* comes with his *bhauji* and has her dance.
Oh, people call him a drummer.
Oh, he is a tabla player, a sarangi player.
Look at the *samdhi*.
Oh, look at the *samdhi*. He is unusually brave.
Look at the *samdhi*.

Scholars—ethnomusicologists—have for decades studied the modality or tonality of traditional songs such as this *gali* sung by Gangajali. The general consensus about diatonic songs from many different cultures is that it is the third and seventh degrees of the scale that are the most flexible. Often they are called neutral intervals as their pitch may lie midway between what we call in the West a major or minor third, or, likewise, a major or minor seventh. As the verses of this song play on, the listener will note that this distinction is not random. Some phrases call for a major third, while others call for a minor third. And some phrases call for a major third in the ascent and a minor third in the descent. Basically, the minor mode suggests sadness and the major mode happiness. So for a Western audience, this song that contains both might be a bit baffling emotionally.

---

"When Jesus traveled on donkey," Umesh asked, "how was he considered?"

"He was considered great," I answered.

"But here the *samdhi* who rides on a donkey, he is not respected," Umesh pointed out. "It says this *samdhi* rides on an elephant. And this *samdhi* is a coachman. Coachman—the person who drives a vehicle."

"What is a panderer (*bharuaa*)?" I asked.

"He is the man who acts as a bodyguard of a prostitute or some dancing girl," Umesh replied. "They were not married at that time, in olden days. He could have sex with her. Drummer means that people have a caste that they dance and play *dholak*," he continued. "It is considered a low caste because he is working for prostitute women. Altogether he used to play for dancing women. Women used to have *sarangiwallah*. But in the court of kings, the sarangi had a good reputation. Nobody teaches sarangi in the city. But girls study tabla and harmonium."

"It used to be a problem of touching animal skin," I said.

"Yeah," Umesh replied. "But it is not anymore. We certainly wash our hands after playing. In olden days, people used big leather bags pulled by the bullocks to irrigate the fields, and people drank water out of that. All people did it. I did it."

I noted that being a musician—a tabla player or a sarangi player—was considered a big insult.

"These women are singing *gali*s for all those people who have come to perform the *tilak*," Gangajali explained. "That he has come riding on an elephant so people say that he is an elephant driver, a coachman, a servant. He has come on an elephant, but this elephant does not belong to him. He is a servant to the elephant, and he has come riding on a donkey. Perhaps he is a washerman. He cleans clothes and makes monkeys dance. He is an acrobat, and he makes his sister dance. He is a damn panderer. He is a tabla player or a *dholki* player. This is the *gali*. This song is for this ritual." Gangajali looked pleased at these absurd insults.

"How did you learn these songs?" we asked.

"Those people who have the desire to sing, they sing songs," Gangajali replied. "Who is happy to do it. Everybody can learn these songs. All these songs are sung in the wedding, so all we people learn them. And those people who love singing and wish to learn singing, he or she learns very quickly. And I composed three or four songs in Bhojpuri such as *bhajan*s to the Lord, *jhumar*, et cetera."

"Do you ever learn words or tunes from filmi songs?" I asked.

"No. I feel free," Gangajali replied. "I keep working. Whatever comes to my mind. I keep humming songs while I'm working, and I compose new songs on whatever topic I like. Sometimes if I am sad, I will compose a *bhajan* for God and will keep singing it and working. I don't even realize when the work is finished or how much work I have done. And this makes people happy.

"You went to the cloth seller," she continued. "That is where I work. When I go there, I keep singing from start to finish. It makes those people happy too. They all remain happy. And young and old children dance to my singing. They all dance while they are playing with me. Yes, and nobody thinks I am old or I am young or I am a child. All the people remain happy. I keep working, and I keep singing."

Gangajali and Sashi seemed to be done singing for the day. Umesh ordered tea, and we carefully packed up the equipment. It was a good day's work—to complete the *tilak* ceremony. Over tea we were mainly silent, or, in any case, whatever small talk had gone on was lost, for the Stellavox open-reel recorder and the Schoeps mic and the mic stand had been broken down for the day. But the Walkman Pro cassette recorder was still quietly running on without a fuss. By 2007, we had not yet transcribed that single cassette. The job, thankfully, like all life work, is never-ending.

FIFTEEN

# THE SONGS BECOME PERSONAL

*At Umesh's house, Karimganj, March 2014*

In March 2014, we did transcribe the little workhorse cassette. The talk was with Sashi, and it was about my sari. Pure nonsense. In those days, I did all my fieldwork wearing a sari. When I first arrived in India in 1986, Umesh and all the women I met made a great fuss about my not wearing a sari. It was a big deal, and people constantly fussed about it. I was comfortable with good Nike sneakers, jeans, and a shirt with lots of pockets. I was dressed for action. Later, on subsequent visits, I slowly began to wear saris, and by 1989, I wore nothing else. Umesh was mightily upset when he realized that I was not very useful in a sari. I could carry the Stellavox over my shoulder, but that was it. He had to manage all the luggage, even small items, by himself. I believe he started to hate my saris. Also, we thought that if I wore saris, people would stop staring at me. In fact, the opposite happened. A white woman in a sari! People had never seen anything like it. I also wore *sindur*, bangles, earrings, and so on—looking like a real Indian married woman. It fascinated onlookers. Strangers stared and stared. All heads turned.

*Back at our apartment, Banaras, September 2007*

Umesh and I looked up from the large file. We had translated three more songs and had been working steadily for some six hours. The work was going well, and Umesh was pleased that he had drawn my attention from my novel to the task at hand.

Hours and hours to translate a few songs. The work was painstaking, even tedious. We were only on page 134 of the four thousand pages. Could we complete this task? Moreover, could we understand the significance of this task? The question comes, who cares about all this—the wedding in eastern India? A sweet lady who had a gift for song? Songs that, everyone told us, were dying out? Is it ethnomusicology? Who would be the audience for such painstaking work, the work of a lifetime? I knew that this book should be easy to read. That it should give voice to the locals—the important people—and not necessarily to the scholar—the bystander. These were thoughts and questions that came to me in September 2007. And then there were other questions. Why? Why do this work? What special message did these women of Indian villages have for the world? The work itself made a beautiful and compelling story, our experiences, Umesh and me. Was that story important? Mostly, such personal relationships are not highlighted in a typical monograph in my field.

I wanted to find a new way. A New Ethnomusicology. A New Ethnomusicology that put authorship in the hands of our teachers in the "field." A New Ethnomusicology that starred our "informants." A New Ethnomusicology that set facts—whatever they are deemed to be—in social, cultural, and geographical contexts in which they were determined to be reality. A New Ethnomusicology that consisted of storytelling. And I was absolutely certain that I wanted my reader to be interrupted again and again—and again—by passages from Anthony Trollope. As physical and cultural violence had been done to Indian people by privileged white people for centuries, so I wanted to trouble my reader. The elephant in the room. I wanted the elephant front and center in this book. And in this book, his name is Anthony Trollope. I wanted storytime. "Things separate from their stories have no meaning. They are only shapes. Of a certain size and color. A certain weight. When their meaning has become lost to us they no longer even have a name. The story on the other hand can never be lost from its place in the world for it is that place."

*The first day continues with Gangajali at the Sarang Hotel, Ballia, July 1989*

"And what do you sing next?" we asked.

Gangajali replied, "We are still doing the *tilak* today. Today I am giving you a whole program of *tilak*. They are seated to eat after performing the *tilak*. I will sing the song that is sung at that time."

Sashi said, "Do not sing any obscene song." I was surprised to hear that from Sashi.

"No," Gangajali replied, "I will sing the famous 'Gopal Gari.' 'Gopal Gari' is sung at the time of food. 'Gopal Gari' is good. And everywhere you go, 'Gopal Gari' will be sung. This is the opening song. Later, women sing obscene *gali*, but this is the opening song."

"So sing the good ones and explain them," Sashi said.

Later, Umesh commented, "I believe that people in the village say 'gari.' But if you read in the books, you will find 'gali.' Gopal is Krishna."

"So is this a *gali* of Krishna?" I asked.

Umesh replied, "I think the men of the *barat* are considered Gopal. And the singing women of the village are considered *gopi*s (milkmaids)."

### SONG 8

*Gopal Gari*

Gopal came by boat.
Gopal came by boat.
Welcome them under the banyan tree.
Yes, welcome them under the banyan tree.
Take the golden cot and lie in the courtyard.
Take the golden cot and lie in the courtyard.
The barber and the *bari* caste person washes their feet.
Yes, the barber and the *bari* caste person washes their feet.
*Dal* (lentils) and rice and bread made of wheat flour.
*Dal* and rice and bread made of wheat flour.
And *parvar*. Yes, and *parvar* vegetable.
And *parvar*. Yes, and *parvar* vegetable.
Krishna Kanhaiya is seated to eat.
Krishna Kanhaiya is seated to eat.
All the girlfriends sing *gali*s.
Yes, all the girlfriends sing *gali*s.
I am the master of all three worlds.
I am the master of all three worlds.
Why are these *gali*s for me?
Yes, why are these *gali*s for me?
If you are the master of three worlds,
If you are the master of three worlds,
Why have you come to your *sasural*?
Yes, why have you come to your *sasural*?
Sing *gali*s for me and *gali*s for my mother.
Sing *gali*s for me and *gali*s for my mother.
I take them by spreading my scarf (in my lap).

Yes, I take them in my lap.
All the girlfriends sing *gali* for me.
All the girlfriends sing *gali* for me.
I take them in my lap.
I take them in my lap.
The grandmother and sister ask, "Did they make yogurt?"
The grandmother and sister ask, "Did they make yogurt?"
What did you eat in your *sasural*?
Yes, what did you eat in your *sasural*?
How did you pass your night in your *sasural*?
How did you pass your night in your *sasural*?
Son, explain it to me.
Son, explain it to me.
My mother-in-law is like the Ganges.
My mother-in-law is like the Ganges.
My sister-in-law is very loving to me.
Yes, my sister-in-law is very loving to me.
Son, you went to your *sasural* for only one night.
Son, you went to your *sasural* for only one night.
Oh, such praise for your mother-in-law.
Yes, such praise for your mother-in-law.
Mother, I swear on your life, I appeal to you.
Mother, I swear on your life, I appeal to you.
I will not go to my *sasural*.
Mother, I will not go to my *sasural*.
You were sworn at, and my sister was sworn at.
You were sworn at, and my sister was sworn at.
I will not go to my *sasural*.
Mother, I will not go to my *sasural*.
Son, your *sasural* will remain for ages and ages.
Son, your *sasural* will remain for ages and ages.
Where *gali*s were sung for me.
Yes, where *gali*s were sung for me.
I thank the fate of Janakpur.
I thank the fate of Janakpur.
Where *gali*s were sung for Dasarath.
Yes, where *gali*s were sung for Dasarath.

This especially beautiful song is essentially a conversation between the bridegroom (who takes the form of Krishna) and his mother, female relatives, and the *gopi*s—his lovers. The conversation is related in sixteen stanzas, each with four phrases. The first line is repeated, both text and tune. The third line is sung to a different tune, and the tune of the fourth is also different, even though the text of line three is repeated in line four. Hence the form of each text stanza is AABC and of each tune stanza is aabb.

Umesh explained, "She thanks the *sasural* people of her son where *galis* were sung for her. Gangajali just added these final four lines to the song—about Dasarath, Ram's father. This *gali* is for Krishna, but perhaps it may also be sung for Ram in a different way. Anyway, she sang it for Ram at the end.

"Actually, most of these songs that must be sung in the wedding are related to the Lord," Umesh continued. "And the wedding is religious, and blessings come from the Lord for that. There are different kinds of *gali*. There are women to man *galis* (men don't sing *galis*). And they feel so to laugh at that time—laughing and eating and enjoying. They can put a personal name in there, and call out individual family members—father, brother, some relatives. Some village people's names are given. So the women call these people by name in song. Like me when I was a child, I couldn't look up when they were singing *galis*. Children get very shy. Children don't hear these words, so their faces just get pink, red, and they begin to laugh too because older people sing *galis*. Other men were laughing. Here in this *gali*, the groom is considered Krishna, and the *barat* people are also Gopal.

"This is a religious *gali* actually," Umesh said. "The *gali* is not sung. They say they have given *gali*, but the *gali* is not anywhere in the song. Similarly, I say to someone, 'I will swear at you, I will swear at you,' but the swear words are not spoken. When he gets home, he praises his *sasural* women, his mother-in-law, brother-in-law's wife, the *sarahaj*. If you are Lord of all three worlds, why did you go to your *sasural*? Oh, you sing *gali* for me and for my mother. I happily take these in my lap. All the *sakhis* (girlfriends), and happily take them in my *patuk*.

"The grandmother and sister ask, 'Was yogurt made there? What did you eat in your *sasural*? And how did you pass your night in your *sasural*? Oh son, explain to me everything properly. Tell me all that has occurred.'

"Now he explains, 'Oh my mother is just as holy as the Ganga, and *sarahaj* is lovable. *Sarahaj* is very loving to me.'

"'Oh, son, you went to your *sasural* for only one night and such praise to your *sasural*. Where is Mother?'

"Then the son says, 'Oh, Mother, for your sake I'll not go to my *sasural* anymore. Oh, Mother, you were sworn at, and my sister was sworn at. I will not go to my *sasural*.'

"Then his mother says, 'Oh, son, your *sasural* people live long, from ages to ages, where the *gali* were sung for us.'

"Now the last four lines are sung for Janakpur," Umesh noted. "Perhaps it is a mistake, perhaps it is from another song, but she does not sing another song that is very related to this."

I said to Gangajali, "You know, this is a long song. Some singers just understand short songs. But this one is very big. I think those others might have forgotten."

"Everybody does not know," Gangajali said. "In fact, we people sing this song everywhere in weddings. Therefore, we people know everything. And some people know three or four songs, and this will do for them."

"They forget," I said. "I think they forget actually. It happens."

Sashi interrupted, "What time is it?"

Umesh replied, "Two o'clock, quarter past two o'clock."

"Will she explain the meaning of this song?" I asked.

"Yes," Umesh said. "Now explain to us something about this song."

Gangajali said, "So after performing *tilak* and after doing everything, all the people who came for *tilak* sit down to have a meal. Then all the ladies sit down on one side to sing *gali*s for them. So after the 'Gopal Gari,' all the other *gali* songs are obscene. But I haven't sung obscene *gali*s. So this song is called 'Gopal Gari.' This is the first *gali*. And this 'Gopal Gari' is sung everywhere while taking food. This song is sung in the very beginning everywhere in Ballia."

Sashi said, "Everywhere in the whole eastern area."

"This *gali* is sung first of all everywhere in the eastern area," Gangajali confirmed. "Therefore, I am giving you the main thing."

"She doesn't need to sing anything unusual," I said. But we were hoping they would sing some rude *gali*s.

"For those people who will listen to this, it will sound good to them," Gangajali said. "They won't feel bad. We people are doing that, singing nice songs. I am giving you the main thing. I am not giving you any songs from here and there. I am giving you the main things that are necessary at the time of the wedding."

Sashi interrupted, "Now have us come tomorrow to sing. Now we are tired."

Umesh sounded surprised. "Now, after only one hour, you got tired?"

"After any work, surely I get tired," Sashi said.

Umesh gave Sashi a bit of an order. "You lay down."

Sashi protested, "Look, three are done."

Gangajali took charge again. "There are thousands of *gali* songs, but after the end of these *gali*s, when people are ready to wash their hands after having eaten, when they are going then, then this song is sung. Oh brother, what thing I have to give, the real thing from the beginning to the end, what I want to give, I am offering. It's not that what I have given until now that I begin to sing obscene songs now. Whether you give or not, I will sing the correct thing. I will not destroy my reputation through bad work.

"So then the ladies sing . . . "

### SONG 9

#### *Gali*

People catch him. The *samdhi* is running away.
People catch him. The *samdhi* is running away.
The damn *samdhi* is asking for a toothpick.
Oh, I will give him a toothpick.
Oh, I will give him a toothpick.
Oh boys, guard his sister.

Oh, I will give him a toothpick.
The damn *samdhi* is asking for paddy straw.
The damn *samdhi* is asking for paddy straw.
Oh, I will give him paddy straw.
Oh, his mother guards the gate.
Oh, I will give him paddy straw.
His sister guards the gate.
Oh, I will give him paddy straw.
Then the damn *samdhi* is asking for a *lota*.
The *tilak* people are crying, "*Lota lota*."
Oh, I will give him a *lota*.
The effeminate man beat them up with a stick.
Oh, I will give a *lota*.
People catch him. The *samdhi* is running away.
People catch him. The *samdhi* is running away.

Like the preceding songs, this *gali* directed at the father-in-law is organized in verses and phrases with different tunes that are sometimes sung only once and at other times repeated. In 1989, we recorded it on my Stellavox SP7 open-reel tape recorder using a crossed pair of Schoeps hypercardioid condenser mics. In 2014, the Archives of Traditional Music at Indiana University digitized this collection, ensuring that the recording of this song would be rescued in the event that the magnetic tape be damaged or destroyed or deteriorated. My three sons grew up with an unreasonable fear of magnets. I warned them over and over not to put any magnet near my tapes. In fact, magnets were pretty much banished from the house.

The Archive for Traditional Music digitized broadcast wav format heard here can now be copied over and over. The Gangajali song files were sent to me from ATM on a hard drive. Copies can be made of copies, and the result is lossless—no quality is lost from copy to copy, as would have been the case working with analog tape. Back in the 1980s, because open-reel tape was so fragile, really the original was only played once to produce a working copy. A scholar would never use the original tape to shuttle back and forth during analysis. For a working trip, such as that in 1989 to meet with Gangajali, I carried with me some two hundred blank five-inch reels of tape. They were very heavy and filled several suitcases. Pretty much I tossed pajamas and a toothbrush on the top and bought what else was needed when I got to Delhi. Excess baggage was a big line item for every research grant. It is difficult to imagine today how this material can be held on a single flash card the size of a postage stamp. Modern digital recording equipment is small and relatively inexpensive. It must be nearly impossible for a young ethnomusicologist in 2019 to imagine what it was like working with open-reel tape. The Stellavox and the mics were worth over $15,000, and the tape itself was costly. Archives and recording companies sympathetic to world music were willing to lend out equipment. Put simply, it took a lot of pure grit.

And then she continued with the next *gali* without a pause, leaving us no time to catch our breath or discuss the funny songs. Here is the next *gali*, again aimed at abusing the father-in-law. After all the expense of the wedding, after the months, if not years, in an exhaustive search for a suitable partner for their child, I reckon hearing these silly insults must come as a kind of soothing relief.

### SONG 10

Oh *samdhi*, leave the payment for our *gali*s on the ground.
*Samdhi*, leave the payment for our *gali*s on the ground.
Oh, our *gali*.
Oh, tie up the payment for our *gali*s in a pouch and take it away.
Collect the money for my *gali*s in a pouch and take it away.
If it does not fit in a pouch,
Put them in a motorcar and take it away.
Oh, put it in the motorcar and take them away.
But *samdhi*, leave the payment for our *gali*s on the ground.
*Samdhi*, leave the payment for our *gali*s on the ground.
Oh, put it in the motorcar and take them away.
But *samdhi*, leave the payment for our *gali*s on the ground.

While collecting these songs was difficult in the 1980s, for scholars working in the 1880s, an amazing decade in the history of ethnomusicology, recording equipment was not available. The Edison Cylinder machine was invented on July 18, 1877, and became available commercially by 1888. So the pioneering comparative ethnomusicologists and psychologists had to rely on their musical training and a good ear and especially on the extreme patience of native artists to repeat their songs over and over. A landmark noted in the history of ethnomusicology is the 1886 article by Carl Stumpf, "*Lieder der Bellakula-Indianer.*" A group of Canadian Bella Coola Indians visited Berlin in 1886. Stumpf heard them and arranged with one of the singers, Nutsiluska, to sit with him for several days to notate his singing. No recording machine was available to them, so Nutsiluska had to repeat his songs over and over while Stumpf painstakingly notated them by hand. First Stumpf noted the overall structure of the song. On a second listening, as Bruno Nettl describes in *The Study of Ethnomusicology* (2015), he notated the main pitches of the song, finding all the while that this work was so challenging that many earlier transcriptions "by ear" done by other scholars might be unreliable. Upon subsequent repeatings by Nutsiluska, he filled in the rhythm and the incidental pitches. Stumpf's article goes on to describe the differences between the tonality of Nutsiluska and the overall features of the Western tempered scale. Nettl calls Stumpf's Bella Coola recordings "descriptive," "the essence of the piece," in that they reflected the average of many slightly different renditions and not the exact analysis of any one rendition.

Stumpf wrote, "I could only put fragments down on paper, on the one hand because I am not a mighty musical stenographer, on the other hand because the communal dances, in which most steps are performed with both feet at the same time, the uninterrupted drum accompaniment and other circumstances (such as . . . the clapping of the jaws of the monstrous wooden masks . . . the constantly swung rattle of the medicine man) interfered. . . . During these proceedings one had, above all, the impression of a heaven uproar, a true devil's music, in the midst of which only here and there distinct tones were drifting" (Nettl, trans. Nettl, 2015).

Carl Stumpf would have liked Gangajali and her willingness to patiently repeat songs, sing for hours on end, and explain her songs. And I know that he would have really liked my Stellavox and those condenser mics. Our sessions with Gangajali were not essentially different from Stumpf's sessions with Nutsiluska—two pairs of listeners and singers working in small rooms, both out of the intended context of the song performance, in both cases somehow cut off from any notion of reality. However, since we were using hi-fi recording equipment, Gangajali only had to sing each song once. And for this circumstance, Umesh and I had the upper hand as we had had the opportunity to participate in dozens and dozens of Hindu weddings in Ballia and environs. Stumpf never had the opportunity to really hang out with the Bella Coola.

Gangajali explained these two *gali* songs. "The women sing this as people are eating, drinking, washing their hands, and going out. Then these *tilak* people have to give something to the singing ladies. So they are going without paying. Then the singers are saying that they have sung *gali*s for them. So offer payment for my *gali* singing before you go. And the *gali* I have given you, tie them in a bundle and take them with you. If they don't fit in a bundle, put them in a motorcar and take them away. Tie them and take them away in an airplane or fill up a truck and take them away."

We were all laughing.

Umesh explained further. "Give me the value of it. The worth of it. I have abused. I have given *gali* to you. Given so many *gali*. Take it in a bundle, take it in a small car. If they don't fit in a small car, carry them in a bus. If they don't fit in a bus, carry them in a plane.

"Women sing *gali* as the men are eating," Umesh said. "These women keep singing *gali*, one after another. People remain seated until all people finish their meal. All must be finished. All must be seated until the last man has finished. Similarly, until all people are served, none will eat. When food and water is served, then they will begin to eat. So women sing from the beginning of this to the end. When the feast is over, and the people begin to go, people help them to wash their hands, and here they sing 'people are running away.'"

"And also I was in one wedding, and so women were singing *gali*, and the singers shouted, 'Tie some rupees in your *angocha* and throw where they are singing,' and the women doubled the money and threw it back to me. So I got paid double."

"Now this is the end of the *tilak*," Gangajali announced.

"The *tilak* is finished," Sashi said. She was always in a rush. "Now is the rest of the wedding."

Gangajali stated, "This was all about the *tilak*, from their arrival at the gate until their departure. Today I have given you the songs of *tilak*. There are so many meaningless *gali* for *tilak*. If all those are sung, then the evening will be full, and there is also no benefit in it—those songs are a useless thing of the world," Gangajali said. I believe she felt very shy to sing the roughest and funniest *gali* today, our first day working together.

Umesh protested a bit. "No, if you give more Bhojpuri *gali*, that could be good."

But Gangajali refused. "This is the end of the Bhojpuri."

"Okay, Bhojpuri or another," Umesh continued to encourage her.

Meanwhile, Sashi was humming a bit to remind Gangajali to sing "He sat on a high platform . . ."

"This is also an important *gali*," Gangajali said.

Sashi really wanted to sing the dirty *gali*s. "Then with shyness, sing this song. Sing one."

Umesh urged her on. "Do finish this reel."

And then Sashi encouraged Gangajali more. "Yes, are you singing? Sing *gali*. Sing two or three *dehati jhumar*, and the reel will finish."

"What boy should I sing it for?" Gangajali asked, gathering her courage with so much support from all of us.

"Any boy," Sashi said. "Call her own name."

"What is the name?" Gangajali asked.

"Whose name is hers, sing *gali*," Sashi said.

"Her name is Helen," Umesh said.

"For her why not sing for her brother?" Sashi really wanted to have a good time at my expense.

"Then no harm is done," Gangajali said.

"Not at all," Umesh said.

"For her, sing about her brother," Sashi said enthusiastically.

"Many women abused her with *gali*," Umesh said. That was certainly true.

"Then all right," Sashi said.

Gangajali was still worried. "Then what happens? I don't know if I will see them in the future or not. Where will I find her?"

Sashi ignored this. "Where is her brother?" she said. "What is the name of her brother?"

"Her brother's name is James," Umesh said. I was silent.

"Sing about Helen and James then," Sashi said. "Begin with the high platform."

And Gangajali began to sing.

SONG 11

*Gali*

Brother James is seated on a high platform.
Brother James is seated on a high platform.
It was broadcast everywhere that he bargains over the price of his sister.
Oh, it was broadcast everywhere that he bargains over the price of his sister.
It was broadcast everywhere that the inspector of police listens to this auction.
It was broadcast everywhere that the inspector of police listens to this auction.
He bids five rupees for the oldest one.
He bids five rupees for the oldest one.
He bids five rupees for Helen.
He bids five rupees for Helen.
He offers a priceless bid for the younger one.
He offers a priceless bid for the younger one.
It was broadcast everywhere that he offers a priceless bid for the younger one.
It was broadcast everywhere that the inspector of police hears your bid.
It was broadcast everywhere that the inspector of police hears your bid.
Oh, he asks one hundred rupees for the older one.
Oh, he asks one hundred rupees for the older one.
He asks a priceless bid for the younger one.
He asks a priceless bid for the younger one.
Alas, it was broadcast everywhere that he asks a priceless bid for the younger one.
It was broadcast everywhere that the inspector of police listens to this auction.
James is seated on the high platform.

"This is a *gali* song," Umesh said. "It is a straight *gali* that maybe James has gone to get married, and the *sasural* people are singing this *gali*. Or suppose you had another brother. The same *gali* can be sung for the younger brother too. *Gali* is *gali*. It can be sung for anyone who comes for the *tilak* or for the *barat*."

Sashi wanted more. "There is much pleasure in the chickpea field. Come on, sing that one."

"Oh, Lord," Gangajali exclaimed.

"Sing that one," Sashi said. "It's no big deal."

And Gangajali sang it.

## SONG 12

*Gali*

There is much pleasure in the chickpea field.
There is much pleasure in the chickpea field.
In the chickpea field.
Potatoes are in the chickpea field.
Oh, the bear took Helen away in the chickpea field.
The bear of Ballia took Helen away in the chickpea field.
There is much pleasure in the chickpea field.
There is much pleasure in the chickpea field.
The cabbage in the chickpea field.
Oh, the washerman of Ballia took Helen away in the chickpea field.
There is much pleasure in the chickpea field.
There is much pleasure in the chickpea field.
The cattle in the chickpea field.
Oh, the barber of Ballia took Helen away in the chickpea field.
There is much pleasure in the chickpea field.
There is much pleasure in the chickpea field.
There is a brickbat in the chickpea field.
There is a brickbat in the chickpea field.
Oh, the horse of Ballia took Helen away in the chickpea field.
There is much pleasure in the chickpea field.
There is much pleasure in the chickpea field.

"A bear taking me off to the chickpea field of Ballia. That's ridiculous," I said. "So, Umesh, what is the deep meaning of this song?"

"So enjoy," he exclaimed. "Have fun in the chickpea field! There is nothing else to say."

Decades later, in April 2017, Umesh told me what part of the female body "chickpea" stands for. I just can't say it here. I really can't!

Sashi wasn't satisfied, and she wanted to go. "Only half. Till now, half."

Umesh urged her politely. "Today you worked only one hour. For this we have come here? You seem to have to go very soon, isn't it?"

"If I don't go, how will my work be done?" Gangajali asked.

"Stay until three o'clock," Sashi suggested. "At three o'clock we people will go."

"If I do not go, my other work will not be done," Gangajali explained. "This work is not hard to do. Then I could give you some time in the evening. I have to see to other things too. I have to look after everything inside the house and outside the house. Friends and relatives come and go. What I have to do inside the house, et cetera."

"Mother of Saroj," Sashi burst in with renewed enthusiasm. "Sing a very good *jhumar* of Lord Krishna. Krishna shouts, 'Have the bangles on.' *Godna* songs, *godna* songs. The reel is only half finished."

"*Matikor*, sing any song of *matikor*," Umesh suggested.

"Not now. It will go in its place," Sashi said. "Everything will be sung in order."

"There is no time," Gangajali said. "I have already told you that I will give you songs from the *tilak* up to the end."

Umesh kept urging. He had a nice way about him. "Now, next, you can sing anything."

"Come on, sing a *jhumar*," Sashi said. "Sing a *godna* (tattoo). Sing the Mohan *bhajan*. Sing so she can fill up her reel."

So Gangajali sang.

### SONG 13

#### *Godna*

Krishna covers himself with the *dhoti*,
And puts on a scarf.
Krishna covers himself with the *dhoti*,
And puts on a scarf.

Sashi interrupted. "This is a *godna* song."

"Yes," Gangajali said.

"This is the tattoo one," Sashi said.

Gangajali continued her song:

Krishna covers himself with the *dhoti*,
And puts on a scarf.
Krishna covers himself with the *dhoti*,
And puts on a scarf.
He transforms himself into a tattoo artist. Oh, tattoo.
Oh, who will have the tattoo?
Oh, who will have the tattoo?
Oh, who will have the tattoo?
Oh, Radhika came out of her own door.
Oh, Radhika came out of her own door.
Oh, tattoo artist, come to my door.
I will get the tattoo.
Oh, tattoo artist, come to my door.
I will get the tattoo.
Oh, tattoo artist, come to my door.
I will get the tattoo.

Oh, then he held my arm.
Oh, he began to ask smilingly,
Oh, then he held my arm.
Oh, he began to ask smilingly,
What kind of tattoo will please you?
Tell me that one.
Radha, what kind of tattoo will please you?
Oh, tell me that.
Oh, tell me the kind of tattoo.
I will draw that tattoo.
A *bharath* vine on my arm (*sic*).
A *bharath* vine on my forehead.
And a Ram vine on my arm.
And a *bharath* vine on my forehead.
And a Ram vine on my arm.
And a Ram vine on my arm.
Oh, tattoo artist, draw Lachhuman and Ram on my chest.
Oh, tattoo artist, write Lachhuman and Ram on my chest.
I will have this tattoo.
I will have a tattoo.
Then make one of Saraswati on my head.
And Ram, oh Ram, on my tongue.
Make one of Saraswati on my head.
And Ram, oh Ram, on my tongue.
Oh, tattoo artist, write the Lord's name (Narayan) on my navel.
I will have this tattoo.
I will have this tattoo.

This song is a dialogue between the tattoo artist (Krishna in disguise) and the lady (Radha) who is requesting tattoos. Essentially, Krishna asks what tattoos she wants and where she wants them, and she answers these questions. The false start at the opening of the song shows how casual our sessions together were and the role of Sashi as some kind of supervisor. Sashi had been expecting another wedding song, and she objected when Gangajali sang a tattoo song. Then she settled in and enjoyed singing the tattoo song with Gangajali.

When listening to this especially beautiful song, one might observe that no single pitch is sung without some sort of decoration or ornamentation. For example, gliding into a main pitch and sliding from one pitch to another are quite easy to hear. There are many tones that fall between the cracks of the piano. This common feature of a great deal of non-Western music was of special interest to another of our pioneers of ethnomusicology, Sir Alexander Ellis (1814–1890). His seminal publication (1885), "On the Musical Scales of Various Nations," was a paper read at a London meeting of the Society of Arts. Ellis would have been delighted to work with Gangajali and would carefully notate the exact pitch of each tone into cents, a measurement that can be used for tiny intervals—as each octave comprises 1,200 cents. With specialized pitch-measuring instruments that he had devised, he examined scales from all around the world. His conclusion has become somewhat of an oath for ethnomusicologists: *"The musical scale is not one, not 'natural,' not even founded necessarily on the laws of the constitution of musical sound so beautifully worked out by Helmholtz, but very diverse, very artificial, and very capricious"* (1885). In his era, this statement was revolutionary, contrary to commonly held notions of natural pitches such as octaves and fifths. Ellis would have taken care to make exact measurements of the glides and ornamentation Gangajali presents in this song.

"This *jhumar* is done," Sashi said. "Now there is just a little bit left on the reel."

"This song is good, this tattoo song," Umesh said.

"Then I will explain this also," Gangajali said. "So the son of Jasoda, Krishna, puts on ladies' clothes like *lahanga* and *orni*. And he takes a basket and goes to Radhika in Banaras in the disguise of a female tattoo artist. And he goes from house to house, asking, 'Will somebody have a tattoo?'

"Radhika Rani came out from her house and asks him to come to her door. 'I want to have a tattoo. Tattoo me.' Then he comes and holds her arm with love. He talks happily, smilingly to her. And he loves her, so he talks to her and asks her what kind of tattoo she wants. 'Tell me what, and I will draw that tattoo.' Then she replies, 'Well, brother, tattoo Saraswati here and tattoo Ram Ram on my tongue. And tattoo Narayan on my navel. Tattoo Bharat on my arm and here tattoo Ram and Lachhuman. I like the tattoo. Draw these tattoos on me.'"

"This is a *jhumar*," Sashi said.

"Yes," Gangajali said. "This is a *jhumar* of God. This is not a human *jhumar*."

"Now sing another one," Umesh urged.

"Right," said Sashi. "Now sing the next *jhumar*. That will finish the reel."

"I will sing the next *jhumar*," Gangajali said.

"Sing! Oh, sing," said Sashi.

"I was found, by the way," Gangajali said. "You found me. We found each other. I met you through the *shadi* (wedding). Otherwise no other lady would sing like this for you. I am telling you the truth that no singer will give you the songs from the beginning to the end like this."

"I came so many thousands of miles to find somebody like you for singing," I said.

"We people have come eight thousand miles," Umesh said.

Then Gangajali was reassuring and stopped watching the reel and the clock. "After all, I don't know why after meeting you that I find so much love. I agreed to work with you. Otherwise I don't do like this. But I don't know why I have love for her in my heart that I am offering these songs."

"Thank you," I said. Some moments during fieldwork are never forgotten.

"Because of the fast today," Gangajali said, "I have not had anything to eat or drink. No. I am not taking any different thing. In such condition I live. In the night, nine, ten, eleven o'clock, I will take some fruit, et cetera. This is for the blessings from God."

"I think you should decide for tomorrow," Umesh said. "Now tell us about tomorrow."

Umesh was trying hard to get these two singers organized. "We need to know what time the next program is so we can meet you and be ready," he said. "Give us a definite time. We need to know every day."

"My time will be in the noon," Gangajali said. "The evening or the morning will not do."

"Okay," I said. "From what time?"

"Yes," Gangajali said. "As that twelve o'clock is the time today, and what we gave, that time will stay the same."

And the ladies left us. And that was the first day with Gangajali of Ballia. We had started to understand each other through the bond of music.

SIXTEEN

# "WE SELL DREAMS"

*Banaras, Sandhya Guesthouse, 2006*

"What is the significance of the *tilak*?" Umesh asked. "We call the mark on the head a *tilak*. A *tika* is a dot. The *tilak* is a line drawn with the ring finger or the thumb. In olden days it was a sign. To make a mark on the head like a *tilak* so the person could feel his responsibility. This was for great kings or for any battle. Then you don't want to show your back in a battle. Either the mother does this, or the wife does this. And when the warrior returned, he was again marked with a *tilak* and then sprinkled with flowers. If you go to Jaipur palace, they have a place for the queen to stand up. When the king used to come in the main door, the queen would sprinkle flowers from the top to welcome his victory.

"So when we arrange weddings, the *barat* is considered the bridegroom's army. And the bridegroom goes with his army to his *sasural* to win his wife. Happily, the bride's father gives them a place to stay, food—everything. As the king used to go to war, they used to have music for them—fighting music, drums. And this wedding *barat* also comes with music.

"In olden days when the *barat* used to go, they used to carry weapons with them. We didn't know if we would run into some bad people on the way, so to face them, people had weapons for their defense. The boy's family used to carry the food for the *barat* in case the girl's family didn't have food for the *barat*. What else does a warrior need to fight? Food for the army, weapons, people. *Dal* means army.

"When women sing Bhojpuri songs, they sing, '*Kahaa dal utarel ho kahawanwa*.' When is the army going to go? Where is the bridegroom's army going to stay?

"Also, in olden days, for the force, they needed elephants to fight with and also horses. They also carried elephants and horses in weddings to show off, as today people bring their best cars. So in the Bhojpuri songs, elephants and horses are often mentioned. And I believe that these songs were made for rich and big people, not for small people, and for an olden age. But slowly other people accepted this as a tradition made for everyone. Kings were surely offering pearls, but simple people don't have pearls, so they offer rice and say it is pearls. Pearls as white as the rice."

"So you think these songs were originally composed by big people?" I asked.

"Yes. Lately they were carried out by everyone, I believe. Why these songs for Rama? Why the songs are not for village people? Rama, King Dasarath, girlfriends, pearls. Why not rice instead of pearls? It is a question in my mind. When I was in the States, I saw a documentary film of Raj Kapoor, and somebody asked him a question, 'Why do you show to Indian people what is not there?' He said, 'Oh, I sell dreams for Indian people.' So the wedding is also like a dream. We accept dreams. We don't accept reality, I believe. The pearls are not real, but we say that these are pearls.

"'We sell dreams,' Kapoor said. Sure. Because something that is shown in the movies is not reality," Umesh continued. "Like the hero meets the girl, they sing five or six songs, and they get married. It is not real life. Rarely do I see movies about the village. If they show a village, it does not look like a village at all. They are shown as sophisticated. I believe there are movie villages. They make them in their studio. And we love to watch these movies, and we never complain that this is not reality. But Kapoor, he was not the first pioneer to make a search about selling dreams in Indian culture. For the wedding in song they mention pearls instead of rice. The door is made out of rubies. Oh, I wish I could have a ruby door. Elephant pearls. What is it? In a way, it shows that these are things that belong to this earth. How many people have seen the pearls and gems? A simple village person has not seen them. But they know these names, these words, these verses, these poems, these songs. They are singing about treasure. Something simple. When the sister says to the brother, 'Open the wealth,' it may only be a few rupees. But she will say, 'Open the wealth.' It is a dream."

SEVENTEEN

# *SAGUNI* SONGS: "THIS NIGHT IS OURS"

*When you use something for your life, it is considered auspicious. Like here in this song, when the yogurt is being made in the new pitcher and the starter is nectar. You can see that pitcher is new, auspicious, and the starter comes as nectar to keep the world running.*

—Umesh

### *Sarang Hotel, Ballia, July 1989, the second day with Gangajali*

As soon as Gangajali and Sashi had left us yesterday afternoon, Umesh and I got straight to work. We broke down the equipment in the proper order. Rescuing the Schoeps mics was first as these were the most delicate and sensitive items we had. Then the Stellavox reel-to-reel recorder. Then we wound up all the cables and folded the mic stands. Finally, we packed up the Walkman Pro cassette recorder. Umesh was in charge of the Walkman Pro, recording all our sessions from before they began until after they ended. It was our backup.

Then came the business of labeling the tapes. It took hours to finish this, given that we could use up to four reels in an hour and that we might work for five hours. Then there were some twenty to twenty-five reels and boxes to label. And five or six cassettes.

After all this, we were pretty worn out. We ate a simple dinner supplied by the hotel and then collapsed into bed.

Today was to be our second session with Gangajali and Sashi. It was hard to decide whether Sashi was ruining everything or making it all comedy and so much fun. And, actually, we really liked Sashi.

So we set up the equipment again—the mics, the mic stands, the recorders, the cables, loading both recorders with tape and fresh batteries. We had Parker Swinger pens on a string around our necks, ready to scribble a number on each cassette, box, or tape reel.

Then we waited. And waited. And eventually they arrived.

We ordered tea for four from the hotel kitchen and then relaxed and chatted and sipped it slowly.

"So yesterday we sang songs for the *tilak*," I said. "And today I want to ask you what comes in the wedding after *tilak*."

Gangajali replied, "I am going to tell you what happens after *tilak*—"

Sashi interrupted. "The tube light is making a lot of noise. The curtain is a bit open. A bit of light will come, so we can see well enough. Then you also have to stop the fan." Sashi had become an expert, overnight, on the sensitivity of condenser microphones.

"You can also easily hear its noise," Umesh said.

"But we are suffering with this heat," Gangajali said.

"Then we will feel the heat," Sashi said.

Umesh said, "No. Meanwhile, we will start. When the song finishes, then we will turn the fan on. When the next song begins, we will turn it off."

"So from time to time," Sashi said.

"*Sagun* takes place after the *tilak* in the house of the bride and the bridegroom," Gangajali explained.

"First will you sing the *sagun* of the boy's side or the girl's side?" Umesh asked.

"The *sagun* can take place on the same day at the boy's and girl's house," Gangajali said. "It can also fall on different days. But the ritual will be the same in each house. The priest comes, and he performs the *sagun* ritual. I mean, having seen his calendar, he tells if this is a good day or a good time. You have to perform the ritual exactly at the right time. Suppose he says to perform the *sagun* ritual Friday at four o'clock in the evening. Then at that time we do the ritual.

"In the home of the bride or groom, the pounding pot and grinder—do you know how it grinds? A big sheet is laid on the ground in the courtyard, and all the neighbor women come and are seated, and women grind the *urad dal* in that grinding wheel. Five women grind turmeric with the grinding stone, and they sing the *sagun* song. I am going to sing that song."

## SONG 14

### *Sagun*

Oh oh augur (soothsayer), oh oh augur,
You bring the omen today.
Oh, because of your omen, augur,
I arrange the wedding.
Oh, because of your omen, augur,
I arrange the wedding.
I make yogurt in the new clay pitcher.
By pouring the starter like nectar,
Oh, because of your yogurt, augur,
I arrange the wedding.
Oh, because of your yogurt, augur,
I arrange the wedding.
Oh augur, with the help of the omen of the rice and *pan*,
Augur, I arrange the wedding.
Oh augur, with the help of the omen of the rice and *pan*,
Augur, I arrange the wedding.
Oh, because of your omen of the rice and pan, augur,
I arrange the wedding.
Because of the omen of the grinding wheel,
I arrange the wedding.
Oh, because of your omen, augur,
I arrange the wedding.
Oh, with the help of the omen of *uradi dal*,
With the omen of the chickpeas,
I arrange the wedding.
Because of your omen, augur,
I arrange the wedding.
With the help of the omen of the mustard oil,
With the help of the omen of the *sindur*,
I arrange the wedding.
Oh, because of your omen, augur,
I arrange the wedding.
Come, come, augur, be seated in my courtyard.
Perform the wedding.
Oh, augur, I perform the wedding of my son.
Oh, augur, I perform the wedding of my daughter.

Umesh and I learned a great deal about this song—later, in 1996 and 1999—on our trips to Mauritius, an island nation in the southern Indian Ocean. Like Trinidad, the British chose Mauritius as a destination for Indian indentured laborers. The East India Company had decided to start its experiment of Coolie indentured labor in 1831 on this verdant tropical island, described by Mark Twain as God's model for heaven. After the Mauritius experiment proved successful, the indenture system quickly spread to Guyana, then to Trinidad and other islands of the Caribbean, parts of Southeast Asia, and eventually to Fiji in 1879.

Every Hindu wedding in Mauritius—every one—begins on a Friday evening with a women's gathering. And these women always sing together this particular *sagun* song first. We came to easily understand that it was very important. The *sagun* can be longer, or it can be shorter, depending on how many auspicious items are recalled by the ladies. But they all remember the important things like the yogurt and the grinding wheel.

And here, Umesh and I had first heard it in the motherland of eastern Uttar Pradesh. There is something absolutely amazing about the durability of these wedding songs across ages and across oceans.

"After this, five married women sit down and grind with the grinder," Gangajali explained. "And they grind the *urad dal* (a type of lentil). Five women grind the turmeric on the stone, and after grinding that, all five women put *sindur* (vermillion) and mustard oil on their heads, and five *laddu* (sweets) are given to each in their *anchal* (the end of the sari), and after this they sing five songs for the Lord. For example, for the Shankar Bhagwan or for Ramji and also for man."

"This *sagun* is an auspicious song," Umesh said. "And those very things, common household items, are used at the wedding time and become sacred and are praised. These items make it auspicious to perform the wedding. The wedding is the auspicious time of the life. When you use something for your life, it is considered auspicious. Like here in this song, when the yogurt is being made in the new pitcher and the starter is nectar. You can see that pitcher is new, auspicious, and the starter comes as nectar to keep the world running.

"*Saguni* is personified here. 'Because of this yogurt, oh *saguni*, I perform this wedding. Due to the auspicious nature of your rice and betel (which has the shape of a heart), I perform the wedding. Because of the auspicious hand-grinding wheel, I perform this wedding.' But all these items are useful for life, Helen. Without the grinding wheel, we have no food. This is auspicious for living on the earth in India. Also, the *dal* and chickpeas, these are also auspicious grains. Then we perform the wedding. Because auspicious mustard oil and the auspicious *sindur*, I perform the wedding. 'Oh come on, oh come on, *saguni*, take a seat in my courtyard and perform the wedding of my son. Oh augur, perform the wedding of my daughter.'

"After the auspicious *sagun* song has been performed," Umesh said, "it is customary for the singers to perform five songs dedicated to Lord Shiva. The marriage of Shiva and Parvati is considered the model for young couples to follow, and often the priest will tell their story on the day of the wedding as the ceremony moves forward."

So, next, Gangajali sang:

### SONG 15

*Sagun—This night is ours*

Have the green green bamboo cut.
Oh, have the temple thatched.
Mahadewa sleeps in it.
He is falling asleep.
Have the green bamboo cut.
Oh, have the temple thatched.
Oh, Mahadewa sleeps in that.
Oh Lord, he is sleeping.
Oh, Mahadewa sleeps in that.
Oh Lord, he is sleeping.
The slave lady sweeps the courtyard,
Oh, the servant.
Girl, go and lay the bed of Shiva.
Oh Lord, he is sleeping.
In the hand of the female servant to a lady *cherii aainin*
And *gowrainin*
(*Two lines are obscure.*)
The girl we told to lay the bed did it.
Oh Lord, he is sleeping.
The girl we told to lay the bed did it.
Oh Lord, he is sleeping.
The girl we told to lay the bed did it.
Oh Lord, he is sleeping.
Oh, she lays the bed with one hand and scatters the flowers.
Oh, Shivaji makes her linger by holding her *anchal.*
Oh, today he wants something.
Oh, Bhola (Shivaji) makes her linger on by holding her *anchal.*
Oh, today he wants something.
There are seven brothers and daughters-in-law in seven houses.
The eighth one is my wife.
The eighth one is my wife.
Shivaji is putting me in deep trouble.
Oh, where is the turmeric paste?

Shivaji is putting me in deep trouble.
Shivaji is putting me in deep trouble.
Oh, where is the turmeric paste?
Mother hears these words, and she cannot bear with them.
Daughter, take the fragrant hair oil,
And the turmeric paste with the fragrant musk smell.
(This musk is said to come from the navel of the deer.)
Daughter, take the fragrant hair oil,
And the turmeric paste with the fragrant musk smell.
Take the turmeric paste in one hand.
She puts the turmeric paste on his leg.
Oh, she puts it on his arm.
Shivaji makes her linger by holding her arm.
Oh, today he wants something.
Oh, guards of the country, be quiet.
Oh dogs, don't bark.
Today I am full of feelings.
I'll take care of your sweet complaint.
Shivaji, today I am full of feelings.
I'll take care of your sweet complaint.

"This is a *sagun*," Gangajali said. "The tent is made of green green bamboo. The cot is laid in it. As the working ladies live in the house to work, Parvati says to them, 'Go and make his bed.'

"He says, 'No, no, you don't make the bed. Your hands are dirty. And she who has ordered you, send her here to lay the bed.' Lord Shankar says to send her.

"Then she comes to lay the bed. But he holds Parvati, and he catches her due to the attachment of two people. Then she says, 'There are seven *bhabi*s in my house, brother, mother—how embarrassing is this to stay with you? Parvati says her mother overhears this talk. The conversation of her daughter and *damad*. So she, the mother, slowly comes and hands Parvati oil and turmeric paste. 'Daughter, take it and go to Shivaji. Whatever he says, serve him.' And he holds her and says, 'Oh guards, don't shout.' He orders dogs and cats to stop barking. 'Today I am in the *kohabar*. Be calm. This night is ours.'"

The tune of this song was special for me because it is the predominant tune in the Bhojpuri repertory from Trinidad. Curiously, I didn't hear it often in the various parts of the Bhojpuri region in India that I had visited. Yes, it did come up from time to time, and this was one of those times. I had often wondered if this sweetly swinging singing tune had replaced some other tunes that had been forgotten in Trinidad. It was questions like these that made the comparative study of the songs of the diaspora and the homeland so interesting—as the study of history always is.

"Oh, I can say so many things about this song," Umesh said. "First of all, these are from the imagination of some poet. We believe that God doesn't need to have sex. He does not have to hold hands with Parvati. We believe that Lord Shiva never takes birth and never dies. He is immortal. My Hindu religious stories tell a different way of having Ganesh and the other son, Kartike. They are sons of Shiva. Religious books don't claim what is sung here in this song.

"The song is auspicious. It gives a taste of a loving pair, a husband and wife, even though growing girls can't understand the relations and the wife. They can think, *What does he want? Food? In bed? At midnight?* A kind of teaching. Nothing bad is mentioned in it."

"In Mauritius the women sang five Shiva songs after the *sagun* song," I said.

"Here too women sing five or six songs for Shiva. They have to sing five *sagun* songs."

Gangajali explained her *sagun* song. "After the *tilak*, the priest sets the date for the *sagun*, the auspicious time for the day. There is a good time and a good day. Then these women perform the *sagun* over there under the wedding tent. That whatever I have sung with betel flowers, chickpeas, lentils, with the grinding wheat, oil—they mark with *sindur*. This work is done under the wedding tent, and altogether they sing five songs to God. And each one takes five sweets in their *anchal* (the end of the sari, considered auspicious because it is used to protect the nursing baby)."

"Does each of them sing five songs?" Umesh asked.

"Five songs," Gangajali replied. "One for Lord Shankar, then one for Ramji, then one for a man, then likewise—five songs."

"Sing all those five," Umesh requested.

Sashi burst into the conversation. "Today the work is done. She will do tomorrow. Eat na! Tea and water. She gets happy suddenly," Sashi shouted. "Sing!"

### SONG 16

#### *Sagun*

Shivaji, there is a wedding in my *naihar* (*naihar* is Gaura's childhood home).  
And there is no invitation for Bhola (Shiva).  
Gaura begins to say,  
"I will go to my *naihar*."  
Oh, then Shiva explains.  
Gaura began to say,  
"I will go to the *yagya* (large sacrificial festival).  
Oh, Shivaji began to explain.  
"If you will go to your *naihar* without an invitation,  
You will not get respect."  
Shivaji explains, "There won't be respect."

Gaura began to insist to Shivaji,
"Oh, I will go to my *naihar*."
Gaura began to insist to Shivaji.
"Oh, I will go to my *naihar*."
"Oh, if you will go to your *naihar* without an invitation,
You will not get respect."
Then Shivaji will get angry,
"Oh, where will you go?"
Then Shivaji will get angry,
"Oh, where will you go?"
Oh Gaura, she went to her *naihar*.
Nobody spoke to her.
Neither mother nor father spoke to her.
Oh, even the townsfolk did not speak to her.
Only sister Ganga spoke to her.
Oh, she got up and gave her a hug.
Gaura got angry at this.
Oh, she went near the large *havan* fire.
Gaura got angry at this.
Oh, she jumped into the *havan* fire.
She burnt to ashes in the fire.
Oh, Shiva got the news.
Shivaji arrived with great anger.
Oh, he destroyed the *yagya*.
Shivaji arrived with great anger.
Oh, then he destroyed the *yagya*.
"Shivaji, accept my request.
Oh, then do not destroy the *yagya*.
Shiviji, I will give you (Ganga) in place of Gaura.
Shiv, oh my *yagya* must not be destroyed.
Shivji, I will give you (Ganga) in place of Gaura.
Oh, do not destroy the *yagya*."

Once again, to my surprise, I heard a familiar melody, a variant of the number one tune from Trinidad. For this song, it was presented in a slightly different form from Song 15, using the lower notes of the octave for some phrases and then the upper parts of the octave for other phrases. Indeed, some songs in Trinidad do just that, shifting from a lower register to a higher register. More normally, however, they stick to the lower pitches of the octave. I suppose that one might use the terms applied to Indian classical music and call the lower melodies the *sthayi* and the higher phrases the *antara*, thereby implying a sort of verse–chorus structure.

"This song looks terrible for those people who do not know the story out of the Purana," Umesh said. "And time to time this story is told by the religious pandit who comes to preach. At the wedding time the wise priest tells some part of this story to the bridegroom and bride both, how to behave, husband and wife together, in their social life. At the same time teaching to the bride, after getting married, when she is in her *sasural* with her husband, then she cannot go to her parents' home without an invitation. So it very clearly tells this lesson.

"When a child takes a birth to a brother, and his sister is in her *sasural*, she can go and tie *raki* (auspicious decorated thread or string bracelet that the sister gives to the brother for his protection). She can go for one day after Diwali when the sister comes to feed the brother. She does not need an invitation for these events. And she will get respect. At any other auspicious time, she must be invited. It must be respectable. It is the brother's duty to go to his sister and take care of her. If she is in trouble, he has to help, and he can go at any time. But she can also send a message to her brother.

"Then tell us about this song?" Umesh said. "Whatever you can explain, that would be really great."

Gangajali began, "So Parvati is saying to Lord Shiva, 'A *yagya* is taking place in my *maica* (mother's home, *naihar*). All the gods are going by the skyway (*aakaas marg*). I will also go.' She insists, 'I will also go.'

"Then Lord Shiva says, 'I don't have an invitation. Nobody has come to take you from here. How can you go without an invitation?'

"'Even then,' she insists, 'I will go. This is my *naihar*. They are my parents. Nobody will drive me out of there or make me feel bad. I will surely go.'

"And the Lord explains, 'You won't get respect if you go somewhere without an invitation. Going with an invitation, people get respect.'

"But after all, Gaura does not pay attention to him. She went to her *maica*. When she reached there, she found all the gods seated. Rishis, munis, everybody is seated. 'There is no place for my Lord Shankar, and nobody is talking to me.' She walks around seeing the *yagya*. And nobody is talking to her, not mother, father, brother, nor *bhauji*. And the Ganga, which flows in every direction, is her sister.

"She gets up, and both sisters meet and hug each other, and Ganga says, 'Why have you come without an invitation? I feel very bad seeing this insult.'

"Gaura gets very angry at this, and the *havan* fire that is made to perform the *havan*, she jumps into it, and having jumped, she burns to ashes.

"The messenger goes and gives Lord Shiva this news. 'In such a situation, mother jumped into the *havan* fire and burned to ashes. And those people did not respect her.'

"As he heard this, Lord Shiva unfastened his hair in anger, and in anger he was consumed. And he destroyed all the *yagya*. He cut off the head of King Himalya and destroyed the *yagya*. All the gods prayed to him to calm down, and this Gaura will be born again. 'We will give you her sister Ganga in the place of Gaura.'

"These songs are sung from *sagun* until the end of *matikor*," Gangajali said. "After digging the dirt during *matikor*, other songs begin. Until the *matikor* is finished, these songs are sung. There are important things. I am telling you what the main songs are. There are hundreds of songs. But which are the important songs, these are the ones I am singing for you."

"But all the songs are important to us," Umesh explained. "We will listen to unimportant songs from you."

"Yes, yes, listen to how many you will hear," Gangajali said. "Here is the next *sagun* song."

### SONG 17

### *Sagun*

The father of Gauradei arrives with a *dhoti* over his shoulder and a *lota* in his hand.
Gaura's father arrives on an auspicious day.
Oh, Gaura, your father arrives on an auspicious day.
Gaura, come and sit on the cot.
Gaura, explain to me your sadness.
Gaura, what kind of sadness are you going through, explain it to me.
Gaura, what kind of sadness are you going through, explain it to me.
*Sas* (mother-in-law) speaks sharply, *nanad* (husband's sister) speaks sharply, the relatives speak sharply.
Shiva speaks sharply in the kitchen.
She is unable to express that pain.
Shiva speaks sharply in the kitchen.
She is unable to express that pain.
Come on Shivaji, sit on the cot.
Shiv, tell me your unhappiness and sadness.
Shiva, take departure of ten days.
Mother cries open-heartedly,
"Shiva, let Gaura take departure of ten days."
Mother cries open-heartedly.
Then Mother, do the *vida* (departure) of Gaura.
Do the *vida* of Gaura.
As Gaura does in *gauna* (departure after the wedding),
Mother fills baskets with rice.
And fills them with sweets.
Mother, give her just as much as is given in the *gauna*.
"Gaura, pardon me for my mistakes.
Gaura, pardon me for my mistakes."
Gaura lives in her *naihar* for ten days.
Then she will come back to her *sasural*.

Gaura lives in her *naihar* for ten days.
Then she will come back to her *sasural.*

The melody of this song is a variation of that of the *saguni* melody of Song 14, "Oh oh augur, oh oh augur." It includes lines of the *sthayi* in the lower portion of the octave and lines of *antara*, lying in the upper pitches of the octave. Although these terms are normally reserved for classical Indian music, they can equally be applied to village song as both flow from the same river, from the village to the courts and cities. The general feel of the song is lively and, one could say, happy, even though the story tells of the unhappiness of the bride living away from her mother. However, the situation is resolved, and the bride is allowed to return to her mother's arms for ten days. This complaint—that the bride longs for her mother's home—is common in everyday life and in song. In her mother's home, her *naihar*, she is free to go about with her face uncovered. Everyone touches her feet. Normally, she gets to wear her new ornaments to show off to the other women of her family, especially if she has returned to attend a wedding or other important function. And, indeed, girls and women gather around to inspect the shiny twenty-two-carat gold necklaces, earrings, bangles, and so forth that the daughter has been given by her husband's family. It is for show. The show is important for the reputation of the family of the bride and for the reputation of the family of the bridegroom. Understanding this relation among reputation, respect, and show is a key to village life.

"This song is of Shivaji," Gangajali explained. "It is a conversation. So Gaura's father has gone to take her back home from her *sasural.* He asks, 'Daughter, tell me what troubles you are having in your *sasural.* So tell me in detail.'

"She says, 'Oh, Father, *sas*, *nanad*, and *jethani*, they all talk tough and rough. And when I cook, then Shivaji also talks tough and rough. And also Gaura tells her father tough talk comes from the side of *sas* and *nanad* and the relatives in the kitchen. I bear with everyone's talk. But I am unable to bear with Lord Shiva's toughness and roughness. And Shiva speaks tough in the kitchen. In the kitchen, when Shiva speaks tough, I can't bear it. Take me to my mother.'

"Then her father talks to Shivaji. 'Oh Lord Shankar, come and sit near me. Listen to what I am saying. Send Gaura Parvati with me for ten days. Her mother is crying a lot to see her. Gaura's mother is crying in her heart, so send Gaura for at least ten days. The mother is heartbroken.'

"Then Shivaji says to his mother, 'Mother, you send Parvati just like you would send her for a *gauna* or a wedding. She must be sent with many things, just like for *gauna*. Send her with a basket full of rice, fruits, sweets, other things, boxes, and so on. Send her with much preparation so she will look good when they see her in her *naihar* so her *naihar* people won't complain to me.'

"And he tells Parvati, 'Stay there for ten days and then come back home. Don't stay longer.'

"When Gaura goes home, then the mother-in-law sends her daughter as if she were going at the time of *gauna*."

"This is told in the name of Shiva," Umesh said. "But this looks real. Father goes to the daughter, talks to the husband of his daughter, and takes her away for ten days. When they send the bride back to her *naihar*, mother-in-law sends baskets of rice and full of sweets and *puri*s or whatever. The mother sends the daughter just as she has done for her *vida* before.

"Mother says, or maybe *bhabi* says, 'Pardon me if I made some fault or some mistake.'

"This song is sung after the *gauna*, maybe after one year or six months, whenever the bride visits her parents. Parents go to visit her and bring her, or her brother goes."

"Why don't we put the fan on for a minute?" Sashi begged. "Please stop the tape so we can get a little air."

After taking a little rest and cooling off with the breeze of the fan, we turned the fan off again, and Gangajali began to sing.

### SONG 18

#### *Sagun/Baithaki*

On the one side is the Ganges, and on the other side is the Jamuna, and in between is sand.
And in between is sand.
On that sand, a yogi is seated, and devotees are seated.
His hair is blowing in the breeze.
His hair is blowing in the breeze.
Oh, daughter Gauradei goes to bring water.
The yogi deluded her.
The yogi deluded her.
Oh, barber and *bariya*, go quickly,
Oh, give the message to father.
Oh, give the message to brother.
Oh, father ran with a shield and sword.
Oh, and brother with a bow and arrow.
Oh, I'll kill the yogis and devotees with this sword.
Oh, he kept deluding my daughter.
He kept my daughter captivated.
I'll kill the yogi and devotees with this arrow.
Oh, he kept my sister captivated.
Father, don't kill the yogi and the devotees.
Father, do not kill them.

Do not punish them.
Brother, don't kill them with a bow and arrow.
Oh brother, the yogi and devotees are written in my fate.
Oh, how can this be changed?
Oh, how can this be changed?

Again, I was surprised to hear yet another popular tune from Trinidad, the tune that normally accompanied the all-important *kanyadan* ceremony on the island. In this version by Gangajali, some of the lines are sung at the lower pitch level—the *sthayi*—and other lines, the *antara* chorus lines, are sung around the fifth degree of the scale. The ladies explained that this melody was for *baithaki* songs. Were many *sagun* songs sung to this lovely melody, mostly with the *sthayi* (verse) and the *antara* (chorus)?

"Actually this song is sung between the confluence of two rivers," Umesh explained. "It is full of sand. One saint or hermit is doing *tapa*s (sacrificial worship). And the king goes to take water from the well. So the mother of the daughter or the *sakhi*s of the girl say, 'The hermit kept the daughter in a yogi's illusion and hypnotized her to accept whatever he said.' So the *sakhi*s say, 'Give the message to the father and mother, barber or *bariya*. You go and tell father, *baba*.'

"The father is running with his sword and shield. The brother is carrying his bow and arrow. 'I'll kill the hermit with this sword and this shield. He kept my daughter deluded.'

"The brother is saying, 'I'll kill that yogi with my bow and arrow. He kept my sister hypnotized.'

"Then Gaura says, 'Oh Father, don't kill this yogi or devotee or whatever he is. Father, don't kill him and don't punish him. Brother, don't kill him with the bow and arrows. This is my fate. He is already from before in my fate. And nobody can erase it.'"

"Ask her the name of the *laya* (melody)," I said. The tune was often sung in Felicity, Trinidad. It came as quite a surprise.

Sashi went to the point. "This is a wedding melody."

"This song is a *baithaki*," Gangajali said. "A *baithaki* of Shivaji."

"In *baithaki*," Sashi said, "*baithaki* is sung only in this *laya*. We know very many *baithaki*." And they began again.

## SONG 19

*Sagun/Baithaki*

Sita is at her door.
Sita makes the garland on a high platform.
Oh, Shri Ram arrived.
Oh, Shri Ram arrived.
Oh, Ram asked the name of her father.
Oh, whose daughter are you? Whose son's wife are you?
Oh, in whose family are you married?
Oh, in whose family are you married?
Oh, I am the loving daughter of King Janak.
I am Dasarath's son's wife.
I am Dasarath's son's wife.
Oh, I am married in Laxman's family.
Oh, Raghubar is my husband.
Oh, Raghubar is my husband.
Ram could not bear with these words.
Oh, *kahar*s (a caste) have been searching the forest where she was sent.
Oh, *kahar*s have been searching the forest where she was sent.
Oh Ram, who is there to take care of me?
In whose hands will you entrust me?
Oh Ram, with whom will I pass my life?
Oh Ram, with whom will I pass my life?
Oh, who am I proud of?
Oh, I will take you in the house of Dasarath.
I will give you into the hands of Konsila.
I will give you into the hands of Konsila.
Oh Sita, you will be proud of me.
Oh, I will pass my life with you.
Oh, I will pass my life with you.

Once again, this song had the same melody as the previous *sagun/baithaki* song (Song 18, "On the one side is the Ganges").

Gangajali began to explain this song. "The platform is called *chautara*, sung here as *chabutara*. So Ram ji arrives. I think the song is meant to be before the wedding. He arrives in the town and moves around in the village. He found Sita making a garland seated in the *chabutara*. And he asks the name of her father.

"'Whose daughter are you, and whose wife are you? And whose family are you married to?'

"She replied, 'I am the dear daughter of Janak, and I am the wife of Dasarath's son, and I am married in the family of Lachhiman. And Raghubar is my husband.'

"As Ram heard these words, he could not bear with them. Then he realized that she is Sita. The *kahar*s kept searching for her in the forest."

Umesh said, "This song shows that Ram was already married when the girl was very small, very tender. When she grew up, then the husband went to take her from her *maica*. And by the way, he reached the same door. He saw a girl making a garland. This was a child marriage. He doesn't recognize that she is his wife. This song is made for that family whose daughter was married as a child, and now she is grown up."

"These songs were already made from ancient times," Sashi said, "not from our period. All this is from before we were born."

Gangajali and Sashi were whispering.

"The plums of the plum tree are forbidden to you," Sashi suggested. "Do not thatch the wedding tent with peepholes."

"How many songs are there for the wedding?" I asked.

"There is no counting them," said Sashi. "Your reels will finish, and they will not end."

(Indeed, this is exactly what happened.)

"The women make the song according to their own way," Gangajali said, "but what I sing, that is correct. And from place to place women sing it to make money. People just sing somehow. They take money, and this is the main thing, and if you sing these songs in the United States, people will wonder where you got them from."

"Indian people will listen to it," Sashi said.

"When people will hear it, they will say this is the right thing," said Gangajali. "'Where did you get it from?'"

"Come on, sing quick," Sashi interrupted.

Gangajali started humming a song.

"What daughter's name should we sing?" Sashi asked. "Take Sapan *beti*."

Gangajali started to laugh.

### SONG 20

#### *Mangal*

Oh, Sapan daughter, beloved to your father.
Oh, Sapan daughter, beloved to your father.
Oh, father has had the basket woven.
Oh, go go daughter to pluck flowers.
Oh, brother has had the basket woven.
Oh, go go daughter to pluck flowers.
Oh, Sapan daughter, beloved to your uncle,
Then uncle has had the basket woven.
Oh, Sapan daughter, beloved to your uncle,
Then uncle has had the basket woven.
Oh, go go daughter to pluck flowers.

Then uncle has had the basket woven.
Oh, go go daughter to pluck flowers.
Oh, Sapan sister, beloved to your brother.
Oh, Sapan sister, beloved to your brother.
Then the brother has had the basket woven.
Then the brother has had the basket woven.
Oh, go go sister to pluck flowers.
Then the brother has had the basket woven.
Oh, go sister to pluck flowers.
Oh, the daughter got tired while plucking flowers.
Oh, the daughter got tired while plucking flowers.
Oh, in that forest daughter sleeps laying her *anchal* on the ground.
Oh, in that forest daughter sleeps laying her *anchal* on the ground.
Oh, Lord, what bridegroom arrived there?
Bridegroom Vijay comes riding on a horse.
Bridegroom Vijay comes riding on a horse.
Oh, girl, get up and tell me why you are sleeping here.
Oh, whose daughter are you?
Oh, whose granddaughter are you?
Oh, and tell me for whom are you plucking these flowers?
Oh, and tell me for whom are you plucking these flowers?
Oh, and tell me for whom are you plucking these flowers?
Oh, I am the daughter of Anrudh Rama.
Oh, I am the daughter of Anrudh Rama.
Oh, my brother had the basket woven for me, so I have come to pluck flowers.
Oh, my brother had the basket woven for me, so I have come to pluck flowers.
Oh, whose grandson are you and whose son?
Oh, whose grandson are you and whose son?
Oh, tell me whose *damad* are you?
Oh, tell me whose *damad* are you?
Oh, I am the son and grandson of Ramchandra.
Oh, I am the son and grandson of Ramchandra.
And *damad* of Anurudh.
Oh, I have come to love you.
And *damad* of Anurudh.
Oh, I have come to love you.
Oh, if you are the *damad* of Anrudh ji.
Oh, if you are the son of King Ram.
Oh, read the religious book in front of me in this forest.
Oh, read the religious book in front of me in this forest.
Oh, read the religious book in front of me in this forest.
Oh, reading and writing is at dawn.
My book was left in Banaras.

Oh, I have become like a sheep before you.
My book was left in Banaras.
Oh, I have become like a sheep before you.

Normally, listening to the previous songs, one might say that Gangajali sang in tune, in as much as that was important to her. But something about the lay of the higher pitches of the *antara* of this particular song seem to cause the tonal center to slip up a bit by the end of each line. On the one hand, Sashi had joined in the singing, and I couldn't help wondering if she, the weaker singer, had caused this problem. On the other hand, each melodic line has an extended range—from more or less the fifth degree below the tonic all the way up to the fifth degree above the tonic—and this may have caused the problem of tonal instability. The area of confusion seems to center around the middle of the *antara* lines when the melody moves ahead very rapidly. But, goodness knows, it may be that all singers slip the tonic upward in this song as it adds to the effect of speeding up with much excitement. So I think it is best to back away from notions of a mistake and think instead in terms of a tune galloping forward. Anybody who has tried to learn a musical instrument knows well how everything can fall apart during those darn fast notes.

In the middle of the song, Sashi stops and asks essentially, "What's next?" This should not be considered a mistake. It happens all the time during weddings as singers orientate themselves. In particular, for songs with repeating lines changing only the name of the relative—father, mother, brother, and so forth—some singer may have to right the ship.

"This song is a *mangal*," Gangajali explained. "After performing *sagun*, five or six more songs are sung—or hundreds. After that, *matikor* takes place.

"So this is the meaning of the song," said Gangajali. "The girl's father or brother has a small basket woven of bamboo. They say, 'Go in the flower garden and pluck flowers. Bring the plucked flowers to offer to the Lord.'

"So the girl goes, and she plucks flowers. While plucking flowers, she gets tired and sleeps there. Then the man to whom she is going to be married comes riding on a horse, and he wakes her up and asks, 'Whose daughter are you, and whose *bahu* are you? Why have you come here?'

"Then she explains, 'My brother and father had this basket woven for me to pluck flowers. But whose son are you? Tell me that. Why have you come?'

"Then he replies, 'I am the son of such and such, and I wandered here without any particular purpose.'

"'Then if you are the son of my *sasur*, then tell me about yourself so that I can recognize that you are the person.'

"Then he explains, 'What should I tell you, because ever since I saw you, I have forgotten everything (that I studied), and I am like a donkey before you.'"

"*Matikor* will take place after this," Sashi said. "And after that, the wedding will take place. Then there will be *kanyadan* songs."

"What comes after the *sagun*?" Umesh asked.

"*Matikor*," Sashi said.

INTERLUDE THREE

# LADY EUSTACE

BEFORE THE UNTIMELY DEATH OF SIR FLORIAN, LIZZIE HAD CONCEIVED a child. So much of her year of mourning coincided with her time of confinement. Trollope offers no details. Of birth and children there is nothing. Of romance, one can expect only that the man puts his arms around the waist of his lady at the time of the proposal. Of money, however, much is explained. The property in Scotland was left to Lizzie for her life. This condition confused our vain little liar, who soon proclaimed to any and all that the "Scotch property" was hers "forever and ever." In point of fact, she was greatly confused about all the details of her late husband's will, even though the lawyers had carefully explained it to her over and over again.

Lizzie had in her possession a necklace, an heirloom, the Eustace diamonds, about which, the book's title indicates, much will be said. The controversy had started as to the proper ownership of the diamonds, and talk among the relatives had also begun until the brother, John, declared, "D—the necklace!"

Umesh had his own thoughts about Lady Eustace. "I don't find any fault in this lady in so many ways," Umesh said. "According to their point of view, there could be. She was found as an orphan, and this vulture lady found her in the street, even though she was related to her. And a child you find in the street, as you found the cat in the street and you tried hard to take its fear off, but still there is fear. So the vulture aunt must have some rules to raise the child, and she carries out her own rules. When she could, she told Lizzie the rules, and Lizzie could not carry it out as she was a child. And Lizzie knew that she is some different lady, not like her father. When she grew up slowly slowly, the old lady, vulture lady, heaps rules over her to make her a better person. And Lizzie thinks this is crap. Vulture lady believes in duty, and that is a big thing. But Lizzie likes so many things that this old lady can't afford. Lizzie is eager to get every good thing that she can get—somehow or other. She does not know the difference between right and wrong. She doesn't know how to manage wealth, money. How much interest they will pay, she does not know. But she has a kind of cunning.

"I found the circumstances of her life were not simple, so she grew up in that bad situation, and she couldn't change herself. On the other hand, the unmarried woman, the aunt, who had never a child of her own, she found it hard to know how to raise a child. She had no experience. She was performing her duty to raise this child, but it does not mean with love. She was thinking she was doing the best, but a child expects something different from their parents.

"The family she came from—the father was addicted to liquor. This man had no right that God had given him a child because he had no way to raise a child properly. So how can I blame her in so many ways that she was bad? Circumstances made it so that she learned to make her way on her own. But, you see, she is clever enough to find a good man to secure her life. She knew she was poor, and her ambition was only to secure her future. Lizzie found a good man who needed love for a little while, and she could fulfill her life's requirement with his help. And she accepted him to love for a dying person. She had come to know that he will die. And she won. Eventually, in a sense, he got a son. And now circumstances will change Lizzie, and she can change into a good woman. This is my feeling. We will see."

### *At Umesh's home, Karimganj, March 8, 2014*

After toast in the village, we read more about Lady Eustace (and had tea, and more tea, and coffee, and buttered toast from the red toaster).

"I'm really thinking about Lizzie," Umesh said. "The description is so great there in English. We say, 'Oh, the girl is really beautiful. Fair complexion. Beautiful eyes like a lake. Only problem is that she has *kanji* eyes—the iris shows that she is the shrewdest woman. Beware of them. It could be true. There is a person in my village that has *kanji* eyes, but he is nice. It is a saying. In poetry, in *Dhola*, if he describes the beauty of a woman, he says, 'Thin lips are beautiful, and she chews *pan* (betel), a diamond is hanging on her nose. When she moves to dance, it dances, it sways when she sways. Oh, black bee drink its honey slowly, not all of the sudden.' Whoever is the man, he is the black bee—the lover. Whoever sees this woman, oh, enjoy slowly slowly. In the village, women cover their heads so only the sweetheart can enjoy it.

"Lizzie has got beautiful ears, she can have beautiful ears hanging with two shining earrings. How can I convert it into ugly? But her ears are short. They should be in the right shape, not big, not short—just suited to the face. Beautiful eyes but also eyebrows. Lizzie has very good eyebrows, very close to each other but not joining. First of all, the author describes the beauty of each part, but then he finds the ugly part. So rishis used to bless a child by seeing features of the face and body.

"What else can we say about the woman Lizzie? While she talks, she gets dimples in both her cheeks. When she talks, she laughs, she has a smile. She has a black mole to her left. We consider this is beautiful. But she is getting it on the left, so she is going to be rich. Lizzie had the intention to be rich. That is why she flirted by her voice, through the reading, to her husband—flirted, yes. And he fell in love only due to the reading of her poetry. When we get married to someone, we must know the background of the person, the family life, and learn the character of the person before. Otherwise love destroys. Love is blind."

EIGHTEEN

# UMESH REMEMBERS CHARLOTTE WISER

CHARLOTTE MELINA VIALL WISER (1892–1981), GRADUATE OF THE UNIversity of Chicago, was sent to India in 1916 as a Presbyterian missionary. There, in Allahabad, the holy city at the site of the confluence of the Ganges and the Jumana rivers, she met William Wiser (1890–1961), also a Presbyterian missionary. They married in December of the same year. They had three sons, now all deceased—Arthur, Alfred, and Edward.

The Wisers spent their early years in India teaching at Allahabad and doing social work in nearby Kanpur. Then, from 1925 to 1930, they settled in village Karimganj in western Uttar Pradesh (called Karimpur in their publications, as pseudonyms were de rigueur in early anthropology). They were sponsored by the North India Mission of the Presbyterian Church of the United States of America. Their classic study of Karimganj, *Behind Mud Walls*, was first published in 1930. In the book, Prakash is Umesh's grandfather. I doubt that there are any anthropology students in the States who have not read it. After William's death in 1961, Charlotte returned again and again to Karimganj, to Umesh's village home, teaching Umesh reading and writing in English and adding chapters to *Behind Mud Walls*. Later, she was joined by a young Susan Snow Wadley, who updated the original text. She too lived in Umesh's village home, and paid Umesh to do a great deal of interviewing and transcribing.

In Karimganj, Charlotte made her home in the house of Umesh's grandfather. She and William had set up the Indian Village Service, a development organization that became a key source for the Block Development Programs.

From the preface of the first edition of *Behind Mud Walls* (1930), the Wisers wrote:

When we came to Karimpur five years ago, to make a survey of the social, religious, and economic life of a fairly typical North Indian village, we were bent on gathering facts by the most direct methods possible. But our new neighbors were not prepared for anything so rapid or impersonal. They refused to help us by any route other than the leisurely one of friendship. The result was that we became engaged in numerous neighborly activities which often led us out of sight of our survey, but which we could not conscientiously refuse. We had learned from our neighbors that the road of friendship and service is courteous and just, if not the most efficient. Those who expected a routine survey—as we did when we started out—gave us up long ago as hopelessly enchanted. But the information collected with the help of our village friends, is a document which we hope will be of some value as source material.

Many of our experiences along the way have been too personal to have a place in a survey. Yet they are too revealing to be discarded. We have set some of them down in this volume for the friends, both Indian and foreign, who have asked us repeatedly to share our village experiences with them.

*In Umesh's house in Karimganj, December 2016*

Umesh was telling me, "One day I asked Dadi, Charlotte Wiser, 'What made you to choose this village to work in? There are so many villages all over Uttar Pradesh.'

"She told me, 'First we had chosen the town Mainpuri to work in and to stay in the mission compound Mainpuri. We went to see the district magistrate of Mainpuri, and we explained to him about my husband's proposed work.'

"The district magistrate, whoever it was in 1925, he suggested that Mr. Wiser visit three particular villages so that then he could choose which one he wanted to work in. William and Charlotte Wiser both went to see these three villages, and Karimganj was found to be the best village to work in.

"Karimganj had a population of different castes—in fact, seventeen different castes—and working farming people lived in the village. It was not very far from the district town Mainpuri and also not too close. William Wiser liked the geographical area of the village. He met with the people, and he decided to work in our village. Mr. Wiser was a sociologist, and he was working on his PhD thesis at Cornell University in Ithaca, New York.

"So they decided to work in Karimganj. Dadi told me that her husband wanted to do some research here with us. This is the way they found my village.

"One day I asked Dadi if she had converted our village sweepers to Christianity because one Karimganj village sweeper person now living in Mainpuri was a Christian. Dadi told me that the Karimganj village sweepers had already become converted before she and her husband arrived. But Charlotte and William Wiser never converted anybody to Christianity, even though basically they were missionaries.

"A long time later, while we were sitting, Dadi and I, in the living room, a village Brahman arrived, and he requested to Dadi that he wanted to be a Christian. Charlotte got very upset and told him very clearly that she did not do this job. She explained that there were in India or in Mainpuri many Christians from whom he could seek this help. And the Brahman insisted. And this was the first time I saw Dadi in anger. Later, the same Brahman went away somewhere from the village, and he returned after two years, appearing as a Naga Baba (who lives naked in the forest). Dadi never saw him in this shape.

"I believe that, being sociologists, they didn't want to make any rules or to disturb or dominate the people in any way.

"I have learned from village people that the Wisers came to the village and pitched their tent in the mango grove that belonged to a Brahman family. It was very close to the sweeper colony. I recall an incident now that my grandmother and grandfather and one of my uncles went to see William Wiser in Ludhyana, Punjab. He was very sick and in the hospital there. My grandfather had gotten stitched a Chester coat for my uncle, who was six months younger than me. When they were ready to go to Punjab, I went along up to the bus stop in Karimganj. In the olden days there were private buses and a *kaccha* (bad, broken) road for Mainpuri. Although my uncle had good clothes on, I did not know what was happening. Suddenly, I realized that they were going farther away, and I began to cry. I was crying crying nonstop crying. The bus came. All the people who were going got into the bus. The bus moved ahead to Mainpuri, and I was crying and running after it. I must have been around six or seven years old. It still hurts me.

"When they returned, my uncle had so many stories to tell them. One of them was that my uncle had a knife, and the clouds were very close to him. He poked the cloud with the knife, and water just fell down on the ground. And I believed it!

"Dadi used to work in my house in two places—in the dining hall and beside the window. Dadi used to sit down in the dining hall at the table, and she used to use a yellow colored pencil with an eraser on top of it. Sometimes she also used a big eraser. She had like a board, and on it there were blank white papers without lines. She began to write very fast, writing writing writing, continuous writing. And for hours she kept writing and writing.

"In the summertime, she sat down next to the window so she could get a small breeze, although it was not enough breeze, but it was something. And she continued writing. I believed whatever she saw she memorized, whatever she learned she wrote continuously, whatever she saw before she might forget. After writing so many pages, she was editing these pages and marking—one place was to go up and making a mark on it, and sometimes she was fixing lines, sometimes moving phrases.

"I was seeing and learning myself. Why is she doing that? Oh, maybe she is shifting that to another place. And I did learn too myself a little bit how to do it. Whenever I write even a letter to someone, I always begin on rough paper so I can edit it and put it in the right way. Although there may be mistakes, I am happy because I have done so much work on my own. At least I do well when I write a letter to someone in Hindi. I really make it perfect. If you take out one word, then the charm is gone. And people appreciate these letters very much.

"After editing, she sat down, and she had a Remington Company typewriter. It was quite big. And she used to type these pages. Hours and hours. And when this typing was over, she sat down once again to edit it. Edit, edit. Then she typed it back. I don't know how many times she used to type those papers back and edit over and again. It was not the intention of mine to count how many times she did it, but I saw her do it.

"One day I asked Dadi, 'Whenever I am studying here or reading here or writing, any kind of noise from inside of the house or outside of the house, I lose my concentration. What is it about you, Dadi? You just keep writing, and I can't do it.'

"She replied, 'Umesh, whenever I write, I write. Even if the room falls on me, I will never know.'

"Now I am writing this, and deep love for Dadi is just floating—how hard, how bigger, how higher—waves are moving in the ocean—is going through my heart. I can't speak. And tears are flowing from my eyes. I believe something I have done real great in my past life so that is the result of it. I found my company with her so that she could live in my house with my family together.

"I can't talk. This is too much for me. I am just back and back in my past life. Long ago. I mean . . . she was so great . . . must have done some great deed . . . I have done in my past life to have her company. . . ."

NINETEEN

# *MATIKOR:* SASHI INTERRUPTS, BUT WE DO NOT HEAR "A MARE HAS PISSED"

*The second day at the Sarang Hotel, Ballia, July 1989*

On the next day, Gangajali arrived fresh for another afternoon of song. We had already swung into the habit of recording for about five hours, filling about twenty five-inch open reels of quarter-inch tape. By that time, Gangajali's voice would tire, and we had much work still to do. Breaking down the equipment, carefully putting those precious mics away, charging all the batteries. Then came the labeling of the tape boxes. I would never do this while Gangajali was singing—that seemed to me to be exceptionally rude. I would just quickly give each tape a temporary number, 1, 2, 3, and so on, to keep them in order.

"Will you sing *matikor* now?" I asked. *Matikor* meant digging in the soil.

Gangajali replied, "So the women come for *matikor* from the village and the house when they are called and the midwife (here we call her *chamain*). She plays a musical instrument (gong, *manar*), and the instrument is worshiped before *matikor.* So women sing the song that I am going to sing."

SONG 21

*Who has pitched the wedding tent?*

Who has pitched the wedding tent?
And who has thatched it?

Oh, at whose door is the music played?
Oh, the gong is worshiped.
Oh, the *chamar* thatched the wedding tent.
Oh, the carpenter pitched it.
The gong is played at the door of Father Anrudh.
Oh, being played, it sounds pleasant.
The gong is played at the door of Father Anrudh.
Oh, being played it sounds pleasant.
Oh, who pitched the wedding tent?
Oh, who thatched it?
Oh, at whose door is the gong played?
Oh, being played because it sounds pleasant.
The carpenter pitched the wedding tent.
Oh, the *chamar* thatched it.
The gong is played at the door of the ancestors.
Oh, being played, it sounds pleasant.
Oh, the gong is played at the door of the ancestors.
Oh, being played, it sounds pleasant.

Compared to the previous song, number 20, "Oh, Sapan daughter, beloved to your father," the melody of this song, 21, is fairly straightforward. Basically, the melody accompanies each long line, with each line having two phrases. The song is quite short, and the tonality is stable. For the moment at least, Sashi seems to have decided to join in the singing, which gives the listener a bit of a sense of how a group of ladies consisting of weaker and stronger singers might sound.

"All women together worship the gong at the door," said Gangajali. "And they begin to move along the way to dig that soil. After worship at the door, they go to dig the soil. This ritual, called *matikor*, is performed to placate the ancestors. Women appease the gods in the upper world so that all the gods of all three worlds will accept this act of worship and come along together and be kind. We pray to the gods, 'Please help us and grant us your protection as I arrange the wedding of my son or daughter.'"

The *matikor* ritual is performed at the house of the bride and also at the home of the groom. Women gather for this ceremony and process to a spot well away from the wedding house, where soil and water are available—often a hand pump, pond, or small drain. This, the digging of holy Mother Earth in preparation for the wedding, is a time for ribald songs and jokes, laughter, and games as participants dance and anoint each other with handfuls of turmeric paste, permanently staining everybody's clothes. Often one or two especially enthusiastic ladies may lead this merriment, slapping paste on the backs of their friends and neighbors as they try to run and escape.

After the small ritual of digging the soil and placing it in a special basket, the women gather in a circle, surrounding those women who are moved to dance—gracefully, with much turning, hands held aloft, describing curves in the air as they twirl and twirl. As they turn and turn, women on the outside of the circle may be eager to step forward and dance, but they feign shyness until they are pushed and pulled to the center and forced to join in the twirling. Waving their hands and undulating their hips, the tone is graceful, also sexual, for Mother Earth has been penetrated by the shovel and is now called upon to bless the marriage.

Women may also sing very sexual *gali* at *matikor.* In Mauritius, the ritual songs for *matikor* have largely been forgotten, but the lusty *matikor gali* are favorites. Manti remembered several very well and performed them for us at the wedding of her niece.

In Trinidad in the 1970s, *matikor* was accompanied by loud tassa drumming and hot dancing. However, today there is no singing—these songs, along with the balance of the Bhojpuri repertory, having been abandoned sometime in the 1970s and '80s. Local scholars explain that the modern chutney songs, so popular in Trinidad now, derived from this mirthful ritual.

In Fiji, the *matikor* ritual may last for over an hour and is celebrated with lusty passion—the singing, the laughing, the dancing, the playful games with turmeric paste. The Bhojpuri language has not died out in Fiji, and the women remember all the songs.

*Gali*, songs of loving insult. They are a favorite of almost all the village women I met in eastern India. In the cloistered world of the village women in eastern India, singing *gali*s is considered great entertainment. It is a very happy experience for everybody. I suppose one day the old traditional songs may be forgotten. But I believe these *gali*s will last forever. In the world of purdah of the Indian wife, *gali*s are a chance to really lash out playfully at menfolk and especially at the male in-laws of their family. It's all in fun. They don't mean it in any kind of anger. I don't think they are acting out inhibitions since they pretty much do that all day anyhow. (One might even suggest that it is the men who are inhibited in as much as they have to cough every time they go into a different room so the women can adjust their veils.)

Often for *gali*, they will sing hidden behind a screen, but they will sing, and they will sing loudly and without inhibition, these days usually with a microphone attached to cheap but huge loudspeakers. Most American guests would think they sound awful, as the distortion of the equipment is so disturbing and the volume is turned all the way up. At weddings, often the women sit on the flat roof of the house and use these microphones and loudspeakers to sing *gali*s while the guests are eating and at other important moments. So it is practically impossible to get a recording of a Bhojpuri song that sounds "nice." But it is all so much fun.

Umesh said, "*Matikor* is a ritual that takes place in eastern Uttar Pradesh and western Bihar, where women go to dig soil from a field nearby the pond or river or where the water is available. This soil is used under the wedding tent to make the miniature *chulha* stove and other ritual items. The *matikor* is a very essential ceremony before beginning any important ritual of the wedding. Women go with their neighbor women and relative women. Children also follow them—girls and boys. Sometimes outside visitor men are also allowed to go along. Otherwise it is completely carried out by women.

"*Matikor* has some four sections, and each section has a different kind of song. The essence of *matikor* is fundamentally important for the wedding rites, for all blessings, all fertility derives ultimately from Mother Earth, according to the Hindu worldview.

"Bachchu Lal of Chapra, Bihar, had said, 'Look, I am telling you. We all eat and drink and become fruitful out of this soil. Therefore, we take the soil in our hands first. We recollect Mother Earth, and we lift her up. Only then can the wedding begin. We are born on this soil, we take it in our hands, we are from it. We take birth from the soil, and henceforth we pray to the soil.'"

"*Matikor* is performed at an auspicious time told by the pandit according to his holy calendar," Gangajali explained. "That could be in the morning, noon, evening, or night, although mostly it takes place in the evening or at night. The women gather, and the barber lady carries a round bamboo basket containing a yellow cloth, turmeric paste, and a *sindhura* (vessel in which the *sindur* is kept) on her head. They also bring a shovel to dig the soil and a *lota* of water. When the women go for *matikor*, songs are sung on the way. As they depart, this is the main song."

### SONG 22

*Matikor, Oh cuckoo, in what forest do you live?*

Oh cuckoo, in what forest do you live?
In what forest do you go?
At which door will you ask, "How are you?"
Go to ask after their well-being.
At which door will you ask, "How are you?"
Go to ask after their well-being.
The cuckoo lives in Brindavan,
And goes in the forest of Nand.
The cuckoo goes to the door of Father Anurudha.
The cuckoo goes to the door of Father Anurudha.
Go to ask after their well-being.
Black cuckoo, oh black cuckoo,
Your beak is green, your beak is green.
Your beak is green, your beak is green.
Cuckoo, in what forest do you live?
In what forest do you go?
Cuckoo, at whose door do you ask, "How are you?"

Goes to ask after their well-being.
The cuckoo lives in Brindavan.
And goes to the forest of Nand.
Cuckoo, at the door of the ancestors,
Ask after their well-being.
Cuckoo, at the door of the ancestors,
Ask, "How are you?"

Most Bhojpuri songs can be understood as a dialogue between two or more people. Hence, it is always important to listen for the voice—who is speaking each line? In this song, the conversation takes a clear question-and-answer form, but the particular people in this conversation are not named. They are implied. So perhaps, as Umesh suggests, the cuckoos are female singers who are asked questions and then give their reply, all in a flock. Question: "Oh cuckoo, in what forest do you live?" And the cuckoos reply, "The cuckoo lives in Brindavan and goes in the forest of Nand." The little story continues, for this is quite a short song, and at the end we learn that the flock of cuckoos is addressing the ancestors. As Gangajali points out, in an actual wedding the song is sung on the way to perform the *matikor* ceremony, and the names of various ancestors will be incorporated into the song in additional verses.

In the late 1930s, William Archer recorded a similar song in the Madhubani area of Hazaribhag district. "O Cuckoo, where is the jungle / where you lived? / And where is the jungle / where you've gone? / Where is the door / where you dance with joy?" Who knows how long such songs have been preserved in aural tradition? But at least for this song, we can assume at least ninety years, and probably much longer—much, much longer.

"All along the way the women will keep singing this song," Gangajali explained. "And those people who have passed away, our ancestors, the women will repeat their names in the song. Whether they have to go one mile or one hundred miles or only a small distance, only this song will be sung."

"This is a religious song with a deep meaning," Umesh said. "The cuckoo is a metaphor. In the song, the cuckoo goes to the door of the ancestors. Then the question comes, 'In what forest does the cuckoo live, and in what forest does the cuckoo go?'

"The cuckoo is a female—even though they are also male, we consider that they are female singers. 'The cuckoo lives in Brindavan and lives in the forest of Nand.' Brindavan is the town of Krishna, and Nand is the father of Krishna. The cuckoo could be Radha, or the cuckoos could be the *gopi*s, the female goatherds that love Krishna and follow him.

"On the other hand, the cuckoo is the mother of relative women of the ancestors of those who are participating in the wedding. The singing ladies, they altogether are the singing cuckoos. Because here it is mentioned that the cuckoo goes to the door of the ancestors to ask after their well-being. The cuckoo means the family female singers. In fact, they have not seen the door of the ancestors.

But when they recite the names of the ancestor in singing their song, they feel that they are at their door.

"Often people have their own worshiping place for the ancestors outside their house," Umesh continued. "They can make it out of mud, out of the stones, or out of bricks and plaster. People assume that their ancestors live around there. And women go up to the platform to sing. Nobody steps on the platform—certainly not with their shoes on.

"There is a banyan tree in my village, and people go there to respect their ancestors. There is a platform made at the bottom of the trunk, and people don't step on it. When people pass by, they join their hands or touch the feet of the tree. They don't piss or spit under the shade of the tree out of respect. There are only certain occasions when people climb in the tree—to hang bells or to hang a pitcher full of water. People say, 'If my job will be done, I will give you bells.' Or they may leave the pitcher of water for the ancestors."

Umesh added, "On Saturday nights I go and light *diya*s using sesame seed oil and a black cotton wick. And I offer water around the tree. I do it after sunset. So the obstacles of my daughter's wedding can be removed after pleasing Lord Hanuman—to get strength and remove obstacles so we can perform my daughter's wedding soon."

Gangajali's friend Sashi interrupted our conversation about the ancestors and Mother Earth. "Sing 'A Mare Has Pissed.' Sing this one. Sing this one!"

"No, no, no, no," Gangajali replied.

"Oh, that is a *gali*, an obscene *gali*," Sashi said.

"Whatever are the important songs, I am singing them and explaining them, not other unimportant songs," Gangajali said. She wanted Sashi to shut up.

Umesh tried to resolve this spat. "If you think singing *gali* is not good, then don't sing *gali*," he said. "If you think singing *gali* is good, that is also good. And if you think singing *gali* would be good, we would be happy to hear them. Do as you wish. But we would like to hear 'A Mare Has Pissed.'"

"For *matikor* they pour some water there out of the pitcher," Gangajali continued, shifting the topic away from 'A Mare Has Pissed.' "And they give a kind of bath to the shovel. They place turmeric paste in five places on its handle. They also put *sindur* on it and offer it rice, betel, and flowers. All the married ladies put *sindur* in their hair, and the five ladies place barley seeds in their *anchal*. Then they dig the soil.

"First the bridegroom's mother digs the soil, and, second, the *nanad*, the sister of the bridegroom, digs. She asks for a donation, a *neg*, for doing it. Whatever anyone can give she accepts, for she feels it is her right to receive something for performing this duty. For without the *nanad*, the wedding could not go forward. She might get a necklace or a watch or rupees as a *neg*. The *neg* is given at that time, and this is the song for this *matikor*."

## SONG 23

### *Matikor*

Where is the yellow soil from?
Where is the shovel from?
Where are the five *suhagin* married ladies from,
Who go to dig the soil?
Where are the five *suhagin* married ladies from,
Who go to dig the soil?
Where are the five married ladies from?
The yellow soil is of Ayodhya.
The shovel is of Janakpur.
The five *suhagin* married ladies are from Ballia,
Who go to dig the soil.
The five married ladies are from Ballia,
Who go to dig the soil.
The five *suhagin* married ladies are from Ballia.

This very short song is about the actual *matikor* ceremony. Five married women perform this ritual. I noticed, over the years, that songs for the actual digging were short or actually absent from some singers' repertories. This holds true for songs in other collections. For example, William Archer reports, "Take up the yellow earth, / O yellow earth / It is with you / that the wedding will go on"—only one short verse. The *matikor* songs I heard in Mauritius always mentioned that the yellow soil should "rise up," but these songs too were very short. In the island diaspora, the most fullsome *matikor* songs were from Fiji, but that is a whole other story half a world away in the South Pacific. In Gangajali's song, again we have questions and answers to questions in what we might a call a call-and-response form. Perhaps the songs for the actual digging are truncated or absent because the women are anticipating the dancing, merrymaking, chasing, fun, and game playing that are about to begin. But I don't really know why this category of songs is short. Perhaps it is because the whole matter of digging up one shovelful of soil really doesn't take very long. But it does seem curious that neither the mother nor the *nanad*—the principal celebrants—are mentioned by name.

"This song has questions and answers," Umesh said. "The entire wedding takes place according to the religious ceremonies, and we usually give the name of Ram and Sita in our wedding songs. In this song, the yellow soil is from Ayodhya, the birthplace of Ram. And the shovel is from Janakpur, the birthplace of Sita. And the ladies of Ballia go to dig the soil. First of all, Ayodhya is the place where the bridegroom is, so the soil is there. And Janakpur is the place where the bride is, so the shovel is there. Instead of saying their own villages, they are putting the names of religious places. But they add Ballia as well, because they belong to Ballia."

In similar fashion, Gangajali sang, "How will the wedding take place without the soil? Oh yellow soil, get up, get up."

SONG 24

*Matikor, Oh get up, get up*

Oh get up, get up.
Oh yellow soil, get up, get up.
How will the wedding take place without the soil?
Oh yellow soil, get up, get up.
How will the wedding take place without the soil?

Now, this song is really short. "Get up, get up. / Oh yellow soil, get up, get up." Only a few simple lines sung to the same repeating melody. And the melody itself is restricted to three pitches of the scale (with a slight hint of a lower note, the dominant, flipping briefly up to the tonic). I'm sure that many would argue that it is wrong in every sense to use words from Western classical music (and also from Indian classical music) to describe features of what some might call a folk song. I would label it as a Bhojpuri woman's song and a rural song, even though these songs have infiltrated towns and cities with the constant movement of peoples from rural farms to urban areas, where they hope to earn a better living. In any case, one might imagine that this Gangajali song is but a remnant of a long and glorious ceremonial song celebrating Mother Earth and explaining the many meanings this takes in rural Hinduism and that there were many other long songs that took up different aspects of the yellow earth rising up. We can imagine that. Or we can also imagine that this shoveling bit never had a song, and singers in India decided there at least should be *some* song, so they devised a few impromptu lines to respect the Earth. Who was there long ago? What did they do? What was their melody? An especially difficult problem in ethnomusicology as those very old songs went with the wind. Or to the daughters. Or to the clouds. In this field, there are so very few fossils.

"This song personifies Mother Earth," Umesh said. "The soil is Mother Earth. 'Get up, get up, Mother Earth. How can the wedding take place without you?'"

Then Sashi said, "What do I know? A little. Tell the white lady a little. Explain to her whatever we have sung, and then let's sing *gali*."

"Not the obscene ones," Gangajali said. "For digging the soil. Five ladies dig there. They all worship first. Now the rest of the women sing *gali* to those who dig the soil."

And they did sing a little *gali*—at my expense.

## SONG 25

### *Gali*

Oh mother, one *ser* of chickpea flour,
Two-and-a-half *ser* of *bariya*.
Mother, one *ser* of chickpea flour,
Two-and-a-half *ser* of *bariya*.

"What is her name?" Gangajali asked.
"Helen," Sashi said.
Gangajali resumed the song.

Oh, all the *bariya* are gone in the garden of Helenji.
I am intoxicated, intoxicated.
I drank marijuana and milk.
I am intoxicated, intoxicated.
I drank marijuana and milk.
Father-in-law is intoxicated, *bhasur* is intoxicated, *jethaniya* is intoxicated.
Father-in-law is intoxicated, *bhasur* is intoxicated, *jethaniya* is intoxicated.

"What is the name of her brother?" Gangajali asked.
"James," Sashi said.
Again the song resumed.

James is intoxicated on a red cot.
(*One line obscure*)
I am intoxicated, intoxicated.
I drank marijuana and milk.
I am intoxicated, intoxicated.
I drank marijuana and milk.

Here is where the fun begins. First of all, the listener will note that Gangajali stopped singing twice to ask Sashi for my name and then for my brother's name. Such interruptions are absolutely typical. During the wedding, women are constantly stopping *gali* songs to insert personal names. For *gali* singing, small boys are sent down to find out the individual names of, say, the bridegroom's parents, his grandfather, his sister, his brothers. If you are in the party of those being abused, I suppose you must dread these little breaks as the next name to be shouted out might be yours.

Some songs are considered "nice" *gali*, and these are what Gangajali sang for us. Other songs are the "dirty" *gali*, and she did not sing any of them. These would be the "Fuck your sister" songs that do turn up in various English collections. Gangajali did not go there, even though "sister-fucker" is an ordinary, everyday swear word in North India, in particular from one guy to another. As Umesh repeated over and again, "She did not go beyond the limit." When we returned to spend time with Gangajali in 1990, she still observed these rules and did not sing the dirty *gali*s. She fully understood that these tapes were going to archives in Delhi and Indiana and that we would be writing a book about them. "She knew her limit. She never stepped beyond her limit."

The exciting insults with our names in this song are reserved for the *antara* lines sung at a higher pitch. The verse, repeated over and over, has a gently rocking melody, as if describing some intoxicated person making their way home. As these songs go, this item has a fairly wide pitch range and a quick tempo. It's a fun song. It's a foolish song. Nobody should be too serious about it. Especially our reader.

"This is a *gali* for you and your brother James," Umesh said. "Everybody got intoxicated—tipsy. So all became intoxicated, the father-in-law, the older brother, and his wife. James also got intoxicated. The red cot is always considered to be the sleeping place for the husband and wife. It means that you slept with your brother. Not on purpose. Because you were both intoxicated."

I was greatly amused, also honored, that they had lovingly insulted me. I showed shock and embarrassment to make them all laugh. Gangajali was having terrific fun. And this is what Sashi had wanted her to sing from the very start.

Then came the next *gali*.

### SONG 26

*Gali*

Black black wolf with gray gray hair.
Black black wolf with gray gray hair.
Oh wolf, where are you going in the dark night?
Oh wolf, where are you going in the dark night?
Where are you going?
I go, I go near to Helen.
I go, I go near to Helen.
Oh, there is my lady spinning the cotton.
Oh, there is my lady spinning the cotton.
Oh, there is my lady spinning the cotton.

When I heard *my* name called out at such a high pitch, I began to wonder, *What's up with this?* Why couldn't my name be buried in the lower and softer lines of the *sthayi*, the verse? The verse lines were sung lower down the scale, while the *antara* lines were higher and more striking. This song moves along at a good clip and, with the repeating words, is quite an effective, funny song to amuse everybody.

"I didn't know you had wolves in India," I said.

“There are,” Umesh said. “Wild dogs. They live in the forest.”

“What kind of reputation do they have?”

“They have a very bad reputation. They strike fear in us. They kill dogs, they kill goats. They can take away children. But this is not a wolf. It is indicating some man, I believe, who is like a wolf. An old man with gray hair.”

I protested, “But I don’t want to sleep with an old wolf.”

“Well, do you want to sleep with James? Do you want to sleep with the old wolf? No, no! That is why it is a *gali*. Perhaps the wolf is a lover. It can’t be your husband.”

“There are hundreds more songs for this occasion,” Gangajali said after performing these two short, simple *gali*. “These *gali* are for the occasion of *matikor*. There are hundreds of *gali*.”

“Now, here a few real dirty *gali* are sung,” Sashi said. “They are not good to sing.”

Our recording session was grinding to a halt at this impasse. Should they sing dirty *gali* or not?

“Do the women dance too?” I asked.

“Yes, yes. Who has feelings in her mind, she dances there,” Gangajali said.

Sashi said, “She—Gangajali—dances very well.”

“I do not dance,” Gangajali said firmly. “The family people dance.”

“No,” Sashi said. “She dances very well, the dances of our area. If you—Umesh—would go out of the room, then she would show her—Helen—the dance. Well, now, turn the topic,” Sashi said. “Suppose now they return.”

They were *not* going to sing the really dirty *gali*. Gangajali was *not* going to dance.

“Now having dug the soil, they get ready to go home,” Gangajali said. “Then at the time of carrying the soil, these few lines of song are famous.”

### SONG 27

#### *Matikor*

I went to dig the soil.
Oh, to dig the soil. Oh sinner *dewar*,
Held my arm, oh *dewar* sinner,
Held my arm, oh *dewar* sinner.
I went to dig the soil,
Oh, to dig the soil. Oh sinner *dewar*,
Held my arm, oh *dewar* sinner,
Held my arm, oh *dewar* sinner.
*Dewar*, let go of my arm. It is tender.
It will get twisted.
*Dewar*, my wrist is tender.
Oh, it will get twisted.

*Dewar*, let go, let go of my tender arm.
Oh, it will get twisted.
*Dewar*, my tender arm will get twisted.
*Dewar*, my fragile bangles will break.
Then *bhauji*, I will replace the bangles.
I will have them put on. Quench my thirst.
Your beautiful *kangan*, oh I will get them fixed.
Your beautiful *kangan*, oh I will get them fixed.
Your beautiful *kangan*, oh I will get them fixed.
Then *bhauji*, I will replace the bangles.
I will have them put on. Quench my thirst.
I will get your beautiful juicy *kangan* fixed.
Your beautiful juicy *kangan*, oh I will get them fixed.

The amusement continues. Whenever Indian songs mention that something is juicy or that somebody wants to quench their thirst, you can be certain that hanky-panky is in progress. Here it is easy enough to understand that the *dewar*, the husband's younger brother, wants his thirst quenched. As this relationship is a "joking relationship," such talk is common enough. A *kangan* is a thick silver bangle, although what a juicy bangle is I can't really tell you. But perhaps you might imagine such a situation.

"At the time of *matikor*, the lady's *dewar* arrived," Gangajali said. "He comes here. He is the younger brother of the bridegroom. He holds her arm. And because of his holding, her bangles break.

"Then she says, 'Oh, why have you held my arm so tightly? My arm has broken, and the bangles are also broken. What will happen?'

"Then he replies, 'Oh *bhauji*, I will let you have better bangles than these. And I will also get your *kangan* that is broken fixed. It is broken. So what?'

"This is a song for after *matikor*."

"Is it a *gali*?" Umesh asked.

"It is a song," Gangajali replied. "This is a *gali* for after digging the soil. When the women begin to move, then this song is sung first."

"This song is very clear," Umesh said. "This is a *gali* between *dewar* and *bhauji*. There is an unusual joking relationship that is allowed between the daughter-in-law (*bhauji*) and her husband's younger brother (*dewar*). This is called the *dewar–bhabi* relationship. There are many songs, especially *jhumar*, that tell of the jokes shared by *dewar* and *bhabi*. These jokes can be quite sexual in nature and still cause no disruption in the joint family. In this song, the *bhauji* goes to dig the soil for the *matikor* ritual, and the *dewar* comes and holds her arm.

"She says, 'Release my tender arm, it will get twisted, and my bangles will break.' He says, 'I will get them fixed.' That is the song. When women go to dig the soil, so boys also go along behind as the women are singing songs. One of the *dewar*s comes up and holds her hand. Then the rest of this story follows. I don't see any deep meaning in the song except its illustration of *dewar–bhabi* jokes."

"Afterward," Gangajali added, "walking on the way, the women sing *jhumar*, whether they have to go a short distance or a long distance. If the way is short, they will only have to sing one *jhumar*, and if they have far to go, they will sing four or five songs."

"Which one will you sing?" Umesh asked.

Gangajali offered only a line of song: "Radha takes the soil of the pitcher in her hand."

"Sing a spicy *jhumar*," Sashi interrupted. "Don't begin with Radha. Oh, sing the bright, spicy *jhumar*!"

The two women began to whisper to each other.

"That song is not in Bhojpuri," Gangajali said.

"Isn't it in Bhojpuri?" Sashi asked.

"No, it is Devanagari," Gangajali said. "She wants Bhojpuri."

Sashi suggested a spicy *jhumar*. "How about 'Hit me'?" she said.

Then Gangajali began to sing.

### SONG 28

### *Jhumar*

Oh sweetheart, I feel great in my parents' home.
Oh sweetheart, I feel great in my parents' home.
Oh sweetheart, I feel great in my parents' home.
Oh, I love my mother, I love my father.
Oh, I love my mother, I love my father.
Sweetheart, I love my younger brother so much.
Sweetheart, I love my younger brother so much.
Oh sweetheart, I feel great in my parents' home.
Oh sweetheart, I feel great in my parents' home.
Oh, I love my brother, I love my *bhauji*.
Oh, I love my brother, I love my *bhauji*.
I love the little nephew very much.
I love the little nephew very much.
Oh sweetheart, I feel great in my parents' home.
Oh sweetheart, I feel great in my parents' home.
I love *puri*s (fried bread). I love *kachori*s (balls of fried lentils).
I love *puris*. I love *kachori*s.
Sweetheart, I love the little sweets very much.
Sweetheart, I love the little sweets very much.
Oh sweetheart, I feel great in my parents' home.
Oh sweetheart, I feel great in my parents' home.
Oh, I love clove, I love cardamom.

Oh, I love clove, I love cardamom.
Oh sweetheart, I love the double bed very much.
Oh sweetheart, I love the double bed very much.
Oh sweetheart, I feel great in my parents' home.
Oh sweetheart, I feel great in my parents' home.
Oh, I love my father-in-law, I love my *bhasur*.
Oh, I love my father-in-law, I love my *bhasur*.
Oh sweetheart, I love little *nanadi* very much.
Oh sweetheart, I love little *nanadi* very much.
Oh sweetheart, I love little *nanadi* very much.
Oh sweetheart, I love little *nanadi* very much.
Oh sweetheart, I feel great in my parents' home.
I love my *jeth*, I love my *jithani*.
I love my *jeth*, I love my *jithani*.
Oh sweetheart, I love my little husband very much.
Oh sweetheart, I love my little husband very much.
Oh sweetheart, I feel great in my parents' home.
Oh sweetheart, I feel great in my parents' home.

This lovely lilting song owes much of its charm to the number three—that is, what is called compound meter. Each main beat is divided into not two but three sub-beats, and when two main beats are joined together, you get the lovely flowing six mini-beat rhythm that in Western classical music is called $\frac{6}{8}$. This time signature is often used for dance music, soothing and flowing melodic lullabies, pastorals, and the like. This darling song gives the sentiments of the wife, who is singing, "I feel great in my parents' home." She emphasizes that she loves her "little husband very much." Yes, a compound rhythm is a very appropriate rhythm for this soft and sweet *gali*. The listener may also be struck by the wordy nature of this song. For the most part, each syllable of the text is set to its own note—syllabic. The opposite would be melismatic, a song in which a vowel is sung over several different pitches, resulting in a more flowing style.

"This is the song that is sung for *matikor* on the way back home," Gangajali said.

"This is a *jhumar* for the very new bride," Umesh explained. "As she arrives at her husband's home, in the beginning she feels very lonely because she has passed her entire childhood in her parents' home. So she is making a complaint to her husband that she likes her *naihar*, her parents' home, the most. And whatever she likes in her *naihar*, she explains. She also tells her husband that she loves to be in her husband's home. She loves her father-in-law and her *bhasur*, her husband's older brother. She also likes her brother-in-law, her *nanad*'s husband. And the question comes, she loves her little sweetheart the most, her little husband. That joke has a double meaning. Her little husband. Just this big. But there is nothing deep in it. Everything is open. It is very clear. She does not want to upset her husband. She balances both families with love."

Gangajali continued her narrative. "After finishing all the songs on the way, they reach the door of the house. And those people, the musicians, the servants, and the maidservants, block the door and ask for a donation.

"'Because you have come back from *matikor*,' they say, 'we demand a donation.' Two rupees, four rupees, five rupees, or ten rupees must be given to them. That is given at the door, and the bridegroom or bride's mother, sister, *bhauji*, and other relatives must give it. After giving the *neg*, then the women come into the courtyard."

I did not observe this interesting custom ever in the islands of the diaspora. But I saw it often in India.

TWENTY

# HELEN'S POUNDING POT

*Continuing at the Sarang Hotel, Ballia, July 1989*

We were all seated in my room in Hotel Sarang, ready to continue.

"Do not sing any obscene *gali*," Sashi said.

"No," Gangajali replied. "Here is the *gali* for pounding the rice. The pounding pot is under the wedding tent. Five women together use the mortar and pound the raw rice, and all the women who participated in the *matikor* are also there. They all sing there at the time of pounding the rice."

## SONG 29

*Gali*

Pound the rice, oh *nitua*, oh pound the rice,
In the mortar of your own sister. Pound rice,
Pound the rice, oh *nitua*, oh pound the rice,
In the mortar of Hem, oh pound rice.
Oh sister, I'm pounding,
Oh sister, I'm pounding,
My pestle got blunt by pounding.
My pestle got blunt by pounding.
Drink the rice water.
Drink the rice water.

Drink the rice water out of Hem's vagina.
Drink the rice water out of Hem's vagina.
Oh sister, I'm drinking, I'm drinking.
Her vagina got tired by stirring.
Her vagina got tired by stirring.

This short rice-pounding song is essentially in duple (or quadruple) meter, which actually is rather unusual for Bhojpuri women's songs. On the contrary, in the West, duple or quadruple meter has dominated much, if not most, music since the eighteenth century. The song is in a neat verse–chorus form, although the melody of the *sthayi* or verse has a range of only a fourth and the melody of the chorus or *antara* the range of a minor third. One might say that the melody of the verse is more exciting than the chorus as it begins up on the fourth degree (fa) and then descends in graceful patterns to the tonic (do). The chorus, with its smaller range, has mostly calm, stepwise movement.

The real point of the song is given in the text, and it is quite naughty. None of the women of this party miss the metaphor of pounding the rice in the mortar with the pestle, which eventually, after lots of pounding, ends up getting blunt. "Keep pounding, keep pounding" is pretty much an insult, isn't it, sisters? Haha. His "pestle got blunt by pounding."

"At every wedding in every house this song will be sung first for rice pounding," Gangajali explained. I was more than a bit amused.

Women among themselves have fun at weddings by singing such ribald *gali* songs. Since these songs are popular at practically all weddings in India, it is curious that they are often absent in weddings in the island diaspora, where humor does not extend beyond the gentle teasing of the *jhumar* and *lachari*. Why are the explicitly sexual *gali* songs never sung in Trinidad, for example? Perhaps these were forgotten over the years. But who could forget songs like these? Perhaps they were discouraged by Hindu reformist organizations such as the Arya Samaj, who served essentially as right-wing Hindu missionaries in these islands. Perhaps they were considered inappropriate as an emblem for a decent and upstanding Indian culture that was specially designed to compete with other cultures on the island for a prominent place in the national spotlight. In Trinidad, East Indians shun Creole calypsos because they are considered lewd, whereas they are proud of clean, wholesome Indian religious songs. East Indians shun Carnival. Many Indo-Trinidadians have mixed feelings about the chutney song-and-dance craze and these new racy songs with their overtly sexual overtones. So, although the particular *gali* brought from India have died out in Trinidad, their esprit, part of the cultural essence of the eastern Indian countryside, lives on in Trinidad in 2019 in chutney.

"This *gali* is sung while the women are playing a drama," Umesh said, "women to women among themselves. There is a lady dressed up like a man, and they call her 'nitua.' So this is a very rough *gali* sung among each other. What should I say? Pound rice in her pounding pot. Something here is very funny. They are comparing things to the human body like the pounding pot is made out of wood or is a hole in the ground and the pounder is made of wood, and they are expressing their thoughts that the pounding pot is just like a woman and the pounder is just like a man—that they are sleeping together.

"'Pound the rice in the pounding pot of Helen.'

"He says, 'Oh sister I'm doing, I am busy doing it.' He says, 'My pounder got tired by stirring it.'

"Then once again the women begin to explain, 'Oh *nitua*, drink the cooked rice water.' All the women understand very clearly what is meant here, but it is said in a hidden way. The rice water indicates what comes out of the human to make a child. 'Drink it out of the woman.'

"And he says, 'Sister, I am drinking it, but her place has got tired by stirring it.'

"This is the song. This is fun among women to women. Now the next song for pounding the rice," Gangajali said.

I prepared for more pounding.

### SONG 30

*Gali*

Verse: Oh, whose mother's pounding pot is deep.
Chorus: Oh mother, Ram Dulari.
Oh mother, love, loving.
Verse: This pounding pot of Helen is deep.
Chorus: Oh mother, Ram Dulari.
Oh mother, love, loving.
Verse: It holds twenty-four kilos of mustard.
Chorus: Oh mother, Ram Dulari.
Oh mother, love, loving.
Verse: It holds 680 pounds of rice.
Chorus: Oh mother, Ram Dulari.
Oh mother, love, loving.
Verse: The rice sounds "chatar-chatar."
Chorus: Oh mother, Ram Dulari.
Oh mother, love, loving.
Verse: It holds 680 pounds of mustard.
Chorus: Oh mother, Ram Dulari.
Oh mother, love, loving.
Verse: Oh, powerful James.
Chorus: Oh mother, Ram Dulari.

Oh mother, love, loving.
Verse: The oil is dripping, making the sound "harara-harara."
Chorus: Oh mother, Ram Dulari.
Oh mother, love, loving.
Verse: Oh, the oil is rubbed on the head of Helen's brother.
Chorus: Oh mother, Ram Dulari.
Oh mother, love, loving.
Verse: The nice smell of the oil.
Chorus: Oh mother, Ram Dulari.
Oh mother, love, loving.

This sweet, simple song has the range of a fourth, from the tonic (do) to the subdominant (fa). It is in a clear verse–chorus structure, although the higher *antara* chorus section does not go higher than fa, the fourth degree of the scale. The point of this short song is not a special melody, but the rhythm and structure are quite interesting. A verse of six or more beats alternates with two chorus lines of two plus two. Toward the end of the song, the last verses get a bit longer, with a couple of lines seeming to have seven, eight, or even nine beats. This flexibility demonstrates how Bhojpuri melodies can be adjusted to accommodate different texts. It is not uncommon, as we have seen in several examples above, to hear two songs with similar but not quite matching melodies. I expect that if one were to make a statistical study of it, one would find lots of texts but a fewer number of melodies to accompany them. At times, scholars during the Raj, in particular Sir George Grierson, claimed that all genres of song had the same melody. This certainly is not true. Perhaps they were thinking in terms of what might be considered a kind of chanting plus the distinctive vocal quality of village women—counting such factors as forming a single homogenous sound or melody. Perhaps recordings were not available, so such scholars had never in fact heard the melodies. Their local appointees who had gone to collect the texts in the countryside might have reported back that the melodies were all just the same. Certainly, after three or four hours of listening to wedding songs in their context, one gets so distracted by the ceremonies themselves, the human nature of mothers and their daughters, fathers and their sons, that one could be excused for having a rather hazy, lazy sense of monotony about the tunes. But with careful listening, it is clear that there are many, many types and styles of different melodies in the Gangajali repertory. In the most general sense, these songs can be considered incantations to make the wedding proceed smoothly and indeed to keep the entire universe running.

"This is a *gali* for the time of pounding the rice," Gangajali explained, without going into any detail. "The *gali* is for you, for your brother, and you, the sister."

“Again the joke is about pounding rice,” Umesh said. “These are village women. What can they think of? And in this song women are singing to women, asking whose pounding pot is deeper. Then these words are added, ‘Oh mother, Ram Dulari’—words are just added to make the chorus of the song. Then it says Helen’s pounding pot is deeper. It takes 680 pounds of mustard.

“These are the wives of farmers,” said Umesh. “They belong to the village, and they know most about agricultural matters. If these songs still remain in the town, it means that India is a country of small villages. So most of the city women know these songs because they got married from village to town, and they bring these songs to the town. This is just harmless fun among women to women. It doesn’t hurt anybody. Even the woman who is played with, she feels happy and playful. She is a close relative of the family whose child is about to get married, either *bua* (father’s sister) or *bhauji* (sister-in-law) or *chachi* (mother’s sister). Women force her to do this drama, and they are happy. When the woman is forced to sit down and make a *chula* (oven) with her legs (sitting and bowing her legs), certainly she will feel shy for a little while, even among women. But she knows that she is making other people happy at the same time. It is a drama. This song is not particular to one wedding. Every wedding has this ritual. So not only one woman will remain the funny one forever.”

TWENTY-ONE

# UMESH EXPLAINS *GALI*

*Banaras, Sandhya Guesthouse, 2006*

"*Gali* is a very old custom in northern India. A *gali* is a song that includes some swearing words, words of abuse directed at men or women of your family or of other families. For example, a *gali* may make fun of the bridegroom's older brother, the *bhasur*—he is lame, I break his leg, I poke out his eyes, and other such insults.

"They also swear by saying that women are sleeping with such and such a person. This is also a type of *gali*. One of our songs says that the girl has not cheeks and she has no breasts and that my brother gave her cheeks and breasts so children are calling Mummy-Papa. This is a true *gali* and is a song of insult, even though no hurt is intended by singing it. It is surely abuse, but it is loving abuse, an affectionate and welcoming form of swearing that brings people close together. In this way, through these amusing insults, the people of the *barat* are brought closer to the family of the bride.

"Certainly, this kind of talk among *bahu*s (wives) does not take place in normal life. A daughter-in-law cannot swear in her courtyard at anyone. In fact, she must cover her face in the presence of her father-in-law and any older men of the family. Usually married women sing *gali*s because married women have a greater knowledge of the world than unmarried girls. Girls must not sing *gali*, they must never swear at their elders and certainly not at their own brother or sister. So the daughters-in-law of the family usually sing *gali* together with relative women and neighbor women.

"Rather than shying from this abuse, men persuade women to sing *gali*s because it is good joking fun. *Gali*s are sung at several important rituals of the marriage ceremony. At the *tilak* ritual, when many gifts are given by the bride's side to the boy's family, it is the turn of the women of the boy's side to sing *gali*s for the *bhasur* (older brother) and *sasur* (father-in-law) of the bridegroom and also to the bride's brother. As the gifts of the *tilak* are brought into the groom's house, then women sing *gali*s. Although the clothes are new, the golden chain is new, and the fruits are very nice, they can be criticized in *gali*.

"*Gali*s are also sung here in this Bhojpuri area when ornaments and clothes for the bride are carried into the bride's courtyard by the men of the groom's side. The women of the girl's side sing *gali*s for the *bhasur* and the *sasur* at this time. Traditionally the most important occasion for *gali* was at the time of the great feast offered for the *barat* as they arrived at the bride's home and were seated and eating in the courtyard. This was in olden times. Men were seated in the courtyard eating, and the women of the bride's family were seated on the flat rooftop singing *galis*. Nowadays food is not served in the courtyard anymore. The tradition has changed. Usually it is served by what we call buffer system, that is to say served outside the courtyard in a tent. So women sing *gali* wherever they find a place and time to sing.

"When women give *gali*s, the intention is never to hurt people, and these *gali*s never hurt anyone. These *gali*s are always intended to give pleasure and to make fun and to joke. But these jokes are not to hurt the person to whom they are given. The target of the *gali* will laugh and smile and enjoy the song. In my area, when women give *gali*s, men throw their *angocha*s (man's cotton scarf) to them up on the roof with some money tied in it to give them for singing *gali*s, and the women toss the *angocha* back with double the money. Women cannot keep the money from the boy's side. It does not happen always, but when it does happen, this is how it goes. This shows that *gali*s are only for fun and laughing, not to make anyone annoyed.

"House people, especially boys, are alert to find out the names of the boy's side people so that the *gali*s can be sung for them personally, with the name inserted in the verse in the appropriate place. And some *barati* people from the boy's side give the name of the girl's side people to sing a *gali* for them. This is all done in jest and is considered funny.

"Although this custom is free and happy, there are certain rules for singing *gali*s stipulating who can abuse whom. The daughter-in-law of the house will not be singing *gali*s for her *sas* (mother-in-law) or *sasur* (father-in-law) or *jeth* (husband's older brother). But she will be singing *gali* for her *nanad* (husband's sister) or her *dewar* (husband's younger brother) or perhaps her *bua* (father's sister). So there are strict rules, although sometimes women break these rules."

## INTERLUDE FOUR

# LUCY MORRIS

THEN WE ARE INTRODUCED TO A NEW CHARACTER, A DELIGHTFUL, ENterprising little lady named Lucy Morris. Confusion presents itself. Who is the heroine of the tale? Trollope is no help on this point. And Trollope makes comedy of the question and fun of himself, the writer.

"*That there shall be any heroine the historian will not take upon himself to assert; but if there be a heroine, that heroine shall not be Lady Eustace. . . . The real heroine, if it be found possible to arrange her drapery for her becomingly, and to put that part which she enacted into properly heroic words, shall stalk in among us at some considerably later period of the narrative, when the writer shall have accustomed himself to the flow of words, and have worked himself up to a state of mind fit for the reception of noble acting and noble speaking. In the meantime, let it be understood that poor little Lucy Morris was a governess in the house of old Lady Fawn.*"

Trollope opens the frame of the story and steps out to chat with the reader for a moment. I have many copies of Trollope's books. But it was only when I was reading that the *copy* became the *book*. I felt Trollope was alive during those moments we spent together. This is what it means to read. It is a performance, it is live, and it can never be done the same way again. The performance is timeless and never-ending. It can be repeated, but it will never be the same experience. The copy is what goes back on the shelf. The book becomes part of your experience.

Lady Fawn, Lucy Morris's mistress, comes to take an important role for the promotion of the drama inasmuch as she was intimately involved with two important romances that Trollope is about to set out for the reader. One is between little Lucy Morris and Frank Greystock, Lizzie's cousin, and of this relationship Lady Fawn did not approve. She explained to Lucy that a governess must not marry or she cannot be a governess—that this union would be ill suited for Lucy and Frank alike. She explained all this to Lucy with great maternal love, a love that was genuine. The other romance was that of Lizzie with Lady Fawn's precious oldest child, her heir and only son, Lord Fawn. Lucy and Lizzie are friends—in as much as Lizzie is capable of friendship—and their lives become entangled, with most of the early action taking place at the Fawn establishment, which was also the home of the Lady's seven unmarried daughters. There is something of comedy in this, that Lady Fawn, with seven unmarried daughters, would take another young lady into her care and that Lizzie should catch the eye of her prize son, the Lord.

Umesh said, "Lucy is the new character in it because she is the governess of the family. And Lizzie is the girl from the beginning who was married to Sir Florian Eustace. Now Lucy falls in love with the barrister, and he is Lizzie's cousin Frank.

"Lady Fawn does not want them to fall in love because as a governess she must remain unmarried. And Lucy and Lizzie knew each other from long ago. They played with each other as children. Lucy got this job with Lady Fawn. Lady Fawn had seven daughters and one son. She is planning that when these girls get raised, she will pass on this governess to her eldest daughter, Mrs. Hittaway.

"Then comes the question of the Sawab. The lady doesn't want her son to be a lover of Lucy. She, Lucy, is thinking to save the Sawab. It is in her mind, and she is prepared to talk about the question of the Sawab. Lord Fawn showed her the new papers concerning the Sawab so Lucy could think them over.

"Now I understand the story fully. The writer paints her character and beauty clearly, that she is beautiful. On the other hand, he is saying she is not beautiful. It is very cleverly done. But he did the opposite with his description of Lizzie. He described her as beautiful but pointed out the small small flaws of each feature."

"Tell me one thing. What do these people know of India?" I asked.

"Nothing really. They know nothing of India, but they are making a decision. Whatever, they want money from the Sawab. Whatever they do, he must pay money if he wants to save himself from going to jail. To save his respect. Otherwise he has to take this money out of his people, ordering more taxes. Never mind if his people dislike him. If he is in jail, who is going to take care of the throne? The British.

"This does not come by itself. In India people are against each other. The East India Company means they were ruling over India for business. Their duty was not to help India, not to save India. Their duty was to save the Empire. Never mind what happens to the subjects of this Empire. Anyhow money must come out of it. It was very wicked in those days. Hindu people wanted to get rid of Muslims of that period. There is no love in hell. Muslims were going very bad in India. At the time, Aurangzeb—he was the real orthodox Muslim—he was ruling India according to the Qur'an. He converted so many people by force. They broke down so many temples. They took money out of the temples. And when he killed his son, the last Mughal emperor, Bahadur Shah Zafar, was a powerless ruler.

"Most of the Hindu kings were against him. They wanted to get rid of this Muslim ruler somehow, and the British were coming from the East, the British were getting power together. A kind of game. They were winning the Empire by divide and rule. They got inside and made trouble in the families sneakily. Then they sent a message—'I can help you out? I can help you. You will be the king, and I will help you.' The king invited them to help on papers. The British made it legal. This business was to hire people from the government of England to do this job. They were making ways and planning ahead. This is the way the entire of India came under British rule.

"We had a system that if the king did not have a child, the king could adopt a child. So various kings had no children in their family—Vijaypur, Jhansi, Satara. These kings had no children, and they were told that they could not have an adopted child. The king of Jhansi was a Brahman from Maharashtra. He came from the south to the north, and his family was from the south. And he had now a child. This is a long story."

"Did any Indian people like the British?"

"Hard to say because I don't know really. Everybody wanted freedom, but they didn't know how to do it. Dr. A. O. Hume, he was the district magistrate of Etawah. He was the one who gave birth to the Congress party—a British person.

"The British were very much hurt by this mutiny (Indian Rebellion of 1857). It went so far, it was hard to control by the British. So a bright person made a way. Make a party and say we want this, this, this. In the very beginning, the president of the party was faithful to the British government. Later some people came and asked for freedom, and it began from there. Actually, Indian people wanted to get rid of Muslim empires to get relief from the Muslims. So Hindu kings joined the British, happily or unhappily.

"And the British did not interrupt in the Hindu social system. Except one or two things. They destroyed the sati (widow burning) system. I said to my grandfather when I was a child learning about sati, 'Oh, Grandfather, it was great that Indian women were dying with their husbands out of love.' He said, 'No, that is not true. They were pushed into the fire to burn with the husband. To save the family property and their dignity.' So sati stopped. This was a great help of the British in India.

"Some people liked the British. Ordinary people who had no jobs, they liked them. The system began from there that when Gandhiji said, a few lawyers fighting for independence won't help. The entire country must fight for freedom. So Gandhiji put on the most simple clothes. He left British clothes. Very clever. Ideas were from before. He made some ideas too, but most were from the back, ideas that had been thought of but not applied.

"Those people who were ruling over India here, they were planning what to do—for some reasons—they were making papers and sending them to the viceroy in Calcutta. And those people signed them, and those were sent to Parliament in London to make decisions.

"But somehow these papers, these blue books, fell in the hands of poor little Lucy Morris. But she has it in her heart to save the Sawab.

"Just so, when Charlotte and William Wiser came to this village, people got scared of them. They were white, and what is the difference between white Americans and white British? And while they, the Wisers, were studying, people were suspicious. But they did work hard to make the correct work. People were lying to them because they were afraid to tell the truth in case their taxes might increase. And the British were helping them.

"But the village Brahmans accepted the Wisers happily. The other castes accepted them later. And they became friends to village people. American people who were here as missionaries knew the most about the rural areas. They were helping people and converting people too."

TWENTY-TWO

# THE *KALAS* AND THE *HARISH*

*The day extends on, back at Hotel Sarang, July 1989*

"Have you sung about rubbing on the turmeric?" Sashi asked.

"How can we sing about rubbing the turmeric?" Gangajali asked. "The *kalas* (wedding pitcher) has to be placed, the *harish* (plow shaft) has to be pitched, the *diya* (clay lamp) has to be lit, the *chauk* (altar) has to be drawn. Aren't there songs for these? Then come the songs for rubbing the turmeric.

"So after pounding the rice, the pandit comes," Gangajali continued. "The barber lady comes and cleans the wedding tent. She plasters under the tent with cow dung. And after plastering she draws the *chauk* with white flour and then places the *kalas* there. Then five married men will pour water in the *kalas* from a bucket or pitcher. On the top of the *kalas* is a shallow dish of barley or rice. On top of that a clay lamp is lit. After grinding the turmeric on the stone, it is put in the little clay pot. There is a song women sing at that time. This is the song for the *kalas* and the *harish*."

### SONG 31

*Oh, now God asks of Siya to take the load*

Oh, now God asks of *Siya* to take the load.
Oh, now ask the *kalas* to take the load.
Oh, why do you ask me, wise people?
Oh, why do you ask me, wise people?

Oh, ask the ancestors to take the load.
Oh, ask the elders to take the load.
Oh, why do you ask me, wise people?
Oh, ask of the *diya*. It will take the load.
Oh, why do you ask me, wise people?
Oh, why do you ask me, wise people?
Oh, ask the gods to take the load.

This call-and-response song has a verse of mostly six beats followed by a chorus of mostly four beats. The pitch reaches as high as the fourth degree and, at the lower end, a neutral seventh. Generally, in traditional rural song (if such generalizations are permitted), one might say that the tonic and the dominant are the most stable pitches of a tune and that the third and seventh degrees are the least stable. Publications about folk songs have put this point forward for over one hundred years now, and broadly speaking, it does still seem to hold. To reflect this instability, writers often refer to a neutral seventh or a neutral third. To explain this phenomenon in Western terms, these pitches are halfway between a melody in a major key and those in a minor key—that is between the cracks of the piano. Neutral thirds and sevenths are common in Bhojpuri women's songs.

A common occurrence in this repertory is that the tonal center may slowly rise in pitch from the beginning of the song or may slowly droop in pitch—as in this example, where the tonic starts around A above middle C and ends around the A-flat above middle C. There is absolutely nothing surprising about this. Without the accompaniment of fixed-pitch instruments, such as the harmonium, pitch drift is common. Indeed, it is to be expected. Typically, this discrepancy is so unremarkable that it passes unnoticed.

Gangajali said, "As the five men pour water in the *kalas* pitcher, women sing that people should put the burden of carrying out this wedding on the gods and ancestors. First, they sing, you humans take care of it. Then the people say, *kalas* (clay pitcher), *harish* (plow shaft), lamp, why are you asking this of us humans? Ask the gods and goddesses and ask the flame and ask God to take the burden.

"So the *kalas* is placed and the water is poured and the lamp is lit on the mouth of the *kalas*. This is the song of the *kalas* and the *harish*. After this, the barber lady will draw the *chauk* (altar) so that the bridegroom or bride may be seated there." The altar, although on the plastered floor, is marked out with a pleasing geometric design drawn on the ground with flour. This holy area is replastered and redrawn with flour between each major part of the ceremony—as many as three or four times a day.

"Here the women are questioning the gods, the ancestors, the flame, the *devijis*—who will take the burden of the *kalas*?" Umesh said. "The gods and ancestors must take the responsibility for the wedding so nothing occurs that is unworthy or wrong. They take the burden of the wedding, and the *kalas* is the symbol of the wedding without which we cannot perform the ceremony. So who will take the weight of the *kalas?* Only the question is posed. No answer is given. They are asking the *kalas*, 'Who will take the load?' The burden means responsibility of not letting occur any unnatural event or any forces from outside to ruin the wedding. This has nothing to do with the financial load, only with the forces of nature."

At the wedding of Ram Sagar Singh's youngest daughter, Umesh and I had witnessed a violent dust storm strike the village just as our friends finished decorating their courtyard. After months of preparation, the wind carried away all the essential ritual items on the spot. Women sing to appease such forces to not strike their wedding. The wedding cannot go forward without these sacred incantations.

As these unhappy thoughts filled our minds, Gangajali continued with a song for the making of the altar.

### SONG 32

*Baliramji has the cow dung brought*

Baliramji has the cow dung brought.
Baliramji has the four-sided altar drawn.
Baliramji has the four-sided altar plastered.
Baliramji has the four-sided altar plastered.
Baliramji has the beautiful *kalas* placed.
Baliramji has the beautiful *kalas* placed.
Baliramji has the beautiful *kalas* placed.
Baliramji has the lamp with four faces lit.
Baliramji has the lamp with four faces lit.
Baliramji has the lamp with four faces lit.
Baliramji has called the wise pandit.
Baliramji has called the wise pandit.
Baliramji has arranged the sandal stool.
Baliramji has seated Ram and Sita.
Baliramji has seated Ram and Sita.
Baliramji has seated Ram and Sita.
Baliramji has seated Ram and Sita.
Oh, Baliramji has him chant religious mantras.
Oh, Baliramji has him chant religious mantras.
Oh Baliramji, the pandit chants mantras.
Oh Baliramji, Ram and Sita's wedding takes place.
Oh Baliramji, Ram and Sita's wedding takes place.

The tonic pitch at the beginning of this song is the A-flat above middle C. During the song, there are so many examples of pitch instability, with the pitches seeming to go sharp or flat for a bit, that it comes as quite a surprise that the tonic pitch at the end of the song is still A-flat. Those notes that sound like steady sustained pitches, in fact, are highly ornamented, and it is often during these ornaments that the pitch seems to go off. I feel that this perception may be a case of Western diatonic-pitched ears listening to a different Indian tuning system. So-called ornamental notes are prominent in this entire repertory of songs. Indeed, there seems to be a total avoidance of a sustained pitch. Little shifts up or down or both are integral to the melodic style. These ornaments (for want of a better word) are not steady and regular as, for example, vibrato is on Western string instruments such as those in a string quartet.

"The barber lady draws the altar now," Gangajali said. "The altar is made with four sides and is plastered with cow dung. The *kalas* is kept there. The lamp is lit on it, and the wise priest has been called.

"And then, after plastering it, the bride or the bridegroom may take a seat at the altar (this ceremony is performed in the courtyard of both families). And the beautiful priest comes there—a good priest, who knows good mantras out of the Vedas and Shastras—those particular mantras that are necessary for worship. This is the song for this moment."

"Baliram is the older brother of Lord Krishna," Umesh explained. "But the word is used here just to make the rhythm of the song. It could be translated instead as 'Oh Lord.' This song tells about the wedding from the beginning to the end—what is done at the altar under the *mandap* (wedding canopy). At the beginning the woman, the barber's wife, plasters the altar with cow dung, which we feel is holy, and draw the *chauk*. After this altar is made, they place the beautiful *kalas*. Thereafter they light the lamp with four faces on the *kalas*. That lamp has four wicks. Then they call the bright priest, the wise priest. And the sandal stool is placed there. Ram and Sita are seated there. Thereafter the mantras are chanted, and the wedding of Ram and Sita takes place. The singer is telling from the beginning to the end how all the wedding takes place in this way, mentioning each event, one after another. These are the main events of the wedding. The rest is drama."

The ladies were tired and ready to end the session for the day.

"What time is it now?" Sashi asked.

"Now it is half past three on this watch," Umesh replied.

"On this watch?" Sashi asked. "Is the watch rubbish? On this watch? What time would it be on another watch?"

"It would be four o'clock on another watch," Gangajali replied. "It takes a little bit of time to sing for the whole wedding. So what? You have come here from so far. Therefore, I will suffer a little bit for you."

*At our apartment, Banaras, September 2007, late afternoon*

So four more songs had been studied, explained, and translated. The work was tiring, tedious, and it was time for a break. Umesh said he would go out for a treat, and he set out down the lane.

He came back with three small packets with three different colored flavors of spicy potato chips. My job was to arrange them artistically on the large *thali* (plate). There were green and red and yellow. Meanwhile, Umesh made tea. We sat down for our simple snack and discussed the day's work. It was a lovely treat. We were alone there, the two of us, and life was what we made of it.

TWENTY-THREE

# ARRANGING A PRIEST

*At our apartment, Banaras, 2007*

As we finished up our tea and spicy chips, I asked Umesh what kind of priest he was seeking for his daughter's wedding.

"Actually, every village has a priest," Umesh said. "And so, when we need it in advance, we tell him that he has to do this wedding. Now if we want a priest from outside, we will tell him long in advance and give him the date. We have also to arrange a vehicle for him to bring him from his home and take him back. So many jobs can be done by a small priest like *tel* (oil) and *haldi* (turmeric) ceremonies before the wedding. But for the wedding itself, you want a good priest under the *mandap* (wedding tent) when the bridegroom comes. A good priest who can speak mantras well, chant mantras well, who knows the rituals that have to be done on time. I also want that he should explain in a proper way Shiva's and Parvati's wedding. And perform the wedding perfectly with the correct mantras. The girl's side gets one priest. And the boy's side's job is to bring one priest. But mostly the boy's side priest doesn't come because they don't have time, because their duty is with the girl's side priest. Some priests are not so clever as to know all the mantras and to say them correctly. A village priest costs ₹300 to ₹400 (about $5.00). Whatever.

"Actually, the priest is paid from the boy's side. The service comes like this. If a girl's side gives the boy's side priest ₹500 ($7.00), the boy's side has to give ₹1,000 ($14.00) to the girl's side priest. Just double. If the girl's side gives the boy's side barber ₹200 ($3.00), then the boy's side has to give the girl's side barber ₹400. Just double. So many people, five or six workers, have to be paid. These days there are less. In olden days, there were as many as nine people who had to be paid under the *mandap* almost at the end. Cash flows like water.

"When the wedding is being performed under the *mandap* at night, the girl's side sends his barber to the *janmassa* (resting place for the groomsmen) to call the responsible person who spends money. So he is under the *mandap* when all this takes place. So that time it is asked, 'What to whom, what should be given?' The priest is finished at that time.

"I would like to hire a priest from Mainpuri. I would like to get my daughter's wedding done under the supervision of a very good priest. Because in the village, the priests are not bright enough. They don't make people work nicely to perform the wedding ritual. So I want it under the supervision of a very good priest. Here in Bhojpur, these people do better than we do in my village."

TWENTY-FOUR

# WEDDING EXPENSES

*At our apartment, Banaras, 2007*

"Also in my area, there is a *gaunra*," Umesh said. "It is claimed by the girl's side from the boy's side. That is expenses of the food and crockery and so on. Usually people don't give it these days. This should be given by the boy's side, but they don't do it anymore. In olden times the *gaunra* was for the working people. This was a ritual. The groom's father gives saris, clothes, and some money to the bride's home. The girl's side asks for it.

"So suppose I asked ₹21,000 ($310.00), then he has to give ₹21,000. It is his duty to give or make a conversation, 'No, this is too much.' Suppose to make an arrangement it should be only ₹15,000. If we agree to ₹15,000 ($220.00), and he gives ₹15,000, the girl's side will refund ₹5,000 ($74.00) for their workers. But whatever happens we cannot disturb relations over money. Because our daughter–sister is going to be part of that family. So if I stir up a problem, that problem might fall on my daughter. But some people do fight, and they take money. If people are good, then never mind, but if people are not good, then problems arise. This is the system—they must pay. If they don't do it, it is their fault. They want all the girl's side to do all their duties, but it is painful if the boy's side doesn't perform their duties. So money is flowing everywhere at the time of the wedding.

"The girl's father may feel that he is robbed. The girl's father can end up with not a single paisa (penny) in his hand. So it happens. People get upset at the end because they end up with nothing, and they cannot please the groom's side. That is so painful. Sometimes the people of the boy's side complain that they were not fed well, they were not taken care of very well, they were not given tea, the tea was cold. Anything—they can make it up. And you can't please five hundred to six hundred people. Something always goes wrong."

TWENTY-FIVE

# THE ISLAND DIASPORA: MY INTRODUCTION TO INDIAN CULTURE FROM FAR AWAY

I HAD NEVER THOUGHT OF WRITING A BOOK SUCH AS THIS—ON INDIA. My specialty is the tropical islands of the Indian diaspora, first Trinidad, then Mauritius, and finally Fiji. It was to these British islands that the poor of eastern Uttar Pradesh, from towns like Ballia, and in western Bihar, men and women like Gangajali, had been gathered up by professional Indian recruiters working for the British. They were marched downriver to Calcutta to sail, they were promised, to the lands of milk and honey to sift for gold. For a man or a woman who has nothing, is caught up in a famine, or has been cast out from his or her family, this fantasy sounded like something. This was the British system of indentured labor, or, as Lord John Russell had called it, "a new system of slavery." It came into being as a natural consequence of African American Emancipation in the British Empire in 1834 and the ensuing labor shortage on these small sugar islands, their economies in ruin as blacks migrated from village to town to seek a brighter future as entrepreneurs.

So these Indians, the so-called "coolies," formed communities, villages, on each of these islands. Indentured laborers, they had endured the torment of the voyage (many died at sea and were buried at sea) and then had worked out their five- or ten-year contracts in the cane fields and freed themselves. Was this better than a life of desperation in eastern India? Only time would tell.

"Coolies" were allotted lousy land, swampland, where they, turning misfortune to fortune, imported the Indian practice of cultivating wet rice. At the conclusion of their indenture, many continued to work in the cane—but for a salary.

Some of the finest singers I met were lower caste cane workers who lived in simple one-room board shacks. The communities were different from one island to the next, but on all three islands, these impoverished people had managed to reconstitute a little India, each in their new island home. India faded like a dream as the generations passed. Customs persisted—foods, dress, names, farming methods, songs, religious customs, and language in Mauritius and Fiji. I witnessed the death of the Bhojpuri language in Trinidad in the 1970s. But as the generations passed, on all the islands, dreams of India faded, and the thoughts of distant cousins in a motherland grew faint.

Trinidad, the most southerly of the Caribbean islands, lies 15 km off the Venezuelan coast and has been the birthplace of unique musical forms—Creole steel band, calypso, and soca, East Indian chutney, and Hispanic *parang*. Trinidad and Tobago gained independence from the United Kingdom in 1962 and is a member of the British Commonwealth. Trinidadian's so-named plural society (population 1,365,000) has two main racial groups: African (43 percent) and East Indian (40 percent). The indigenous American Indian population (Arawak and Carib) died tragically from European-borne viruses during the period of Spanish rule (1498–1797), and Tobago was not settled before the arrival of Columbus (1498). During British rule, slaves from West Africa (until Emancipation in 1838) and East Indian indentured laborers (1845–1917) were conscribed to the island's sugarcane plantations. These immigrants contributed their languages, religions, and music to the modern cultural mosaic. English is the official language, and French patois (Creole) and Bhojpuri died out by the end of the twentieth century. The statistics for religion further illustrate the fascination of this nation—Roman Catholic (32 percent), Hindu (36 percent), Protestant (29 percent), and Muslim (6 percent). The mixed ethnic composition, the multiplicity of religions, and the contrasting cultural backgrounds of the island's inhabitants have drawn generations of anthropologists and ethnomusicologists to study—and luxuriate—on these popular tropical tourist resort islands with pristine white-sand beaches and verdant interiors.

The forebears of today's 470,524 Trinidadian East Indians (a segment of some 30.8 million South Asians living overseas) were brought between 1845 and 1917. Many remained, and in 2019, their descendants still mainly occupy the swampy land along the western coast and the central interior county of Caroni, Trinidad. Nowadays, there are large populations of East Indians in major North American cities such as New York, Miami, Toronto, and others. These "twice-migrants" have a remarkably holistic view of globalism.

Nearly all East Indians speak English as their first language, yet until recent decades, they sang songs in an Indian language—Hindi, Sanskrit, and Bhojpuri, the language which served as a lingua franca on the old plantations. Bhojpuri is still remembered in the names of foods, kitchen utensils, farming equipment, animal names, ritual objects, and kinship terms.

The music of these impoverished immigrants is first described in logs of the ships that transported laborers from the Indian ports, Calcutta and Madras, to these islands around the globe. There amid the tallies of epidemic and death are glimpses of Indian village song: "the Madrassee is a lively singing fellow," "the Coolies are very musical," "should be permitted to play their drums till 8 bells," "coolies on deck all day, singing and dancing in the evening," "coolies having some native games and war-dances." Over the 150 years since these communities were established on islands of the Atlantic, Indian, and Pacific Oceans, they abandoned the inflexible aspects of their Indian culture, such as caste and the jajmani patronage system, but have enshrined in music their abiding love of eastern folkways.

North Indian village songs in Bhojpuri were still sung in Trinidad as recently as the 1970s and 1980s, including *byah ke git* and *lachari* (wedding songs), *godna* (tattooing), *sohar* (childbirth), *kajari* (rainy season), and *chautal* (springtime festival of Phagua or Holi).

The Hindu three-day marriage ceremony included thirty to forty unaccompanied *byah ke git*, describing the marriage of Ram and Sita as told in the Hindu epic the *Ramcharitmanas* ("The Lake of the Acts of Rama"), by the illustrious Gosvami Tulsidas (1552–1623). Or perhaps, Tulsidas was much influenced by the women's rural songs of his time. The strophic texts of wedding songs are in leader–chorus style, sung by groups of older women in an antique (but creolized) Bhojpuri of nineteenth-century India. Much like the Bhojpuri songs in India, the island songs typically had undulating melodies of a limited range, in duple meter or an easy swinging alternation of twos and threes (as with *kaharwa tal*, eight beats, or *dipchandi tal*, fourteen beats). Women singing at weddings used a full-throated, sing-shout style with a low tessitura, typical of village singing in India. For the arrival of the groomsmen, the *barat*, they sang, "In the evening six stars come out, the evening star comes out in the middle of the night. Ram has come to wed, his friends and four brothers. On the bridegroom's forehead, there is a beautiful crown, around his neck he has the garland of five colors, in his ears earrings are resplendent, the sandalwood paste adorns his forehead, his lips are red with the betel leaves. Ram has come to wed." And for the wedding night they sang, "In the evening the clouds come in the sky, and at midnight it starts to rain. Mother, open the sandalwood door and let Ram enter the *kohabar*. Mother, open the sandalwood door and let Sita enter the *kohabar*."

Those old Bhojpuri wedding songs prove to be strikingly similar to those of Ghazipur, Gorakhpur, Ballia, Varanasi, Mau, and Azamgarh districts of Uttar Pradesh, India, including that for the ceremony of *kanyadan* (donation of the virgin daughter), for the dusting of the red *sindur* (vermilion) powder in the parting of the bride's hair, and for the couple entering the *kohabar* (sacred chamber).

*Lachari*—amusing and gently teasing songs performed by half a dozen to a dozen women—were sung at the bridegroom's home during cooking, the wedding feasts, and long delays while the rites were performed. *Lachari* derived from nineteenth-century Indian *jhumar*, dancing songs of eastern India. *Lachari* are accompanied by the double-headed *dholak* drum and instruments such as *manjeera* finger cymbals, the *dantal* stick idiophone (now lost from India), tambourines, and shak-shak rattles. The playful *lachari* call to mind an olden India, where women found their fun in private and sang away frustrations of male dominance with affectionate good humor—"How can I blink at him? He is my husband. I will curse him with night blindness, I will dispel the curse by offering my breast, he is walking down the road with his balls swinging. Oh, I love him!" But the musicologist must report that these traditional song genres have mainly been forgotten in Trinidad (some still survive in the backwaters of Guyana and Suriname), as have some of the ceremonials they accompanied. In 2019, it is sad to report that they have passed on.

The most illustrious East Indian from Trinidad is the late novelist and Nobel Prize winner V. S. Naipaul (1932–2018). Hailing from Chaguanas in County Caroni, V. S. Naipaul wrote, "In India I know I am a stranger; but increasingly I understand that my Indian memories, the memories of that India which lived on into my childhood in Trinidad, are like trapdoors into a bottomless past." A dark and rather bitter genius, Naipaul does not write fondly of Trinidad or even of India.

At the end, he made his home in London, where I expect he felt somehow comfortable—as anybody might. In any case, his early novel *A House for Mr. Biswas* is the great masterpiece of English literature of the twentieth century. And I was proud to have recorded his aunts singing the granny music from Chaguanas for me in 1974. These, for me, are dear memories. Now they, his maternal aunts, the Permanand sisters, have passed on, but their songs have been preserved for the ages and are held at the Archives for Traditional Music of Indiana University in Bloomington, Indiana, and at the Archives and Research Centre for Ethnomusicology, Gurgaon, India, just south of New Delhi. It was a life mission for me to repatriate recordings from the diaspora to the motherland, and Dr. Shubha Chaudhuri helped me achieve this mission every step of the way. My other life mission was to discover, if I could, these very songs in the countryside of eastern India. And, with the help of Umesh, I was able to do this.

Naipaul's books on India include *An Area of Darkness*, *India: A Wounded Civilization*, and *India: A Million Mutinies Now*. In the first, he writes of the return to his ancestral village, Mahadewa Dube. There they have the old photos, and his visit is a topic of local history that was lovingly told to us by his family, detail by detail. Their version pretty much matched the version Naipaul tells in *An Area of Darkness*.

Mauritius, a remote Indian Ocean island with a postcolonial French ambiance, has fostered a repertory of Bhojpuri song different from that of Trinidad. Despite 158 years of British rule, English language and culture had little impact on Franco-Mauritian plantation lords or on their indentured Indian cane laborers. Today, the French-Bhojpuri Creole language fascinates linguists, and traditional

Bhojpuri songs for life rites and religious festivals are sung throughout the year—a treasure for scholars of the Indo-Caribbean, where spoken Bhojpuri and the song repertory it supported have mostly died out. Most of the Bhojpuri songs in Mauritius match those we collected in western Bihar. Hundreds of these songs have survived, with their rich texts and undulating melodies. Umesh immediately took to Mauritius, and the Indian people there took to him. As for me, on the other hand, they just assumed that I was a French tourist.

In recent times, leaders in Mauritius are promoting Hindi as their ancestral language. Unfortunately, this is false as their mother tongue was Bhojpuri. Nevertheless, they have chosen the more modern language, Hindi. It will be very interesting to see what results from the whole government of India project of sending Hindi teachers to Mauritius.

Fiji, a Melanesian island archipelago of some 330 islands in the southwest Pacific, is a multiethnic nation of about 800,000, including 51 percent indigenous Fijians and 43 percent Indo-Fijians. Between 1879 and 1916, some 60,965 Indians, known locally as "girmitiyas" for the "girmit" or "contract," were brought from South Asia to work on the Australian-owned sugarcane plantations. The full set of 60,965 passes is extant and indicates that these émigrés came from diverse caste backgrounds and represented a cross-section of the rural neighborhoods of the Bhojpuri-speaking regions of Uttar Pradesh, including Hindus, Muslims, and tribal peoples. Characterized by contemporary officials as "harlots of the empire," "flotsam of humanity," and a "floating caravan of barbarian tourists," these travelers faced a life of toil and poverty in Fiji. Although their labor formed the foundation of the islands' sugar-based economy, Indo-Fijians were despised by the indigenous Fijian population and have been the victims, since their arrival, of systematic racial discrimination. The British government, under pressure from Indian nationalists, ended the indentured labor system in 1916, and the system came to a final halt in 1920.

The Indo-Fijians settled mainly in the sugarcane belts on the larger islands of Viti Levu and Vanua Levu to the north. They soon outnumbered the indigenous Melanesians, although this trend was reversed due to mass emigration of Indians following the two coups d'état of 1987 and several other coups thereafter. The indigenous Fijians, who claimed 90 percent of the land by unalienable right, put extreme racist policies in place. Land leases held by Indo-Fijians began to expire in the 1990s, leaving many individuals and families without employment and homeless. Prospects for the Fijian sugar industry became bleak. A third coup in 2000 ushered in a period of renewed discrimination against Indians with the institution of apartheid-like measures. Indian businesses were looted, Parliament stormed, and the Indian prime minister, Mahendra Chaudhry, held hostage by the rebel leader George Speight.

The rhetoric of the indigenous Fijians fueled racial hatred when they claimed that the indigenous population is the host community in Fiji. "We reserve the right to expect all visiting communities, regardless of how long they've been here, to at least assimilate with us, understand the culture and try to fit in," Speight said. "As far as our Indian brothers are concerned, that has not happened. . . . We fear that in our country, it's not so much a hate of the Indians but a fear of our host culture and everything unique about ourselves being eroded to the extent that it could be lost." The economy was soon in crisis with the sugar and garment industries losing millions of dollars. For eight weeks Indians were subject to robbing, looting, and rape, and many skilled professional Indo-Fijians emigrated to Australia, New Zealand, Canada, and the United States.

In 2006, a coup d'état by the military ousted the civilian government, and the country was ruled by decree until the fair and free elections of September 2014. With this election, some modicum of freedom of the press and freedom of assembly is slowly being restored. The fate of Indo-Fijians certainly seems in peril at the time of writing. One can conclude that the descendants of Indians sent to Trinidad and Mauritius fared well but those of Fiji did not.

Three former British colonies, all tropical islands with multiracial societies and sugarcane plantation economies, constitute a unique setting for musical comparison and present the unusual possibility of examining changes in a single repertory of songs in different settings.

The newly arrived Coolies were first divided into groups—the shovel gang or cane-cutting gang (who did the digging, clearing, and planting) and the weeding gang (the women and weaker men). Coolies worked by the task, and those who could not complete an entire task forfeited their whole day's wage. For a member of the shovel gang—these, the strongest men—a day's task would be eighty to ninety cane holes five feet by five feet (in heavy soil), or 150 cane holes (in light soil). The working day began before daybreak and ended at sunset or later for those manning the Dickensian sugar mills of the Victorian era. Women worked beside their menfolk. It was only after the wretched Coolies had marked their thumb print on the contract ratifying this, the "meanest and weakest of bonds" (Kingsley)—after their identification papers had been issued, after they had been shown to their quarters on the Coolie line, had been assigned to a work gang, had been defeated by the heat of the midday, hands raw, then hardened from the cane, after they had been beaten, fined, jailed, after rations had been withheld—only then the realization came that they had not crossed *sat samundar par* and the seventh sea to paradise, that the beautiful Queen was not to be found, that indeed they had been forced across the black water, across *kalapani* into exile, and that for these voyagers, these island homes were a world of slavery.

So it was truly said—
Fare forward, travellers! not escaping from the past
Into different lives, or into any future;
You are not the same people who left that station

Or who will arrive at any terminus,
While the narrowing rails slide together behind you;
And on the deck of the drumming liner
Watching the furrow that widens behind you,
You shall not think "the past is finished"
Or "the future is before us."

T. S. Eliot
"The Dry Salvages," III
*Four Quartets*

I alternated trips to those tropical rum islands, lazing in burlap sugarcane-bag hammocks and hanging out with the grannies of the place, combined with arduous trips to India, searching in the overpowering heat of the summer wedding season for the songs sung on the islands and matching them up with those of their motherland and the grannies of that place. It was never my intention to write about what I first saw as the torment of poverty and sorrow that I found in India. But now, with greater understanding, India has become my second home.

INTERLUDE FIVE

# FRANK GREYSTOCK

*At our apartment, Banaras, 2007*

Storytime again. Umesh and I could escape from work and worries and read Trollope. Chapter 4, Frank Greystock. We had two candidates for heroine—Lizzie Eustace, the vixen, who lied even when she herself did not know she was lying, and Lucy Morris, who was considered by Lady Fawn to be "a treasure," a little woman who spoke her mind firmly but did not have the beauty (or the jewelry) of a Lizzie Eustace.

But what of the heroes of our story? Here Frank Greystock is introduced. Only son of the Dean at Bobsborough, he was in fact poor. His father had an income of £1,500 a year but also had three daughters to marry off. And he, Frank, directed himself toward a profession that "is not often lucrative at first. He had been called to the Bar—and had gone." His main work was in Bobsborough, but he was occasionally up in London, where he found himself drawn to a more extravagant lifestyle than might be prudent for a man of his means. "Tailors, robe-makers, and booksellers gave him trust." At the age of twenty-eight, four years into his work in the law, he met Lucy Morris at the deanery.

Will this be a romance? We are told that he was on the winning side of a complex legal case that rewarded him with a certain degree of money and position. Hence, he was much admired and was recruited to stand as a conservative candidate for Parliament from Bobsborough. He did, and he won the seat. This position added polish to his metal, but still it was clear that he must marry money.

His mother warned him against an alliance with Lucy Morris, as did Lady Fawn. Angry at being bossed by older women, he soon realized that his higher position required money all the more—to have a fancy address and be accepted in the high circles of London society. An alliance with Lucy Morris, treasure though she was, would be a bar to these aspirations.

It was then that Uncle John Eustace, brother of the late Sir Florian and Frank's intimate friend, dropped Lizzie's name into their conversation.

"We could trust you—with the child and all of it," John argued. Lizzie was Frank's first cousin. Frank argued that she was destined to become the betrothed of Lord Fawn of the deanery. John said, "Never." It is then that we learn that Mr. Camperdown, who figures large in this tale, has been after Lady Eustace to settle certain matters of the Eustace estate.

Trollope jokes, "*Dramatists, when they write their plays, have a delightful privilege of prefixing a list of their personages;—and the dramatists of old used to tell us who was in love with whom, and what were the blood relationships of all the persons. In such a narrative as this, any proceeding of that kind would be unusual—and therefore the poor narrator has been driven to expend his four first chapters in the mere task of introducing his characters. He regrets the length of these introductions, and will now begin at once the action of his story.*"

Umesh said, "This person who is the big barrister, he is related to Lizzie. They are first cousins. And he is interested in Lucy. And this barrister likes Lucy. And where Lucy works, those people are against—very much against—letting her get married. So the Fawn family wants to keep Lucy away from the barrister, Frank. If she gets married they will lose this nice working lady from the family.

"But she is not that kind of woman, to stick to one place and lose her rights. She gets upset when she is warned not to talk to this Frank, who gave her the 'bluebooks' from Parliament. These English parliamentarians consider that they don't know anything about Indian people very much, how they run their country. But they are playing with the papers, to take away money from the Sawab or put him in prison.

"In this circumstance either he has to collect money somehow or other from his subjects or go to prison. If he charges a lot of taxes, he will also be accused of being a bad ruler and be in trouble with his people. And if he does not pay to the East India Company, then the British government will put him in prison. Anyway, to make these kings less wealthy, they must not have too much wealth so they could have enough money to raise the military or the police against the British government. If a person has money and a brain, he can create people to work for him. By using money, by using words, by giving them powerful slogans, using their social system, using their religion, telling them about their poverty, showing them they are like slaves, so many things. If he takes money from his people and gives it away to the British people, then the British government will also accuse him because he is charging money and his people are dying of hunger. This is a trick.

"The kings of India at the British time were puppets of the British government. They had no right to have a military. They were just tax collectors. The land tax collector paid to the British government and kept out of that some money for the people who were working for that and for their kingdom. The British liked those people who were devoted and faithful to them. And one who was not faithful was a threat to them. Easy way—to increase tax and put the king in trouble.

"My village belonged to one *zamidar*. We also called him *raja* (king), but he was not. He was a big *zamidar*, and in 1901 he sold half the village to Awagarh State. And half of it went to Gyaprasad Trust, Kanpur. There was a fight between these two factions, Gyaprasad and Awagarh State. I was in the Awagarh Trust—most of the Brahmans lived on this side. Awaghara was clever. So the road in the middle of the village divided the village. The eastern side belonged to Awagarh Trust, and western side belonged to Gyaprasad Trust. There was a court case. In those days, farmers could not go to court because the land belonged to the *zamidar* or king.

"I think they, the British, said you just pay it, or you go to prison. Perhaps the Sawab couldn't pay because he was paying for so many people working for him.

"Law and politics was the same in India as in England," Umesh said. "This law was made for Indian people. Muslim people and Western people had different courts. The Western court was for white people. It was in Connaught. But Muslim people, they have the same court with different laws. British people tried not to touch the social system. Missionaries came, and they helped people and converted them into Christianity.

"So on top at that time, the British were ruling over India, and the law was not carried out by the people, or, if they broke the law, they were punished by the government through the courts. The Supreme Court was in England. If there was a serious case, only those people could go to England who had money. At the time of justice, it was seen whether it was in favor of the government or it was not. So if it was not in the favor of the government, then people were punished. Suppose a man was doing something. Although he was not guilty, he was punished as if he were guilty. Justice was unjust. For example, Bhagat Singh blasted small bombs in the Indian Parliament to show the anger of the Indian people. No one was hurt. And he was hanged to death."

Umesh saw how Lizzie loved those diamonds.

"Language is different, culture is different, ornaments are of a different type," Umesh said. "But men and women are the same on the Earth. The culture of woman or man is similar all over the world, having and loving ornaments, hiding ornaments, and the position of the ornaments. And it seems that the love feelings for ornaments look like the same in India and in England. And the action of women for ornaments, to cry and show the love for her past husband in remembrance of him, is equal. Tears come. But these are crocodile tears.

"This book by Trollope also tells the rules and social system of the time, of the society and of the nation. There are three people. The person who has ornaments, the person who keeps the ornaments, and the lawyer. They trust each other, and they need each other. If the lawyer loses the Eustace account, he will lose everything. And if the jeweler loses the necklace, they will be out of business.

"Now Lady Eustace is thinking to get married, and she has castles in the air. Although she loves these jewels and everything, she has a fantasy of being in love with someone that she can give away all these things to him. She is also thinking how to save, not to let the necklace go elsewhere. So she is thinking of a heavy metal box so she can shift the necklace in it, even though she could barely lift the box.

"But she does not know to whom she should love. She is just thinking. Will she lose the property after she gets married to another person? Will she lose the money she gets from the Scotch property if she marries another person? She doesn't know. But she is reaching one point. That she can give away everything for love.

"Did people need money to arrange weddings in those days in England? No, but they married for money. How could they find out if people had money or not? Everybody in the society knew the answers to these questions.

"You can have a title but no money. Such is Lord Fawn. He has a big title, Lord, but no money. But Lizzie, who has some money, would like the title.

"Better to go for title. If she goes for the title, the money might come someday. But these people who have a high title have to live in high society without money to support such a lifestyle. Like I am Brahman. I will remain Brahman. No one can take this title from me. But it is very hard to live as a Brahman with no money."

TWENTY-SIX

# GRANNY MUSIC

SO I HAD NEVER INTENDED TO WRITE A BOOK ABOUT INDIA, "AN AREA of darkness," "a wounded civilization." But gradually I had learned that there indeed was happiness and beauty in this torment of India, and I was discovering the joy of India. The whole movement against Orientalism moved me. India was not the rustic, exotic but dark and dreary and mysterious land that I had described in my earlier book, *Music of Hindu Trinidad: Songs from the India Diaspora* (Chicago 1998). Even so, it had never occurred to me to write about India, the torment or the joy. Mine was for sure a happier task, for I sought to write about the pleasures of these three sugar and rum islands of the diaspora. They were easier than India in so many ways. Creature comforts were to be had—plumbing and electricity. There were usually toilets when you needed a toilet.

But it soon became clear to me, in all these settings, in India and in the islands, that it was the grannies of all these places that were the tradition bearers. They had the knowledge. They certainly had the songs. If the music of the world is, say, 100 percent, then I would estimate that 70 to 80 percent of it is in the hands of the grannies. They sit in the corner, alone or sometimes in groups, in rows or circles, and sing, sometimes softly, sometimes in full voice, as life and ceremony go on. They comment on the passing scene, preserve ideas from lost days, sing as they learned from their grannies, and make fun of everything. They protect their world, their families with incantations to the gods. In India, they believe, and people generally believe, that this constant singing keeps the world running. Their songs are full of repetition and are structured around repetition. They are often story songs, usually in the form of a dialogue, often between family members. Their setting is important, for they always relate to a specific situation, generally offering commentary on the action or on the role of the gods in the lives and actions of these farmers. The grannies, they carry the traditions to the next generation of girls, soon enough in the sweep of time to become grannies. It is not seamless, and new items are constantly introduced, especially by the girls and also by the grannies themselves. But as it is happening, in the moment of performance, it is all new. In this evergreen state, these songs have lived on and have been passed on, granny to girl, granny to girl. Should we grieve if songs are forgotten? Probably not.

I myself witnessed the death of these songs in Trinidad. It was happenstance that I was there in the 1970s to record the dying of an old tradition. It was certainly sad to witness. But the Trinidadians are forever inventive and have created new Bhojpuri music called chutney and have also developed the art of tassa drum playing far beyond that of their counterparts in India. These new forms of East Indian Caribbean music have become a craze over the whole island, and they have spread to neighboring countries including Suriname and Guyana. Chutney has its origins in the *matikor* ceremony of the wedding, with its ribald singing and dancing. In Trinidad, chutney is performed at every wedding, together with tassa drumming by the men, a form that does not need the Bhojpuri language to survive. The chutney songs are in a local Bhojpuri with Hindi and Creole sprinkled in. Pure English chutney is also greatly appreciated by the East Indian audience. Hindi speakers find Trinidadian chutney texts extremely difficult to translate because they are sung in the remembered island Bhojpuri Creole mixed with English. There is also a lot of slang. There are lots of island-wide chutney competitions and tassa competitions, championships, and grand prizes. There are trophies. There is a queen of chutney, d'Rani, and a king of chutney, d'Raja. With the advent of social media, Trinidadians have developed an orthography for their own distinctive island dialect of English. You can read it on Facebook.

Culture created in Trinidad, the "local," is especially prized these days. Some of the singers are young, some not so young—for the grannies of any place will not sit silent. It's recreation, it's fun, and it's creation. Nothing grows old in this forever world of song.

TWENTY-SEVEN

# ETHNOMUSICOLOGY

THE ESSENTIAL MESSAGE OF *STORYTIME IN INDIA* IS "'THE INFORMANT' as author." Here is a notion that, I believe, all ethnomusicologists are adopting—to give real voice to those local folk who understand their music better than we do and certainly from a more interesting perspective.

A second message is that the violence of colonialism and postcolonialism should be in the reader's face. So our reader here is faced with passages of *The Eustace Diamonds*, a deceptively lighthearted story from the era of British colonialism in India. Hence, the ethnographic flow of our story is violently interrupted by the colonial, the postcolonial, notions of the other, and thoughts about ownership and authorship.

Even with such serious issues in the forefront, *Storytime in India* is meant to be a lighthearted, reader-friendly storybook, with Gangajali's songs from Ballia at its ethnographic heart. It seems to me that of late ethnomusicology has become so serious that it is sometimes dull and also difficult to understand. We all hate jargon, but, in fact, we can find the definition of most terms of that jargon in a dictionary. It is neologism, assigning a new meaning for an existing word, that is the biggest problem we face in our scholarly writing and at papers at our annual meetings. Webster's Dictionary is no help. This results in scholarly articles and books that are essentially impossible to understand—with the exception of an in-group. Isn't it true that the writing up of our scholarship, our choice of fashion words, on Indian music is beyond the reach of Indian musicians, to say nothing about the general Indian reader? Our writing in ethnomusicology should be clear, direct, and understandable. If we were all to embrace this notion, perhaps ethnomusicology would be elevated beyond the mocking joke, "Oh, God, your daughter got a PhD in . . . ethnomusicology??"

In conjunction with clear expression, we also should immediately improve our standards for field recordings. Most teenagers have in their bedrooms better equipment than ethnomusicologists normally use in the field, wherever that may be. I have learned that serious scholars even use their iPhones for field recordings. I feel shame at the national meetings of the Society for Ethnomusicology that musical examples are played in mono and that nobody notices or cares. This is unacceptable. SEM needs to buy its own equipment. We should not settle for a hotel sound system designed for a business meeting. If we wish to be taken seriously, we must take ourselves seriously. We could start slowly. Perhaps buy hi-fi stereo equipment for one room, and at each meeting designate one room as The Percy Grainger Room. Scholars who care about such matters could compete to present their papers in The Percy Grainger Room. This simple idea wouldn't cost much, and it would perhaps open the eyes and ears of our members.

So there is no excuse for lousy recordings any more than there is an excuse for dry, dull writing that is impossible for a general reader to understand. In all our travels, near to or far from home, we never have a dull day. We stumble upon stories, wonderful stories. Stories, drama, conflict, affection, love, misunderstandings, above all music, and many a painful goodbye, many a joyous hello. We would all like to hear each other's stories. "Things separate from their stories have no meaning. They are only shapes. Of a certain size and color. A certain weight. When their meaning has become lost to us they no longer even have a name. The story on the other hand can never be lost from its place in the world for it is that place."

But the ethnographic heart of this volume remains granny music. Grannies singing at weddings in eastern India. The grannies never did quit. But did we ethnomusicologists quit them? It would make a wonderful topic for a book—*Granny Music*. So, ethnomusicologists, don't you too have a joyful story to tell? Are there not characters in your drama? Tell us your tale from faraway. Tell us your tale from home. What story did you find? Did you read great literature, great stories, as you did your research? Did you find in a Trollope or a Mailer or a Hemingway a creature like Lizzie Eustace to illumine your way to great storytelling? Reading great fiction has been found to enhance the human capacity for empathy and to open our eyes to all manner of wonder. Martha Nussbaum has been putting this idea forth for decades. "You can't really change the heart without telling a story." (TLS 2012)

The songs of Gangajali were a fantastic sample of this granny music. Indeed, she had long gray hair, was slender (or "dry" as the Indians say for older women), and she had grandchildren. Here in our apartment we had twelve heavy files with the Gangajali songs. Four thousand pages of granny music.

TWENTY-EIGHT

# THE TURMERIC IS PLEASING

*Sarang Hotel, Ballia, afternoon of another hot day, July 1989*

"There are several people when we normally sing," Gangajali was explaining as we finished our tea. "Some of the songs are sung by them and some by others. So we take turns. They 'hang on' with their throat. This supports the singing. They 'hang on.' Therefore, it takes less strength to sing in a group than it does with just two of us alone here.

"Now we will sing the turmeric song for the women," she said. "First I will sing the song, and after the turmeric ritual there will be the *chumawan* ritual, the kissing ritual. Women kiss with rice."

"Come on, sing for the turmeric," Sashi said.

"Now henceforward they keep putting the turmeric. The priest performs the first ritual of *haldi* (turmeric). Henceforth, five men perform the ritual. Once these people perform the *haldi*, then five women also perform the ritual. So the songs for the men and the priest are different. And ladies' songs are also different. We sing for the priest, for the men, and for the women. This is the song for the priest."

## SONG 33

*Haldi: Oh, who grows the turmeric*

Oh, who grows the turmeric (*haldi*)?
And who rubs it on?
Oh, who grows the turmeric?
And who rubs the turmeric?
Oh, on whom is the turmeric rubbed?
The turmeric is pleasing.
Oh, on whose head is the turmeric being put?
The turmeric is pleasing.
Oh, the *koirini* has grown the turmeric,
And the priest buys it.
Oh, the *koirini* grows the turmeric,
And Father Anurudha buys it.
It is put on Sapanji's head.
The turmeric is pleasing.
Oh, it is put on daughter Sapana's head.
The turmeric is pleasing.
Oh, who grows the turmeric?
What father uses it?
Oh, on whose head is it put?
The turmeric is pleasing.
Oh, Father Anurudha.
The *koirini* grows the turmeric.
Father Anurudha rubs the turmeric.
Oh, the *koirini* grows the turmeric.
Father Fate rubs the turmeric.
Oh, it is put on the head of daughter Sapan.
The turmeric is pleasing.

Basically, this tune has a pitch range of a major third (that is, to our ears it sounds like it is in a major or happy key). The pulse is strong and clear throughout, but there are opportunities where the pulse accommodates a longer word that shouldn't really fit. Examples are on the words "Anurudha baba" (six syllables) and later on with "Sapanaa betiyaa ke" (seven syllables). It came as a bit is a surprise, knowing that these long words had been tucked in, that when I set my metronome at quarter note = 94, it all fit together rather nicely. I had thought that the Bhojpuri words with extra syllables, some from the language itself and others from the musical flow, were jammed into one or two beats. Words like the bride's name, *Sapanaa* (three syllables), are often shortened to *Sapan* (two syllables), and *betiya* (daughter, three syllables) is often abbreviated as simply *beti* (two syllables). This is the opposite of a very common practice in Bhojpuri song of adding syllables to contribute to the melismatic flow of a smooth, flowing vocal line, hence the loving *betiya* instead of the rather abrupt *beti.*

A basic problem in transcribing this entire repertory is that in the Bhojpuri language words are often extended with the addition of syllables such as *ba* or *wa*. Add to that the addition of a long *a* at the end of a word to extend it into the flowing melody and you have a major distortion of the text that would puzzle one who knew only Hindi (*khariboli*) as is spoken in New Delhi. Archer puts it nicely that Bhojpuri is "characterized by long drawled vowels, its fondness for labials, and its musical rhythms. An English which favored words like 'candle,' 'dangle,' 'ladle,' and 'meddle' would be an appropriate analogy. Bhojpuri lends itself nicely to song. Even the simplest of songs can strike the ear in a very beautiful way."

Of course, Modern Standard Hindi is, in fact, a much newer language than Bhojpuri, which has ancient roots. The fourth most spoken language in the world, Modern Standard Hindi is spoken by 54 percent of the population of India. Hindi began to be standardized in the late nineteenth century, and a standardized system of writing was also developed. As late as 1954, a commission was set up to establish an official grammar for Hindi and was released in 1958 as *A Basic Grammar for Modern Hindi*.

Bhojpuri, on the other hand, was historically written in Kaythai script, mainly for official and court documents that date back to the sixteenth century. However, around 1894, a changeover to Devanagri script was underway, right in the midst of the British system of indentured Coolie labor. The indentured laborers who sailed out from Calcutta to the islands of the diaspora wrote in Kaythai and some also in Devanagari script. The Bhojpuri language itself has four basic pitch levels. Ballia is considered to be a center of Southern Standard Bhojpuri, also known as Shahabadi and Chapariyah.

The fight is on in the island diaspora to preserve traditional Bhojpuri from the modern influx of Hindi teachers and their New Delhi Hindi language, often sent out by the government of India. For example, Bhojpuri language has died out in Trinidad, but Hindi is taught in the East Indian schools. In Mauritius, spoken and sung Bhojpuri is also dying out in favor of standard Hindi and, more importantly, French and French Creole. In Fiji, the desperate land tenure situation has forced mass emigration so that the number of Bhojpuri speakers has dwindled. But I heard a lot of Bhojpuri spoken and sung in the outer large island of Vanua Levu. I expect one would find communities of expat Fiji Indians in Australia speaking Bhojpuri. International organizations such as GOPIO (Global Organization of People of Indian Origin), founded in 1989, promote conferences and especially the preservation of the Bhojpuri languages. GOPIO has a nice Facebook page.

"The turmeric ritual is performed at auspicious times given by the priest," Gangajali explained. "Generally, it is begun three or five days before the wedding. We call these 'empty' days before the wedding, *manara*. *Manara* means the middle empty days. So that was the song for the priest and for the men."

Umesh said, "In India as in Mauritius, the *haldi* ceremony is done for both bride and bridegroom at each of their houses. Turmeric is an aryuvedic medicine. For the Indian complexion, when it is rubbed on the body it makes the skin yellowish—a golden body. It looks more beautiful than the usual complexion. When turmeric is rubbed on the skin, it has also flour mixed in it. It takes the dirt and dead skin off the body and cleans the body so it becomes smooth and golden so the groom and bride will look beautiful.

"Once this ritual begins, thereafter the bride and bridegroom do not go out of the home. The families believe that the young couple is very tender now, and any bad spirit can attack them. Maybe there is a scientific reason that if the skin is very clean, even a small suntan can hit the body and make them sick or darken the body.

"So here the song says, 'who grows the turmeric' and 'who buys it' and 'by whom is it put on' and 'to whom is it put on?' So it looks beautiful. It is also mentioned that the *koirin* is the caste lady who grows the turmeric, and Anurdh Baba—that is to say some family person—buys the turmeric and offers it to the bride or bridegroom so it looks beautiful."

Gangajali explained, "This is a song for the men and the priest at the time of performing the turmeric ritual. It is sung both on the bride's side and the bridegroom's side. But only this song will be sung. And whatever name the bride or bridegroom has, it will be put into the song. Girls have also composed turmeric songs to filmi tunes. These are really fake songs. This is the real main song.

"For the women, here is another main turmeric song. There are lots of imitation songs taken from films. But this one is from Ballia."

### SONG 34

#### *Haldi: Koirini-koirini, you are my queen*

*Koirini-koirini*, you are my queen.
From where is the turmeric that is rubbed on today?
From where is the turmeric that is rubbed on today?
*Telin-telin*, you are my queen.
From where is the oil that is being used today?
From where is the oil that is being used today?
Our daughter Sapan is very tender.
She cannot bear the turmeric fumes.
She cannot bear the turmeric fumes.
Our daughter Sapan is very tender.
She cannot bear the oil fumes.
She cannot bear the oil fumes.

This short song is in a simple verse–chorus form, with the principal word sustained at the beginning of each verse. The chorus is mostly syllabic, with one word per note. Hence, because of this phrasing, the important people—the turmeric grower lady (*koirini-koirini*), the oil presser lady (*telini-telini*), and the bride (*Sapan beti*), are repeated slowly and thereby given special emphasis. These are the principal people that move the wedding forward as the rubbing of turmeric mixed with oil is an essential ritual performed at both the home of the bride and the home of the bridegroom.

The tonic pitch of the song is relatively low at A below middle C. Also, much of the melodic movement takes part in the lower part of the octave, beginning on the little leaps from the dominant (sol) up to the tonic (do). However, when the important actors are named, the *koirini*, the *telini*, and *Sapan beti*, the melody goes up to the fourth degree above the tonic (fa) so that the main characters stand out on the higher pitch.

"In the Bhojpuri area of India, the *koirini* is the turmeric-grower lady," Umesh explained, "and her job is to supply the family with turmeric at the time of the wedding. According to the social system of jajmani, she supports herself by serving several families who pay her wages. These payments amount to more than the value of the turmeric, because this is how the jajmani system operates. In Mauritius, they remember this old Indian custom and the jajmani social system and sing of the koirini, even though turmeric is not grown on the island.

"So in India, all categories of people participate in the wedding. They also work all around the year for these families, and they get fair wages for this work. But wedding time is a happy time for the boy and the girl's family so, out of this happiness, the *koirini* is paid more. The boy's side has to pay more to the turmeric grower than the girl's side because everybody in the community understands that the parents of girls will be spending a lot of money for the wedding. So it is considered good to give financial help to the girl's side for the wedding. On the other hand, the groom's side gets money from the bride's side in the dowry, so they are expected to pay more for these services.

"The *telin* is the oil presser lady," Umesh continued. "The poet says, 'You are a queen to me. My bride is very tender, she is unable to bear with the fumes of the oil.' The *koirini* brings the turmeric, and the *telin* lady brings the mustard oil for the family. In India and in the diaspora, oil and turmeric are both mixed together to rub onto the bodies of both the bride and bridegroom in their homes. At wedding time this turmeric and this ritual of the oil are considered very auspicious."

## SONG 35

### *Haldi*

Rub the turmeric on the loving bride,
Together, all five girlfriends.
Rub the turmeric on the loving bride.
Put it on her hands and on her entire body.
Put turmeric on her entire body.
Save her hair a little.
Together, all five girlfriends.
Save her hair a little.
Together, all five girlfriends.
Rub turmeric on my bride.
All together, all five girlfriends.
Put it on her hands and on her entire body.
Put it on her hands and on her entire body.
Save her eyes a little.
All together, all five girlfriends.
Save her glasses a little.
All together, all five girlfriends.
Rub the turmeric on my bride.
All together, all five girlfriends.
Put it on her feet and on her entire body.
Put it on her feet and on her entire body.
Save her clothes a little.
All together, all five girlfriends.
Save her clothes a little.
All together, all five girlfriends.
Rub turmeric on my bride.
All together, all five girlfriends.

This song has quite a strong pulse in duple meter as it should, being a form of a work song. While the ladies are singing, five girlfriends are working hard rubbing the turmeric and oil on the seated bride—arms, legs, as much as modesty will allow—as everybody is watching. Yes, it is a bit of a mess, this ritual, and anybody who has ever had a mustard stain knows well enough that turmeric simply can't be washed out of clothes. Ever.

The initial tempo at quarter note = 92 speeds up slightly as the song moves along. As it is in the major mode, this little item has quite a happy and lilting feel about it, emphasized as the verse lines begin up a major third above the tonic. The verse line jumps from the tonic to the third degree and right up to the dominant (sol) and then gives a little surprise while descending as the fourth degree is sharpened (which in solfeggio would be sung as "fi"), adding just that bit more cheerfulness to the song.

“This is for the women,” Gangajali explained.

“We women when we get together we all sing very many loud songs in a flock,” said Sashi. “We sing in a very fast voice.” (By “fast,” I believe she meant “loud.”) “Yes, we people sing together happily a lot—swaying, dancing, and swinging (*jhum-jhum*). There are so many people together. Many people sing together and enjoy it a lot.”

“Women will say to one another, ‘Well, perform the turmeric ritual,’” said Gangajali. “Put it on in such a way that it doesn’t go in her eyes and her clothes don’t get dirty and her hair doesn’t get messed up.”

“Here is a song that shows how many people together rub the turmeric on the bride,” Umesh explained. “In this area it is mentioned that five girls do it. The paste that is rubbed on the body is also called *ubtan*. So here in Ballia five girls together rub the *ubtan* on the girl. The songs also give the instruction to put turmeric everywhere but save her hair, her eyes, her glasses, and her clothes. Usually at the time of the turmeric ritual, everyday clothes are worn—nothing fancy. Advice is given in the song. Beware of these things so she will not be harmed. It is important not to get the turmeric in her hair because it would be necessary to wash it out with soap, and there is a chemical reaction between the soap and the turmeric that turns the skin dark.”

“To put turmeric is an auspicious work,” Gangajali explained.

“For auspicious work, we people use turmeric,” said Sashi.

“There is no wedding without turmeric,” said Gangajali. “This is the Indian body. It doesn’t become pure until you apply the turmeric. Yes, the body won’t be holy until the turmeric is put on. Until the turmeric is not put, any auspicious work, occasion, or worship cannot take place.”

INTERLUDE SIX

# THE EUSTACE NECKLACE

*At our apartment, Banaras, bedtime again, 2007*

Chapter 5. Here we learn more about Mr. Camperdown, family lawyer for the Eustace estate. He was keen to get back from Lizzie a spectacular diamond necklace. That Lizzie had it, he considered robbery. He enumerated her various holdings mentioned in the will to Uncle John Eustace and insisted that that was certainly enough to satisfy the young widow, who, after all, had nothing to start out with.

"She has got the whole of the Ayrshire property for her life. She goes about and tells everybody it's hers to sell tomorrow if she pleases to sell it!" Camperdown was no friend of Lizzie, and Lizzie was certainly no friend of Camperdown. He, Camperdown, had opposed the marriage to Sir Florian and had advised Florian not to lavish so much on her in his will. It was only after Sir Florian's death that the matter of the necklace arose in the mind of Camperdown. The Eustace family jewelers, Messrs Garnett, had told him that Sir Florian had withdrawn the most valuable jewels from their care before he traveled with Lady Eustace on the fatal trip to Naples.

Lizzie protested all this fuss with a simple claim. "My husband gave me a necklace, and they want me to give it back." She had engaged the firm of Messrs Mowbray and Mopus. That this was a disreputable firm can easily be told by the names Trollope chose for them. Camperdown held them in complete disdain. Camperdown wrote to Lady Eustace in polite but firm terms, asking for the return of the necklace (worth £10,000 he claimed) and mentioning previous letters to her that she had left unanswered. He warned her of pending legal action if she did not reply and comply. Lizzie opened the letter but read only the signature. She pondered the matter for a couple of days and then put in an order for a strong box, which, when it arrived, was almost too heavy for her to carry up the stairs to her bedroom.

In fact, she was not sure if the manner in which her husband had handed her the necklace made it hers or not. Once she had read the letter a single time, she read it a dozen times. How she longed for a close confidante with whom to talk over this troublesome matter. Then she determined that the safest course was not to provide any answer at all.

Would she go to prison? Would her estate in Scotland be taken from her? She could not confide in Mowbray and Mopus, for she too knew they were untrustworthy, just as she knew that Camperdown was "as respectable as the Bank of England." If only there had been a friend who would give her the advice she wanted to hear. She recalled her relationship with the late Sir Florian, how it had been a loveless marriage, and began again to dream of a handsome Corsair, a pirate like the character in Lord Byron's *The Corsair* (1814). Then her thoughts turned to Lord Fawn. "It would also be very nice to be a peeress—so that she might, without any doubt, be one of the great ladies of London."

*"But she was quite alive to a suspicion that she was not altogether strong in her position. The bishop's people and the dean's people didn't quite trust her. The Camperdowns and the Garnetts utterly distrusted her. The Mopuses and the Benjamins were more familiar than they would have been with a really great lady. She was sharp enough to understand all this. Should it be Lord Fawn or should it be a Corsair? The worst of Lord Fawn was the undoubted fact that he was not himself a great man. He could, no doubt, make his wife a peeress; but he was poor, encumbered with a host of sisters, dull as a bluebook, and possessed of little beyond his peerage to recommend him. If she could only find a peer, unmarried, with a dash of the Corsair about him! In the meantime, what was she to do about the jewels?"*

Entertaining dreams of the romantic Corsair, "The door opened and Lord Fawn was announced."

India plays a small and ridiculous role in this long tale of money and greed, for Lord Fawn was the Under Secretary for the India Minister.

*"The Sawab's case is coming on in the House of Commons this very night. . . . Your cousin, Mr. Greystock, is going to ask the question in the house."* Lord Fawn began explaining the rules of Parliament to Lizzie and her house companion, Miss Macnulty. *"Lord Fawn had just worked himself round to the case of the Sawab again, when Frank Greystock entered the room."*

*"'You intend to ask your question about the Sawab tonight?' asked Lord Fawn, with intense interest—feeling that, had it been his lot to perform that task before he went to his couch, he would at this moment have been preparing his little speech."*

*"But Frank Greystock had not come to his cousin's house to talk of the Prince of the Mygawb territory. When his friend Eustace had suggested to him that he should marry the widow, he had ridiculed the idea;—but nevertheless he had thought of it a good deal. . . . He was a rising young man, one of those whose names began to be much in the*

*mouths of other men;—but still he was poor. . . . He wanted just such a lift in the world as a wife with an income would give him."*

As for Frank, there was no doubt that Lucy Morris was the "mistress of his heart." Yet he was not looking for love but, rather, station. He thought of asking Lizzie tomorrow—or even today—to be his wife. Lizzie was contemplating similar thoughts. Frank was "not exactly a Corsair;—but he was a man who had certain Corsair propensities." She preferred Greystock to Lord Fawn and believed that he, Frank, would have her keep the necklace, whereas the dull Lord Fawn would insist that she return it. She did not know at the time that Camperdown was also the Fawn family lawyer. Lord Fawn finally took his leave, and Frank was on the verge of taking Lizzie in his arms, when Miss Macnulty rushed into the room with the news that Lady Linlithgow, the "vulturess," was in the parlor!

Umesh loved chapter 5. He loved the comedy and laughed out loud about the situation of Lizzie and her two lovers, Frank Greystock, her cousin and member of the House of Commons, and Lord Fawn, a member of the House of Lords. "This is neither tragedy nor comedy," he said. "It is both mixed together. It is happy and sad things applying both. What the future will tell about this novel, I don't know. So the vulturess is coming upstairs. She is bringing a big message. She couldn't come to give a happy message to this girl. Both were unhappy with each other. But the vulturess was doing her duty. That she is coming is a bad message to Lady Eustace. I don't think she is bringing good news, but whether she is bringing good news or bad news, both are helpful to this girl. Her arrival is really shocking. The vulturess is coming as a messenger, and you can never ignore the message.

"Both Frank and Lord Fawn are in a kind of love with Lizzie because both are poor, and they want a rich woman to get married with. So both lovers are with Lizzie. Lord Fawn has a taxi with the meter running, but he is not leaving. He has an idea to say something to Lizzie, so he could go inside and talk. Lizzie is also imagining at the same time to talk.

"There is no talk," Umesh said. "There is one thing, only to run. Don't take your mind off from the serious topic.

"Lizzie is a poor girl and being taken care of by the vulturess. And it grew that she hates to whom she calls vulturess. This vulturess is just paying duty, not love, and a child needs love to grow, not just duty. That is why this girl, Lizzie, got disturbed. The lady was only doing her duty by the child.

"Like I have a duty to raise my children. If they don't get love out of me, they can't grow freely their minds. They will get disturbed too. What happens when the child gets neither love nor duty from their father? Who can know better than I, Umesh, do? But I am lucky to have in my childhood my grandfather and Charlotte Wiser.

"Lord Fawn left because the meter was running. And Frank appeared before Lizzie. He just wanted to say about love, and suddenly Miss McNulty, she came running to give the message that vulturess was there. Enough to think about for Lizzie! Now she can think what is coming now. Frank was about to say, 'Will you be my wife?' And she appeared before he could say it, she came rushing, dashing to give a message. Especially she is coming unexpectedly without taking any permission, that was the most important thing.

"This author is doing the same as Indian dramatists. Similarly, when Indian people play drama, they stop at the place where people don't want them to stop. What is next? What is next? The people are eager. This author is doing the same thing. If he does not do it, who will read ahead? Create suspense for the next. What is next?"

TWENTY-NINE

# HEAT

HERE WE MUST PAUSE AND SET THE SCENE AGAIN. THE YEAR WAS 1989. It was summer, wedding season, and it was hot. We had started that year in Bihar, on the outskirts of Chapra, a district town in western Bihar. Then we had set out for Ballia in eastern Uttar Pradesh, arriving on July 11. The monsoon had not yet arrived, and it was still the height of the wedding season. Unbearably hot. Unbearably hot.

*Writing* that, *reading* that, *saying* that doesn't make you *feel* that. As we were moving from place to place in the '80s and '90s, there was no remedy except to wear pure cotton, sit under the ceiling fan, drink lots of bottled water—perhaps four liters a day—and, during the power cuts—and they were regular and frequent—sit absolutely still in the exact spot—a spot that any Indian could easily locate—where there was any sort of breeze or cross draft.

Now in 2007, in our Banaras apartment, even Umesh agreed that there was no such spot, no breezeway to solace us. We measured the outdoor summer temperature at 120 degrees, day after day. It was real, and I gave out. It was the power cuts that destroyed me. In Banaras in 2007, they were every day, seven days a week, from 10:00 a.m. to 2:00 p.m. The height of the heat. No fans, no breeze. It gave me such a sense of fear, anxiety, and panicky claustrophobia that I was gleeful when they finally broke down the wall of my room to install the air conditioner for which I had paid a queen's ransom—some $400.00.

Umesh devised a temporary fix that he arranged for me while all this was being organized. He had me put on my pajamas, no underclothes, just cotton shorts and a T-shirt, and lie down. Then he soaked his lightest cotton *angocha* in water and laid it over me. Ah, relief. He told me not to move—and I didn't move.

The *angocha* covered my entire face and head too. But the relief was short-lived. Within a few minutes, the *angocha* completely dried. And Umesh, who was on the lookout for this, took it and soaked it again, wrung it out again, and repeated the exercise. It's not that he saved my life. But he saved my *mind*. I was seeking an escape, and he had found a way. To escape the heat, I was immobilized and completely dependent on him. He supplied an escape, and my anxiety eased up a bit.

After an hour or two of this, I would go and take a cold bath. That meant filling up the plastic bucket in the bathroom (there was no shower) and using the matching plastic cup to pour the tepid water over my whole body. Though the water was not cold at this point in the day, it provided instant but momentary relief. Most important was getting my hair soaking wet. I would brush it back and let it dry. Once dry, I would dash back to the bucket, lean over, and douse it again. Umesh really *did not* approve of this, but he facilitated it all because he assumed that my coming from a land of snow—and that circumstance combined with my white skin—might cause me to have special problems with the heat. He was just as hot, just as uncomfortable as I was, but he was much stronger than me in enduring the unendurable.

When the fan slowly sprang to life after two o'clock, it was pure relief. Later, once the wall had been mended and the air conditioner installed, that was wonderful. But, of course, it too did not function during the power cuts.

Umesh had the concept that he could keep the fans going through the power cuts if we bought a high-voltage battery. He was very eager to do this, and I shared in his excitement. It took days to organize this battery. The idea was that it would charge up during the hours when the power was on. Then it would discharge to run the fans from ten to two. It would not be powerful enough to run the air conditioner.

Our first attempt failed. Umesh declared the battery was faulty and had a great argument with the vendor. He won the argument and got us a new battery that did work. So that day, when the power cut came at ten, he switched us over to the battery. We shut down the front room fans and retreated to my room, which only had one fan. And, voilà, the fan turned. Slowly, slowly, but it turned.

We had put in three ceiling fans, two in his large front room and one in my smaller, more private, back room. We felt, for the moment, even for the hour, we had found victory over the heat. But by twelve noon, the battery was fully discharged, and we were still stuck with the two most intense hours of the noon heat. It seemed especially cruel, this timing of the power cut around the height of the sun in the sky.

It is amusing to remember how we always made sure that we had had enough toast before ten o'clock, when the power went out. We always lingered over morning tea and toast, and it sometimes, ofttimes, led to more tea and toast. On these mornings, in 2007 to 2008, from around seven until ten o'clock, Umesh told me the secrets of the Indian village. We could talk and listen to each other forever. Under shared food, shared accommodation, and shared adversity, and in the presence of music we both loved, we grew close.

THIRTY

# KISSING

*Once again in Ballia, Hotel Sarang, July 1989*

"Now the turmeric is performed," Gangajali said. "Now, whether it is a boy or a girl, we place rice in their cupped hands. And on that rice, we place something made out of gold, such as an earring or a ring. And then we put *laddu*, *gur*, or sweets, any sweets, in it. After this, five women, either married or unmarried, do the *chumawan* kissing ritual. Whether it is the boy being kissed or the girl, this next song will be sung. So after giving rice, gold, and sweets in the cupped hands of the bridegroom or bride, women perform the ritual—the mother kisses, the sister kisses, his or her *bhabi* kisses, the female neighbors kiss, all women kiss."

### SONG 36

*Chumawan*

Green green dub grass and cupped hands full of rice.
Mother goes to kiss Sapan Dei.
Mother goes to kiss sweetheart Sapan,
As she kisses her, similarly she blesses her.
Live long my bride or bridegroom, one hundred thousand years.
Live long my bride or bridegroom, one hundred thousand years.

The singers offer only a short part of this song, as in the actual wedding it would be repeated over and again during the sometimes long and drawn-out *chumawan* ritual. I was surprised to find out that, once again, the song had begun on a lower pitch, again the A below middle C, as we have had for several songs now. Perhaps Gangajali and Sashi just got this particular tonic pitch fixed in their minds and continued with it, even though we paused after each song, turned the fan on, and chatted.

"Who kisses first?" Umesh asked.

"The mother kisses first," Gangajali said. "Thereafter the sister then the *bhabi*. These are two songs for the *chumawan* kissing ritual. This particular *chumawan* song is for the bridegroom. Mother does the *chumawan*. Then because she is full of happiness, she gives away her golden bangles, and she gives away some money for her own son. And in much happiness, people offer loving abuse in this song. They give away things such as a *bichhuaa* and an ornament for the waist. The women move around here and there, swinging and jumping because my sister or my brother is being married.

"Some *chumawan* songs also express joking and fun. For example, when the mother goes for *chumawan*, she gives away her golden bangles out of happiness. And when the bride or groom's *bhabi* goes for *chumawan*, she offers her breast to give pleasure out of her body ('give away your sensuality slowly slowly'). On the other hand, it also says that when the sister goes for *chumawan*, she is walking funny, shaking her skirt, showing off her pretty *lahanga* dress."

"*Chumawan* means 'kissing,'" Umesh said. "The *chumawan* ritual is performed throughout the wedding after every major rite. Usually it is done by women, sometimes girls, and in some places all participants. For example, in Mauritius, all do the *chumawan*. It is considered a very important ritual.

"The girlfriend takes rice from the cupped hands of the bride and holds it pinched in the fingers of both hands and touches the rice to the feet, knees, shoulders, and forehead of the bride or bridegroom. Then the girlfriend kisses the rice in her pinched fingers. This action is done five times. And green *dub* grass is also used in this ceremony. The song shows that with the *dub* grass and the rice, *chumawan* takes place and that the bride or bridegroom are blessed and wished a long life."

## SONG 37

### *Chumawan: Kissing the boy slowly slowly*

Kissing the boy slowly slowly.
Kissing the boy slowly slowly.
*Suhagin* (happily married) mother goes out after kissing.
*Suhagin* mother goes out after kissing.
Generously give away golden bangles slowly slowly.
Generously give away golden bangles slowly slowly.
*Suhagin bhabi* goes out after kissing.
*Suhagin bhabi* goes out after kissing.
Generously give away your sensuality slowly slowly.
Generously give away your sensuality slowly slowly.
Kissing the boy slowly slowly.
Kissing the boy slowly slowly.
*Suhagin* sister goes out after kissing.
*Suhagin* sister goes out after kissing.
Shake your dress invitingly slowly slowly.
Shake your dress invitingly slowly slowly.
Kissing the boy slowly slowly.
Kissing the boy slowly slowly.

Although the text of this song keeps emphasizing slowly, slowly, in fact it is sung in the same tempo range as most of the other songs, that is a quarter note = 92 mm. The song sounds as if it is in the minor mode as it has a flattened third degree, and the seventh degree, below the tonic, is also lowered. At a stretch, one might call these neutral thirds and sevenths but probably not as they seem pretty fixed as lowered pitches. Once again, the tonic is approximately the A below middle C.

The song has a verse–chorus, *sthayi–antara* structure, the most prominent feature of which falls on the words "slowly slowly (*dhire-dhire*)," which drops down to the sixth pitch (la) below the tonic (do) and then to the flattened seventh degree. Every line in the song is repeated, doubling the length and allowing time for the job of rubbing the turmeric to be completed.

THIRTY-ONE

# THE BRIDE AND GROOM GO TO THE *KOHABAR*

*Still at the Sarang Hotel, Ballia, with Gangajali and Sashi, July 1989*

"Following the kissing ritual, the family escorts the bride or bridegroom into the ritual chamber called the *kohabar*," Gangajali explained. "It is the place of the gods. By using a little red soil and turmeric, we draw a picture on the wall with different types of flowers, birds, and the palanquin that the bridegroom or bride sits in. We also make a house there for the gods and goddesses. The bride or bridegroom is led there, where they can put down their handfuls of rice. So we take the boy or girl away from the altar to the *kohabar* singing this song."

SONG 38

*Kohabar: This new kohabar is made of bronze and brass*

This new *kohabar* is made of bronze and brass.
This new *kohabar* is made of bronze and brass.
The forehead is shining like ruby.
The forehead is shining like ruby.
Daughter Sapan Rani sleeps in the same *kohabar*.
When bridegroom Vijay is alone.
When bridegroom Vijay is alone.
Bridegroom Vijay sleeps in the same *kohabar*.

When bride Sapan is alone.
When bride Sapan is alone.
The mother of the bridegroom goes to awake.
Get up son, day breaks.
Get up son, day breaks.
Oh, I give away such a mother in the hand of *samdhi*.
At midnight, she is saying it is daybreak.
At midnight, she is saying it is daybreak.

The tonic has changed in this song to a flattened D-flat just above middle C, and the tempo settles in at approximately quarter note = 94mm. The verses of the song are sung once, and then the chorus line is sung and then repeated. Then comes another line of verse, then down to the chorus and its repetition, and so on. In this *kohabar* song, the verse is sung at higher pitches, ranging mainly from the tonic up to the minor third above the tonic, while the chorus line dips all the way down to the subdominant (fa) below the tonic, and the song ends on the dominant pitch below the tonic (sol). This represents a change from the norm in which the verse or *sthayi* is at a lower pitch level and the chorus or *antara* at a higher level. Although these terms are borrowed from Western music and Indian classical music, they are helpful to explain the sound of the melody.

"The *kohabar* is made in the room where the family women have called all the gods, all the ancestors, to participate in the wedding," Umesh said. "A drawing is made on the wall there, and the *devi*s and ancestors are thought to be residing there for the duration of the wedding. So after performing each essential ritual, the bride and groom are sent to the *kohabar* for the blessings of the *devi*s and ancestors."

Gangajali said, "A *kohabar* is made in both houses—at the daughter's parents' home and the groom's parents' home. In both places the gods and goddesses are worshiped. So before the wedding, at the bridegroom's side a *kohabar* is made, and all the natural forces are captured there. The same is done in the house of the bride. After performing the wedding ritual, the bride and bridegroom are carried into the *kohabar* at the bride's home. But the door is stopped by the girls to get money from the groom. This is their *neg*. He pays something and they let them go into the *kohabar* with the old woman. And she worships there, some ritual, and they come out of the *kohabar*. When the bride and groom both come to the groom's house, they are carried into the *kohabar* there, and the bride is kept in the *kohabar*, and the groom is out after performing some rituals. After a certain time, the *kangan* (ritual bracelet) of both bride and groom are untied, and she can come out of the *kohabar*. And the gods and goddesses are released from the *kohabar*. The day that the *kakkan*s are untied, in the evening singing takes place, and women make the bride sing and dance. Meanwhile the groom is waiting in some room until midnight and cursing these women. Then the bride is carried to the gate of the room where he sleeps, and some *bhabi*, she pushes the bride inside.

"And they are there. The groom may be asleep. She may have to wake him up. Then she presses his legs because he is very tired. And she has been given a cup of warm milk to take to him. The groom should have with him some sweets to offer her. And the night passes.

"In the morning the mother-in-law quietly calls her to get up so she can go to the bathroom before anybody can see. And she must not remain with her husband in the cot until 10:00 in the morning. She is a new bride. She has to behave as a new bride.

"This song is explaining that after the wedding the bridegroom goes into the *kohabar*. So the mother tries to say that very little darkness remains and it is time to get up and out so that nobody can see them due to modesty. There is much modesty and shyness at the time of the wedding. Then the mother says it will soon be daybreak. 'You get up and go out. What will people think or say?'

"Then he speaks due to laziness and anger and says to his mother, 'You are such a mother that what to say? That what to do to her. It is midnight right now. Where is the morning?' He thinks it is midnight and does not realize that morning is breaking."

THIRTY-TWO

# THE BLUE BLUE HORSE

*The session at the Sarang Hotel moves along, Ballia, a hot July day, 1989*

"Women sing songs after the *kohabar* ritual—spontaneous songs," Gangajali explained. People are seated in the courtyard, and songs are sung from now until the wedding day—for example, *sahana* and *banda–bandi* songs are sung."

"How do you distinguish between *sahana* and *banda–bandi* songs?" Umesh asked.

"Are we foreign?" asked Sashi. "We are of Ballia, this very place. So we know! Weddings take place here."

Gangajali said, "Following the *kohabar* ritual, as the wedding day draws near, women sing *sahana* songs. There is no particular fixed time for these. They are usually performed for two days. These songs can also be sung after the marriage. Songs of this type can be sung in so many tunes. Although they are *sahana*s, they are also considered *banna–banni*—songs for the bridegroom and bride.

"I am going to sing the main *sahana* for you now."

SONG 39

*Sahana: The blue colt of the blue blue horse*

The blue colt of the blue blue horse,
Oh, the blue colt.

Asks for green green *dub* grass.
Oh, the blue colt.
Asks for green green *dub* grass, asks.
Bridegroom Vijay rides on the back, having mounted on one side,
Bridegroom Vijay rides.
Oh father, father is holding the reins.
Oh father, father is holding the reins.
Oh, father, father let go. Let go of the reins of the horse,
Of the reins of the horse.
I go to the country of her birthplace. I go.
I go to the country of the loving bride,
I go to the country of her loving brother.
The blue colt of the blue blue horse,
The blue colt.
Asks for green green *dub* grass.
Asks for green green *dub* grass.
Bridegroom Vijay rides on the back, having mounted on one side,
On one side.
Oh *chacha* (mother's brother), *chacha* is holding the reins.
Oh *chacha*, *chacha* is holding the reins.
Uncle, let go. Let go of the reins of the horse,
Of the reins of the horse.
I go to the country of my own sweetheart. I go.
The loving bridegroom's country.
The blue colt of the blue blue horse.
The blue colt.
The blue colt.
The blue colt asks for green green *dub* grass.
He asks for green *dub* grass.
Bridegroom Vijay rides on the back, having mounted on one side.
Bridegroom Vijay rides on the back.
Oh brother, brother is holding the reins.
Oh *jija*, *jija* is holding the reins.
Oh *phupha* (father's sister), *phupha* is holding the reins.
Brother, let go. Let go of the reins of the horse.
Let go of the reins of the horse.
Brother, I go to the country of my sweetheart.
I go to the country of my own sweetheart.
*Jija*, let go. Let go of the reins of the horse,
Of the reins of the colt. I go.
The reins of the sweetheart.
Mother, I go to the country of my sweetheart.
Mother, I go to the country of my sweetheart.
Oh *phupha*, let go. Let go of the reins of the horse,

Of the reins of the colt.
Father, I go to the country of my sweetheart.
Brother, I go to the country of my sweetheart.
Mother, I go to the country of my sweetheart.

This is my favorite song, both the poem and the tune. Gangajali stresses that this is a very, very old *sahana*, and it does have that olden feel, standing out from the other songs.

This song is constructed of four main phrases that we can label A, B, C, and D. The first words for the A phrase, which open the song, are "*lili-lili ghorawaa* (blue blue horse)." This phrase begins on the second degree (re) of the scale and rises up quickly to the fifth (sol). Phrase B follows immediately on "*ke lili re bacherawa*" (blue colt), starting up on the fifth degree and descending a bit to the second degree. Next, the B phrase is repeated. Then comes the stunning C phrase, stunning because it starts square on the tonic with three strikingly sweet sustained notes—perhaps we could say half notes of two beats as opposed to the quarter notes of the rest of the song. The first C phrase has the text, *mangela*, with each syllable sustained. The final D phrase follows immediately and ends the stanza solidly on the tonic—which is approximately F# above middle C.

In 2017, when I began to play the 1989 recording of "The Blue Blue Horse," I could easily see Umesh's form change. He closed his eyes. His breathing slowed and became very even. He waved his head from side to side for what must have been for him special lines of the Bhojpuri, as if this song was going deep in him.

"This song was stepping down deep inside me," he said. "It changes. It depends. As much as good words are used by a composer, it is good. But if the singer is not good or if it is not sung well, it cannot affect a person's heart. With a few good words and the singer putting them nicely in song, then it touches the heart. At that time when I was listening, I was not observing myself. I was just thinking and going deep into my feelings. When I heard it in 1989, maybe it had not gone deep because we were working in so many ways, having tea, sometimes Sashi said something, changing tape reels—interruptions came from different places.

"But now I am here. We are only with three people—the sound of Gangajali, you, and me. It took me back in time. I was just feeling that Gangajali was sitting in front of me. In my mind, she was just there. I was seeing her even although my eyes were closed. The sound brought Gangajali to us. At first it didn't take me to Ballia or to Hotel Sarang. I could just see her face and her singing and her waving hands, her lips, face, sari, everything. Yes, I could see everything. The brain makes a figure. I was not seeing this machine. I was here, right here. I could see her face.

"If I memorize some poem, I see the words on the page. But for Gangajali, I was seeing her form. I saw her singing years back, and the sound was just like hers. Nothing different. When you are listening, you don't pay attention to any obstructions that are there. When I was hearing the song, I was not seeing you. I was not thinking of you or this apartment. I was just seeing Gangajali before me singing. It happens to people. When we are concentrating, we can only see one thing. I believe I was falling into meditation for a little while. If only the ears are working or words—ears and words in combination work together. And sometimes ears, brain, and eyes work together. But for this time, hearing 'The Blue Blue Horse,' the ears and brain, I was seeing her by my brain, not by my eyes. It was not in the past, I knew the song was there and Gangajali was with us.

"Then I went back. It seemed like I was thirty-five years old. After a little while, she was there, and a quiet place is here. Then we were in Hotel Sarang. The song is really really much enchanting. It also depends what kind of feelings a person has. If a person is religious, and religion gives her the most comfort. And some people are like the social songs—they charm them, of their culture.

"At the worst time of life, the cure is only music. The worst time for a person when he or she loses her beloved, and knowingly or unknowingly the bereaved sing in their mind and heart. They are just not only crying. They are singing. And those are sorrow songs. Never mind if it gives any meaning to other people or not. But it solaces the mind and heart of the person. These tears solace a person's heart, because if tears don't come—we want that a person to cry—because if they don't cry, they will lose their mind and heart."

Then Umesh dropped off into a deep quiet sleep. He is lying very still, motionless. I do not know what world he has gone to now. I do not know where he is, even though his form is lying on the couch in the living room in total exhaustion, after explaining the role of music in the human heart.

"Yours is a quite long and beautiful song," Umesh said.

"Yes," Gangajali replied. "This song is from the very olden period. I don't know how old this *sahana* is, but it is very old.

"So, in this song, the bridegroom goes to his *sasural* riding on a horse, according to his own wish. His father begins to ride the horse. So his father, brother, or his *chacha*, *phupha*, or *jija* holds the reins, asking, 'where are you going?' Riding on the horse, he says, 'Let me go. I am going to the one who is loving to her mother, beloved of her father, beloved of her brother, and beloved to me. I am going to her. Do not hold my horse. Let me go.'"

*Back at our apartment, Banaras, September 2007*

While translating "The Blue Blue Horse," Umesh and I fell into conversation. After working on this song, Umesh had a lot on his mind.

"Krishna is blue," he said. "It means dark, *shamlya*. It is not black, it is blue—black and blue mixed together. So when we say 'blue blue horse,' it means mixed with black and blue. They are very shining. They glow in the sun. Beautiful. We get these kinds of horses."

"What does it mean, 'Bridegroom Vijay rides on the back on one side'?" I asked.

"It means that he mounts the horse from one side. Nobody gets on the horse from the back. It is from the side. The right or left *karbat*. Like we sleep. Sometimes it is on the left *karbat*, and sometimes it is on the right *karbat*.

"Why does the horse only ask for *dub* grass?" Umesh asked. "First of all this grass can be found all around the year. Other grasses are seasonal grasses. You cannot get them around the year. *Dub* grass is the most powerful and healthy grass for animals. Its roots are not very deep but spread all over on top of the soil. This grass does not die easily. If it is dry for six months, if you irrigate it, it will begin to grow. When we mark off the fields, *dub* grass grows on the banks that divide them. It lives longer than any other grass. It is the most useful grass in daily life.

"The song is unusual because it depicts the groom going to seek out his wife in the village of her birth, her *naihar*. This village is also referred to from his point of view as his *sasural*, the home of his in-laws. Maybe he is going to pay a visit to his *sasural*, and his family people do not want to let him go. Actually, this does not happen usually. Sometimes the groom wants to go, and the father refuses, but an Indian man normally won't say, 'I am going to my loving wife.' These are quite shy words for an Indian husband.

"This is a nice song composed by women, who have put the feelings of a man in a nice and right way. When he says 'let me go, let me go, release the reins,' it means that there is a kind of force not letting him go, keeping him from his wife's house. In real life, men make different excuses to go to their *sasural*, and this song puts it very nicely. It shows the importance of the social system here, that the father can't stop his son from going anywhere, even to his wife's village. The groom must have permission to pay a visit to the *naihar* of his wife. Altogether it shows the importance of the joint family. The father is the master of the house. It is a nice song, a beautiful song, beautifully done. When you read this song in English, for me it is heart touching. How can it be in the Bhojpuri?"

### *Again at the Sarang Hotel, Ballia, 1989*

The song session continued.

"Oh," Umesh said to Gangajali, "sing one more old *banna–banni* in your own language—Bhojpuri."

Gangajali began another popular *sahana* sung at wedding time.

#### SONG 40

##### *Sahana*

The bridegroom has a string of pearls.
The bridegroom has a string of pearls.
The bridegroom has a string of pearls.
The crown looks beautiful on the bridegroom's head.
The crown looks beautiful on the bridegroom's head.
He is fixing the earrings from time to time.
Look, he is fixing the earrings from time to time.
The bridegroom has a string of pearls.
The bridegroom has a string of pearls.
The gold looks beautiful on the ears of the bridegroom.
The gold looks beautiful on the ears of the bridegroom.
He fixes the earrings from time to time.
He fixes the earrings from time to time.
The bridegroom has a string of pearls.
The bridegroom has a string of pearls.
The garments look beautiful on the body of the bridegroom.
The garments look beautiful on the body of the bridegroom.
He fixes his clothes from time to time.
Look, he fixes his clothes from time to time.
The bridegroom has a string of pearls.
The bridegroom has a string of pearls.
The *mehindi* looks beautiful on the feet of the bridegroom.
The socks look beautiful on the feet of the bridegroom.
He fixes his shoes from time to time.
He fixes the *mehindi* from time to time.
The bridegroom has a string of pearls.
The bridegroom has a string of pearls.
The bridegroom has pearls on the bed of the bridegroom.
The horse looks beautiful bearing the bridegroom.
The horse looks beautiful bearing the bridegroom.
He fixes his saddle from time to time.
Look, he fixes his saddle from time to time.
The bridegroom has a string of pearls.
The bridegroom has a string of pearls.

The bride looks beautiful in the bed of the bridegroom.
The bride looks beautiful in the bed of the bridegroom.
She fixes her veil from time to time.
Look, she fixes her makeup from time to time.
The bridegroom has a string of pearls.
The bridegroom has a string of pearls.

For this song, we find that the tonic is around F. But so much of the melodic activity is based on the dominant note (sol) that one is tempted to rather assign that note as the tonic. There are two main melodic lines that we may call A and B. At the outset, melody A is repeated five times. This is followed by melody B, at a higher pitch, repeated twice. Then we return to melody A, which is repeated four times, and then back to melody B, and so forth. For the last note of the song, Gangajali sings a lovely departing melisma.

The tonality of these Bhojpuri songs is in no way related to our tonic sol-fa system of solfeggio as invented by Guido d'Arezzo, a Benedictine monk (991–992–after 1033), neither to our Western major or minor scales, or even to older modes of church music in the Middle Ages. The study of the grammar of these Bhojpuri melodies is quite a worthwhile study in and of itself.

Umesh said, "This song tells the adornment of the bridegroom, what he put on in those days, what he used to go on, like a horse, ornaments, *mehindi*, garments, crown. I think shoes and socks were added later. I do not think they were used in those olden times. The bridegroom ties his shoelaces, which is quite funny. It also shows how the bride is beautified. There is no hidden meaning in this song. That he ends up in the bed with his love is a bit of a surprise. The construction of the song shows that he is dressed so and so. It does not lead naturally to the bed. Then all of the sudden she concludes the song."

"After singing *sahana* women sing *jhumar* according to their own wish," Gangajali explained. "I am going to sing a *jhumar* type involving God. This is the *jhumar* of Mohan."

### SONG 41

#### *Jhumar*

Mohan, let me go, Mohan, let me go.
Mohan, let me go to sell yogurt in the market of Madhuwan,
To sell yogurt in Madhuwan.
Mohan, why have you blocked my way?
Mohan, why have you blocked my way?

Mohan, why are you forcing me?
Mohan, let me go to sell yogurt in the market of Madhuwan.
Mohan, let me go to sell yogurt in the market of Madhuwan.
Oh, if you are hungry, eat yogurt.
I will not give you butter.
If you are hungry, eat yogurt.
I will not give you butter.
If you quarrel, I will quarrel with you.
If you quarrel, I will quarrel with you,
Oh son of Yasoda.
Mohan, let me go to sell yogurt in the market of Madhuwan.
Mohan, let me go to sell yogurt in the market of Madhuwan.
First, my arms got tired.
Second, my mind is troubled.
First, my arms got tired.
Second, my mind is troubled.
Third, my girlfriends are gone.
Oh Krishna, third, my girlfriends are lost.
My house is lonely.
Mohan, let me go to sell yogurt in Madhuwan,
To sell yogurt in Madhuwan.
First, I feel like breaking the flute and throwing it away in the Jamuna.
First, I feel like breaking the flute and throwing it away in the Jamuna.
But second, Mohan, I have deep feelings.
Second, Mohan, I have deep feelings.
Oh, your body is tender.
Mohan, let me go to sell yogurt in Madhuwan,
To sell yogurt in Madhuwan.
Kanhaiya makes a paper boat.
Kanhaiya makes a paper boat.
Moving, moving, the boat went in the Jamuna.
Moving, moving the boat went in the Jamuna.
Radha plays *jhijhiri*.
Radha plays *jhijhiri*.
Kanhaiya plays Holi.
Mohan, let me go sell yogurt in Madhuwan.
Mohan, let me go to sell yogurt in Madhuwan.

This song has two main melodic sections, and each lyrical line can be divided into two phrases. So, if we follow them, section I, phrase A opens the song, phrase B completes the line, phrase C brings a slightly different line, and phrase B completes the couplet. Then the melody moves on to section II, with phrase F, then E and F repeated, and so forth. Sections I and II alternate until the story of the song has been told.

The whole song leaves one rather lazy and relaxed as this rather silly quarrel between Mohan (Krishna) and Radha, the milkmaid, carries on. Essentially Mohan is playful, while Radha has a job to get on with. So, in fact, it is all about teasing. Suddenly, a game begins. This is a section II passage. Krishna quickly creates a paper boat. Moving forward, the boat sails in the Jamuna river. Radha plays a game called *jhijhiri*, circling the boat playfully. Goodness knows what this play is intended to mean. Then, after a couple of lines on this new topic, Radha resumes begging Krishna to let her go and sell yogurt in Madhuwan, and these few phrases, returning to the phrases of section I, close out the song.

"This is a *jhumar* of Radha and Krishna," Gangajali said. "Queen Radha goes to sell yogurt, and she is going from Barsana to Gokula. She is going to Mathura. Kanhaiya stops her on the way, and he quarrels and holds her back. Then she says, 'Let me go to sell yogurt. I am getting late. First, my house remains lonely. Second, my girlfriends are left behind. And I got tired. My mind is restless. Let me go to sell yogurt. If you are hungry, then take a little to eat. Ah, yes, but I won't let you have butter. I have to sell butter for a lot of money. If you insist, eat yogurt.'

"Then she says in anger, 'I feel such anger that I would like to break your flute and throw it in the Jamuna. But what should I do? I feel attachment. Oh, I feel like being kind to you since you are very tender and beautiful. That is why I don't feel like beating you up or breaking your flute. Let me go to sell yogurt.'"

### SONG 42

#### *Jhumar*

Father, I am sixteen years old.
Father, I am sixteen years old.
Father has searched for a *damad* eighty years old.
Father has searched for a *damad* eighty years old.
The old man asks for food upstairs.
Father, the old man asks for food upstairs.
Father, I feel embarrassed to go upstairs.
Father, I feel embarrassed to go to the old man.
The girlfriends of childhood ask, who is he to you?
The girlfriends of childhood ask, who is he to you?
Father, out of embarrassment, I say he is my father-in-law.
Father, out of embarrassment, I say he is my father-in-law.
Father, the old man upstairs asks for a jug of water.
Father, the old man upstairs asks for a jug of water.

Father, I feel embarrassed to go upstairs.
Father, I feel embarrassed to give him water to drink.
The girlfriends of childhood ask, who is he to you?
Father, people ask, who is this old man to you?
Father, out of embarrassment, I say he is my father-in-law.
Father, out of embarrassment, I say he is my father-in-law.
Father, I am sixteen years old.
Father, I am sixteen years old.
Father has searched for a *damad* eighty years old.
Father has searched for a *damad* eighty years old.
The old man upstairs asks for betel leaf.
The old man upstairs asks for betel leaf.
Father, I feel embarrassed to go upstairs.
Father, I feel embarrassed to offer him the betel leaf.
Father, all the villagers ask, who is this old man to you?
Father, the same aged friends ask, who is he to you?
Out of embarrassment, I say he is my father-in-law.
Father, the old man upstairs asks for a bed.
Father, the old man upstairs asks for a bed.
Father, I feel embarrassed to sleep with him.
Father, I feel embarrassed to sleep with him.
Father, all the villagers ask, who is this old man to you?
Father, all the villagers ask, who is this old man to you?
Father, out of embarrassment, I say he is my father-in-law.
Father, out of embarrassment, I say he is my father-in-law.

This jokey, amusing song about a June/December wedding is fun for everyone. The structure is very simple. Each line of text has a line of melody. Tune A, repeated twice, starts the song. Then the *antara* or chorus phrase on tune B takes over and is repeated twice. And then back to tune A, again repeated twice, and so forth, alternating between the two lines. The tunes are both lively, starting around an A-flat and hovering a lot around the fifth dominant degree (sol) in tune A and around the subdominant (fa) degree in tune B. So the lines opening with the words *baba* ("father") on the higher fifth degree (sol) are those of tune A and the lines, also sometimes opening with the words *baba* but on the lower subdominant pitch (fa), are those of tune B.

Only pausing for a quick breath, Gangajali continued with the next song, also a *jhumar*.

## SONG 43

### *Jhumar*

Whose heart should I solace?
There are three men in the room at a time.
Whose heart should I solace?
There are three men in the room at a time.
There are three men in the room at a time.
There are three men in the room at a time.
Whose heart should I solace?
There are three men in the room at a time.
There is food for one person in the room.
There is food for one person in the room.
To whom, to whom, to whom, to whom should I serve?
There are three men in the room at a time.
To whom, to whom, to whom, to whom should I serve?
There are three men in the room at a time.
Whose heart should I solace?
There are three men in the room at a time.
Whose heart should I solace?
There are three men in the room at a time.
There is one jug of water in the room.
There is one jug of water in the room.
To whom, to whom, to whom, to whom should I serve water?
There are three men in the room at a time.
To whom, to whom, to whom, to whom should I serve water?
There are three men in the room at a time.
Whose heart should I solace?
There are three men in the room at a time.
Whose heart should I solace?
There are three men in the room at a time.
There is one betel leaf in one room.
There is one betel leaf in one room.
To whom, to whom, to whom, to whom should I serve?
There are three men in the room at a time.
To whom, to whom, to whom, to whom should I serve?
Whose heart should I solace?
There are three men in the room at a time.
Whose heart should I solace?
There are three men in the room at a time.
Whose heart should I solace?
There are three men in the room at a time.
There is one double bed in the room.
There are three men in the room at a time.

There is one double bed in the room.
With whom, with whom, with whom, with whom should I sleep?
There are three men in the room at a time.
With whom, with whom, with whom, with whom should I sleep?
Whose heart should I solace?
There are three men in the room at a time.
Whose heart should I solace?
There are three men in the room at a time.
Whose heart should I solace?
There are three men in the room at a time.

This is a really hard song to sing in tune. After a few unsteady phrases, however, Gangajali and Sashi settle into a reasonably in-tune performance. The song is, of course, a joke and features jokey alliterative text syllables: *kekar-kekar, tin-tin, tin-ni-tin-ni, char-char,* and especially the silly phrase *ke-ke-ke-ke* (to whom? to whom? to whom? to whom?). The listener can easily identify three different tunes or musical sentences. Tune A, the *sthayi*, begins below the tonic as we have come to expect. Tune B, the first line of the *antara*, is at a higher level. Most dramatic is tune C, which is sung way up on the sixth degree (la) to the repeated syllables *ke-ke-ke-ke*. It's hard to miss these high points. Cheerful. The song is cheerful.

An Indian wedding is a time of great stress, the stress of so much cash flowing out of your hand in a short day, the stress of maintaining polite and respectful relations with the in-law family, the stress, for the bride's parents, of losing a much-loved daughter. Will there be enough food? Enough plates? Enough cups? Enough snacks? Will the tea be hot? Will the *barat* enjoy the food? Will there be water for everybody? Will there be some natural disaster such as a dust storm? Driving rain? The attack of a cobra? Have all the spirits been appeased?

Music, song, is used by the womenfolk to appease the spirits, and, likewise, music is used to calm the heart of the bride's mother and the heart of the bride, who moves through all these ceremonies like a limp rag doll, head bowed.

"This is a *jhumar*," Sashi explained.

"This is the meaning of it," Gangajali said. "As there is a room, a room like this. We four are sitting in here. Or only there are three seated here. I have food for one person in a dish, and there are three people to eat. All three are asking to eat. And I am asking what should I do now?

How can I serve all those three people? How to feed all three? All three say, 'We will eat.' All three say, 'We will drink water.' There is water only in a jug, only one glass, and all three have to drink. How to have them drink? She says, 'There is only one double bed, and they are all to sleep on it. And how to put all three on one bed?' This is the meaning of it."

## SONG 44

### *Bhajan*

Sit down, Saint Udhau, sit on the bed.
Oh, sit down, Saint Udhau, sit on the bed.
Oh, explain this to Krishna thoroughly.
Oh, my Saint Udhau.
Explain this to Krishna thoroughly.
Oh, my Saint Udhau,
Then Udhau falls in love,
Leaves love.
Then Udhau falls in love,
Breaks up love.
He is gone and seated in Mathura,
Oh, my Saint Udhau.
He is gone and seated in Mathura,
Oh, my Saint Udhau.
When, if I had known,
Krishna would deceive me.
Udhau, if I had known,
Krishna would deceive me,
I would not have loved him,
Oh, my Saint Udhau.
I would not have loved him.
Explain this to Krishna thoroughly.
Explain this to Krishna thoroughly.
Oh, my (Saint) Udhau.
There is the shade of the *kadam* tree at the bank of the river, Udhauji.
There is the shade of the *kadam* tree at the bank of the river, Udhauji.
We go to take water every day.
Oh, my Saint Udhau.
We go to take water every day.
Oh, my Saint Udhau.
Explain this to Krishna thoroughly.
Oh, my Saint Udhau,
Explain this to Krishna thoroughly.
Oh, my Saint Udhau,
Udhauji, as the fish out of water flips.
Udhauji, as the fish out of water flips.
Similarly, I flip night and day.
Oh, my Saint Udhau,
Explain this to Krishna thoroughly.
Oh, my Saint Udhau.
Explain this to Krishna thoroughly.

Oh, my Saint Udhau.
Udhauji, as the cuckoo sings,
The cuckoo of the forest,
Udhauji, as the cuckoo sings,
The cuckoo of the forest,
My heart also sings like that.
Oh, my Saint Udhau.
My heart also sings like that.
Oh, my Saint Udhau.
Explain this to Krishna thoroughly.
Oh, my Saint Udhau.
Explain this to Krishna thoroughly.
Oh, my Saint Udhau.
Udhauji, as it rains in Sawan and Bhadauaa,
Udhauji, as it rains in Sawan and Bhadauaa,
Similarly, my eyes rain with tears.
Oh, my Saint Udhau.
Similarly, my eyes rain with tears.
Oh, my Saint Udhau.
Explain this to Krishna thoroughly.
Oh, my Saint Udhau.

This song has a dramatic beginning at the top of the vocal range and comes tumbling down an octave to the lower tonic in one musical sentence: "Sit down, Saint Udhau, sit on the bed." In fact, each verse of the song, set to a number of various tunes, is lovely and difficult to sing. A listener might just wish to settle back with their eyes closed and listen to the song—phrase to phrase. Before long, they might notice that there are no sustained plain pitches—that is, each sustained pitch is decorated by a bouquet of ornaments. Perhaps the notion of a single sustained pitch does not exist in this repertory. Pitches are not sung without their ornaments. Following on from this, why should we hold to the notion that any song in this repertory has sustained pitches? But, rather, all notes are decorated, and, further, the decorations are, in fact, part of the pitch concept.

In Western notation, we could indicate glissandi, grace notes, melismas, vibrato (slow or fast), sliding into a pitch from above or from below. Perhaps these Bhojpuri melodies are more like a piece of homespun, with a bit of thickness here and a bit of thinness there, and it is these very irregularities that are in fact the regularities, the identifying feature of the homespun fabric. By this analogy, however, I do not mean to suggest that these songs are rustic, whatever this might mean, that they are rough-hewn, simple, or folk, whatever that might mean.

"This is a *bhajan*," Gangajali explained. "And this is the meaning of this song. When leaving Radha behind, Kandhaiya went to Mathura. Then, after several days, he sends Udhauji to Gokul and brings the news from Radhe and the other *gopi*s. So Udhauji comes to these people. And they tell him of their pain. 'When he wanted to go to leave us, when he wanted to break his love with us, then why did he love us? Why did he give us people so much love? Without him, day and night, we people sit at the bank of the river bank and wait for him, wondering when will he come, when will he come.'

"As the fish dries without water and flips, as a fish out of water, she will die from flipping. Similarly, we flip like a fish without water, without him. When we will die. And as the cuckoo sings in the garden for rain, similarly, we people coo for him, like the cuckoo. Brokenhearted for him, we suffocate when he had to leave Gokula. Then why did he love us so much? Saint Udhau, go and explain this to him. This is the meaning of this song."

### SONG 45

#### *Bhajan*

I have become a devotee of my own Mohan.
I have become a devotee of my own Mohan.
I have become a devotee of my own Mohan.
I have become a devotee of my own Mohan.
I have become a devotee of my own Mohan.
I have become a devotee of my own Mohan.
My body and mind are fully devoted to Krishna.
My body and mind are fully devoted to Krishna.
I am fully devoted to Ram.
I am fully devoted to Ram.
I have become a devotee of my own Mohan.
I have become a devotee of my own Mohan.
Krishna's form is blue.
Mohan's form is blue.
Krishna is blue.
Mohan's form is blue.
In the temple of my heart,
I have seated him in the temple of my heart.
Krishna's form, Krishna's form, Krishna's form.
I have become a devotee of my own Mohan.
I have become a devotee of my own Mohan.
Become a devotee. I have become a devotee.

I have become a devotee.
I have become a devotee of my own Mohan.
I broke up with my family.
I have turned my back on the world.
I broke up with my family.
I have turned my back on the world.
I broke up with my family.
I have turned my back on the world.
I broke up with my family.
I have turned my back on the world.
Now I have offered my body and soul,
Now I have offered my body and soul,
To the feet of the Lord.
I have become a devotee of my own Mohan.
I have become a devotee of my own Mohan.
Never mind if they make fun,
Never mind if the entire world makes fun of me.
I have become a devotee,
I have become a devotee of my own Mohan.

This song is personal. She is trying to move the listener as she herself is moved to sing it. This song is sung with so much passion, with so much devotion, from the very heart of Gangajali.

One element, repetition, overrides the performances of all the Bhojpuri women's songs. You can easily hear the repetition that structures this song. Women repeat lines many times. This is for several reasons. It helps them to learn and remember the songs. Someone who does not know the song can join in after she has heard the lines a few times. The songs are often sung in leader–chorus style. There will be one woman who is the leader. She will sing the line, and the group or chorus will repeat it after her. Sometimes the leader is not a single woman but a group of women. This also helps to strengthen the memory of the songs. At a wedding, there need only be a single strong singer who can be the leader in order for the singing to be successful and for the tradition to survive. The leader will be a woman who is known for having a strong and clear voice and for knowing a lot of songs.

"I composed this song myself," Gangajali explained.

Umesh said, "This is not only a *bhajan* for Krishna. She is composing the song herself. Sometimes some girl fell in love with someone. It can be one-side love. To get the attention of the boy, this song can be sung. I have become your yogini of Krishna. Krishna is the name of whom she loves. Anyone can understand that this song is sung for a sweetheart. Because if anyone makes fun of me, I don't care. I have become a yogini of my Krishna.

"This is quite a long song. While she sings this song, she is on a little high, but the pitch is little bit shaking like this, and she is floating a new melody as she holds the note, through the help of the throat. It sounds so beautiful. It is so sweet. Sometimes people don't have words, and I am one of them. I have not learned the words for music. But I know what I hear because this is also based on my religious love for Lord Krishna."

THIRTY-THREE

# UMESH TELLS THE KRISHNA STORY

*Our apartment in Banaras, one morning, 2007*

"So Mohan is Krishna?" I asked Umesh.

"Mohan is Krishna," he replied. "We believe that Krishna is a god, and he is the son of Basudev and Deviki, who were imprisoned by Kans, the king of Mathura. Kans was the *mama*, the maternal uncle to Krishna.

"Krishna was born in prison. In fact, he just appeared in a radiant glow, for he was an avatar, an avatar of Lord Vishnu. And the story tells that he was the seventh child of his mother. At his birth, the doors of the prison opened by themselves, and the breeze blew so sweetly, so perfumed, that the guards fell asleep, and the handcuffs were opened. And from nowhere the words came, 'Take this boy to the house of Yasoda. There is a girl. Bring the girl from there here.' And Basudev took the babe in his *sup*, his winnowing basket, on his head. And it was the time of rain, so the Jamuna was flooded. He found a place to ford the river, but as soon as he was crossing, the Jamuna flooded more because the great river wanted to touch the feet of Lord Krishna. When the father began to drown, Krishna just touched his foot down into the water, and, all of the sudden, the Jamuna went down, and a way was given for Basudev to cross. Basudev went to Nand Baba's house."

"This story is too complicated," I complained.

"Just a little bit more," Umesh said. "How Krishna got there. Basudev took the child to the house of Nand. He found the door open, and they knew Yasoda had given birth to a daughter. But Basudev exchanged the girl with Krishna, and Krishna was left in Nand's house. He brought the baby girl back to the prison. So Nand and Yasoda raised Krishna, believing he was their son."

"What happened to the baby girl?" I asked.

"As soon as they got back to the prison, the handcuffs were tied up, and all the doors were closed, and gatekeepers got up, and all of the sudden the wail of a child was heard throughout the building. So a message of this birth was given to King Kans. So the king came and took the girl out of their hands to kill her. As soon as he held one of her legs to throw her on the ground, the girl slipped out of his hand and flew into the sky. Thunder roared, and lightning crackled. And a great loud voice came from the sky from the baby girl. We call that voice *akash-vani* (we also use this word for broadcasting). The voice boomed, 'Oh, Kans, you wanted to kill me. Your killer is already born.'

"When Krishna grew to be a young boy," he continued, "he began stealing butter and yogurt from house to house. He fed this to his friends and fed himself too. Deeply the concept was not to let butter, milk, or yogurt go to Mathura to the people of Kans—for his soldiers and other people. You eat it here in Gokul, become healthy and strong. So still today in the families of Ahirs, they mostly don't sell yogurt and milk. They can sell ghee but not milk and yogurt."

"But I thought Ahirs were the caste of cattle minders," I said.

"If you keep interrupting my story, I will lose my enthusiasm for it," Umesh complained.

"We can tell more of the Krishna story when we come to the next Krishna song," I said.

"Let me come back to Krishna's childhood," he said. "Krishna met with the wives and daughters of the milk sellers, the *gwala*s. They are called *gwala* here in this Bhojpuri area. Well, these women are called *gopi*s, and they played a great role in the life of Krishna. The job of the *gopi*s was to sell milk, yogurt, or butter to the townspeople. So when these *gopi*s went to sell all these things, Krishna stopped them not to let them go, and if they didn't stop, he took their yogurt and butter, fed himself, and fed his friends. This is the tale told here in this song. But, as the song tells, the *gopi*s liked Krishna the most because he was charming, he played the flute, and also played several amusing games. He did miracles. He did so many other things. He was God.

"So the *gopal*s, the boy cowherds, also liked him because he fed them, lived with them in the forest, went to graze cows with them, played at the Jamuna River with them, and did so many other deeds together with them. Among all of these deeds, the story of Kanhaiya is very famous."

"Kanhaiya is another name for Krishna?" I asked.

"Yes. Kanhaiya, Bansidhar (who plays the flute), Muralidhar (who plays the small flute), Gopinath (who is the lord of the *gopi*s), Nandalala (son of Nand), Girdhar (who keeps the mountain on his pinkie), Nagnath (who has the bridle of the snake)—he has thousands of names."

INTERLUDE SEVEN

# LADY LINLITHGOW'S MISSION, THE SAWAB OF MYGAWB

*At our apartment, Banaras, 2007*

As the days passed at our apartment, we had to make up ways to amuse ourselves. There was no television and no radio and no Internet and no cell phones. But we had books. So *The Eustace Diamonds* became an important form of entertainment for us, and we looked forward to storytime.

*"Lady Eustace had been so surprised by the announcement that hitherto she had not spoken a word. The quarrel between her and her aunt had been of such a nature that it had seemed to be impossible that the old countess should come to Mount Street. Lizzie had certainly behaved very badly to her aunt;—about as badly as a young woman could behave to an old woman. She had accepted bread, and shelter, and the very clothes on her back from her aunt's bounty, and had rejected even the hand of her benefactress the first moment that she had bread and shelter and clothes of her own. And here was Lady Linlithgow downstairs in the parlour, and sending up her love to her niece! 'I won't see her!' said Lizzie."*

Frank escaped from the scene via the back door, and Lizzie begged Miss Macnulty to remain beside her. Lizzie prepared herself for combat.

Umesh said, "As the Lady Linlithgow gets inside the house, in the room, Lizzie is thinking that she has come here to create trouble. She is suspicious that why she has come? Miss Mcnulty is sent out so they could talk. Lady Linlithgow tells her that she has been sent here to Lizzie by Mr. Camperdown to tell Lizzie to give away the diamond necklace since she is the closest person to Lizzie."

Umesh went on. "Oh, Lizzie gets upset hearing this, and says, 'No! This belongs to me, my husband has given this to me.' And Lady Linlithgow gives three reasons of the social system why she could not have the diamond necklace or she could be in prison. These are the Eustace heirloom jewels, and they cannot be given to anyone, and they cannot be sold. A widow cannot wear this. If she marries a second time, the new husband won't permit her to have this on because it is disgrace for him. Then what is the point of having this necklace? So give it away. This shows the social system of the time will not permit Lizzie to keep the diamond necklace.

"There is long talk between Lady Linlithgow and Lizzie, and over and again, she is trying to tell Lizzie give away the necklace either to the jeweler, the person who keeps it, lawyer, or to a family member. But Lizzie insists that it belongs to her because this was given by her husband, and this is hers. She wants to keep it to pass on to her son. And the vulturess thinks this is ridiculous. 'You don't care even about your own child.' And she—Lizzie—warns her to not say that she does not care of her son. 'Mind what you are saying. Shut up!' Lady Linlithgow tells her that she is just performing her duty and that duty is to explain the facts that what will happen if she does not return this diamond necklace. She will be in prison. Lady Linlithgow also explains that Lizzie is thinking that whatever the lawyer sends, Lizzie thinks it is like a barking dog. It makes Lizzie to think over it. And she does not have an answer.

"And she calls Miss Mcnulty in and asks like an order to show the way out to the vulturess. She also asks Miss Mcnulty, 'Perhaps you have heard all these words.' After hearing all this conversation, since she was asked to give her point of view, Miss Mcnulty also says better to give away the diamond necklace. It shows the real character of Miss Mcnulty. She doesn't want to let Lizzie be in trouble. So Lizzie cannot accept any advice against giving away the diamond necklace. So she says to this supporting lady, 'Get away.' She sends her away. To whom can Lizzie turn to as a friend? Which one is the best for her? One is just like a rock, as powerful as a house. This was Frank. One is another poor creature. This was Lord Fawn."

THIRTY-FOUR

# AND LOVE

*At our apartment, Banaras, 2007*

When we finished the chapter, I rested, and Umesh turned to carefully working on the Gangajali files, checking the transcriptions against the compact cassette copies. We translated and translated for hours each day. And days passed.

We went on in this manner for weeks. The routine was healing. The milkman, boiling milk, chai, buttered toast, Gangajali, Trollope, Lizzie Eustace, diamonds, court cases, castles in Scotland, castles in the air, greed, theft, colonial violence.

My mind began to free itself from the academy and from any thoughts of ethnomusicology. To me it all blurred and became story—fiction or nonfiction, the only story I knew how to tell, my story with my impressions and my understanding, my insights. I was just a storyteller.

"Things separate from their stories have no meaning. They are only shapes. Of a certain size and color. A certain weight. When their meaning has become lost to us they no longer even have a name. The story on the other hand can never be lost from its place in the world for it is that place."

As Umesh and I traveled around India, late into the night in the villages, after I had gone to bed with the women, he would sit outside and talk to the men. They all loved stories, family stories, sensational stories. They would all love the suspense and intrigue of Trollope.

Trollope saw the passing scene as a comedy. He had a comfortable middle-class life in England, Ireland, and on his many overseas travels. Umesh saw the passing scene as tragedy, the performance, however possible, of one's duty (dharma) at the risk of one's karma. There was little thought of joy, true happiness, or true love.

In the village, love, especially romance, was a joke. Nobody took it seriously. Nobody ever thought of it as a sound basis for marriage. It was the matching of horoscopes, the matching of families and caste, the matching of respective wealth, the investigation of the respective properties, and, in particular, the job prospects of the boy that were under serious consideration. This is the nature of the Hindu arranged marriage.

There is very little divorce in India. Families thrive in their various ways. Love, indeed, may come into the picture, but it comes as an afterthought. It happens that a man may mention that, after whatever time, he fell in love with his wife. Such was the nature of the arranged marriage. At this point, when the farmer could not be coaxed out of the courtyard, out of the bedroom containing his wife, the women laughed. They had conquered another man, a good farmer, and they rejoiced and laughed. In quite private moments, Umesh told me how exactly this had happened to him, and I remembered the details of these conversations carefully and committed them to my heart.

THIRTY-FIVE

# KABIR

*Sarang Hotel, Ballia, July 16, 1989, third session with Gangajali*

It came to be that, by our third session, Gangajali would like to begin a day's singing with one of her favorite *bhajan*s, and we soon fell into that habit. But I wasn't expecting the song she chose this day.

### SONG 46

*Kabir*

The Lord has woven the sheet with much effort.
The Lord has woven the sheet with much effort.
The Lord has woven the sheet with much effort.
Lord, with much effort.
Oh, what is made from the loom,
What is made from the skein of thread?
What is made from the loom,
What is made from the skein of thread?
What is the string made of?
Of what is the string from which the sheet is woven?
The Lord has woven the sheet with much effort.
With much effort.
Lord, with much effort.

The Lord has woven the sheet with much effort.
With much effort.
Lord, with much effort.
The skeleton is made of bones.
And the loom is made out of flesh.
The skeleton is made of bones.
And the loom is made out of flesh.
The skeleton is made of bones.
And the loom is made out of flesh.
And the loom is made out of flesh.
The sheet is woven with the threads of the breath of life.
The sheet is woven with the threads of the breath of life.
The Lord has woven the sheet with much effort.
Lord, with much effort.
Gods, man, and the saints are woven of the same sheet.
Gods, man, and the saints are woven of the same sheet.
Having covered the skeleton with the skin,
You stained the character.
Having covered the skeleton with the skin,
You stained the character.
The Lord has woven the sheet with much effort.
The Lord has woven the sheet with much effort.
Oh, oh, oh, with the same sheet,
Mira's body was made of the same sheet.
Miraji was covered up,
Miraji was covered up.
Oh, oh, oh, having covered with much effort,
She kept the sheet stainless with much effort.
The Lord has woven the sheet with much effort,
With much effort.
Oh, this *bhajan*, oh, oh, oh,
Oh, Gangajali sings this *bhajan*,
Gangajali sings,
Having sung the Lord's *bhajan* in her heart.
Having sung the Lord's *bhajan* in her heart.
The Lord has woven the sheet with much effort,
Lord, with much effort.

I was soon to learn that although this song bewildered me, it spoke straight to the heart of both Umesh and Gangajali. What is involved here is emotion. Having understood the text, and it is a difficult text, one can clearly hear that Gangajali sang this particular song with a great deal of emotion. It is a *nirgun bhajan*, *nirgun* indicating that the song is dedicated to "God without form." The opposite of *nirgun* is *sagun*, God with form, as for example Shiva, Ganesh, Krishna, Ram, and so on. These gods can be represented in the form of *murti*s—icons, such as paintings and statues. That you can hear in the singing Gangajali's emotions and devotions makes this song so very special.

Scholars, philosophers, thinkers have puzzled for millennia about the relationship between emotion and music. But for particular ideas on this topic, let us turn to Oliver Sachs. In his 2007 book, *Musicophilia*, he says, "For many of us, indeed, the emotions induced by music may be overwhelming." This is how, I believe, Gangajali felt while singing this Kabir *bhajan*. "A number of my friends who are intensely sensitive to music cannot have it on as background when they work; they must attend to music completely or turn it off, for it is too powerful to allow them to focus on other mental activities." Sachs continues, "States of ecstasy and rapture may lie in wait for us if we give ourselves totally to music; a common scene during the 1950s was to see entire audiences swooning in response to Frank Sinatra or Elvis Presley—seized by an emotional and perhaps erotic excitement so intense as to induce fainting. Wagner, too, was a master of the musical manipulations of emotions, and this, perhaps, is a reason why his music is so intoxicating to some and so disturbing to others."

Gangajali paused, and she explained the meaning of the song for us. "This *bhajan* tells how God has constructed our body, how he had constructed such a beautiful and priceless body of a man. If a man or woman chooses the wrong path or does bad work, then the people will laugh at them. They will say how dirty the person is and how corrupt the person is. Even to say his name is a sin. And if this body does worship, *bhajan*, charity, or any good work, then people will say how great this is. How wonderful it is. If we turn this God-given body to evil work, once it is stained it lasts. It cannot be removed for the entire life. It never goes. This is the meaning of this song."

"It is very heart-touching," Umesh said.

I found it strange and kept silent.

"We will always remember this song," he added. "Whenever we begin some work, we will begin with a *bhajan*."

"Yes, I know many *bhajan*s," Gangajali replied. "I remember *bhajan*s day and night and keep singing *bhajan*s. I don't realize how much work I have done. I recall *bhajan*s constantly and keep working in my mind. Or I hum or sing out loud. I don't know whether I have eaten or not. I don't realize how much work I have done."

Gangajali rested after saying these important words, and I reflected on the curious nature of Hinduism, whose depths had always eluded me. How could this unusual, esoteric song find a place in the heart of *my* musical world—as Umesh had promised Gangajali? But I was pleased to think that my ethnomusicological work had brought me to India, to Ballia, and to her, to work with this highly gifted singer, appreciate her aesthetic, and to nurture, reward, and preserve her vast repertory. If, indeed, "The skeleton is of bones and the loom is made out of flesh," I would have to deal with that too.

Umesh said, "The Lord has made this great body with much effort. What kind of thread is this body woven from, what things are used to make this body? *Tante* is a string made out of goatskin. This is fully personification. It says this bone is *tante* and the flesh is *birny*. So on the string of bones with the *birny* of flesh and its string of breath, this body is made. I believe this poem could be by Kabir, and Kabir was a weaver. The song is in the style of Kabir and is called a *nirgun bhajan*.

"There are two forms of God, *sagun* and *nirgun*. For the *sagun*, God takes form, and for the *nirgun*, God is formless. Kabir worshiped the *nirgun* God, the God without form. Around Banaras, so many people know about *nirgun*. When we visited Banpurwa so many people sang *nirgun bhajan*s.

"Kabir lived in Banaras," he continued. "He was born to a widow Brahman lady. And to hide her embarrassment, she left the baby at the bank of the Ganges River. So a weaver found the boy, and he raised the child to be a weaver.

"Kabir was a hardworking person. He composed songs although he was illiterate. He lived in the same period as Tulsidas—around the seventeenth century. He had a wife and children. But he went to die elsewhere, outside Banaras, to a particular location that was considered unlucky because it was believed that if somebody died in that place, they would go to hell. So to break this myth, he went to die there.

"So Kabir was raised by a weaver, and he was a weaver. So in his song here he is comparing life to weaving. It is a metaphor.

"Nothing is typical in here. He is saying the bone is string and the flesh is the skein of thread, and we take the breath, this is the real string—it goes in and out. This is the real thread—breathing is the thread. This is how we live. The songs of Kabir are always very complicated.

"So although I love this song very much, it is always hard to make meaning out of Kabir's poems. This happens to be an easy one. There are so many that I can't explain at all.

"Kabir makes the point, 'the same body covered all the gods, humans, and rishis, they are all covered by the same sheet.' It means these great beings have the same kind of form as we do. After receiving this body that God had created, we have stained it with sins. At the end Gangajali put her name in the song as the singer. After singing this song she says that she will keep it deep in her heart."

After I got home to the United States and was preparing this book, I had a chance to listen to my field tapes over and again. I found that on this, the beginning of the third day of recording, Gangajali was putting so much more emotion into her songs than on the previous days. The songs had many sustained notes with glorious melismas sung over sustained vowels. Singing lines such as "oh, oh, oh" with such delicacy and feeling. I believe she had accustomed herself to the strangeness of our meeting like this, in a hotel room, and that we had had a meeting of minds about what we were doing. She sang her very best, and now, as I hear this song in 2018, it brings me to tears. I suppose it has indeed become the heart of my musical world.

THIRTY-SIX

# GREAT NOVELS AND LESSER NOVELS

*Back at our apartment, Banaras, 2007*

"But, Helen," Umesh commented one morning, "you didn't come to India to read novels." For Umesh, novels were pulp fiction read secretly by unmarried girls, the Harlequin romances, all neatly arranged to have 189 pages (by adjusting the leading and font size). I have made girlfriends all around the world by swapping Harlequin romances. It happened first in Trinidad in the 1970s with Matti's sister, Kamini, and later with her daughter-in-law (Matti didn't approve of these novels either). Then in India at the archive, there was a hidden box of what were known as "shits." I borrowed some of these cheap romances from the box and also brought some for the box. In Mauritius, all the shits were in French, and I didn't bother. But there they were again in Fiji, and, of course, they were abundant in England, where I had lived for fifteen years. England was their home of origin, I suppose. It thus should come as no surprise that shits could be found throughout the Commonwealth and have caught favor in the United States. Girls read them and, especially, grannies read them. I read them. They are the sex of old age.

"No, Umesh," I admitted. "I didn't come to India to read novels. But these novels are classical and very important." (I had read *War and Peace* and *Moby Dick* and Keay's *India* and many others.) "In fact, they are literature, and they are studied by important scholars in universities."

Umesh didn't believe me as, to improve his English, he had taken to reading one of my Danielle Steele books. But I gave in, and he read the Danielle Steele book to me out loud every evening, chapter by chapter, as a form of entertainment. Storytime was always a real treat. As Umesh got into the Danielle Steele, he came to agree with me that these were excellent books and that possibly she also was a classical writer whose works were studied in universities by important professors. I promised him that the next book would be *our* book and would also have his name on it, and I suppose he worried a bit about how he could rise to the level of a Danielle Steele.

But those words haunted me a bit as the days passed and I was just reading Trollope. "You didn't come to India to read novels." Or did I? I had long felt that reading classical literature went hand in hand with good observation, clear thinking, ideas flowing from one to the next, stimulating for a restless imagination, and eventually leading to good writing or, in any case, to good storytelling.

THIRTY-SEVEN

# TRAPPING THE FAMILY GODS

*Once again at the Sarang Hotel, Ballia, July 1989*

"Before the wedding, people prepare their homes for a religious ceremony," Gangajali explained. "Many jobs are required for the women to do. For example, they make *laddu* of rice flour. They keep chickpea *dal* and the same stone and *lori* (grinder) in the room that they have designated as the *kohabar*. This is where the bride and bridegroom will be seated so many times during the wedding after coming away from the holy altar. Five married ladies sit in there to invite the ancestors and gods. In each of their *anchal*s, there is some chickpea *dal* and *laddu*. They all put *sindur* in the parting of their hair. These five place the *dal* of chickpeas on the stone, and all five hold the grinder and grind it back and forth. They grind wearing yellow clothes and are all covered with a red sheet. All the five women must grind slowly slowly, and their body must not shake. Only their hands move. Like this—slowly slowly. Then this song is sung by the other women. All this is for the gods and ancestors. And the five women, without making a sound, keep slowly slowly moving this grinding stone in their hands while the other women sing this."

## SONG 47

### *Invocation*

Oh, Brahma resides in heaven.
Oh, I invite him.
Oh, I also invite his wife, Barmainiji.
Oh, Vishnuji resides in heaven.
I also invite him.
Oh, I also invite his wife, Mother Laxmi.
Oh, Shankarji resides in Kailaas.
I also invite him.
Oh, I also invite his wife, Gaura Parvati.
Oh, Bradinathji resides in Bradinath.
I also invite him.
Shri Ramji resides in Ayodhya.
I also invite him.
I also invite Mother Janki (Sita).
Oh, Tubarkanath resides in Hardwaar.
I also invite him.
Oh, Gorakhnath resides in Gorakhpur.
I also invite him.
I also invite his wife.
Oh, Mother Ganga resides on the Earth.
I also invite her.
Oh, I also invite her sister, Mother Sarajun.
Mother Kali resides in Kolkata.
I also invite her.
Oh, I also invite her devotee, Father Bhaironath.
Bhairug Baba resides in Ballia.
I also invite him.
I also invite his brother, Dardar Muni.
Balishwarnath resides in Ballia.
I also invite him.
I also invite his sister, Mother Haisati.

### SPOKEN

This is for the Gods.

One might be tempted to call this song a chant or an invocation. All text lines are sung to a single melody within a very narrow pitch range, hovering around the tonic. Gangajali does not take artistic freedom whatsoever in the singing. There are very few, if any, so-called ornaments or melismas. We can call it syllabic, a note for each syllable. The work of this song is so serious that I believe that what we might consider the more musical features of a song are left behind. There is no verse–chorus structure, no contrasting line sung at a higher pitch level, no euphonious combination of rhyming words, and absolutely no teasing. Gangajali here is inviting the gods, one by one, to attend the wedding. She invites them into the *kohabar* ritual chamber, and the ladies there trap them in a sacred painting that they draw.

I suppose one might say that all these songs sound the same, but that clearly is not true. This song is deadly serious, and the success of the wedding depends upon it. Other songs have joking and teasing. Some are sexy and fun. Some are extremely emotional. This song is formal. It must be sung correctly. It is for the gods. In this way, these songs and these singing women keep the world running.

"This is for the gods, as many as there are, they are invited," Gangajali explained. "I have invited all these since we are now going to arrange the wedding. All you gods, come and remain here. Oversee everything, and take care of our wedding. By singing this thereafter, all the gods are trapped inside the house. So the five married women remain seated and covered with the red cloth, and all the gods are trapped. After all, these gods should be kind to us. Protect us and don't disturb us here. Be alert."

"Trapped means to be shut in," Umesh said. "Invite them in and trap them there and say, 'I am closing you in.' Fire—Agni, rain, storm, scorpions, and snakes, whatever those who can be trouble while the wedding takes place from the beginning to the end, they are trapped in so there won't be trouble from any side."

"In the next song I am going to trap other forces," Gangajali explained. "The rain, big ants, small ants, scorpions, snakes, winnowing baskets, strainers, mortar and pestle, big pans, fire. Now I am going to trap all these forces so that they don't interrupt the wedding."

### SONG 48

Dust storm and rain and clouds,
You be kind to us.
You big ants, little ants, honey bees,
You be kind.
Oh, snakes, centipedes, wild scorpions,
You also be kind.
Oh, winnowing basket, strainer, mortar, and pestle,
You also be kind.
Oh, Father Bitan Baba seated under the eve,

You also be kind.
Oh, oven, you also be kind.
Oh, fire, rain, and pan,
You also be kind.

On the copy of our translation of this song, Umesh wrote at the top, "Real Bhojpuri!" And it certainly is. Listen carefully to all the words that end in *ba*, *wa*, and *yah*. These are the Bhojpuri endings for various nouns and verbs. So you can imagine that these soft sounds make Bhojpuri a very musical language. For example, in Hindi the word for winnowing basket is *sup*, while in Bhojpuri it is *supawa*. Similarly, the word for rain in Hindi, *pani*, is rendered in this Bhojpuri song text, *paniyan*, again a very soft flowing musical word.

Once again, the singer is performing an invocation, hence the very simple melody, the same as for the previous song—structure with a limited melodic range. Gangajali is appealing to the spirits of the winnowing basket, strainer, mortar and pestle, the snakes, centipedes, and wild scorpions, the big ants, little ants, and the honey bees—these spirits could all destroy the wedding, hence the singer's chantlike invocation. The usual verse–chorus structure is absent, and the song is sung at a very low part of Gangajali's tessitura, meaning her comfortable singing range. It does indeed feel odd to be using Italian musical terms to describe a Bhojpuri melody.

Gangajali explained the meaning of this song. "As many storms, rains may come as the wedding takes place, or as the *barat* is arriving, we seek protection. Whatever is taking place in the wedding tent must be protected. As it rains, as the dust storm rages, so everything breaks and goes here and there. Or the centipede bites anyone. Or the scorpion or snake bites anyone. This song requests them to get out of the house. Somebody's house might catch fire. Therefore, I pray for all these that you gods and forces remain in your place. Do not disturb anything. Thereafter the women take off the sheet from the five married ladies."

"Yes," Umesh replied. "For Ram Sagar's wedding, it happened at the same time when they pitched the tent, and everything was going well that night. They were ready for the *barat* to arrive, and then the dust storm suddenly came out of nowhere. Everything like the tent went upside down. The lights were destroyed, the tent was destroyed. The tables and chairs were sent up flying, everything went here and there. It was also drizzling. We were hiding ourselves under the tin shade so that our recording instruments and cameras would not get wet. People were all around his verandah. It is surprising, but usually it happens on the very day that we arrange the wedding. A similar thing happened at my niece Bina's wedding. There was a storm and then rain. The *barat* had arrived, and then when people were going to eat, all of the sudden the storm came, and it began drizzling. All the charm was destroyed, finished. I have seen several weddings like this. So the fear is always there for people, so women try to do something to keep these forces under control.

"Well, who can control nature? We can protect ourselves against some forces, but we cannot control nature. We could hire a big marriage hall, and then if a storm came, nothing would be disturbed. But people are slaves to nature.

"It is the belief of North Indian people that whatever they are doing to trap the deities and gods and ancestors, they do their job. If something goes wrong like a dust storm or snakebite, it means that either we made a big mistake or that we couldn't trap them well. It was not done properly. Perhaps there was some woman who had her period. She must not be there at the worshiping place because she is considered unholy. She can't go to the temple. She must stop worshiping for three days."

Gangajali's next song was something of a mystery.

### SONG 49

*Pittar-nyota*

What is the grinding stone made of?
What kind of *dal* is it?
Oh, pretty lady.
What is the grinding stone made of?
What kind of *dal* is it?
Oh, pretty lady.
The grinding stone goes "gasar-gasar."
Oh, pretty lady.
The *sil* is made out of stone.
The *dal* is of gram.
Oh, pretty lady.
The grinding stone goes "gasar-gasar."
Oh, pretty lady.
The grinding stone goes "gasar-gasar."
Oh, pretty lady.

### SPOKEN

So women grind. So all women are singing this:

What are these made of?

SUNG

The grinding stone is made out of stone,
The *dal* is made of gram,
Oh, pretty lady.
The grinding stone goes "gasar-gasar."
Oh, pretty lady. (abrupt cut)

Suddenly, Gangajali stopped singing. Apparently, the remainder of the song contained obscene words that she did not want the world to hear.

Once again, the tessitura of this song is very low in Gangajali's vocal range. The melody is quite simple and is repeated for every line of the text. The typical verse–chorus form is absent in this song. In fact, practically all the musical niceties are absent, I believe, because this song is a heartfelt prayer to the spirits to be kind, to let the wedding be successful. As a prayer, it does not require fancy tunes or lively rhythms. Indeed, they would not be suitable. You can also hear the lack of overt emotion in Gangajali's voice as she delivers each line in exactly the correct way, as in a rather somber ceremony.

"This is *pittar-nyota*," Umesh said. "An invitation to the ancestors. The song is very short. Is it possible that this is a *gali* that she did not want to finish. It includes some words that we do not usually say. One is *diljaniya,* which means 'heart lady.' We don't say this word. We've translated this as 'Oh, pretty lady,' but in fact I'm not sure what this word means."

INTERLUDE EIGHT

# MR. BURKE'S SPEECHES

THE SCENE SHIFTS TO FAWN COURT AND THE INNER THOUGHTS OF OUR young Lucy's heart and mind. She had disliked being told that as a governess she ought not to fall in love, in love in particular with Frank Greystock. Lady Fawn did not have that right, even though she treated Lucy well. But the truth of it was that though she had given her heart over to Frank Greystock, no such declamation had come from his side.

Elsewhere, in the House of Commons, the object of her heart's desire was making an argument on behalf of the Sawab of Mygawb.

*"Had not Frank belonged to the party that was out, and had not the resistance to the Sawab's claim come from the party that was in, Frank would not probably have cared much about the prince. We may be sure that he would not have troubled himself to read a line of that very dull and long pamphlet of which he had to make himself the master before he could venture to stir in the matter, had not the road of Opposition been open to him in that direction. But what exertion will not a politician make with the view of getting the point of his lance within the joints of his enemies' harness. Frank made his speech, and made it very well. It was just the case for a lawyer. . . . The Indian minister of the day, Lord Fawn's chief, had determined, after much anxious consideration, that it was his duty to resist the claim; and then, for resisting it he was attacked. Had he yielded to the claim, the attack would have been as venomous, and very probably would have come from the same quarter. . . . It is thus that the war is waged. Frank Greystock took up the Sawab's case, and would have drawn mingled tears and indignation from his hearers, had not his hearers all known the conditions of the contest. On neither side did the hearers care much for the Sawab's claims, but they felt that Greystock was making good his own claims to some future reward from his party. He was very hard on the*

*minister—and he was hard also upon Lord Fawn, stating the cruelty of Government ascendancy had never been put forward as a doctrine in plainer terms than those that had been used in 'another place' in reference to the wrongs of this poor ill-used native chieftain. This was very grievous to Lord Fawn, who had personally desired to favour the ill-used chieftain;—and harder again because he and Greystock were intimate with each other. He felt the thing keenly."*

At Fawn Court, the affairs of the Sawab were discussed by the sisters and by Lucy. "Miss Fawn had already told Lucy that her brother was very angry with Mr. Greystock. Now Lucy's sympathies were all with Frank and the Sawab. She had endeavoured, indeed, and partially succeeded in perverting the Under-Secretary," this being Lord Fawn himself. "There had been a time when the poor Sawab had been in favour at Fawn Court." Lucy fought for her Frank: "I think the prince is being used very ill—that he is being deprived of his own property, that he is kept out of his rights just because he is weak, and I am very glad that there is some one to speak up for him."

After a considerable exchange of words among Lord Fawn, Lady Fawn, the daughters, and Lucy, she, Lucy, rushed out of the room and collapsed in tears. When Lady Fawn found her sitting alone in the girl's schoolroom, in the dark and without a candle, she reminded Lucy that Frank Greystock, a member of Parliament, could never marry a governess. But through her tears, Lucy declared, "It is no use, Lady Fawn. I do love him, and I don't mean to try to give it up!' Lady Fawn stood silent for a moment, and then suggested that it would be better for them both to go to bed. During that minute she had been unable to decide what she had better say or do in the present emergency."

Umesh enjoyed this chapter about politics. He said, "At that time this is the social system in the British Empire to have a governess in the family who is not supposed to be married. They must be a maid for the rest of their life. They must be obedient and devoted to the family where they live. It shows that they are not mistreated. According to this story, Lady Fawn accepts her as a daughter. Although she wants her blood daughters to be married, she dismissed this adopted daughter from married social life. Lady Fawn says she loves Lucy, but she loves Lucy as a servant, not as her own daughter. Her daughters have rights, maybe in property, to get married. And Lucy can't have those. So when she says she loves her as a daughter, it is fake. She likes Lucy, she wants to keep Lucy at home because she is nice and kind and a good person by heart. Lady Fawn does not want to lose her. At the same time, she doesn't want Frank to marry with this maid.

"Before, the family was in favor of the Sawab as well as was Lucy. Lucy is not a part of the Parliament. Lord Fawn is given the job to go against the Sawab. But for Lucy, this doesn't change her mind because of the decision made by the boss of Lord Fawn. So she speaks in favor of the Sawab. She wants to go to what she feels is right. And the feeling of this family does not mean anything. They have to go with what Lord Fawn's boss says. So when Frank Greystock gets this job—he is already a barrister as well as an elected member of Parliament—she accepts this challenge to not let hurt the Sawab. The mother of the family is very much concerned that Lucy is in love with Frank, and she hates it because she is going to lose this nice woman, a real good devoted person. What person would like to lose such a person who is an outsider yet fully devoted to the family? At the same time, Lucy is turning against this family by telling that there should be justice in favor of the Sawab. Lady Fawn also has a kind of jealousy that who was a great friend of her son has turned against her son in Parliament, and Lucy is in love with him. His speech is published in the *Times*, the newspaper. Lucy reads it, every word. She is happy that the person to whom she loves is feeling the same way she does. She reads that Lord Fawn is criticized. The speech is against Lord Fawn. The Lord must have made a speech. Until he gets the words, how can Frank speak that the words are wrong? The Lord has already pleaded against the Sawab, that is why he gave a speech or made a paper against the Sawab. And this is discussed in the family. This discussion takes place in the family between Lady Fawn and Lucy and the Fawn daughters. And Lucy is very clear to say that it was great to speak in favor of Sawab. Lord Fawn and Lady Fawn just try to put her down. What does she know about the history of speeches made by great leaders? And this is the time that tears begin to drip down from Lucy because she does not know about the history of such speeches. Lucy runs upstairs from the room and misses Lady Fawn's sermon at nine o'clock. Then Lady Fawn goes upstairs, and she finds Lucy alone in the schoolroom in the dark. Then the conversation begins. Lucy did say sorry because downstairs she had spoken something tough in favor of the Sawab and against Lord Fawn. She might lose her job, and she has no place to go right now. Then Lady Fawn solaced her in several ways by telling, 'You are just like a daughter, we love you my dear dear little Lucy,' to make her inferior. Then Lucy says, 'I love Frank.' And Lady Fawn is speechless and considers this an emergency. She announced to go to bed, both herself and Lucy."

## THIRTY-EIGHT

# HELEN CONTRACTS TYPHOID

*At our apartment, Banaras, one September evening, 2007*

"It's diarrhea," I told Umesh. I was embarrassed. "It's just started. And, actually, I'm not feeling so well. Let me go take my temperature."

When I saw it was up a few degrees, I was alarmed. That was not a good sign. That particular combination of symptoms always meant something in India, something pretty bad, even fatal.

I recalled with fear the episode of falling so terribly ill in the interior town of Mau in 1990. During that episode, my urine had turned the color of black tea. Umesh didn't believe me until I brought some in a glass to show him. He was alarmed. After a great effort, he found a car to hire. His concept was to get me south to Ghazipur that night and then rent another car to get me west to Banaras the following morning. From there, we could fly to Delhi. I don't recall much about that trip. And from Delhi, he could put me on a flight home. Never had I felt so far from safe medical care. I do remember that, at every stop, every night, Umesh called for the doctor. I would be examined and given a handful of pills to take, which I did. In the morning in Ghazipur, I work up with a terrible rash. I'm allergic to penicillin, and most likely that had been one of those pills. I didn't care in the least. I felt so sick.

Umesh did save me, got me to Delhi, and we, for the first time ever, took our two rooms in a *three-star* hotel with air conditioning. The doctor came to me every day and also a beautiful young Christian nurse from Kerala. They took blood.

It was not hepatitis—in fact there was no diagnosis whatsoever. Obviously, my liver was inflamed, but the cause was unknown. The doctor threatened to forbid me from flying home I was so sick. But Umesh managed to get me on a flight, and I left India, still very ill. He did the right thing. He saved me. Even after treatment in the United States, we never discovered what the illness was. That I had been very sick, there was no doubt. That I did not have hepatitis, there was also no doubt. That I began to recover slowly was a great relief.

Now, in 2007, these memories, vague though they were, alarmed me. Umesh got me into a taxi, and we rushed over to the large Heritage Hospital, near the Banaras Hindu University. It was not far from our apartment.

I was shown into the office of the top doctor on duty, ahead of many dozens of Indians waiting for help on the floor of the lobby. It was unfair. I was *white.*

I was taken to a private room. It had a hospital bed for me and a raised platform for my family member to sleep on. This would be Umesh. No patient checks into an Indian hospital alone. A family member is needed to bring meals and to tend to many other matters—buying the medicine, keeping track of the medicine schedule, making notes about what the doctor says, helping the patient to the bathroom. Even a toothbrush, a facecloth, some light reading. Umesh made all this possible. As in the small district towns in 1990, the doctor on call gave me a handful of pills and got me on an IV drip immediately. They drew blood.

"It's typhoid," the doctor announced in the morning. "You'll need to go on a course of strong antibiotics."

"But I'm allergic to most antibiotics," I replied, and I listed the ones I could recall: penicillin, erythromycin, tetracycline, sulfa, and so on.

"Not to worry," the doctor said. "We have newer antibiotics that will cure this." And, indeed, they did.

It was curious because I had taken typhoid prophylaxis in the form of pills about three years prior. They must have just worn off. Looking back, the case was mild—horrible but mild—so they may have still been somewhat effective.

In Indian hospitals, everybody is hooked to an IV, and medicines are administrated that way. In my case it was necessary to tackle this quickly and directly. The combination of diarrhea and IV is not an easy one to manage. I took Imodium around the clock but to no effect. I was surprised, for this staple of the India traveler's first aid kit had never failed me before. Umesh helped me to the bathroom and stood with his back turned, holding up my IV.

Umesh served me night and day. But there was a bright side for him, for this special private room had a flat-screen TV. We watched old English movies, mainly from the 1980s. One after the other, we watched them. When nothing good was on, Umesh read chapters from his Danielle Steele book for me. He brought me clean, safe food from outside. Many street vendors worked outside the hospital, for all the patients needed to be fed. Umesh found the best, a *masala dosa* stand that was very crowded. He even managed to get ones for me without chilies.

*Masala dosa* is a delicious South Indian food that has become very popular in North India. They consist of a potato and pea mixture flavored with onions and garlic and spices stuffed inside a freshly fried and extremely thin crispy rice pancake. The pancake, which was over a foot in diameter, was folded in half to contain the filling. They were fresh and delicious. Umesh brought me Cokes and orange soda to drink and handmade Indian sweets as a treat. He kept an eye on our apartment but always spent the night in my room to take care of me.

I began to wonder how friends who don't travel with an Indian colleague ever managed.

So with this wonderful, resourceful man taking charge of my care, and with the expert medical care I received at Heritage Hospital (what a surprise for me), I recovered. If you find yourself in an Indian hospital, it is not the end, especially if you are white. More on this color prejudice below, when the time comes for me to take Umesh to the same hospital.

THIRTY-NINE

# GETTING THE *SIRI* AT THE HOME OF THE POTTER

*At the Sarang Hotel, Ballia, July 1989*

"After singing this last song in the *kohabar*, all these people get up," Gangajali said. "Then they go out for the next ritual. They will go to fetch the *siri* clay pot. This is a special ceremony performed on the boy's side. The women go to the house of the potter to perform this ritual, for the *siri* is made out of clay. The *siri* ritual is performed in this area, in Ballia district and in some other areas. So women are gathered to go to the potter with a basket containing a yellow sari, rice, flour in a leaf dish, *dal*, rupees, paisa, and mustard oil. They take these things to the home of the potter and gather around the potter's wheel. As they are going along the way, they sing songs from when they depart until they arrive. Here is one such song."

SONG 50

*Matikor*

Oh cuckoo, in what forest do you live?
In what forest do you go?
At which door will you ask how are you?

Go and ask the news.
The cuckoo lives in the forest of Nand,
She goes to Brindavan.
The cuckoo goes to the door of Anrudha Baba.
She goes to ask the news.
The cuckoo goes to the door of Faute Baba.
She goes to ask the news.
Black cuckoo, oh black cuckoo,
Your beak is green.
Cuckoo, in what forest do you live?
In what forest do you go?
Cuckoo, at whose door do you ask?
Go to ask the news.
The cuckoo lives in the forest of Nand,
And goes to Brindavan.
Cuckoo, at the door of the ancestors, ask the news.
Cuckoo, at the door of the ancestors, ask the news.
Cuckoo, in what forest do you live?
In what forest do you go?
Cuckoo, at whose door do you ask?
Go to ask the news.
The cuckoo lives in the forest of Nand,
And goes to Brindavan.
The cuckoo goes to the door of the goddesses,
Goes to ask the news.
The cuckoo goes to the door of the gods,
Goes to ask the news.
Black cuckoo, oh black cuckoo,
Your beak is green.
The cuckoo sings sweet songs.

The tune for this song is so similar to tune number one from Trinidad that it is tempting to say they are the same. Well, they are—but not quite. Most of the phrases here are sung in the lower part of Gangajali's tessitura. Phrase B moves to the upper part of the octave, lending spirit and liveliness to the presentation.

Similar tunes here and there. When are two songs "the same" songs? When they share what is basically the same text? When they share the same melody? When they share neither text nor tune, but the essential story of the song is the same?

Do songs of a particular genre all have the same tunes? In our book here, we have found that they do not. For example, each *tilak* melody is different than the others and so on—for *sagun*, *gali*, *matikor*, *chumawan*, and more. Scholars have argued these points for over a century, beginning with the notion of Sir George Grierson (1886), eminent linguist, that songs in one genre all had the same tunes. Scholars following on after, lacking his linguistic expertise, have both maintained and disclaimed this particular idea about tunes. In the late 1980s and early 1990s, Wadley and also Marcus found tunes within a genre to be the same, or—and I am guessing here—at least similar. In 1967, an Indian ethnomusicologist, Trilochan Pande, found that Bhojpuri *sohar*s all had the same tunes, even if the words had to be run together or elongated to suit this particular tune. In 1964, the linguist John Gumperz found that the tunes (which he called ragas) were few and that they generally corresponded to specific genres. This entire discussion has been followed up in 2000 by the anthropologist Edward O. Henry, who discussed the above scholars and more and went on to analyze many tunes and texts that he had collected in the Bhojpuri region.

I believe that this discussion among scholars will continue as the years pass, as tunes are forgotten and exciting new filmi tunes are incorporated into the rural repertory. Some singers, such as Gangajali, compose their own tunes, further enriching any sort of scholarly analysis.

"So this is the song of the cuckoo," Gangajali explained. "At the time of going to the home of the potter, this song is sung. The cuckoo that says 'koo koo' at the tree branch, this song is of the same cuckoo. This song is also sung along the way when the women go to dig soil for the *matikor* ritual. So for both occasions, this song is sung."

"What is the *siri*?" I asked.

"It is round, but it is not a pot," Gangajali explained. "The potter takes a lump of clay on his wheel and makes the form of a small man and a small ladder. Then he pokes barley seeds into these forms on all sides. We call the man Balbhaddar. He is a kind of god that the potter makes and gives to the women. So two women take clay dishes in their hands. One has Balbhaddar and the ladder placed inside it, and the other serves as the lid. They turn the lid upside down on the dish, hiding Balbhaddar and the ladder inside, and then the two dishes are sealed together all around. Then the women prepare to return home. The yellow sari for the bride is held aloft by one woman in the front and one in the back, and the women carrying the *siri* walk in the shade of it. This sari is the first sari the bride will put on to get married. If a person has money, they have a sari decorated with special threads. It may have a moonlight *gota* shining border of silver or gold embroidery. If they are poor people, they use only a simple yellow sari."

"These traditions are very old," Umesh said, "but they keep changing too. I believe that people did not want to abandon their ancient beliefs, for example, the belief in a small clay man named Balbhaddar, that existed in the time from before. So many things in the wedding are not done by the priest. Actually, the priest plays a small role. Other customs are important. So they kept these ancient symbols and incorporate them in their ceremonies even to this day.

"Often our festivals and rituals incorporate such symbols. For example, on Janamastami women draw Krishna playing flute on the hood of a cobra. They use paint made out of some carbon and rice powder and draw on the wall. For Karava Chauth they draw a big picture on the wall with the sun, moon, a man and women, household things. These are all symbols. We do this to control nature, and we do this because we have always done this from ancient times. So for these Bhojpuri people, the wedding cannot take place without the clay man and the clay ladder. They have deep meaning."

"Before leaving the potter's house, women make offerings," said Gangajali. "According to their financial situation, they might offer something fancy and expensive like ornaments, a blouse, *lahanga*, ₹100 or ₹150, anything. But poor people do not offer such things. Rich and poor, all perform this ritual. After offering, the potter returns the things into the hands of the women. Then the women return from there after taking all those things. But *gali* are sung there for the potter at the time of receiving the *siri*."

### SONG 51

*Gali*

Potter lady, come out in the courtyard.
Oh potter lady, come out in the courtyard.
Your brother who is your husband has come.
Your anklets are jingling.
Your brother who is your husband has come.
Your anklets are jingling.
Oh potter lady, come out in the courtyard.
Oh potter lady, come out.
Your brother who is your husband has come.
Your anklets are jingling.
Oh, I take you in the courtyard.
Oh, I take you in the courtyard.
I greet your brother at the door.
Your anklets are jingling.
I greet your brother at the door.
Your anklets are jingling.
Greet your brother.
The potter lady sits on a high stool.
The potter lady sits on a high stool.
And she turns upside down.
Your anklets are jingling.

Oh, she turns upside down.
Your anklets are jingling
Oh, her brother got inside from outside.
Oh, her brother got inside from outside.
He lifts her up in his lap.
Your anklets are jingling.
He lifts her up in his lap.
Your anklets are jingling.
Oh, if a girl is born, *kanyadan* will be given.
If a girl is born, *kanyadan* will be given.
And happy songs for a son.
Your anklets are jingling.
Oh, play happy songs for the son.
Your anklets are jingling.
Oh, potter lady, come out in the courtyard.
Oh, potter lady, come out in the courtyard.
Your brother who is your husband has come.
Your anklets are jingling.

What a cheerful, uptempo song. And sure enough, it is a little *gali*, or, since it is rather long, a mildly abusive *gali*. Not spicy, just sweet. Jingling anklets, happy songs for the son, a potter lady wife turned upside down. On a high stool on her brother's lap! At least while this cheerful and ridiculous song is being sung, the stress of the wedding ceremony is relieved.

"So the ladies are singing for the potter lady, asking her to come out of the house," Gangajali said. "Look, your brother has arrived. So in the place of the husband, the brother stood there. The brother has changed into a husband in this *gali*. She cannot come out. So she is seated on a stool. Then she falls down. The brother goes and lifts her up. Then the women say that if a daughter is born, you will give *kanyadan*. And if a son is born by your brother, then joyful songs will be played. This is a *gali*, a song of loving abuse."

"This is a *gali*," Umesh said. "If women sing *gali*, although they are very rough, it does not hurt anyone, and people just say it is women, and they laugh at these songs. People may feel shy or embarrassed, but they never get hurt by these *gali*. Men don't laugh but just enjoy them, but the children burst into laughter. So here the women go the potter's house to get *siri* in a group while singing on the way. When they reach at the door of the potter, they sing this *gali*. 'Oh lady potter, come out. Your brother who is your husband has arrived.' Then they sing a kind of chorus, 'your anklets are jingling, your anklets are jingling.' So this is a part of the jajmani system to get every caste involved in the wedding. Finally, they sing when you get the child, if it is a girl, give *kanyadan*, and if a boy is born, sing happy songs.

"Actually, these women go mostly to those people who work for them, and this is a very good example of the jajmani system, that it is not important that small people need big people, but here you can see the big people need the small people very much. They are dependent on them. And a very important point: they go to ask for *suhhag* from these people, which means the happiness of married life. *Suhagin* is the happily married wife. And the woman is grateful to the Lord if her husband is living. This is a great blessing from the Lord. And who offers them, the grain parcher, potter, washerman, oil presser, and other people. They go singing happily, seeking *suhhag* for their daughter."

"On the walk home, women will sing happy songs, *jhumar* all the way," Gangajali said. "Whether the way is finished in one song or a hundred songs, until they arrive at home, they will sing. Here is a *jhumar* of Ram and Sita."

### SONG 52

*Jhumar*

Glancing Ram, glancing Ram,
Glancing at Sita.
Oh, Ram is glancing,
Glancing at Mother Sita.
Oh, Ram is glancing,
Glancing Ram, oh glancing Ram,
Glancing at Janki (Sita).
Ram is glancing.
Mother Sita goes to pluck flowers.
On the way Raghuraiya ran into her.
Oh, Ram is glancing,
Glancing at Sita.
Oh, Ram is glancing,
Glancing at Sita.
Oh, Sita also glanced,
And their eyes became one.
Sita and Ram's eyes became one.
He didn't blink.
Oh, Ram is glancing.
She didn't blink.
Oh, Ram is glancing,
Glancing at Sita.

Oh, Ram is glancing,
Glancing at Janki.
Oh, Ram is glancing.
Janki goes to worship Gauri.
Janki goes to worship Gauri.
On the way Raghuraiya ran into her.
Oh, Ram is glancing.
On the way Raghuraiya ran into her.
Oh, Ram is glancing.
Sunainan asks the news about Sita.
Sunainan asks the news about Sita.
How did you get so late?
Oh, Ram is glancing.
How did you get so late?
Oh, Ram is glancing,
Glancing at Sita.
Oh, Ram is glancing,
Glancing at Sita.
Mother, it became noon while I was plucking flowers.
Mother, it became noon while I was plucking flowers.
Midnight passed while I was worshiping.
Midnight passed while I was worshiping.
Oh, Ram is glancing,
Glancing at Sita.
Oh, Ram is glancing,
Glancing at Sita.

This lilting song is driven by the triplets that form its compound rhythm. Best compared to Western $\frac{6}{8}$ rhythm, this *git* emphasizes a repetition of long-short, long-short, long-short, long—lah-li, lah-li, lah-li, lah. Each triplet constitutes one beat, and the rhythm is constructed of two triplets, hence duple time. So altogether, duple time subdivided by triplets matches $\frac{6}{8}$ time. It's hard not to feel cheerful as you listen here.

Clearly, Gangajali is the leader, and you can hear Sashi leaning on her as she follows. This strong singer with her clear, loud confidence as weak singers lean is a pattern that you hear through the Bhojpuri region and doubtless throughout India and perhaps across the world. It is natural for a group of women to have one or two strong singers and other weaker singers to pick up the line or sing the chorus. The constant repetition helps the weaker singers learn the song. The chorus gives the strong singer a chance to rest a bit.

"Janki is going to pluck flowers in the flower garden," Gangajali explained. "And Ram is also going to pluck flowers. And both of them meet each other in the flower garden. And Mother Sita is so beautiful that in each hair of her body *kamdev* is there. There is such a kind of beauty in Mother Janki. No devi is more beautiful than she. Ram falls in love with such beauty. He stood still as a statue, and Mother's gaze fell. But he didn't blink. He remained staring, and between both of them, they didn't realize when the day passed and night fell.

"Midnight came. When they come to their senses, both of them went to their homes. But when she went home, Mother Sunayana scolds her. 'Why did you come so late, young daughter? You went out for flowers in the flower garden and midnight passed. What were you doing there? To whose house did you go?' So she replied, 'Mother, by plucking flowers all the day passed in the flower garden. And midnight passed while I was worshiping Durga and Gauri. So I got late.'"

"This is from the Ramayan composed by Tulsidas," Umesh explained. "This can be from other books also. This is the time when Ram is in Janakpur, and he goes to get married. And Sitaji goes to worship Gauri. This is the first time Ram and Sita meet each other. When they meet, they cannot move, they do not blink their eyes. Ram keeps an eye on Sita wherever she goes. Ram goes to pluck flowers for his guru for worship. And they meet each other in that flower garden where Gauri's temple is located. This also concerns the social system. The mother asks Sita, 'Why were you late?' Her role is to keep an eye on Sita. Sita does not tell her mother that she met Ram in this song. She hides this fact."

FORTY

# "MY HUSBAND IS THE INSPECTOR OF POLICE"

*The day continues at the Sarang Hotel, Ballia, July 1989*

The heat in the small hotel room was unbearable. We all decided to take a break, stop the Stellavox, and turn on the fan.

Then Gangajali sang another song. Fan off. Stellavox on.

### SONG 53

*Gali*

By sleeping, by sleeping,
By sleeping, by sleeping.
Destroyed life, by sleeping, by sleeping.
So, by sleeping, by sleeping,
Destroyed life, by sleeping, by sleeping.
So, by sleeping, by sleeping,
Son, by sleeping, by sleeping,
Destroyed life by sleeping.
So, by sleeping, by sleeping,
Destroyed life by sleeping.
He does not obey his parents, his parents.
He does not obey his parents.
He does not obey his parents.

You kept swaying.
Son, you are going along the way,
Swaying, swaying (wasting time).
Destroyed life by sleeping, by sleeping.
Destroyed life by sleeping, by sleeping.
Son, by sleeping, by sleeping,
You destroyed life.
By sleeping, by sleeping,
You destroyed life.
Son, by sleeping, by sleeping,
You destroyed life.
He does not obey his brother and *bhauji*.
Oh son, you do not obey your mother, do not obey.
Oh son, you do not obey your mother and *bhauji*, do not obey.
Goes around with friends,
Swaying, swaying (happily?).
Son, you give away wealth to your friends,
Foolishly, foolishly.
Destroyed life by sleeping, by sleeping.
Son, by sleeping, by sleeping.
Destroyed life by sleeping, by sleeping, destroyed life.
Does not give away a single paisa to a beggar.
Does not give away a single paisa to a beggar.
You drink liquor,
Swaying, swaying (happily?),
Son, you drink liquor.
Swaying, swaying.
Destroyed life by sleeping, by sleeping.
Destroyed life by sleeping, by sleeping.
Life . . .
By sleeping, by sleeping,
Son, by sleeping, by sleeping.
Destroyed life by sleeping, by sleeping.
Destroyed life.

A lovely easy swinging duple melody, again based on subdivisions of three ($\frac{6}{8}$). The distinctive feature is the constant repetition of the words, "*sooii-sooii . . . sooii-sooii*" (by sleeping, by sleeping—wasting time by being lazy, by sleeping).

This song has two main phrases that alternate throughout the song. As we have seen before, phrase A is sung to the lower notes of the octave and phrase B to the upper notes of the octave, forming a very basic *sthayi–antara* structure. The song begins and ends with phrase A.

"So the women are still going on the way. They haven't reached home yet. Then they sing one more song. This is a *bhabi–dewar* song," Gangajali was explaining.

"The next song has this meaning. The *bhauji* eats rice. She does not eat vegetables. She does not eat dal. She was eating rice and thin yogurt in her house. That watery yogurt and rice chokes her. So she says to him, 'Oh *dewarji*, have me drink a little water quickly. Thin yogurt and rice have choked me.' So the *dewar* quickly has her drink water. But her teeth shine like pearls. So while having her drink water, he fell in love with her. So she says, 'Why have you fallen in love with me?' After drinking water, she went to her bed and slept. But the *dewar* fell in love, so he opens the door and gets inside the room. 'Oh *bhauji*, are you awake or asleep?' *Bhauji* wakes up and looks at the *dewar*. She knew that the cheating *dewar* would surely come. She awakens, and she says, 'Oh *dewarji*, why are you peeping? I want to assure you that your brother, my husband, works in the court. He is a police inspector. He is a police deputy. He will tie you up and send you to prison. Send you behind bars. What do you know? He will string you up.' Then he replies, 'Oh *bhauji*, you be quiet. How can you tie me up? Oh, I have earned so much money. I will spend so much money in the court or district town that he will release me. Nobody can do anything to me.'"

### SONG 54

#### *Gali*

I ate leftover rice with watery yogurt.
I ate leftover rice with watery yogurt.
Oh *dewar*, don't break your heart.
Have her drink water.
Do not break your heart.
While I was drinking water, my teeth were shining.
While I was drinking water, my teeth were shining.
My teeth shine like diamonds and pearls.
My teeth shine like diamonds and pearls.
The *dewar* falls in love.
My teeth shine like diamonds and pearls.
The *dewar* falls in love.
My teeth shine like diamonds and pearls.
The *dewar* falls in love.
I kept sleeping in the Bhusahul's house,
By using the thatched screen.
I kept sleeping in the Bhusahul's house,
By using the thatched screen.
From the other side of the thatched screen,
The *dewar* is giving signals.
From the other side of the thatched screen,

The *dewar* is giving signals.
Oh *dewar*, why are you giving signals?
Oh *dewar*, why are you giving signals?
My sweetheart is employed by the court.
I will have you jailed.
My sweetheart is employed by the court.
I will have you jailed.
I will have you jailed, *dewar*.
I will have you strung up.
I will have you jailed, *dewar*.
I will have you strung up.
My husband is the inspector of police.
I will have you jailed.
My husband is the inspector of police.
I will have you jailed.
Oh *bhauji*, how can you send me behind bars?
Oh *bhauji*, how can you send me behind bars?
*Bhauji*, I will give away buried rupees.
*Bhauji*, I will give away buried rupees.
*Bhauji*, I will give away buried rupees.

"This is a song of *dewar–bhabi* relations," Umesh explained. "A jokey song. The *bhabi* is asking her *dewar* don't break your heart. Give me water and quench your thirst."

Bhojpuri songs are classified according to the time they are sung—the time of the year they are sung or by the specific ritual for which they are sung. This *gali* could be sung on several different occasions. Songs sung during the construction of the wedding tent (*marawa*) are called wedding tent songs (*marawa git*). Songs for the ritual of the application of vermillion powder (*sindur dan*) are called *sindur dan git*. Certain songs are categorized by the time of year they are sung. *Kajali* are sung during the monsoon. *Phagua* are sung during February. Other categories also come into play. Songs can be categorized, in another example, as *bhajans*, which can be further broken up into *devi git, nirgun bhajan*, *Hanuman bhajan*, and so forth.

Gangajali explained, "This is a joking kind of song that can be sung any time. It is a *jhumar* type. This song is sung on happy occasions."

Gangajali continued her narration of the events of the Bhojpuri wedding. "So the women arrive home with the *siri*. And where the *kohabar* is made, they carry this *siri* and place it there. After placing it, *sahana* will be sung. Thereafter more *sahana* and *jhumar* will also be sung. As much as they like, they may sing, play instruments, dance, and jump with happiness."

"What is the difference between *sahana* and *jhumar*?" I asked.

"There is a difference," Gangajali said. "*Jhumar* is sung at every place at the time of dancing and singing. *Jhumar* can be of the bridegroom and bride.

Everywhere they are sung. They are sung for joking fun. But *sahana* are sung only at the time of the wedding. *Sahana* will be sung for the bridegroom and bride at wedding time.

"Here is a *sahana* that is sung following the *siri* ritual."

### SONG 55

#### *Sahana*

Oh gardener lady, put the henna full of color on my Radhe.
Oh gardener lady, put the henna full of color on my Radhe.
Oh gardener lady, put the henna full of color on my Radhe.
Where is the henna planted?
Where is the henna planted?
Oh gardener lady, where are the flowers planted for my Radhe?
Oh gardener lady, where are the flowers planted for my Radhe?
Oh gardener lady, put the henna full of color on my Radhe.
Oh gardener lady, I will have the henna planted in the lower field.
Oh gardener lady, I will have the henna planted in the lower field.
Oh gardener lady, I will have the pomegranate flower planted in the upper field for my Radhe.
Oh gardener lady, I will have the pomegranate flower planted in the upper field for my Radhe.
Gardener lady, put the henna full of color on my Radhe.
Gardener lady, put the henna full of color on my Radhe.
Gardener lady, with what will I irrigate the henna?
Gardener lady, with what will I irrigate the pomegranate flower for my Radhe?
Gardener lady, with what will I irrigate the pomegranate flower for my Radhe?
Gardener lady, put the henna full of color on my Radhe.
Gardener lady, I will irrigate the henna with water.
Gardener lady, I will irrigate the henna with water.
Oh gardener lady, I will irrigate the pomegranate flower with milk for my Radhe.
Oh gardener lady, I will irrigate the pomegranate flower with milk for my Radhe.
Gardener lady, put the henna full of color on my Radhe.
Gardener lady, put the henna full of color on my Radhe.
Oh, what is the knife made of with which I cut the henna?
Oh, what is the knife made of with which I cut the henna?
Oh, what is the pomegranate flower made of?
Oh gardener lady, for my Radhe.
Oh, what is the pomegranate flower made of?

Oh gardener lady, for my Radhe.
Oh gardener lady, put the henna full of color on my Radhe.
Oh, I cut the henna with the silver knife.
Oh, I cut the henna with the silver knife.
Oh, I cut the pomegranate flower with the golden knife.
Oh gardener lady, for my Radhe.
Oh, I cut the pomegranate flower with the golden knife.
Gardener lady, for my Radhe.
Oh gardener lady, put the henna full of color on my Radhe.
Oh, I grind the henna very firmly.
Oh, I grind the henna very firmly.
Pick up the *rerawa* leaf.
Gardener lady, for my Radhe.
Pick up the *rerawa* leaf.
Gardener lady, for my Radhe.
Oh gardener lady, put the henna full of color on my Radhe.
I fully decorate the bride's hands.
I fully decorate the bride's hands.
Oh, I decorate the bridegroom's pinky.
Gardener lady, for my Radhe.
Oh, I decorate the bridegroom's pinky.
Gardener lady, for my Radhe.
Oh gardener lady, put the henna full of color on my Radhe.

"In this *sahana*, the gardener lady is being called on for help to bring the henna for the bride," Gangajali explained. "For example, singers explain the role of the oil presser in the wedding. The oil presser's wife brings the oil for us to mix with the turmeric. We use this to rub on the bride and groom. 'Oil presser lady (*telin*), you are very talented.' The barber is also very important. So is the barber's wife. Before the wedding the barber must come to cut the hair, also to cut the nails. During the wedding the barber's wife will bring the turmeric. She will put the turmeric on the people. Also, she will perform the ceremony to take off the evil eye. She puts the auspicious red paste on the feet of the groom."

As the years pass, and villagers emigrate to large cities, it is more and more difficult to find such caste specialists. Still, the songs mention them—but for how long?

"This is a song about the henna," Umesh explained. "And it explains about Radhe, Krishna's lover. This song is composed for Radhe to have the henna put on by the gardener lady. It is explaining where to plant the henna and where pomegranate flowers are planted. So this is a description of nature and its use for beautifying a woman, and henna is also part of nature because it is a plant, and its leaves have color. Natural and also related to agricultural issues.

"The questions are asked. How to plant it? How to irrigate it? So she concludes the song with this, that the bride is painted with hands full of henna, and the groom only one finger, the pinky. Why are they relating these pomegranate flowers with the henna? Because the henna changes into the color of the pomegranate—red. So they are put together in this song."

"That was a *sahana*, whereas here is an example of a religious *jhumar*," Gangajali said.

### SONG 56

*Jhumar*

The fair takes place in Janakpur.
In my heart, I want to see it.
The fair takes place in Janakpur.
In my heart, I want to see it.
I want to see it.
Oh, I want to see it.
Oh, I want to see it.
The fair takes place in Janakpur.
In my heart, I want to see it.
The fair takes place in Janakpur.
In my heart, I want to see it.
King Janak arranges a *swayamvar.*
King Janak arranges a *swayamvar.*
He has placed a heavy bow and arrow.
In my heart, I want to see it.
He has placed a heavy bow and arrow.
In my heart, I want to see it.
The fair takes place in Janakpur.
In my heart, I want to see it.
The fair takes place in Janakpur.
In my heart, I want to see it.
All the kings arrived from far far away.
All the kings arrived from far far away.
Kings arrived, emperors arrived.
Kings arrived, emperors arrived.
The fair takes place in Janakpur.
In my heart, I want to see it.
The fair takes place in Janakpur.
In my heart, I want to see it.
Rishis, gods, munis,

Rawan also arrived.
Rishis, gods, munis,
Rawan also arrived.
They could not move the bow a single inch.
In my heart, I want to see it.
They could not move the bow a single inch.
In my heart, I want to see it.
The fair takes place in Janakpur,
In my heart, I want to see it.
The fair takes place in Janakpur,
In my heart, I want to see it.
The sadhu arrived with a gray gray beard.
The sadhu arrived with a gray gray beard.
He brought two disciples with him.
In my heart, I want to see it.
He brought two disciples with him.
In my heart, I want to see it.
The fair takes place in Janakpur.
In my heart, I want to see it.
The fair takes place in Janakpur.
In my heart, I want to see it.
Oh, Lakhan pushes the ground down.
Oh, Lakhan pushes the ground down.
Ram breaks (the bow) into nine pieces.
In my heart, I want to see it.
Ram breaks (the bow) into nine pieces.
In my heart, I want to see it.
The fair takes place in Janakpur.
In my heart, I want to see it.
Sita moves holding the victory garland.
Mother (Sita) came out holding the victory garland.
Sitaji came out holding the victory garland.
Sitaji came out holding the victory garland,
Along with two or four girlfriends.
In my heart, I want to see it.
Along with two or four girlfriends.
In my heart, I want to see it.
Along with two or four girlfriends.
In my heart, I want to see it.
The fair takes place in Janakpur.
In my heart, I want to see it.
She places the victory garland around Raghubar's neck.
She places the victory garland around Raghubar's neck.
The gods sprinkle flowers.

In my heart, I want to see it.
The gods cry, "Victory, victory."
In my heart, I want to see it.
The fair takes place in Janakpur.
In my heart, I want to see it.
Mother has to offer the victory garland.
Mother has to offer the victory garland.
Sita becomes his wife.
In my heart, I want to see it.
Sita becomes his wife.
In my heart, I want to see it.
The fair takes place in Janakpur.
In my heart, I want to see it.
I want to see it.
Oh, I want to see it.
I want to see it.
Oh, I want to see it.
In my heart, I want to see it.
The fair takes place in Janakpur.
In my heart, I want to see it.

This lilting song, with an enthusiastic chorus about the fair in Janakpur, suggests something like the Western $\frac{6}{8}$ time signature. But there are so many words and so many syllables that it would seem that the 6 little beats may be 7 or may be 5 depending on the verse and the number of syllables in the words. For sure the song is syllabic, with one short note for each quickly pronounced syllable, and altogether the impression is of rushing forward. To Western ears this song sounds happy because mainly it is in the major mode.

This story is of immense importance in Hinduism. It is a story that has been told and retold in religious texts, songs, dramas, and in village storytelling. All the unmarried kings and princes gather at the court of King Janak for a *swayamvar*, a ceremony for Sita (Janki) to select her husband. A challenging task, lifting the ancient mighty bow of Shiva, was set for each prince, as Gangajali tells, and her explanation gives even more information about this story than the song itself. The victor is Lord Ram, and Sita places the victory garland around his neck, choosing him as her husband.

Gangajali explained this happy song. "So Janakji, King Janak, arranged a *swayamvar* (assembly of kings) for Janki. And placed a very heavy bow. Whichever king could break the bow, Sita would be married to him. Kings from many different countries, the princes of the entire Earth, even Rawan, arrived. The gods also came. But nobody could move the bow or even shake it. To break it seemed impossible. It did not move even an inch. And one of the rishis arrived via Bagasar after making Aahilya out of stone and killing Tarika. Vishwamitrji arrives with both princes, Ram and Lakhan, from Ayodhya to Janakpur. Now it is told there to the Lord that everybody got tired now. You people go.

Laximanji is out of the form of a snake. He takes the load of the Earth. In other incarnations God Snake (Sheshh Naag) is taking the load of the Earth. Vishnu Bhagwan rests on the snake. So this is the same avatar that became Laxman. So Laxmanji pushed the Earth down with his foot. If Ram will break the bow, the Earth will turn upside-down. So it will be *paralaya*, the never-ending water world. Therefore, Laxmanji pushed the Earth down with his toe so the Earth would not shake. Nobody could move the bow a single inch, and Ram broke it into nine pieces. And then Mother Janki comes out with her girlfriends, holding a victory garland. She turns and places the garland around his neck. The gods get happy in the world of the gods. It rains flowers from above. She gets married to him. Mother Janki becomes his wife and queen.

"Yes, yes, this is a *jhumar*. This song is also for God. We only sing it on happy occasions. Whenever we people dance, we sing this song. We sit down and play musical instruments to sing it. We also sing it on the way. We sing it everywhere."

"This song gives a lovely explanation of the marriage of Ram and Sita, how it was held and why it was held," Umesh explained. "It was not an ordinary marriage. Janakpur is the kingdom where King Janak rules. He has a daughter Sita. So he called all the kings of the world at that time and they came to participate in the *swayamvar*. The *swayamvar* is an assembly of kings in which the bride has the right to choose a husband for herself. In this case it is slightly different. Here the promise was made by Janak that whoever could lift the very old bow of Lord Shiva, only he would be able to get married with Sita. All the other kings had a chance to test the bow, to lift it. And none of the kings could even move it slightly, even the distance of a sesame seed, as we say in Hindi. King Dasarath's sons were also invited by Janak, and they reached in the assembly with their guru, Vishwamitra. So Ram had a chance at last to lift it up. This bow was so heavy that if somebody lifted it up, the Earth would tremble. This point is not mentioned in the song. So his brother Laxman was there, whom we know as an avatar of Sheshh Naag, who is holding the Earth on his hood. So Laxman himself pushed the Earth down with his toe, and it was made easier for Ram to lift the bow and not let tremble the Earth. When he lifted up the bow, it was so old that it broke into three parts. Some accounts mention nine parts, as in this song. Other accounts mention three parts."

## INTERLUDE NINE

# THE CONQUERING HERO COMES

ON THURSDAY EVENING, ONLY THE UNANTICIPATED ARRIVAL OF LADY Linlithgow had interrupted Frank's purpose to ask Lizzie to be his wife. And he had promised to return "on the morrow." But on that Friday, he never arrived.

*"She had been quite sure that the offer was about to be made when that odious old harridan had come in and disturbed everything. Indeed, the offer had been all but made. She had felt the premonitory flutter, had asked herself the important question—and had answered it. She had told herself that the thing would do. Frank was not the exact hero that her fancy had painted—but he was sufficiently heroic. Everybody said that he would work his way up to the top of the tree, and become a rich man. At any rate she had resolved; and then Lady Linlithgow had come in! Surely he would come on the Sunday."*

Frank did not come on the Sunday, but on that day, at four o'clock, after his weekly family visit in Richmond, Lord Fawn called. He found Lizzie alone, Lizzie having dismissed the unfortunate Miss Macnulty on three consecutive days.

*"'My dear,' she would say, 'the best friends in the world shouldn't always be together; should they? Wouldn't you like to go to the Horticultural?' Then Miss Macnulty would go to the Horticultural—or else into her own bedroom."*

Lord Fawn took time to collect his thoughts. He wished to explain his circumstances, his financial circumstances, clearly to Lizzie.

"Ah—I myself am a poor man;—for my rank I mean."

Then followed an exchange in which Lord Fawn carefully explained, point by point, his financial circumstances. Lizzie misunderstood at every step. His property was in Ireland, he explained, but there was no place on it, for it had been "allowed to tumble down."

*"It's about five thousand a year, and out of that my mother has half for her life."*

*"What an excellent family arrangement," said Lizzie.*

*"In this manner the conversation rambled on a bit, with awkward silences in between each remark as the other party scrambled for a suitable reply. Then, came the critical moment.*

*"I have told you everything about myself which I was bound, as a man of honour, to tell before I—I—I—In short, you know what I mean."*

Although Lord Fawn couldn't find the words, in fact, he begged her hand in marriage, and she begged for an hour to think it over.

He suggested calling again, "on Monday, or Tuesday, or Wednesday?"

*"But Lizzie was too magnanimous for this. 'Lord Fawn,' she said, rising, 'you have paid me the highest compliment that a man can pay a woman. Coming from you it is doubly precious; first, because of your character and secondly—'*

*'Why secondly?'*

*'Secondly, because I can love you.' This was said in her lowest whisper.*

*Then Lord Fawn put his arm around Lizzie's waist and kissed her on the forehead.*

*'I shall write to my mother tonight. . . . And she will come to you at once, I am sure.'*

*And he took his leave.*

*"'Lady Fawn,' she said to herself."*

"Are there two types of owl?" Umesh asked. "In India owl means a stupid person. Are there smart owls? This seems like an Indian story. If something goes wrong in India, we say, 'Oh, You are an owl!'—to make someone shut up. Lizzie says Lord Fawn is an owl. I think now she has feelings she has lost her husband. Tears are coming because she is having problems now. She is having problems about this necklace. And she believes that if her husband had been living, she wouldn't have them. Although she didn't love this person to whom she married, but those problems arise after his death, giving tears, not unto the love of her husband. At that time, she was not aware of these troubles. She had not the understanding of being a widow. She wants to believe the necklace belongs to her. In fact, she knows that the necklace was not given to her by her husband forever. But she keeps insisting to keep the diamond necklace somehow or another because it is very precious. And her desire is to be rich forever, so she had married the young man Florian Eustace.

"Lizzie was getting angry because Frank didn't appear for several days, and she felt annoyed, and was counting day by day, and she was also angry that she was finished up with him. And this Lord Fawn was home, and he had breakfast and announced his departure. The Fawn family women were upset because they thought that something was happening between Lord Fawn and Lucy. Something was taking place. They accused everything to poor Lucy, while he was thinking to go and see Lizzie. Lord Fawn went to visit Lizzie, and when he got there and Lizzie is alone there, she welcomes Lord Fawn warmly and asks about poor Lucy. And she is also trying to preach that kind of living on the Earth and trying to catch these stars. She is a poor Lucy, and she is reaching to marry Frank while she is a servant. So she just forgets her own self, what condition she was in. It looks ridiculous, doesn't it? And finally, slowly Lord Fawn begins to tell Lizzie all about himself—what he does have, what he does not have. Similarly, he tells that he has property in Ireland—no house there, for the house is broken down. So the family gets £5,000 from it, and he gets half of that money. The rest of the half goes to his mother and sisters. So that is his money.

"While he was talking, Lizzie began to tell about her son. This was quite annoying to Lord Fawn. How she had to take care of this son until he was twenty-one. And she introduces several other topics, interrupting while he is trying to speak and tell Lizzie his feelings, standing and putting his hand on his heart. And at the same time, he is just slurring something and is unable to say something about love. He wants to propose, but the words won't come out of his mouth. Finally, he says that he loves her and that he is willing to take care of her and her son. And she asks for one hour so she could think over it. And suddenly he picks up his hat to go. Lizzie realized that he was leaving immediately, and she accepted him. He puts his hand around her waist and kisses her on her forehead because he is playing gentleman, and the hat is already in his hand to leave. But he wants to stay, but the hat is in his hand, so he first 'disencumbers' himself of the hat. He wants to use both his hands to make this love talk go to its conclusion. He said, 'Dearest Lizzie,' and she said, 'Dearest Frederick,' and she lay her head on his chest. So the wife has to be of equal size or shorter. He can't be smaller.

"I don't think she understood his financial condition so far. Does she really want to marry this person? She is just playing between these two men. In fact, Frank is a better person for this girl to use as he is a lawyer as well. She doesn't have to pay any money. If she marries this lawyer, she has free cost of barrister, and she doesn't have to pay. She thinks this Lord Fawn is like an owl, but she has never said anything like this about Frank. Whatever she feels, she has surely called Lord Fawn foolish and worse. She feels in herself that he is a dull, stupid owl. Even then she believes that something is better than nothing. As she thinks, 'One bird is in the hand, and the other is in the bush.'"

FORTY-ONE

# THE EVIL EYE

*Again at the Sarang Hotel, Ballia, July 1989*

"This next is a song for the ritual bathing of the bridegroom," said Gangajali. "It tells how King Dasarath has dug the tank. King Dasarath has the pond dug and has the *ghat* made for Ram to take a bath. And the servants, the water-pulling people of Queen Kosilia, bring the water to the boy. Ram is asking, what is the meaning of this bath? So the people say the body gets holy after taking this bath. The body gets holy. Whatever sin or guilt that had been done, all will wash away. Whatever the sin and fault are there, all those flow away with this water of the body."

## SONG 57

*Nacchu Nahawan*

Whose ancestor dug the *ghat* and had it made?
Oh, what is filled by the water-pulling people (*kahar*)?
Oh, who is taking a bath?
Oh, what is filled by the water-pulling people?
Oh, who is taking a bath?
King Dasarath had the tank dug and had the *ghat* made.
The water-pulling people filled the water for Queen Kosilia.

Then Ram takes a bath.
The water-pulling people filled the water for Queen Kosilia.
Then Ram takes a bath.
Shivaji asks the secret meaning, asks of Gaura Dei.
"Gaura, what is the meaning of this bath?
So explain it to me."
"Gaura, what is the meaning of this bath?
So explain it to me."
"Listen, Lord Mahadev.
Oh Bholahinathji.
Shivaji, it is the effect of this bath,
The sins are washed away."
"Shivaji, it is the effect of this bath,
The sins are washed away.
The sin is pardoned and flows away."

"As the boy begins his bath, he washes his head," Gangajali explained. "His mother covers him with her *anchal*, the protective end of her sari, as he bathes. His mother collects some of the water from washing his head in one of her hands and pours it into a special pot made for that purpose by the potter. Rupees are dropped in the pot, and marks of *sindur* are made on it. Then the pot is covered with a lid and sealed with dough by the barber lady.

"After the boy takes a bath, there is a little ritual," Gangajali continued. "The mother, sister, *bhabi*, all these people have a fire in a clay pot and sprinkle caraway seeds (*jiwain*) on it. They turn it over on the ground. The bridegroom will break it with his foot. Then he crosses that area. After breaking that fire, the bridegroom will go inside his courtyard. Then the mother takes off the evil eye with sugar and caraway seeds. The house is full of women. After taking a bath with turmeric and so on, my son has become beautiful. This is a vulnerable time. We must be careful that nobody has given him the evil eye.

"The pot with the bath water is given to the barber, who carries it in the *barat* on that very night, the night of the wedding. When the *barat* reaches the village of the girl's side, then the ritual of *nacchu nahawan* of the bride takes place. As the *barat* arrives in the village, the groom's barber steps out first with the pot containing the bridegroom's bath water. He hands it to the barber for the girl's side, who in turn gives it to his wife to take into the bride's courtyard. The bride takes a bath with soap and cleans herself well. But at the end she is given a bath out of that special water, the water with which the bridegroom washed his head."

Returning to the songs and rituals of the boy's side, his mother blesses him after his bath, as described in the song that follows.

## SONG 58

*Parichhawan*

Mother blesses him with mustard and caraway seeds.
Look, nobody can give him the evil eye.
Nobody can give the evil eye to the beautiful bridegroom.
Mother blesses him with mustard and caraway seeds.
Oh, nobody can give him the evil eye.
Nobody can give the boy the evil eye.
Oh, nobody can give the evil eye to the beautiful bridegroom.
*Bhauji* blesses him with mustard and caraway seeds.
Oh look, nobody can give the evil eye.
Oh, nobody can give the evil eye to the beautiful bridegroom.
Oh, nobody can give the evil eye to the boy.
Sister blesses him with mustard and caraway seeds.
Oh look, nobody can give him the evil eye.
Oh, nobody can give the evil eye to the beautiful bridegroom.
Oh, nobody can give the evil eye to the boy.
*Bua* blesses him with mustard and caraway seeds.
*Dadi* blesses him with mustard and caraway seeds.
*Nani* blesses him with mustard and caraway seeds.
Oh look, nobody can give him the evil eye.
Oh, nobody can give the evil eye to the beautiful bridegroom.
Oh, nobody can give the evil eye to the boy.

"The fire is placed in a clay pot," Gangajali said. "So these women think if somebody has already given the evil eye, then come on, let us take off the evil eye quickly. Otherwise, something will go wrong. How beautiful my son is looking because he has taken a bath in the turmeric and how beautiful he is. So his mother, *bhabi*, sister, *dadi*, *nani*, whoever is there, each of them blesses him five times and throws the caraway seeds in the fire. So if anyone has cast the evil eye, that magic spell will burn in the fire. After circling their hands, they throw the caraway seeds in the fire, and it burns."

"As superstitions have developed all over the world about so many things," Umesh explained, "Indian people have the same very deep, very similar, as deep as touching wood. I never saw any American saying something when he or she is supposed to touch the wood and she or he hasn't done it. Similarly, Indian people have one or two or three hundreds of superstitions in their life. Some people carry them out, and some people don't care. But surely some are so powerful as touching wood.

"If you see someone's child in northern India, whether he is handsome or beautiful or not, but to make him or her feel comfortable and you say even false, 'How beautiful this child is,' she wouldn't say anything to you, but surely the mother or sister or family person's eyes will get alert all of the sudden, and her job will be to take the child home to the family people all of the sudden and tell them to take the *nazar* off of the child. So then, all of the sudden, action will be taken. The wife's sister or his mother will bring red dry big chilies, and one or two women will circle them around the child's head and then throw the chilies in the fire. Even then, if a child gets the *nazar* and it gets sick, some person who takes the *nazar* in the village, he will be called. And he uses a broom or a piece of the broom. The mother sits down on the ground with the child in her lap, and the man sits two or three feet in front of her. And he begins to move the broom around the child while speaking some mantras. And then sometimes he also hits the broom on the ground three or four times. This is one way of doing it. Another way some people use a neem branch with leaves that can be easily handled. And he does the same as he does with the broom. So this is the way of protecting the child. But similarly, when you give a vaccine, the mother puts a dark mark on his forehead to one side or on the chin, so whoever sees the child, before he appreciates him, he will see the ugly black mark on his face. Although he will feel that he is a great nice beautiful child in this way, he won't get the evil eye because he will see the ugly mark there. This is a precaution for taking vaccines, for not getting the evil eye. The mother, after giving the child a bath, putting him in beautiful clothes, everything nice, the mother will put a dark mark somewhere so the person can't escape seeing the dark mark. The mother also makes a black mark in the middle of both soles of his feet, so whenever the person comes from far away and the child lies down, he will see the dark thing first.

"When you are traveling in India, even you will be seeing in several places several trucks hang up an old leather shoe in the grill down to the mudguard and also one at the back of the truck too. Drivers do this so the truck or their business won't get the evil eye. They decorate the new truck carefully, in detail with paint, and they don't want the truck to get *nazar*. You must be seeing several rickshaw pullers hang shoes on the back of the rickshaw. The concept is the same. And it is always mentioned in several places.

"*Buri najar bale tera munh kala*. It means, oh evil eye person, your face is dark. It means you are disgraced. Whenever people are in trouble with the spirits," Umesh explained, "if I'm there, I always explain to them that there is no harm from getting help from the *ojah*, the person who takes the evil eye off, and also suppose he has a different illness that is beyond the *ojah*, go to the doctor. Do both. If I say okay, stick with the *ojah*, it is not fair. The problem comes for poor people who cannot afford with a lot of money, so they get the help from the *ojah* free of cost. This is a free service. In return the *ojah* gets respect. They also feel that if they will begin to charge money, they won't be beneficial for people. In this way, they cannot charge money because they will lose the effect of their mantras. Also, time to time, when you go to some shop or house, you will see lemons and chilies hanging in one corner at the door so his business will not get the evil eye or maybe some bad spirit will not enter in that place."

"So the Hindu world is full of bad spirits?" I asked.

Umesh burst into laughter. "All the world is full of spirits. Some are good, and some are bad. And most of the world believes in the spirits. After death, these are the spirits of dead people. They can be good, or they can be bad. How you think that if a human is good or bad that the spirits can be good or bad? Why are they ghosts? People believe in spirits all over the world, either Christian, Muslim, or Hindu. Maybe they don't believe, who don't believe in God. Most people who believe in God, they believe in spirits. So the majority of these spirits are dead people. Some are bad, some are very good, some are very helpful."

FORTY-TWO

# UMESH GETS MALARIA

*At our apartment, Banaras, 2007*

It's hard to believe how horrible malaria is until you witness it firsthand. Malaria is a protozoan infection generally brought on by the bite of an infected female of the *Anopheles* genus of mosquito. Mainly, these mosquitoes feed at night. There are several forms of malaria, and it is important to quickly diagnose through a blood test which form the patient has. Some forms, such as *falciparum* malaria and several other deadly types, can be fatal after only a day, so prompt diagnosis and treatment are essential.

Malaria attacks the patient in cycles. When Umesh realized he had been infected, he explained to me exactly what was about to happen to him and what I was to do. There would be hours when he felt chilled beyond belief, and I was to gather up all his sweaters and all the quilts in the apartment for this phase. Then would follow periods of very high fever and intense sweating and a desperate need to find a cool place. This too could last for several hours. This cycle would probably occur every day until the disease cleared his system—or killed him.

I have never seen anybody so sick. The chills were horrible. I gathered up all the sweaters and quilts, but this seemed to be of no avail. He just kept shivering uncontrollably. After this phase passed, he would begin to sweat, and he stripped down to his T-shirt and *lungi* and fanned himself. His fever rose to 106 degrees. I was desperate, called Narayan, and rushed him immediately to the hospital, where they could perform the needed tests and provide care and medicine.

I had received such special treatment in Heritage Hospital that it came as a complete shock that they were quite casual about Umesh's condition. I begged for the private room that I had had, but they simply dispensed some white pills to be taken every four hours and sent him home. I fought with them. They refused to admit Umesh. I was in a complete panic. If only it were me that had fallen ill, I would have been admitted into the hospital immediately.

Color prejudice is great in India. Umesh is a color that Indians prefer. It is called wheatish, and is fairly light. In joking he would compare his skin to mine and call himself black. I always objected and said that I was pale and he was healthy and that he was a Brahman after all. Other Indians are very dark and are called blue. This is considered much lower than the wheatish Indians. When a baby is born, the first thing a father looks for is the complexion of the child. If he is wheatish, he expects his child to be wheatish. If the child is dark, the wife is accused of adultery.

So I had to take Umesh home and care for him as best I could. It occurred to me that my air-conditioned room would be of great help in the hours of sweating and high fever. I knew from watching American TV dramas that they even packed patients in ice to lower a fever. But Umesh was afraid. That was mixing the hot high fever with a cold air-conditioned room. There was no reasoning with him and no point trying to make a point when his mind was made up. We clung to the pills the hospital had dispensed. Later I learned that they were only 325 mgs of Paracetemol. I could have helped him so much more if I had known this. I myself could have easily given him up to 2,000 mg of Paracetemol a day and added ibuprofen 800 mg a day. These could have been alternated so that he was receiving fever-reducing medication every three hours. I could stay up all night and be sure that he was getting at least some relief for his fever. There are also various medicines for treating bad cases of malaria. To me Umesh's case seemed as bad as it could get.

Umesh had had malaria many times before. I loved this man so, partly because of his uncanny ability to endure the unendurable. He managed the heat and helped me. He supported me during my typhoid. He carried the luggage. He bossed the cook. He arranged our transportation. He was everything to me. And he made the toast.

When he was in the greatest need, I could hardly help him. I felt depressed and useless. The least I could do was stay by his side and give him water when he needed water, food when he needed food (not often during this malaria battle), administer his pills on time, keep track of his temperature, keep track of the length of time the chills lasted and then how long the sweating lasted, and finally offer the comfort of my company and my affection. I could not get him into an Indian hospital because his skin was brown, and malaria was such a common affliction.

FORTY-THREE

# "THE ELEPHANT IS ADORNED, THE HORSE IS ADORNED"

*At the Sarang Hotel, Ballia, July 16, 1989, afternoon*

"Now *gali* are sung for the boy," Gangajali said. "They also take *gur*, and they bless and feed the boy. Either it is *buniyan* or *gur*, whatever sweet thing is there is fed in his mouth. And when *bhabi* feeds, she teases, offering it to him and suddenly putting it in her own mouth. So jokes and laughing take place here. It is a lighthearted time."

SONG 59

*Gali*

Eat *gur* from your mother and sister.
Oh, give the bridegroom to *samdhi*.
Eat *gur* from *bhabi*.
Oh, give the bridegroom to *samdhi*.
Eat *gur* from your sister.
Oh, give the bridegroom to *samdhi*.

This short teasing song is just a little *gali* for the bridegroom. As he puts on his clothes his womenfolk goof around and joke with him. Here, Gangajali only sings three verses of two lines each, although the song could be longer if she wanted to mention another female relative. The song is cheerful as the topic is playful, and we can enjoy a pretty stable duple meter.

"This song is also a *gali*," Umesh explained. "It is a very short song. This song seems to be special to Ballia. It was not sung for us in nearby Chapra, Bihar, last month, for example. This is sung at the time the bridegroom is getting dressed. While dressing, the bridegroom is given sweets to eat. The *bhabi* offers sweets, and then at the last moment pops them into her own mouth. It is a *gali* because it says give the bridegroom to the *samdhi*. They are trying to make the song charming because they put fun, play, swearing altogether in the song. This reduces the mental pressure of the wedding preparations for all the participants. Certainly, there are special women who know these songs to sing."

"Then the bridegroom is moving," Gangajali said. "He is going where he has to put on his clothes. So all his clothes are kept there. His sister's husband will dress him, his *jija,* but not in a simple way. He will be given a *neg* (donation). Until then, the *jija* will remain seated in his place and will not dress him. Then his *sas* will come, and according to her financial situation, she will give him a watch, a golden chain, or ₹200 or ₹400, or she gives ₹100 or ₹51. If the bridegroom's family is poor, he is given ₹11 or ₹51. Only then will he dress him. Otherwise the bridegroom will remain seated, undressed. 'Dress him please. Come on, I will pay you in the future.'

"Now he is seated naked," Gangajali continued. "Take his clothes so you can dress him.' Then the *sali* and girlfriends play the *dholak* drum here and then sing *sahana*."

This sounds unusual, that he is seated naked. In fact, he is wearing handmade cotton shorts. Indian men wear them all summer in their courtyard, so the bridegroom here is not feeling ashamed.

### SONG 60

#### *Sahana*

Bridegroom Vijay is seated on the stage.
Look, he must not be given the evil eye.
Nobody can give the evil eye to the beautiful bridegroom.
Nobody can give the evil eye to the boy.
On the stage, the bridegroom puts on his garments.
On the stage, the bridegroom puts on his garments.
Nobody can give the evil eye to the beautiful bridegroom.
Nobody can give the evil eye to the boy.
On the stage, the bridegroom puts on a watch.
On the stage, the bridegroom puts on a watch.
Oh look, he must not be given the evil eye.
Nobody can give the evil eye to the beautiful bridegroom.
Nobody can give the evil eye to the boy.

On the stage, the bridegroom puts on his socks.
On the stage, the bridegroom puts on his *dhoti*.
Oh look, he must not be given the evil eye.
Nobody can give the evil eye to the beautiful bridegroom.
On the stage, the bridegroom puts on his socks.
On the stage, the bridegroom puts on his shoes.
Oh look, he must not be given the evil eye.
Nobody can give the evil eye to the beautiful bridegroom.
On the stage, the bridegroom puts on his turban.
On the stage, the bridegroom puts on his turban.
Oh look, he must not be given the evil eye.
Nobody can give the evil eye to the beautiful bridegroom.
On the stage, the bridegroom puts on his crown.
On the stage, the bridegroom puts on his crown.
Oh look, he must not be given the evil eye.
Nobody can give the evil eye to the beautiful bridegroom.
On the stage, he puts on his *tilak*.
On the stage, he puts on his *tilak*.
Oh look, he must not be given the evil eye.
Nobody can give the evil eye to the beautiful bridegroom.

Concern about protecting the bridegroom from the evil eye continues here in this lovely *sahana*. The song is divided into eight stanzas, each describing the item of clothing that the bridegroom is putting on. For these, the opening one or two lines of the stanza, the melody is ascending and lies above the main pitch. For the rest of the stanza, which mentions the evil eye in each line, the melody descends and lies below the main pitch. This is a bit of word painting here, where the flow of the melody reflects the meaning of the words. Ascending as he puts on his shoes, descending with the mention of the evil eye. This musical trick, "word painting," was very common in the Italian Renaissance madrigal. Here we can see that word painting is an idea that may occur to different composers around the world in different eras. It seems to me that it is almost natural to sing ascending high melodies when describing cheerful topics and to sing descending low melodies when describing their opposite. Hence, Gangajali has built a mini drama in this song. On any given day, for all of us, the forces of good and evil are tugging, and so this foundational balance between the two is expressed in a fine way in this song.

"This is sung as he dresses," said Gangajali. "As he puts on his undershirt, as he puts on his *kurta*, as he puts on his watch, turban, crown, *tilak*, socks, and shoes. This is the song for this time."

"This song explains that the bridegroom is seated on the high platform, the stage, and anyone can see him there," Umesh explained. "But, look, he must not get the evil eye. He is protected from bad spirits and the evil eye by a small piece of iron that is inside his *kakkan*, tied on his wrist."

SONG 61

*Parichhawan*

The elephant is adorned, the horse is adorned.
Oh, Phate Baba is adorned.
Oh father, adorn the *barat* nicely.
Gentlemen will come in a bunch.
Oh father, adorn the *barat* nicely.
Gentlemen will come in a bunch.
I will spread the *anchal*.
I will lay the cot.
I will sprinkle flowers.
Oh father, I will fan slowly slowly,
So I can keep the gentlemen at home.
Oh father, I will fan nicely,
So I can keep father's home.
The elephant is adorned, the horse is adorned.
Oh Father Anurudh,
Oh father, we have many *barati* people.
They will loot father's house.
Oh father, we have many *barati* people.
They will loot brother's house.
I will spread the *anchal*.
I will sprinkle flowers.
I will shake the fan.
Oh brother, in such a way I will explain to my sweetheart.
I will keep my brother's home.
Oh brother, in such a way I will explain to my sweetheart.
I will keep my brother's home.
The elephant is adorned, the horse is adorned.
Oh *chacha* Piarath is adorned.
Oh uncle, the *barati* people are still there.
They will loot the uncle's house.
Oh uncle, the *barati* people are still there.
They will loot the uncle's house.
I will spread the *anchal*.
I will sprinkle flowers.
I will shake the fan.
Oh uncle, in that way I will do all for father-in-law.
So I can keep my uncle's home.

Like so many of Gangajali's songs, this one has a higher melody and a lower melody. Probably, this is one of the easiest ways to compose a nice song, by having a repeating question-and-answer type of swing to it. For this song, "The elephant is adorned, the horse is adorned" always marks the beginning of the new stanza and the high melody. Also the three lines, "I will spread the *anchal*," "I will sprinkle flowers," and "I will shake the fan," mark the beginning of a new stanza and the high melody. The remaining lines that are interspersed discuss looting and are sung to the lower melody. In fact, "loot" in English actually is a loan word from the Hindi and Bhojpuri languages, and if you listen carefully you can make it out. It is so nice to be able to catch just one word in a foreign language. Imagine how delightful these songs would sound if you knew all the words.

"I think this song is from the bride's side," Umesh explained. "It also says that before the *barat* departs, adorn the horses and elephants, what they use for saddles, fake flowers, and the elephant is painted in so many ways. Oh, father, the *barat* is adorned very well. Gentlemen gather. I will spread the cot, sprinkle flowers on it. Oh, father, I will gently shake the fan. Keep the gentleman at the father's home."

"All the way this song will be sung," Gangajali explained.

"What kind of song is that?" I asked.

"This is a song when the *barat* is ready to arrive, and the bride's people are there," Gangajali replied. "And the bride's family have begun to move out from their house."

"So is this song from the girl's side or from the boy's side?" Umesh asked.

"This song is from the bride's side by adding the appropriate names," Gangajali said. "Now the bride's side people think that the *barat* is coming. How will we keep the *barat*? So the girl says, 'Don't get upset since they are coming. I will do something like this. I will make them happy by serving them. Your house will not be looted.' The *barat* moves as the military moves. The bride's side people say it—that 'the military is coming.' They fear that their house will be robbed. This song is for the way. This is a *parichhawan* song.

"Once the bridegroom is adorned and the evil eye is cast off," Gangajali explained, "the nail cutting ritual takes place at the altar. The barber lady clips his nails and puts color on his feet. Following this ritual, the crown is tied onto the head of the bridegroom. The *barat* is ready and leaves the house. Mother has rice in her *anchal*, in a small knot, collected from the *matikor* ritual. She has had it since that day until this day. It has not been untied. And from the day of the wedding until the wedding is over she will not untie it. After the wedding, when the bride comes to the house, when the son returns, then at the bank of the Ganges his *kakkan* will be untied. Only then will she untie that rice and offer it to all the gods by throwing it in the Ganges."

"When the boy goes to the bride's home to be married, how does the mother say goodbye to her son?" Umesh asked.

"Ma covers the bridegroom with her *anchal*," Gangajali replied. "She takes him to the taxi and has him sit inside. She has rice in her other hand to sprinkle. A rich mother would have coins to throw. Or if the mother is poor, she throws rice and sweets. The taxi is waiting there, and to perform the important *parichhawan* ritual they have to go to the Baleshwar temple. She covers him with her *anchal* so nobody can see her son, or if somebody looks at him he will remain under her protection. No gods from the air, no witchcraft, no ghosts, nobody will catch him. Therefore, covering him carefully with her *anchal*, she has him sit in the taxi.

"After seating him, the door is closed. And a lot of music is played from behind. All the women are going. The mother is moving with her *anchal*, covering the boy. The bridegroom goes slowly ahead in the taxi and mother throws rice on him—like this—from behind. And up to the temple of Baleshwar, even if it is one hundred *kos* (approximately two hundred miles) far, she will be throwing rice ahead. The rice that is thrown on the taxi belongs to the gods. So he will remain protected."

"Do you realize that some people have forgotten their old traditions nowadays," asked Umesh.

"No, no," Gangajali replied. "She does not forget. Where the work is for the *anchal*, she will use her *anchal*. She will not forget, whether she is poor or illiterate. In case she is crazy other people will explain to her to do it in this way. This is the main point of Bhojpuri culture. I'm not giving you from hither and thither. It is very accurate. Wherever you hear about this place, you will hear this song. At the beginning, first of all. This thing you will hear first of all. After this you can hear any other song, but this one is first, whatever I am saying."

"She does not feel sad. As a mother feels comfort having a small child at her breast, she feels comfort when she holds him to her chest. She gets much pleasure after holding him to her heart. She cannot do this when the child becomes older. How can she when the child becomes taller than the mother. But at the moment, it reminds her of his or her baby period. She will not do this after marriage. After marriage, the child does not belong to his mother. Now he is given to the bride. Now he belongs to others. Then the mother won't do this."

"Then how is the mother happy then?" asked Umesh.

"She gets happiness because she thinks my son has become two from one. He will be three, four, and five out of two. He will carry my family ahead. The family will increase. So she is entirely happy. This is pure happiness, for my son is going to get married today and he will come back home with his wife. How it will fill up the house with the daughter-in-law, with wealth, and thereafter my grandson will come. Great grandchildren will come, and so on."

"The bridegroom is dressed," Umesh said. "What is next?"

"He goes for *parichhawan*," said Gangajali. "The taxi of the bridegroom is moving slowly, and the mother is following behind and throwing rice slowly, and the other women follow her. And up in front are all the musical instrument players and the dancers. The band plays, the *barat* goes, and the women follow them while singing songs."

"Does the band go ahead of the mother or behind her," asked Umesh.

"In front," Gangajali replied. "Women sing songs from behind."

FORTY-FOUR

# PREPARING FOR WINTER

*At our apartment, Banaras, 2007*

October had passed, and it was now early November.

"It is time to prepare for winter," Umesh announced. "We have to arrange for quilts."

"Quilts?"

"Yes, quilts. We will not make it through the winter nights without quilts. You must come out today and watch them made and take pictures. Now you will see the snow in Banaras."

Umesh took us to the quilt market not far from our apartment. The first step was to pick a fabric. One fabric for the top, and one for the bottom. He selected his, and I picked something pretty for me.

"We'll wait to watch them puffing the cotton," he said.

A truly amazing process. The two sides of the quilt are sewn together around the edges. Then the puffed cotton—it did look like snow—was spread evenly across the quilt, which was turned inside out. Then the craftsmen carefully turned the quilt right side out, and it was very puffy and filled with cotton. Then they took the puffed quilt and stitched tying links to hold the cotton in and to hold the front to the back. It was spectacular.

People think of India as a very hot country. But the winters, though short, are very cold. By mid-November winter really starts, and by Christmas it is hard to get anything done for the cold. January can be very foggy, and February welcomes the beginning of springlike weather.

Because the winter season is short, Indians don't generally buy winter coats. I certainly hadn't brought one with me. They dress in layers, and I followed their example. The trick is to put on your clothes—all your clothes—at the same time. Sweats under your trousers, T-shirts under a couple of sweaters, a wooly hat. A couple of pairs of socks. During winter, all Indian people look fat, puffy. But it's just the layering of the clothes. Then you can snuggle up under your handmade quilt and feel warm. By following these rules, I wasn't cold.

Bathing in the winter presents a special problem, at least it did for me. All we had in our apartment was cold running water. Umesh bathed with no problem every morning in the ice-cold water with his bucket and cup. I couldn't manage it.

Umesh went off to the market and came back with a large and unusual electrical gizmo that reminded me of the little tea-making immersion units that are sold in the West.

"This is for heating water in your bucket," he explained. Every day he prepared this hot water for me. He watched over the bucket until the water reached the right temperature for bathing. Then he removed the immersion unit and carried the bucket into my bathroom.

It was cold taking off your layers of clothes. But the warm water from the bucket was delightful, and I used my cup to pour water all over my head and body and then washed and rinsed my hair. When the precious hot water was all used up, I dried myself with my towel and shivering began the tedious job of putting on layers and layers of clothes again—fresh, clean clothes.

I was dependent on the kindness of Umesh. India is tough for anyone. A Westerner needs help. I learned that I was not very tough and that I certainly needed a great deal of help. I've seen Indian mothers bathe their kids—who are crying their heads off—in the cold water of the winter. I suppose Indians grow up used to what to me seemed like torture. But no Indian would go for a day without a morning bath. A great value is placed by Hindus on personal hygiene.

The quilts were a big success. In the morning, Umesh would bring his into my room and wrap himself up in it. And I was wrapped up in mine. Then we would have our tea and toast and our morning conversation until the power cut came at ten o'clock. Thus, we could continue our work on the Gangajali songs. We had spent only five days in July 1989 with Gangajali. It was taking months to realize the meaning of these amazing songs. We worked on speedily, and the completed pages mounted up—500, 750, even 1,000 pages.

The battery on my Mac computer had completely died, so I could only do the typing part of this work while there was power. The power cuts from ten to two continued on during the winter, but then they were not so troublesome.

We continued our daily routine of tea and toast. Ramwati came every day to clean and cook our lunch. We continued to read our Trollope together, savoring every line. And we worked on the Gangajali songs.

Because I was in the throes of grief, I just wanted to stick to our daily routine—tea and toast, bathing, working on translations, reading, our lunch, working again on translations, reading more Trollope, perhaps an afternoon snack from the shop at the end of the lane as a treat (Umesh didn't really like Ramwati's cooking), a light dinner—leftovers from lunch—more Trollope. Then Umesh would read to me from his Danielle Steele book, and then came bedtime.

FORTY-FIVE

# "SEXY SWEETHEART DRINKS SLOWLY SLOWLY"

*Another noontime meeting at Hotel Sarang, Ballia, 1989*

"Next the *imali* ritual takes place," Gangajali explained. "During this, the bridegroom's mother is seated behind the bridegroom. The bridegroom's *mama*, the brother of his mother, brings a sari that is placed on the mother's head. The crown of the bridegroom is placed on top of that. And the barber takes five mango leaves. They are bitten by the boy. The stem of the leaf is given to bite. The bridegroom will bite the stem, and he will spit it on the palm of his mother. Then the *mama* will drop water on her hand. And the mother will drink the spitted stem with the water. Then he will ask his sister, 'Oh, sister, you are drinking water. Are you satisfied?' She will reply, 'Yes, brother, I am satisfied.'

"During the *imali* ritual this song is sung," she explained.

## SONG 62

### *Parichhawan*

Honorable mother comes out for performing *parichhawan*.
Holding the *sinaura* and *arti* in her hand.
Holding the *sinaura* and *arti* in her hand.
Mother does *parichhawan* of the crown of the head of the bridegroom.
A *tilak* on the forehead is made for the bridegroom.

A *tilak* on the forehead is made for the bridegroom.
The crown for the head is the sandal for the heart.
*Parichhawan* is performed of the bridegroom's forehead.
Oh, *parichhawan* is performed of the bridegroom's forehead.
*Bhauji* comes out to perform *parichhawan*.
Holding the *sinaura* and *arti* in her hand.
Holding the *sinaura* and *arti* in her hand.
*Bhauji* does *parichhawan* of the crown on the head of the bridegroom.
A *tilak* on the forehead is made for the bridegroom.
The crown of the head is the sandal of the heart.
*Parichhawan* is performed of the bridegroom's forehead.
*Parichhawan* is performed of the bridegroom's forehead.
Sister comes out to perform *parichhawan*.
Holding the *sinaura* and *arti* in her hand.
Holding the *sinaura* and *arti* in her hand.
Sister does *parichhawan* of the crown of the head of the bridegroom.
A *tilak* on the forehead is made for the bridegroom.
The crown of the head is the sandal of the heart.
*Parichhawan* is performed of the bridegroom's forehead.
*Bua* comes out to perform *parichhawan*.
Holding the *sinaura* and *arti* in her hand.
Holding the *sinaura* and *arti* in her hand.
*Bua* does *parichhawan* of the crown of the head of the bridegroom.
A *tilak* on the forehead is made for the bridegroom.
The crown of the head is the sandal of the heart.
*Parichhawan* is performed of the bridegroom's forehead.
*Parichhawan* is performed of the bridegroom's forehead.

"So the mother has done *parichhawan*, the *bua* has done *parichhawan*, the sister has done *parichhawan*, *bhauji* has done *parichhawan*, all women have done the *parichhawan* in this way."

Umesh said, "In this song women ask for whom the mother is doing *parichhawan*, for whom the sister is doing *parichhawan*, for whom the *bhauji* is doing *parichhawan*. She says the crown of the bridegroom is a piece of my heart. That is my heart. What a lovely thing this is. Then the mother puts *kajal* on the eyes of her son. And a jug of water is given to the bridegroom to have his mother drink. And he asks, 'Mother, are you happy? I am going. Are you happy?' She replies, 'Yes, son, I am very happy.' There is a song for this."

### SONG 63

Son, you are going to marry Gaura.
What can you give me in return for my milk?
What can you give me in return for my milk?

Son, you are going to marry Gaura.
What can you give me in return for my milk?
What can you give me in return for my milk?
In return for my milk?
Mother, I cannot pay you back for your milk.
Mother, I cannot pay.
Take from me the worth of the pain of childbirth.
Take from me the worth of the pain of childbirth.
Mother, I will be a slave to my father.
And my bride will be your slave.
And my bride will be your slave.

Gangajali explained this short song further. "So the mother says, 'You are going to get married. But the milk I have fed you out of my breast, you sucked my blood to feed you and raise you. You are going and leaving me behind. What will you give me in return for it?' Then he replies, 'I cannot repay you the value of your milk. But whatever trouble you have gone through, you gave me birth. I will surely give you the return of it by serving you.' It means that I will serve my parents. I will help you wherever you are. And my wife will remain your slave. She will live under your foot. She will serve you."

"So the mother is unhappy here at the time of putting the *kajal*?" Umesh asked.

"No, no," Gangajali replied.

"Why?" Umesh asked. "She gets upset, and she asks, 'What do you give me in return for my milk?' So is she happy or unhappy?"

"She is saying this in happiness," Gangajali replied. "There is no sadness in any place."

"But if we go deep into it, is she happy or sad?" Umesh asked.

"She is sad and happy both," Gangajali said. "Happy and sad both."

"Because all her rights have finished," Sashi said. "The daughter-in-law's rights begin. So the mother gets sad."

"From here the mother's rights finish," Gangajali said. "Now she has given him into the hand of another."

"So she gets a little sad," Sashi said.

"So what are you giving me in return for my milk?" Gangajali said. "So he says, 'I will be a servant to my father, and my wife will remain your slave. She will serve you.'"

"The main thing is that the feeling comes from the mother's side," Umesh said. "How can I have those feelings that mother has? Only by telling someone how she feels do we know it. Mother knows better than anyone else. Even I believe she doesn't know why she is crying, either out of happiness or sadness."

## SONG 64

Neem tree, you are bitter.
The cool breeze blows.
The cool breeze blows.
Bridegroom Vijay is standing under it.
Tears are flowing from his eyes.
Bridegroom Vijay is standing under it.
Tears are flowing from his eyes.
The father asks secretly,
Son, why are tears flowing?
Son, is there little music and only a few musical instruments,
So the gentlemen are unhappy?
Or son, has the wealth become little?
Son, why are tears flowing?
Father, there is much music and many musical instruments.
But the gentlemen have become unhappy.
But the gentlemen have become unhappy.
This brother Raghubar of mine,
He became powerful.
We are five brothers.
Oh, I'll go alone.
Son, the musicians will go with you,
And the *barati* people.
And the *barati* people.
The *bahanuiya* goes moving the whisk.
Then how are you going alone?
The *bahanuiya* goes moving the whisk.
Then how are you going alone?
The *barati* people will get wealth, and the musicians will get *nachhabar* (ritual of giving money to musicians).
And the musicians will get *nachhabar.*
The *bahanuiya* will get the yellow *dhoti.*
Son, you will get the bride.
*Bahanuiya* will get the yellow *dhoti.*
You will get the bride.
Oh son, how are you alone?

Gangajali explained this song. "The bridegroom stands here under a tree, and he thinks, 'I have five brothers, and I am alone. How shall I go such a long way alone?' He is crying. The tears are flowing out of his eyes. His father comes and asks, 'Son, why are you crying? Why are tears flowing out of your eyes?' Then the son replies, 'Father, I am going alone, and my brothers are not with me. And nobody else is available for help. How can I go alone?' The father says, 'Oh, son, you are not alone. There are two or three pairs of musical instruments with you. This is a musical band. All the *barati* people are with you. Your *jija* will go with you, shaking that fly whisk. All will go, and you will get wealth and the bride. Your *bahanoi* will get a yellow *dhoti*. Son, you will come back home with a bride. Why are you crying?'"

Umesh said, "She is mentioning crying, but the word crying does not appear in the song. The brothers are not going, and he is feeling deeply sad. There can be so many problems, and the brothers may not want to participate in the wedding. So the groom is getting upset, crying, 'Even having five brothers, I am alone going to wed by myself,' when usually all the family men participate in the wedding, the *barat*. It is considered the strength of the family. The *barat* is an army. The brothers are leaders of this army. And how many jobs the brothers might do, someone else will be doing. If the youngest brother is left and the older brothers do not participate, it is very very painful. Suppose there is an older brother getting married, the younger brothers go. In a way, this is a duty of the older brother to take care of the younger's wedding. It's the father's job to supervise the work of the wedding, dividing it among his sons. Without his sons he has to request other people to help—with pain—because there is so much work in the wedding. That is the meaning of it."

"Now after *parichhawan* the bridegroom gets in his taxi with the musicians and the musical instruments and the *barati* people," Gangajali explained. "Women come back from the temple to their home. Now the bridegroom moves ahead. 'Leave him. He is going.'"

"The bridegroom goes in his *barat*," Umesh said.

"He moves, and he is going," Gangajali said. "But now the women are coming back to their homes. While coming back all the women hold hands and sing *jhumar* on the way with great happiness. They dance and sing *jhumar*. As they come back to their homes, they sing."

### SONG 65

#### *Jhumar*

The tamarind leaves move slowly slowly (repeated five times).
Sweetheart, I serve food in a golden dish (repeated three times).
I serve food.
I serve food in a golden dish.
Oh, sexy sweetheart.
Sexy sweetheart eats slowly slowly.
Sexy sweetheart eats slowly slowly.
The tamarind leaves move slowly slowly.
The tamarind leaves move slowly slowly.
The *jhanjhar* jug and the water out of the pitcher.
The *jhanjhar* jug and the water out of the pitcher.
Water out of the pitcher.

Water out of the pitcher.
Oh, sexy sweetheart drinks slowly slowly.
Sexy sweetheart drinks slowly slowly.
The tamarind leaves move slowly slowly.
The tamarind leaves move slowly slowly.
I made a betel with clove and cardamom.
I made a betel with clove and cardamom.
Oh, sexy sweetheart.
Sexy sweetheart chews slowly slowly (repeated three times).
The tamarind leaves move slowly slowly.
The tamarind leaves move slowly slowly.
The bed is laid with thousands of marigold flowers.
I laid the bed by plucking buds.
Sweetheart, I laid the bed, I laid the bed.
I laid the bed, I laid the bed.
Oh, sexy sweetheart, aah.
Sexy sweetheart sleeps slowly slowly.
Sexy sweetheart sleeps slowly slowly.
The tamarind leaves move slowly slowly.
The tamarind leaves move slowly slowly.

"So women from the *barat* side come back," Gangajali said. "*Jhumar*, this is a *jhumar*. Those songs that are sung on the way. This is the meaning of this *jhumar*. What is slowly shaking the leaves of the branch? How slowly slowly? The tamarind leaves. This is a high tree of tamarind. They are not so big when they are full of fruit. The bunches are close to each other.

"The breeze is blowing very slowly. As the breeze blows, how nice it feels to the body. There is enthusiasm. And they sing for that. That I have cooked a meal for you. And what a season. The breeze is blowing slowly slowly. You have this food slowly slowly. And I have also filled up the water jug and placed it for you to drink. There is also betel ready for you. Chew it. Look, I have laid the bed. So slowly go to sleep."

FORTY-SIX

# THE *JALUAA*

*We continue our song session at the Sarang Hotel, July 1989*

"Now women go inside the house," Gangajali said. "And water is carried in a jug. The barber lady drops some stone tin in the jug that she has picked up on the way. And where the plow shaft and the *kalas* have been placed, five married women will walk around them five times. As they walk they will keep shaking the jug with the piece of stone in it. They will keep shaking it to make a sound and will sing a song. Here they sing *gali* songs."

### SONG 66

*Gali*

Oh my feelings. All the men have gone in the *barat*.
Oh my feelings. All the married men have gone in the *barat*.
Oh my feelings. The husbands of all have gone in the *barat*.
Oh my feelings. Everyone's place is on a fast.
Oh my feelings. Let the *barati* people come.
Oh my feelings. There will be a guest for everyone's place.
Oh my feelings. There will be a guest for everyone's place.

SPOKEN

"Only this remained."

"This is a *gali*," Gangajali said. "This is a very dirty *gali*. I haven't sung all of it. I hid it. It is saying that all the bridegrooms have gone in the *barat*, and only the women remain at home. And they went crazy. So they say, 'Don't get excited. Be calm. The *barat* will be back.' Then all the women will get their husbands back. And everyone's wish will be fulfilled.

"Oh, there is much pleasure in it. There is much fun here. There is much joking and fun. The *gali* is sung with the names of everyone put in it. This is just among women. Men are not there. So the women are singing and playing instruments after doing all the rituals in the courtyard."

This song has a single melodic line that is repeated over and over for each line of the text. The range is only that of a minor 3rd, so essentially the song is simple to sing. This performance sounds very cautious and reserved. I believe that Gangajali was so concerned to not sing the dirty lines that she held back even singing these "clean" opening lines. To understand how this song would sound in an actual wedding, I believe we need to imagine a large group of women in a noisy group joining in on this simple repeated melody hurling insults, telling dirty jokes, and laughing and laughing. In capturing songs during an actual wedding the atmosphere and mood is accurately represented, but the clarity of the song texts is drowned out. We had many such recordings. For this song, Gangajali was singing alone in a hotel room. The text is clear but we have totally lost the atmosphere of the occasion. Choices and compromise. That is fieldwork.

It would seem that Gangajali's struggle to sing for us only "good" songs and to omit "bad" songs like the preceding *gali* was troubling her mind, as she immediately went on to perform a lovely bhajan without further comment. We felt that it was entirely up to her what songs she chose to sing. She knew these tapes would be going in archives and that they would go in this book. The choice was hers.

### SONG 67

#### *Bhajan*

Oh Lord, I got so much trouble after forgetting you.
Lord, I got so much trouble after forgetting you.
Lord, I got so much trouble after forgetting you.
Lord, I got so much trouble after forgetting you.
Oh Lord, I got so much trouble after forgetting you.
The people of the world are misers.
The people of the world are misers.
The people of the world are misers.
The people of the world are misers.
I lost the priceless soul by forgetting you.
Lord, I got so much trouble after forgetting you.
I lost the priceless soul by forgetting you.
Lord, I got so much trouble after forgetting you.

Lord, I got so much trouble after forgetting you.
The entire world has forgotten your preaching.
The entire world has forgotten your preaching.
Being worldly, I lost the priceless soul.
Lord, I got so much trouble after forgetting you.
Lord, I got so much trouble.
I saw the priceless actions of this world.
Lord, I got so much trouble after forgetting you.
Lord, I got so much trouble after forgetting you.
Lord, I got so much trouble after forgetting you.
Being lovers, the worldly people lost.
Being lovers, the worldly people lost.
Being lovers, the worldly people lost.
They did not identify the movement of fate.
They did not identify the movement of fate.
Oh Lord, I am thirsty for the stream of your nectar.
Lord, I got so much trouble after forgetting you.
Lord, I got so much trouble after forgetting you.
After I forgot you, after forgetting you.
Lord, after forgetting you, after forgetting you,
Lord, I got so much trouble after forgetting you.
Lord, I got so much trouble after forgetting you.
Due to sex, anger, and miserliness, I destroyed my own world.
Due to sex, anger, and miserliness, I destroyed my own world.
I destroyed my own world.
I destroyed my own world.
Lord I come . . .
Oh oh oh oh Lord, I live.
Lord, I live on your foundation.
Lord, I have gotten such trouble after forgetting you.
Lord, I got so much trouble after forgetting you.
All the people of the world have forgotten your preaching.
All the people of the world have forgotten your preaching.
Being worldly, I lost the priceless soul.
Being worldly, I lost the priceless soul.
The string of fate rings with the help of the string of sin.
The string of fate rings with the help of the string of sin.
Lord, I got so much trouble after forgetting you.
Lord, I got so much trouble after forgetting you.

I believe that his lovely flowing and ornamented devotional song was composed by Gangajali herself. Some lines are sung at a lower level, and some, rather surprisingly, at a much higher level with melismas gliding over several pitches. Gangajali told us how she sang such at her jobs when she was doing housework and also when cleaning in the cloth store where she worked every morning.

As her mind settled, Gangajali proceeded to tell about the *jaluaa*, the drama and play performed by the bridegroom's family women while the wedding is taking place, deep in the night, at the bride's home. She said, "Then the women will keep awake all the night. The women will not sleep. All the women, whether there are one hundred or two hundred or ten or five, they will keep awake all night. And they will do their work according to their schedule."

"What kind of schedule do they have?" Umesh asked.

"They have games and dramas," Gangajali replied. "Dancing and singing. We people call it *jaluaa*. For *jaluaa* we have different types of games, dramas, dancing, and singing. Women consider it auspicious for the bride and bridegroom. For one popular drama, they imitate a child in the womb—they tie a cloth on their stomach. Then they sing songs about it. They sing songs for all ten months. And then they deliver the child. As the boy is delivered, that boy is beautiful. He is made out of dough and wrapped in a cloth. Oh, his arms are long, his feet are long. He will do to his *bua* like this (obscene). He will do to his grandmother like this (obscene).

"This is an auspicious thing, and this is a ritual of this place. At the other side, at the bride's house, the wedding is taking place. And here, at the bridegroom's house, this thing is taking place. We consider it auspicious. It takes place in every house, whether the people are rich or poor."

"You will not sing the songs because I am sitting here," Umesh said.

"I will sing, but I will not bring dirt into it. I will sing it veiled ('purdah').

"So when the wedding is taking place on the girl's side, only then will the women play drama. On the bride's side, the bridegroom will sit down under the *mandap* to get married. On the boy's side, the women will remain awake all the night and will do this drama. The wedding will take place under the *mandap*. The women play drama here. We people play with each other. We play a game and keep talking. This is the first number.

"The new new daughter-in-law asks from her *sas*, her mother-in-law, 'How is rice planted? How is it reaped? How is the *soha* to it? How is it pounded? How will we beat it? How will we transport it from the field? How will we winnow it?'

"The *chin* is round round yellow yellow rice," Gangajali said. "We call it 'mara.' It is grown here.

"So the daughter-in-law is saying to her mother-in-law, mother-in-law. . . ." Gangajali paused. "Is somebody listening from outside?" she whispered. "So the daughter-in-law says to the mother-in-law."

Gangajali began singing in a whisper lest the hotel people would hear this funny song.

## SONG 68

### *Jaluaa*

Oh how, oh how,
Oh how, oh how, mother-in-law, how is the rice planted?
Oh how, oh how, mother-in-law, how is the rice planted?
Oh, like this, oh, like this,
Oh, like this, like this, daughter-in-law, rice is planted like this.
Oh how, oh how,
Oh how, oh how, mother-in-law, how does the rice grow?
Oh how, oh how, mother-in-law, how does the rice grow?
Oh, like this, oh,
Oh, like this, like this, daughter-in-law, rice is grown like this.
Oh, like this, like this, daughter-in-law, rice is grown like this.
Oh how, oh how,
Oh how, oh how, mother-in-law, how does the rice become fruitful?
Oh daughter-in-law, it is fruitful like this, like this.

"Then the mother-in-law explains," Gangajali said.

Oh, like this, oh, like this,
Oh, like this, like this, daughter-in-law, the rice becomes fruitful like this.
Oh, like this, like this, daughter-in-law, the rice becomes fruitful like this.
Oh how, oh how,
Oh how, oh how, mother-in-law, how will I reap the rice?
Oh how, oh how, mother-in-law, how will I reap the rice?
Oh, like this, oh, like this,
Oh, like this, like this, daughter-in-law, you reap the rice like this.
Oh how, oh how,
Oh how, oh how, mother-in-law, oh how do I bundle up the rice?
Oh how, oh how, mother-in-law, oh how do I bundle up the rice?
Oh daughter-in-law, like this, like this,
Oh, like this, like this, daughter-in-law, you bundle up the rice like this.
Oh how, oh how?
Oh how, oh how, mother-in-law, how will I transport the bundle?
Oh, like this, like this, daughter-in-law.
Oh, like this, like this, daughter-in-law, you transport the bundle like this.
Oh how, oh how.
Oh how, oh how, mother-in-law, oh how do I thresh the rice?
Oh, like this, like this, daughter-in-law.

"We hold the stick like this. A long long stick," Gangajali said. "We take something, we pound it, we sing and dance."

Oh, like this, like this, daughter-in-law,
Oh, like this, like this daughter-in-law, you thresh the rice like this.

"Any lady, any woman who pulls her veil down to here (covering her face), she will make a daughter-in-law," Gangajali explained. "And one lady will become the mother-in-law and will remain standing there. She will ask her:"

Oh how, oh how, mother-in-law,
Oh how, oh how, mother-in-law, oh how do I winnow the rice?

"Now people shake the winnowing basket. We get it from the house."

Like this, like this, daughter-in-law, you winnow the rice like this, oh daughter-in-law.
Oh how, oh how, mother-in-law, how do I pound the rice?

"We people take a stick like a mortar. We take something. We pound it, and we sing and dance."

Oh, like this, like this, daughter-in-law, you pound the rice like this.
Oh how, oh how, mother-in-law, how do I cook the rice?

"Whoever is *bua* or *bhauji* to the boy, we will seat her like this. We will seat her entirely like this," and Gangajali demonstrated how she could place her legs to form an Indian clay oven (*chula*). "Means 'I'll make her a *chula* (obscene).' We laugh a lot. Here we sing entire *gali*s. We beat her like this. From the front and from the back. And we sing *gali*s for her, that her *chula* is very shallow. Water is flowing, and all wooden sticks are getting wet. And how can we cook rice on it? Then somebody says to her,"

There are no teeth in your mouth.
Daughter-in-law, blow it with much strength, or she will catch wood (obscene).
Oh how, oh how, mother-in-law, how do I make the oven?
Oh how, oh how, mother-in-law, how do I make the oven?
Oh, like this, like this, daughter-in-law, you make the oven like this.
Oh, like this, like this, daughter-in-law, you make the oven like this.
Oh how, oh how, mother-in-law, how do I place the oven?

"People will seat her like this. And will place two or four wooden sticks there. On it the entire *ganta*. They will shake it, and there is much laughing here."

Oh, like this, like this, daughter-in-law, you have to place the oven like this.

Oh, like this, like this, daughter-in-law, you have to place the oven like
this.
Oh how, oh how, mother-in-law, how do I cook the rice?
Oh how, oh how, mother-in-law, how do I cook the rice?

"In one jug filled up with *puris* and rice. And they will put it on."

Oh like this, like this, daughter-in-law, you cook rice like this.

"Then they say,"

Oh how, oh how, mother-in-law,
How do I serve the rice water to mother-in-law?

"They fake-spread cooked rice in a dish to let the rice water run off. And the hot hot rice water is served in front of mother-in-law."

Oh, like this, like this, daughter-in-law, you serve the rice water to
mother-in-law like this.
Oh how, oh how, mother-in-law, how do I serve food to *nanad*?
Mother-in-law, how do I serve *nanad*?
Oh, like this, like this, serve like this to *nanad*.

"We people take it in a dish like this and place in near the *nanad*. Like this, like this. Take it away, eat, and run away from here."

Oh, like this, like this, daughter-in-law, you serve food to *nanad* like this.
Oh, like this, like this, daughter-in-law, you serve food to *nanad* like this.
Oh how, oh how, how do I serve food to my sweetheart?

"To her husband."

Oh how, oh how, mother-in-law, how do I serve food to my husband?

"So for her husband she cooks food with much effort, and they push the rice. There is much laughter here. There is a big joke here."

Oh like this, like this, daughter-in-law,
You serve food to your sweetheart like this.

"Then some women ask, 'Why do you serve that hot rice water to your mother-in-law? You tricked your *nanad* into going away like any other person, and how nicely you are offering rice to your husband (obscene) with pushing pushing.'

"Then she replies, 'My husband is useful to me. Shouldn't I feed him? What is her use to me? My husband will remain with me. He will live with me all of my life.' Yes. There are so many other links in it. Hidden obscene lines. Dirty dirty."

*(Song 68 ends here, but the conversation continues.)*

"So this is one drama of the *jaluaa*. Inside of it there is much dance and play and drama, laughter, jokes, in the middle of it. It is full of all those qualities. In the boy's house on the wedding night, *jaluaa* takes place.

"The *barat* is going to the house of the bride. Now in the house of the groom, all the menfolk have gone. Women remain awake all night. They play drama and remain awake. And the lamp is lit on the *kalas*. All the night they will keep filling the lamp with oil so it won't be quenched. Two wicks will remain lit in that lamp. When the time will come to get married, the flame of both wicks will meet each other in the lamp in the house of the bridegroom. Then people will say the wedding is taking place now. When both flames come close, then it is said that now the wedding is taking place.

"This is of the mother-in-law and daughter-in-law. That is why it is the main thing in it. There are so many kinds of different games like this. When they have to keep awake all the night, then there are different types of games. Only then the night will pass.

"So then the daughter-in-law gets pregnant. Then she says:"

### SONG 69

### *Jaluaa*

She could not understand the first month.
Oh, she could not understand.
Oh mother, the second month begins.
Oh mother-in-law, the second month begins.
Then the third month begins.
I could not understand the second month.
I could not understand, could not understand that it began.
Oh mother-in-law, the third month has begun.
Oh mother-in-law, the third month has begun.
Mother-in-law, then I could not understand the third month.
Mother-in-law, the fourth month begins.

### SPOKEN

"Then the daughter-in-law says to her *nanad*, 'Oh *nanad*, you go to the market. I feel like eating green green chilies. I feel like eating sweets. And I feel like eating radish. And bring the big, sour, green mangos. I also feel like eating it. You go to the market. And I feel like eating radish. And bring the big sour green mango. I also feel like eating it. You go to the market.

"Then she says:"

SUNG

I could not understand the fourth month.
Oh, I could not understand.
Mother-in-law, it began.
Oh, now the sixth month begins.
Oh mother-in-law, the sixth month begins.
Mother-in-law, I could not understand the sixth month.
I could not understand that it began.
Oh mother-in-law, the seventh month begins.
Oh mother-in-law, the seventh month begins.

SPOKEN

"The daughter-in-law says, 'Oh mother-in-law, I cannot walk in high and low places. Oh mother-in-law, I cannot get onto my cot. Mother-in-law, I cannot plaster the kitchen. Mother-in-law, how can I clean pots? I cannot do it. So mother-in-law, you go to the market. Bring these things for me. I feel like eating them.'"

(SINGING RESUMES)

I could not understand the seventh month.
I could not understand that it began.

(REEL CHANGE)

Oh mother-in-law, the eighth month begins.
Oh mother-in-law, the eighth month begins.
I could not understand the eighth month.
I could not understand that it began.
Oh mother-in-law, the ninth month begins.
Oh mother-in-law, the ninth month begins.
Then I could not understand the ninth month.
I could not understand that it began.
Oh mother-in-law, the tenth month begins.
Oh mother-in-law, the tenth month begins.

(SINGING ENDS)

This story moves ahead in spoken form even after the sung portion has finished. It offers the listener a glimpse of an entirely different genre of music.

"The daughter-in-law realizes that she has made a grave mistake.

"The daughter-in-law says, 'Oh my mother-in-law, you go and call the midwife.' Here we call her *chamaini*—who delivers the child. If the midwife does not succeed, then we go to the doctor. We will go to the *memm* (government midwife).

"'Oh mother-in-law, go and call the *chamaini*,' the daughter-in-law says.

"The mother-in-law says to the midwife, 'Oh mother, oh mother of Jankiya, my daughter-in-law is going to have a baby. You come on and have a look.'

"Then the midwife replies, 'I will not go to your daughter-in-law.'

"The mother-in-law asks, 'Why will you not go?'

"The midwife replies, 'What will I do there? She never gave anything to me. The daughter-in-law is very miserly. I will not go to do her work to deliver a boy or a girl to her. Listen, I went to her on the day of Holi. Then she gave me bread cooked out of *mahua* and gave the vegetables of *karmi*. Well, does somebody eat *mahua* bread and vegetables of *karmi* at the time of Holi?'

"So the mother-in-law asks the daughter-in-law, 'Oh daughter-in-law, what had you given the *chamaini* to eat?'

"The daughter-in-law replies, 'Oh mother-in-law, I gave her cooked *mahua*. I gave her the vegetables of *karmi*.'

"The mother-in-law, horrified, asks, 'What else did you give her? What did you eat?'

"The daughter-in-law replies, 'Mother-in-law, I ate sweets and *puris*.'

"'Do you deserve to eat these things, and did she deserve to eat *mahua*?' asks the mother-in-law.

"'If she will not eat *mahua*, then what else will she eat?' replies the daughter-in-law. 'Oh, does she deserve to eat *puri*s? Come on, come on, mother-in-law, call someone. I am dying of pain. Mother-in-law, call the *chamaini*. Now I will cook such big *puri*s for her. And also I will give her *laddu*, sweets, and a yellow sari to put on. You will give her to dress up. Her husband to put on (*words obscure*). Mother-in-law, I touch your feet.'

"And she cries, 'Please call her quickly. Now I will die.'

"This is about the birth of a boy. Now, so many women also dress up like Ayurvedic doctors. They continue the games and dramas."

> Oh, I am a very wise doctor from Patna.
> I am ready to remove the evil spell.

"The women imitate doctors.

"'I am a doctor.'

"'I am a doctor.'

"'I am a doctor.'

"'I am a doctor.'

"Somebody can have the evil spell removed from the ear, have the evil spell removed from the arm, have the arthritis removed, and help with childbirth.

"'I am a doctor.'

"'I am a doctor.'

"'I am a doctor.'

"'Oh doctor, come here. Oh doctor, come here. Oh doctor, listen. Brother, my daughter-in-law is in much trouble. Come on doctor, let's check her. Oh, what are your fees?'

"The doctor replies, 'Oh sister, my fees are ₹1,400' (pronounced just like the words "screw you" in Bhojpuri).

"'Oh brother, your fees are ₹1,400. Oh come on, come on, you take ₹1,300. Come on, please check my daughter-in-law a bit.'

"So the doctor goes and checks her. He loses control over himself.

"The daughter-in-law cries, 'Oh mother, oh mother, this doctor is very adulterous. Make him go very quickly. Beat him up and make him go.'

"The next one comes. The doctor sahab has come. Oh, the doctor sahab has come.

"The mother-in-law says, 'My son's wife is in a little pain. She is going to give birth to a child. Doctor sahab, check her a bit. Doctor, what are your fees?"

"'Oh mother of Monikaya, my fees are ₹1,400' (again, 'screw you')

"'Oh no, no,' the mother-in-law replies. '₹1,400 is much. I won't give it. Take ₹1,300. My brother, check her a bit.'

"So the doctor sahab came and delivered the child. Here we people sing many songs. This song is a little bit dirty. The doctor delivered the baby.

"Now the *chamaini* takes the child and drops oil on him. She put him to sleep and rubs oil on his head and feet. She pours the oil on the child and pulls his legs.

"The daughter-in-law squeezes him a little bit. And pulls his legs so he will be tall. She makes his legs long.

"The mother-in-law shouts, 'Oh, my daughter-in-law, you are pulling his arms. Oh, daughter-in-law, you are pulling his arms. Oh daughter-in-law, why are you pulling his arms? What will you do if his arm breaks?'

"'Oh mother-in-law, what do you know? My husband explained to me that to hold his arm a bit and make them longer. My mother has made my arms smaller. Isn't it that I will take the money from on top of the cupboard by jumping? So pull the legs slowly, squeezing.'

"'Oh daughter-in-law, what kind of daughter-in-law are you? Oh daughter-in-law, why are you breaking the leg of the child?'

"'Oh mother-in-law, you shut up! You are just an idiot! By pulling his legs, I'm making him taller.'

"So all of a sudden she gets up and sits on the motorcycle. She says, 'Why do you put *kajal* around his eyes with the finger, not with the elbow?'

"'Oh daughter-in-law, you are crazy. Is *kajal* put around the eyes with the elbow?

"'So mother-in-law, this is the way to put *kajal* with the elbow. That my son's eyes will be bigger, just like mango halves. Whenever he winks, thirteen girls will fall down.'

"'Oh daughter-in-law, what kind of person are you? You want to keep oil on the head of a child? You put it on your head and get a massage.'

"'Oh mother-in-law, I won't put oil on me. Stay calm. Your son asked me. You live well. If a smell comes, I will not return home. Therefore, I am making myself ready in advance.'

"So the child has been born, and the other side singer women, due to much happiness, they sing and play *dholak*. This drama is of this place."

### SONG 70

*Sohar*

Oh, Nandala is born.
Govindalal is born.
Look, Nandala is born.
Govindalal is born.
Oh, listen to me, my great mother-in-law.
Oh, listen to me, my great mother-in-law.
Appease the gods quickly.
Govindalal is born.
Mother-in-law, appease the gods quickly.
Govindalal is born.
Nandalal is born.
Govindalal is born.
Oh, listen to me, my married lady friend.
Oh listen to me, my married lady friend.
Oh, quickly cook the *halua*.
Govindalal is born.
Oh, quickly grind the *pipari*.
Govindalal is born.
Nandalal is born.
Govindalal is born.
Oh, listen to me, my great *nanad*.
Oh, listen to me, my great *nanad*.
Oh, quickly play the *thariya* (metal plate).
Govindalal is born.
Oh, quickly play the *thariya*.
Nandalal is born.
Nandalal is born.
Govindalal is born.
Oh, listen to me, my great *dewar*.
Oh, listen to me, my great *dewar*.
Oh, play the flute quickly.
Govindalal is born.
Oh, play the flute quickly.
Govindalal is born.

Oh, play the flute quickly.
Govindalal is born.
Oh, listen to me, great *bhashhur.*
Have the tent pitched at the door.
Oh, listen to me, great *bhashhur.*
Have the tent pitched at the door.
Govindalal is born.
Nandalal is born.
Govindalal is born.
Oh, listen to me, my great father-in-law.
Oh, listen to me, my great father-in-law.
Quickly have the olden coin looted.
Govindalal is born.
Oh, quickly have the dancing girl dance.
Govindalal is born.
Nandalal is born.
Govindalal is born.

"Usually in *sohar* for a son," Umesh explained, "the birth of the human child is related to the birth of the Lord. In this case, the birth of Govindalal and Nandalal—two names of Krishna—are mentioned. Here, although the birth is of a simple person, it is mentioned that the Lord, son of Nand, that is Krishna Nandalal, was born. Thereafter, in the song it is mentioned that the job of everyone is given by the mother for the child—by cooking, grinding spices, and making *halua.* Thereafter, for happiness, women play the *thali* to show that the son is born. The *dewar*'s job is to play the flute after the birth of the child. The older man, the *bhasur,* has the job to have the tent pitched. The father-in-law has looted the golden coins, meaning that he has given them away freely to poor people. And quickly call the dancing woman to dance to show happiness at the birth. Although this *sohar* is sung here in a drama, the song shows that it is not drama at all. This is a real song that is sung when a child is born."

"This is a *sohar,*" Gangajali said. "When the boy is born, this is the main song. The first number. Thereafter there are many songs. But mainly only this song is sung in the beginning when a son is born.

"There are five *sohar* at the occasion of this *jaluaa,*" Gangajali explained. "But I will not sing five *sohar.* I will sing two or three *sohar.* Thereafter I will sing two *khilauna.* So by adding, there will be five."

### SONG 71

*Sohar*

Oh, Sita asks for Janakpur as a *naihar,*
And Ajudhya as a *sasural.*

Oh, Ajudhya as a *sasural.*
Oh, Sita asks for Janakpur as a *naihar,*
And Ajudhya as a *sasural.*
Ajudhya as a *sasural.*
The first boon Sita asks.
Whatever pleases her.
Whatever pleases her.
My Sita asks for Janakpur as a *naihar,*
Ajudhya as a *sasural.*
Oh, Ajudhya as a *sasural.*
Then, the second boon Sita asks,
Whatever pleases her,
Oh, whatever pleases her.
My Sita asks,
Dasarath as a father-in-law.
Oh, Kosilla as a mother-in-law,
Oh, Kosilla as a mother-in-law.
My Sita asks for,
King Dasarath as a father-in-law,
Kosilla as a mother-in-law,
Kosilla as a mother-in-law.
Then, the third boon Sita asks,
(*one line obscure*)
Oh, my Sita asks for,
Oh, Ram as a husband.
And Lachhan as a *dewar,*
Oh, Lachhan as a *dewar.*
Then Sita asks for the fourth boon,
Whatever pleases her,
Oh, whatever pleases her.
My Sita asks for,
Hanuman as a helper.
(*two lines obscure*)
Sita asks for the fifth boon.
My Sita asks,
A sandalwood altar.
A yellow sari to put on,
Oh, a yellow sari to put on.

In this song, we hear again one of Gangajali's favorite melodies. "This is also a *sohar,*" said Gangajali. "*Sohar* of Shri Ramchandra. Of God. Of Ramji. Jankiji asks, 'I want Janak as a father and Janakpur as a *naihar.* And Ajudhya as a *sasural.* And for my father Janakji. And as father-in-law, King Dasarath.'

"Well, all the *bahu*s of this place ask the same. 'And I want Kosilla as a mother-in-law.'

"And what kind of husband does she want? Like Ram. And what kind of *dewar*? Like Laxman. And a kingdom. Like Ajudhya.

"'And a sandal altar, and I sit on it with my son wearing a yellow sari. I want such a kingdom.'

"Oh, every woman wants like this for herself," Gangajali said.

Umesh said, "The Ramayan is such a thing, it is from before the Lord came on this Earth and also after his arrival. Until his *lila*, as Brahma gave wisdom to Valmiki, through the lamp, that he will be writing for the past and the future. He had such power. Whatever Ram was going to do, he wrote in advance. And whatever he is doing can easily be read. So we people think we sing *sohar* with the name of the Lord. Whatever the Lord has done, similarly the people are doing according to the Ramayan. Those who follow this religion, they are acting similarly and doing similarly. And those who do not follow, they do according to their foolish wish, that is to say, nothing good will come out of it. They do not understand what is the Lord. And who is bigger and who is smaller. And what is the meaning of the Lord's statue. They do not understand the meaning of the stone. We also sing the name of the Lord. We also sing *sohar* with the name of the Lord. We sing *bhajan* and *sohar*. We sing *jhumar*. Also adding the name of the man, we sing *sohar*, we sing *bhajan*, we sing *kilauna*. We begin with the Lord's name first. Then we sing with the names of the people. We begin with the name of the Lord because the first action is for him. Having reached on this Earth, whatever has begun is done by him, so we people are doing it."

Umesh said, "This *sohar* is about Sita. Sita asked a boon from someone. She worshiped and asked for several boons to be granted. It seems that this song comes from the time before Sita was born because it mentions that she wishes for Janakpur as a *naihar*—her birthplace. This *sohar* explains the Hindu feelings about rebirth. If they do good deeds, they ask for boons, and they get them in the next birth. This is the belief of Hindu people, that whatever people earn in this life they gain in the next life, either good or bad. If they have done good, they lead a better life in the next birth. If they have done bad against religion or humanity, they are punished in the next birth.

"Sita also asks for Dasarath as a father-in-law and Kausilla as a mother-in-law. She also asks for a husband like Ram and a *dewar* like Laxman. Here she asks for Hanuman as a helper. And at the end she asks for a sandalwood altar and a dark yellow sari."

Gangajali sang the next *sohar*:

### SONG 72

*Sohar*

*(Fan on at the beginning. You will hear when Sashi turns it off.)*

The cuckoo is black (meaning "ugly"),
But her voice is sweet.

My cuckoo, your song sounds beautiful.
And it attracts the world of the gods.
Oh cuckoo, your song sounds pleasant.
And it attracts the world of the gods.
You attract Vishnu of Gaya.
And Banimadhaunu of Pryag (Allahabad).
Oh cuckoo, you attract Kanhaiya of Gokul,
Oh, and Dasarath of Ayodhya.
Oh cuckoo, you attract Kanhaiya of Gokula,
Oh, and King Dasarath of Awadh.
Oh cuckoo, you attract Kanhaiya of Gokula,
Oh, and King Dasarath of Awadh.
So, Queen Kausila is seated on a cot.
King Dasarath is seated on the throne.
King Dasarath is seated on the throne.
Oh cuckoo, your song is beautiful, beautiful.
And it attracts the world of the gods.
Oh Kausila, what fast have you kept,
That you got Ram as fruit?
Oh, that you got Ram as fruit?
Queen Kausila is seated on the cot.
King Dasarath is seated on the throne.
King Dasarath is seated on the throne.
Oh, what a fast have you kept for the son,
That you got Ram as fruit?
Oh, that you got Ram as fruit?
Oh Kausila, what fast have you kept,
That you got the son as a fruit?
Oh, that you got the son as a fruit?
Every day I got up and took a bath in the Ganges,
And touched the feet of the sun,
Oh, and touched the feet of the sun.
My husband lit a lamp to *tulsi* (basil).
I got Ram as a fruit.
I got Ram as a fruit.
Oh, the King worshiped the basil.
He got Ram as a fruit.
He got Ram as a fruit.
I took a bath in the month of Mangh,
And I kept so many fasts,
Oh, I kept so many fasts.
My sweetheart kept a fast.
That my sweetheart kept a fast on Sundays according to the laws.
So, I got Ram as a fruit,
Oh, I got Ram as a fruit.

(HESITATION)

I fed the hungry Brahmans,
And gave clothes to the naked.
Oh, and gave clothes to the naked,
Oh my sweetheart, I brought *rukhe* (obscure) to the barren lady.
So, I got the son as a fruit.
Oh my sweetheart, I (obscure) to the barren lady.
I got the son as a fruit.
Oh, I got the son as a fruit.
Whoever sings this *sohar*,
Whoever sings this *sohar* of Ram,
Oh, whoever sings and has to listen,
Oh my son, he goes to heaven.
I got the son as a fruit.
Oh, I got Ram as a fruit.

"The cuckoo is a bird," Gangajali said. "She sings in the jungle and forest. She sings such a lovely sweet song that all those in the world of the gods are attracted to her. So Queen Kausilla, wife of Dasarath, is seated on a cot. And she has the avatar Ram in her womb. So the king is very happy. And he says that 'Queen, what kind of deeds have you done that you have given birth to four beautiful sons? How did you give birth to such beautiful and brave sons?' So the Queen replies, 'Oh King, oh master, I get up early in the morning before the sun rises,' means at four o'clock. 'I take a bath in the Ganges. And I offer water to Mother Basil. I worship her. I lit a lamp there. Therefore, being happy, I am given Ram as a son, and I kept a fast according to the rules. I do Sundays according to the rules.' *Itwar* is called 'Sunday Monday.' 'I kept the fast for twenty-four hours without a grain and water. I keep a fast. I worship them. And I offer clothes to the naked. Whoever is hungry, I feed him. I keep him happy. If there is someone's ugly and dirty child, I take him in my lap with love and play with him. Therefore, being happy, God has given such a son. I got Ram as a son.'"

"It is a language, just like a telegram," said Umesh. "Something is written a little bit. Now the job is for another person to understand. Now try to understand all the letters through the telegram. The songs are similar. One line is written, and from it you can write an entire book.

"I believe that here in this song the cuckoo is the lady who gives birth to a child. You can say in real life it shows that although she is black and she does not look beautiful, but her voice is sweet. Indian people believe black things are not beautiful. So the cuckoo is also black. But when she speaks, we love it. The singing is so sweet it also pleases the gods. So the woman pleases everyone because of her actions. The poet then begins to mention that the cuckoo is a real bird and that the cuckoo is everywhere in every house, all over the world. Like Gajdhyaar, the Vishnu of Gaya was attracted, Benimadhau of Prayag whose wives are here called cuckoo. Then Kanhaiya of Gokul is also mentioned together with the cuckoo. Then the poet says that King Dasarath is seated on the throne, and Kosilla Rani is seated on a cot in Awadh. They ask, 'Oh cuckoo, your sweet voice and you attract the world of the gods.' And he asks his wife, 'Oh Kosilla, what fast have you kept so you got a son like Ram?' Then she replies, 'Oh, I took a bath in the Ganges, worshiped the sun, lit a lamp to the holy basil, so I got Ram as a son. I also took a bath in the month of Mangh and also kept a fast, and I have kept the fast according to the rules, so I got Ram as a son. I fed the hungry Brahmans and gave clothes to those who were naked. So I got Ram as a son.' It says that 'whoever sings this *sohar* of Ram will go straight to heaven.' So this song shows what our good actions are to take in life and to be religious in order to get a great child."

FORTY-SEVEN

# THE STORY OF KRISHNA AND THE CROCODILE: A SONG WITH MANY MANY STORIES

*Gangajali sang on as the evening closed in, Sarang Hotel, Ballia, July 1989*

### SONG 73

*Sohar*

Mother Jasoda goes to take a bath.
Krishna cries.
Oh, Krishna cries.
Oh mother, I will also come along to take a bath.
I will also have a holy vision of the Jamuna.
Oh, I will also have a holy vision of the Jamuna.
Oh, Queen Jasoda requested.
Oh, listen to me, son,
Oh son, there is a crocodile in the Jamuna.
He will eat you up.
Oh, the crocodile will eat you up.
Oh mother, I will turn myself into a turtle.
She went to the saint.
Oh, went to the saint.

Oh my mother, fill up the water jug with water.
It dried out.
I did not see the crocodile.
I want to see the crocodile.
Oh, I want to see the crocodile.
Oh, I turned myself into a turtle.
Oh, I have churned the sea.
Oh, I have churned the sea.
Even then my mother, I haven't seen the crocodile.
Oh, I want to see the crocodile.
Oh, I want to see the crocodile.
Oh, I turned myself into a pig.
Oh, I stole the Earth.
Oh mother, even then I haven't seen the crocodile.
Oh, I want to see the crocodile.
Oh, I want to see the crocodile.
Oh, I turned myself into a pig.
Oh, I went to the underground world.
Oh, I went to the underground world.
My mother, even then I haven't seen the crocodile.
Oh, I want to see the crocodile.
Oh, I want to see the crocodile.
I turned myself into Baman (a short God).
Oh, I went to King Bali.
Oh, I went to King Bali.
Oh, my mother, I measured all fourteen worlds.
I haven't seen the crocodile.
Oh, I haven't seen the crocodile.
I turned myself into Ram.
I went to Lanka.
Oh, I went to Lanka.
Oh my mother, I killed Rawan and came back home.
Oh, I haven't seen the crocodile.
I want to see the crocodile.
Oh, I want to see the crocodile.
Oh, I turned myself into Krishna.
Oh, I went to Gokhul.
Oh, I went to Mathura.
Oh, my mother, I killed King Kans and came back home.
I haven't seen the crocodile.
I want to see the crocodile.
Oh, I turned myself into a child.
Oh, I have come to your lap.
Oh, I have come to your lap.

Oh my mother, I still haven't seen the crocodile.
I want to see the crocodile.
Oh, I want to see the crocodile.
Queen Jasoda replied politely,
Listen, my son.
Oh listen, my son.
Oh son, your *lila* (holy play) is unlimited.
The crocodile is nothing.
Oh, the crocodile is nothing.

This is a song that is all about the words, the story, and not the melody. Without knowing Bhojpuri and without knowing the stories referred to in the song, this piece can sound monotonous. To make an absurd connection, it reminds me of the recitative passages of classical opera, the conversational matter that links the real songs, the arias. For any composer, this is always an important question. What is important here, the melody or the text? For most of Gangajali's songs, the melody is very important and exhibits a great deal of musical variety. By comparison, the melody here seems to drone on and on and become boring to those who do not understand Bhojpuri. But the story moves forward quickly, moving from incarnation to incarnation.

"This is also a *sohar*," Gangajali said. "This is a *sohar* for Krishna. The other one was for Ram. Jasoda is going to take a bath in the Jamuna. Krishna says, 'Oh mother, I will also come along to do *darshan* (holy vision) of the Jamuna.' Isn't it true that we tell children a lie? We tell them there is a *baba*, there is *bhakanuan* (obscure). It will bite you. That is, he will bite you. 'Run away, stay at home, he will catch you. I am going now.' Then Jasodaji says, 'Oh son, in the Jamuna is a big big crocodile. He will eat you up. Do not go to the Jamuna. I will return right after taking a bath.' Then the Lord says, Krishna says, 'Oh mother, I was born as a fish. I turned into a fish and went in the saint's water pot, the water of the saint's water jug when the saint was taking a bath. He was thinking that how such a big fish could live in the water.' Then the Lord replies, 'I am testing you.' When we people offer water to Lord Sun, so he begins to offer the water. So in the form of a fish, the Lord came into his cupped hands.

"Then the saint says, 'Oh, he has come under my protection. I won't leave him.' In such water of his water pot he keeps the fish. And he puts water in it and keeps pouring. Oh, the Lord in the form of a fish gets bigger and bigger, and the water pot burst. So the saint says, 'Is this a fish or something else, brother?' Then he meditates on the Lord to see. He has a great revelation. When he sees with his wisdom, then he recognized the form, and he says, 'Oh Lord, pardon my mistake. I forgot to recognize you.' Then he released him. Then he says, 'I went near the *muni*s. I absorbed the water of the water pot. Even then I haven't seen the crocodile. And you are saying that the crocodile will catch you. I will come to see surely. Oh, I took the form of a turtle. You will have heard it. I churned the sea. Even then I have not seen the crocodile. And I took the form of Baman. I went to

King Bali, and I measured fourteen worlds in two steps. Even then I haven't seen the crocodile. And I took the form of Braah (a pig). I went in the underground world. And I brought the Earth and established it in its place. Even then I didn't see the crocodile. I took the form of Ram avatar. And I went from forest to forest. I went to Lanka. I killed brave Rawan and came back home. I haven't seen the crocodile. I took the form of Krishna, and I killed brave Kans, and I came back. And being like a child, I'm in your lap. What is the crocodile? I will surely see it.'

"So she feels defeated. She recognizes that this is not a child. He is God. He is the Lord. So she joins her hands and prays, 'Oh child, I told you a lie that the crocodile will catch you. Your *lila* is unknown and unlimited. Nobody can understand it. In this world, in all three worlds, nobody can understand your ways. Does somebody know the *lila* of the Lord?'"

"In this composition, all the religious books come together to form a song," Umesh said. "Each story, each line, has a book that should accompany it. This song is *really something.*

"As sometimes the mother does not want to take her child with her, so mother Jasoda goes to take a bath in the Jamuna. Krishna cries, and he requests his mother, 'I would like to go to take *darshan* of the Jamuna with you.' Then the mother Jasoda told him politely, 'My son, listen to me, the crocodile has come in the Jamuna, and he will eat you up.'

"Here a new story begins. Krishna says, 'Mother, I made myself as a fish and went to the *muni*. Oh mother, I drank the water of the jug in which the *muni* carries water. But this *kamandal* was magical and never dried, but I drank all the water of it. But I did not see the crocodile. So I want to see the crocodile.

"'I have made myself as a tortoise.' This is another story out of the *Puranas.* All these stories are from different books. This story comes when the gods were churning the sea of milk, the *chhir sagar.* While the gods were churning the sea, they had some mountain to put in the sea to churn it. The Lord made himself into a tortoise and went down into the Earth to hold the mountain on his back. 'Even then I did not see the crocodile there. I want to see the crocodile.'

"Then another story begins. 'Oh mother, I made myself as a pig. When somebody had stolen the Earth, I took the Earth out from the underground world.' You will see sometimes a picture of the Lord as a pig with the Earth on his two horns.

"Then another story begins. 'Oh mother, I have made myself as Baman and went to King Bali.' Lord Baman is measured with the height of a finger. He was fifty-two fingers high. He came to King Bali as a Brahman, and Bali offered to him. So Baman asked that he wanted three feet of Earth out of Bali's kingdom. Baman measured all the sky with one foot, the Earth with the second foot, and the underground world with the third foot. So nothing was left. But he gave this to Baman. Actually, Baman was the Lord. He says, 'Oh, I have made myself in the form of Baman, but I have not seen the crocodile.'

"Then another story begins. 'I have made myself the entire universe, but I haven't seen the crocodile. I wish to see the crocodile.'

"Then another story. 'I took for myself the form of Ram and went to Lanka. I killed Rawan, and I came home. But I have not seen the crocodile. I want to see the crocodile.'

"Then are more thoughts of the poet. The story turns to the future. 'I took a birth as Gokul. Oh, I went to Mathura. I killed Kans, and I came home. But I haven't seen the crocodile. I want to see the crocodile.'

"'Mother I have taken the form of a child and came into your lap. Even then, Mother, I haven't seen the crocodile. I want to see the crocodile.' And mother Jasoda politely told to her son, 'Oh son, your *lila* is unlimited. The crocodile is nothing actually.'

"In this *sohar* the poet has collected almost all the forms that Lord has taken in Hinduism. It also shows that the Lord can take any form—pig, man, fish, whatever is there. He has unlimited power."

FORTY-EIGHT

# UMESH TELLS THE REMAINDER OF THE KRISHNA STORY

*At our apartment, one winter evening, Banaras, 2007*

"So I was telling you about the life of Krishna," Umesh said. "This song gives you a glimpse of many episodes in his various incarnations. When Kans held the leg of the baby girl and started to beat her on the stone, she slipped out of his hand and went into space. And a voice was heard. We call this voice *akasvani*, which means the 'voice from the sky.' The voice said, 'Oh Kans, you wanted to kill me, but the person who will kill you has been born.' So Krishna was born to kill Kans.

"After hearing this, Kans got scared, and he did not know where the child had taken birth who was going to kill him. So he ordered his secret agents to make a search for the child and bring him to the king. So, the same-aged children were brought, and they were killed. But he had no courage to touch Krishna because Nand was also a powerful person.

"Kans made so many other attempts to kill Krishna. He sent Putana, a magic woman who could change her form. She made herself beautiful and went to Nand's house. Krishna saw her and smiled. This woman had already poisoned the nipple of her breast. She got inside the house and took the child into her lap. Yasoda thought she is someone from nearby that we know. Putana kept playing with the child, and slowly she gave him her breast to his mouth. Krishna held her breast with both of his hands. Instead of milk, he began to suck the life out of her body. And she flew in the air with Krishna. She just went into the sky and fell far away to the ground. She got bigger like a giant, and Krishna was playing with her just like a child. And people ran to see the child, and they thought this demon wanted to kill the child, and somehow that child was saved.

"Krishna was growing and playing among the *gopi*s, doing his *lila*, grazing cows, playing the flute. He was playing ball, and the ball fell into Lake Kalidah. Krishna jumped into this lake, and a very poisonous snake named Kali was living in it. This fearful snake had many hoods. Krishna fashioned a bridle for the nose of the snake to prevent it from biting. It is often depicted that Krishna is dancing on the head of a many-hooded snake, playing his flute.

"Another story is that the *gopi*s used to take a bath naked in the Jamuna. The god Varuna lives in the water. So Krishna stole the clothes of the *gopi*s and went into the tree to teach them not to take a bath naked in front of Varuna.

"When people used to worship Indra, the Lord of Rain, Krishna told people to worship Goberdhan because they were grazing the cows and getting food from there. Because of this, Indra got very angry, and the pouring rain began. And Krishna held the mountain on his little finger and saved people from the rain under the mountain.

"When Krishna grew bigger there was the last attempt by Kans to kill him. Krishna and his brother Balram were invited by King Kans to participate in wrestling. Kans had many healthy wrestlers there. When Krishna left for Mathura, he reached the door of the stadium. Kans had already settled there, and his wild, drunken elephants were at the gate. Krishna got there and held the trunks of the elephants and killed them. He went on straight to the wrestling field where Kans was seated. And he killed Kans."

FORTY-NINE

# MORE *JALUAA* SONGS AND STORIES

*We remain in the Sarang Hotel, Ballia, 1989, as Gangajali sings more songs for childbirth*

Now that the dough baby, a son, has been "born," the women's drama continues. Just as they would for a human child, they sing *khilauna* and *sohar*, genres that are expressly sung around six days or twelve days after childbirth. In this example, you can hear the word "khilauna" being sung if you listen carefully. Throughout the song, pairs of lines sung at a higher pitch are contrasted with pairs of lines at a lower pitch. The lines at the higher pitch mark the beginning of each new stanza. During the song, Gangajali starts to cough, and she and Sashi both unwrap cough drops. Nevertheless, once they are finished, they resume the song. Again, such commonplace events are not considered "mistakes" as such, because things happen and the singing can just proceed.

### SONG 74

*Khilauna*

*(Gangajali has a coughing problem and opens a cough drop.)*

The toy seller lady goes from lane to lane.
The toy seller lady goes from lane to lane.

For her son,
Will somebody buy a toy for their son?
Will somebody buy a toy for their son?
Will somebody buy a toy for their son?
The toy seller lady goes from lane to lane.
The toy seller lady goes from lane to lane.
For her son,
Will somebody buy a toy for their son?
Will somebody buy a toy for their son?
Mother Jasoda comes out of the house.
Mother Jasoda comes out of the house.
I will buy a toy for my son.
I will buy a toy for my son.
I will buy.
I will buy a toy for my son.
I will buy a toy for my son.
What kind of toys do you bring for my son?
What kind of toys do you bring for my son?
The toy seller lady goes from lane to lane.
The toy seller lady goes from lane to lane.
For her son,
Will somebody buy a toy for their son?
Will somebody buy a toy for their son?
Mother Jasoda comes out of the house.
Mother Jasoda comes out of the house.
I will buy.
What kind of toys do you bring for my son?
What kind of toys do you bring for my son?
What kind of toys do you bring for brother?
Married grandmother comes out of the house.
Married grandmother comes out of the house.
What do you bring?
What kind of toys do you bring for the boy?
What kind of toys do you bring for the boy?
I bring rattles and small sticks and silky toys.
I bring the silky toys.
I bring the chutney toy for the son.
I bring the chutney toy for the son.
The golden plate is full of pearls.
The golden plate is full of pearls.
Then toy seller lady,
Toy seller lady, take the payment from my son.
Toy seller lady, take the payment from my son.
Mother, may your son live for ages and ages.

Mother, may your son live for ages and ages.
I will bring every day.
I will bring toys for the son every day.
I will bring toys for the son every day.

"This is a *khilauna*," Gangajali explained. "This is the first *khilauna* when children were born in the house. The toy seller lady, having toys in the basket, is going around the neighborhood. 'Oh, who will buy for a child? Will somebody buy a toy for their son?' Then Jasoda comes out of her house and says, 'Come on, sister, I will take the toy for my son.' So she buys a toy. And with happiness she offers a dish full of pearls. Oh, because of much happiness the toy seller lady blesses her son. 'Your child will live for ages and ages, and I will come every day with toys for your son.'"

### SONG 75

*Khilauna*

So Nandalalaji dances.
His mother has him dance.
So Nandalala dances.
His mother has him dance.
His mother has him dance.
Nandalala dances.
His mother has him dance, his mother has him dance.
Nandalala dances.
His mother has him dance.
Nandalala dances.
Jasoda is teaching him to hold the fingers.
Jasoda is teaching him to hold the fingers.
He thumps his feet to move ahead.
Kanhaiya steps ahead, Kanhaiya.
Nandalala dances.
His mother has him dance.
Nandalala dances.
On this side Mathura, on the other side Gokula.
Kanhaiya holds the current in the middle.
Nandalala dances.
His mother has him dance.
The butter and cream is in the golden bowl.
Happily feeds, his mother happily feeds him.
Nandalala dances.
His mother has him dance.
Nandalala dances.
The sandalwood swing and the chain of flowers.

And Kanhaiya swings in it.
His mother swings him.
Nandalala dances.
His mother has him dance.
Nandalala dances.
His mother has him dance.
Time to time Mohan,
From the home of Jasoda,
Places fruit at the bank of the Jumana.
Places fruit.
Nandalala dances.
His mother has him dance.
Nandalala dances.
When I go to sell yogurt in Mathura town,
When I go to sell yogurt in Mathura town,
Nandalala breaks my pitcher along the way.
Breaks Nandalala.
Nandalala dances.
His mother has him dance.
I went to complain,
In the courtyard of Jasoda.
I went to complain,
In the courtyard of Jasoda.
Oh mother, you do not refuse your Kanhaiya.
Your Kanhaiya.
Nandalala dances.
His mother has him dance.
Nandalala dances.
His mother has him dance.
Butter-seller lady, you are a liar.
Butter-seller lady, you are a liar.
And by caste, you are a liar.
Butter-seller lady, you are a liar.
And by caste, you are a liar.
My son is swinging in the swing until now.
My son swings.
Nandalala dances.
His mother has him dance.

"Her son has become older now," Gangajali explained. "So people think, 'When will he walk?' We teach him to walk by holding out a finger. Then doing like this 'thump-thump,' 'tum-tum-tum-tum.' The child walks. How beautiful he looks. Then they begin to walk and play. Then Mother Jasoda swings him in the sandalwood hammock. She feeds him butter and cream. She puts him to sleep. And then he just disappears from the hammock. In one home he is in the hammock, and in another, in a big form, he plays flute at the Jamuna. He entices the *gopi*s. He breaks his pitcher of water. He keeps breaking these pots. So the girlfriends say, 'Let us go to complain in Jasoda's house.' So the *gopi*s come to complain. Mother Jasoda replies, 'Oh, my son is so small, and I fed him, and he is sleeping in the hammock. You *gopi*s are liars. Even your caste are liars. You keep adding water in yogurt and buttermilk.' And they say, "I swear by Ram, I swear by my son there is no water in it. My yogurt is good. You take it.' 'By caste you are liars. You go to your home. My son is sleeping in the hammock.' This is the meaning of the *khilauna*."

Gangajali continued explaining the *jaluaa*. "The child we have delivered in the *jaluaa*, out of happiness for that, we sing *sohar*. And then we sing *khilauna* after *sohar*. Then some *jhumar* and some *bhajan*s. We sing very many songs. Generally, we sing five *sohar*, five *khilauna*, five *sohar*, five *bhajan*—these many."

The sound of the next song is disturbed throughout by the noise of the overhead fan. It was July and the rains had started. It was just so darn hot and humid that working with the fan off felt almost impossible. But we did it. But in this next song you will easily hear how much wind disturbance the fan created, muddying the entire performance.

### SONG 76

#### *Jhumar*

*(fan on)*

Oh my *bhaujiya* smiles like a flower.
Oh my *bhaujiya* smiles like a flower.
Oh my *bhaujiya* smiles like a flower.
*Bhauji*, brother has brought one *tika* for your forehead.
Oh my *bhaujiya,*
The *dewar* will have leaves fit on it.
Oh my *bhaujiya*, the brother will have leaves fit on it,
Oh my *bhaujiya*, she smiles like a flower.
Oh my *bhaujiya*, she smiles like a flower.
Then *bhauji*, the older brother will bring droplet earrings for your ears.
Oh my *bhaujiya*, little brother will have the nose ring made.
Oh my *bhaujiya*, little brother will have the nose ring made.
Oh my *bhaujiya,*
Oh my *bhaujiya*, she smiles like a flower.
Oh my *bhaujiya*, she smiles like a flower.
Then *bhauji*, the older brother will bring golden bangles for your hands.

Oh my *bhauji*, little brother will bring flowers for your hair.
Oh my *bhauji*, little brother will bring flowers for your hair.
Oh my *bhaujiya*, she smiles like a flower.
Oh my *bhaujiya*, she smiles like a flower.
*Bhaujiya*, the older brother will bring anklets for your feet.
Oh my *bhaujiya*, the little brother will bring toe rings.
Oh my *bhaujiya*, the little brother will have the ankle bells attached.
Oh my *bhaujiya*, she smiles like a flower.
Oh my *bhaujiya*, she smiles like a flower.
Oh my *bhaujiya*, the older brother will bring the southern scarf.
The little brother will have the bodice stitched.
Oh my bhaujiya, the little brother will have the bodice stitched.
Oh my *bhaujiya*, she smiles like a flower.

"So all the women of the house and of the neighborhood are sitting and singing and waking all the night for the *jaluaa*," Gangajali said. "When the *jaluaa* is born, *sohar* and *khilauna* are sung. We will make the form of the *jaluaa* this big, out of dough, and we will wrap him in a new cloth. We will draw ear, nose, hair, everything for him in that form, just like a boy. And all those women and those who are dancing play the drama. Those who do the drama, the child is given to every lap, one after another. And every woman will take him in her lap with love. And whoever has one paisa, one rupee, ten rupees, ₹50, ₹100 (from pennies to $1.50), they bless and offer it. They give blessings to the child. The money is given to the woman who does this drama. And when they are finished, we take the child where we have made the *kohabar*. We place the child in the *kohabar*, where he will remain all night.

"When the bridegroom and bride will come back home after the wedding, the child will *not* be shown to them. Before their arrival, it will be hidden. And whatever women are there, they will go to their own home now. And the women of the house, if there is time to sleep, if there is a little time to rest, the sun has not risen yet, they will take a little sleep, or they will get busy with their work. Outsider or neighbor women, when they go to their home, this much sweet or *gur* (raw sugar) and rice is given to them. We call it *muri*. It is made out of rice. It is parched. Puffed rice. So that rice and three or four pieces of sweets are given to all women. And mustard oil is also put on their head, and *sindur* is rubbed in their parting like this. All women go to their home. Now they wait for when the bride and bridegroom will arrive. They quickly cook *puri*s and *khir*, 'Do this, do that, we have to feed the *barat*.'"

And these activities lead us to the end of the musical accompaniment, for the moment, of the wedding for the family of the bridegroom.

"Next I will explain the program from the bride's side," Gangajali promised.

## INTERLUDE TEN

# SHOWING WHAT THE MISS FAWNS SAID AND WHAT MRS. HITTAWAY THOUGHT

ON THE FOLLOWING DAY, LORD FAWN WENT TO HIS MOTHER AT FAWN Court. He was satisfied that he had explained his circumstances honorably and exactly to Lizzie Eustace. Should any questions arise, he could refer back to those honest words he had slowly and carefully set out. Of the details of Lizzie's wealth, he knew much—of her estate in Scotland and the £8,000 she had inherited, probably most of it already spent, he bemoaned.

*"Lord Fawn thought a great deal about money. Being a poor man, filling a place fit only for rich men, he had been driven to think of money, and had become self-denying and parsimonious—perhaps we may say hungry and close-fisted. Such a condition of character is the natural consequence of such a position. There is, probably, no man who becomes naturally so hard in regard to money as he who is bound to live among rich men, who is not rich himself, and who is yet honest. The weight of the work of life in these circumstances is so crushing, requires such continued thought, and makes itself so continually felt, that the mind of the sufferer is never free from the contamination of sixpences."*

Lord Fawn and his mother agreed that she would invite Lizzie and her little boy for a visit to Fawn Court. Lord Fawn, who had failed twice in his love affairs, was eager to succeed this time and thus had not given a great deal of thought to the character of Lady Eustace.

*"But, for aught he knew, she might be afflicted by every vice to which a woman can be subject. In truth, she was afflicted by so many, that the addition of all the others could hardly have made her worse than she was. She had never sacrificed her beauty to a lover—she had never sacrificed anything to anybody—nor did she drink. It would be*

*difficult, perhaps to say anything else in her favour; and yet Lord Fawn was quite content to marry her, not having seen any reason why she should not make a good wife. Nor had Sir Florian seen any reason;—but she had broken Sir Florian's heart."*

The seven sisters were eager to gossip about the choice their brother had made.

*"'She is very beautiful,' said Lydia, the fifth.*

*"And clever,' said Cecilia, the sixth.*

*"'Beauty and cleverness won't make a good wife,' said Amelia, who was the wise one of the family.*

*"Augusta Hittaway, Lady Fawn's eldest daughter, exclaimed, 'You don't mean it! . . . She is the greatest vixen in all London. . . . And such a liar. . . . You don't know her mamma.'*

*"'It's my belief that she is over head and ears in debt again. But I'll learn. And when I have found out, I shall not scruple to tell Frederic. . . . The long and the short of it is this mamma, that I've heard quite enough about Lady Eustace to feel certain that Frederic would live to repent it.'"*

Naturally, this news greatly distressed Lady Fawn. But she determined to carry out her mission to visit Lizzie that very day. Lizzie *"fully intended to make a conquest of her future mother-in-law and sister-in-law;—for the note that had come up to her from the India Office had told her that Augusta would accompany Lady Fawn."*

*"'Dear, dear Lady Fawn!' she said, throwing herself into the arms and nestling herself against the bosom of the old lady. . . . Her manner was almost perfect. Perhaps there was a little too much of gesture, too much gliding motion, too violent an appeal with the eyes, too close a pressure of the hand. No suspicion, however, of all this would have touched Lady Fawn had she come to Mount Street without calling in Warwick Square on the way. But those horrible words of her daughter were ringing in her ears, and she did not know how to conduct herself."*

Lizzie had hidden her French novels and had placed a small white Bible in a conspicuous spot on the table. She had put on quite a show. It was agreed, with some discomfort on the part of both parties, that she would come down to Fawn Court the following week and stay for a fortnight.

*"'Nasty, stupid, dull puritanical drones,' Lizzie said to herself, once alone. 'If he don't like it, he may lump it. After all, it's no such great catch.'"*

"Lord Fawn returned home in the morning," Umesh said, "and he is taking breakfast and tells his mother, Lady Fawn, that he is engaged to Lady Eustace. He is telling this while he is putting a spoonful of egg in his mouth. I think this kind of conversation took place in those days in the families, so these small details are very meaningful. It also makes a person read it. He tells his mother to go and see Lady Eustace and 'take one of my sisters with you.' Lady Fawn is happy with that. And he leaves. 'I suppose you will want to see Clara (Mrs. Hittaway) he said.'

"While Lady Fawn goes to meet Lizzie, she meets first with Clara, who is her married daughter and a wise woman. Lady Fawn tells her daughter that her brother is engaged and she is going to see his fiancée. Clara asks, 'Who is she?' And she replies, 'Lizzie Eustace.'

"All of the sudden Clara takes a big breath. *Oh Dear! She is a vixen!* How could he think to marry her? She gets really upset and says so many things: you can find out thousands of criticisms of such a bad woman. She is full of faults, and it is hard to find any goodness in her. She also says she will make an inspection of Lizzie's past. Clara, the sister, says, 'I will tell Frederic all the information about Lizzie.' She says, 'The marriage will last two years. She has already killed one in six months who married her to live longer. How long is Frederic going to live?' Now, Lady Fawn goes to Lizzie Eustace, and Lizzie Eustace does not leave any of her weaknesses on top so she will be considered bad. She puts her hair lock up (that she uses to make people flutter). She uses her favorite perfume and places the Bible on the table, which can be easily seen but is a bit hidden—and so many other things. For the social person, to see the Bible on the table pleases—that this person goes through the Bible teachings, so she must be a good woman.

"As soon as Lizzie greets Lady Fawn, she smells an unusual fragrance from her forehead wrinkles. Lizzie has a yucky kind of feeling. Lady Fawn and Lizzie go inside, and Lizzie tries to make such good conversation by telling her that 'Oh, she will call her "Mother."' Lady Fawn never says, 'Yes, you may call me Mother.' She never accepts it. And Lizzie does all the work with such excitement that it confuses Lady Fawn. There is so much other talk. And Lizzie holds the Bible against her heart and says, 'This will be my guide.' This is the absolutely fake talk of hers. So now, since Lady Fawn had already been warned by her daughter Clara, she was inspecting everything very carefully and making her decision and thinking over each point. She went back to Clara's house to pick up her daughter. Clara asks if she loves Lady Lizzie, and Lady Fawn replies, 'Did I ever say that? But she is coming to my home for a fortnight. We will see.'

"And the last thing, she never tells Clara about the Bible she saw there, but Lady Fawn never forgets it. It is my concept that the person who says I swear for this, for this, for this,—mostly they are liars. Otherwise people can trust a person if they think that their talking is true. An honest person doesn't have to swear over and again."

## FIFTY

# CHARLOTTE WISER LEAVES KARIMGANJ

*Umesh at his home in Karimganj, aged twenty-seven*

"When Dadi was leaving, she was distributing her things, giving them away. I was sitting here in the dining room and reading some book. Dadi appeared and handed me her watch and also a red Parker fountain pen made out of gold and made in England, and she said, 'This is for you.'

"And all of the sudden it occurred to me for the first time—I had no way of thinking that she will not come back soon. When she left India at this time, now I feel that she knew that she would not be able to continue living in the village. She was old. I couldn't feel that she would not come back to live here. I thought she was here forever. Yeah, I thought she was here forever and that I never would feel lonely. But she returned in 1976, during the Emergency period in India. Indira Gandhi was the prime minister. And she came in a wheelchair—oh, she was in a wheelchair in the village. She couldn't hear me properly, and she used artificial tears to drop in her eyes. But she could see."

"And oh, she was happy, very happy. She was here with Dana, her grandson, Ray, her granddaughter, and Ray's husband, David, and Allen, the oldest grandson of Dadi, and Susan, Allen's wife. She is my *bhabi*. She joked with me a lot. She offered me a bit of her soda, and I drank it all! Like a boy. I was about twenty-seven years old.

"And the village people used to ask her, 'Memsabh, when will you come back?' And each time she said, 'The Lord knows,' '*Ishwar janta hai*.' This was the only time when I saw her in a wheelchair in the village and the only time I saw her in trouser and shirt. Before she always wore a white sari or a white long skirt and a white blouse. But after 1976 she never came back to the village thereafter or to India thereafter."

FIFTY-ONE

# WEDDING NIGHT

*With Gangajali and Sashi, the Sarang Hotel, another hot day in July 1989*

This next song is characterized by lines that begin with a small upward leap followed by a gradual downward descent. The melancholy words of the bride leaving her parent's home are nicely matched by the downward melodic drifts in the melody.

### SONG 77

*Lachari*

Oh father, why have you planted the dense garden?
Why have you planted the flower garden?
Why have you planted the flower garden?
Oh father, why have you arranged my wedding?
Oh Lord, why have I been sent to my husband's home?
Oh Lord, why have I been sent to my husband's home?
Oh, daughter is plucking flowers in the flower garden.
Oh Lord, the garden is planted for the shade.
Oh Lord, the garden is planted for the shade.
Oh daughter, my thigh became holy because of your marriage.
Oh Lord, I have performed the *gauna* ritual to get holy ashes.

Oh Lord, I have performed the *gauna* ritual to get holy ashes.
Oh father, that is why you have arranged my *gauna*.
Oh Lord, my dream became fulfilled.
Oh Lord, my dream became fulfilled.
Oh father, I left my *buiahua* in the *kohabar.*
Oh Lord, I have gone after leaving my parent's home.
Oh Lord, I have gone after leaving my parent's home.
Oh father, you haven't sent a single letter or any news.
Oh Lord, you have not listened to my news.
Oh Lord, you have not listened to my news.
Oh father, for what reason have you brought me on this Earth?
Oh Lord, for what reason have you raised me?
Oh daughter, let the fair begin in Hajipur.
I will change your fate.
Oh father, bronze and brass, these can be changed.
Oh Lord, how can you change my fate?

"This is the meaning of this *lachari,*" Gangajali said. "The girl is talking to her father. 'Oh, Father'—in our side people call their father *babu* or *babuji*. 'Why did you arrange my marriage? And why did you plant this flower garden?' The father replies, 'Oh daughter, if anyone gets tired, he can sit in its shade. That is to say, whoever is in trouble can get protection from my family. Therefore, I have planted a garden for the shade. And I have planted the flower garden so whenever you want to, you can pluck flowers and offer them.' 'Oh Father, why have you arranged my wedding and *gauna*?' 'Daughter, I have arranged your marriage because of giving birth to a daughter so my thigh can become holy.' When I perform *kanyadan*, at that moment my thigh becomes holy, and *gubte* means to endure worldly sadness–happiness. The *gauna* is performed to send out the daughter to her *sasural* a second time. Everybody gets the happiness of worldly life. She says to her father, 'Oh Father, what kind of fate do I have? What kind of deed have I done that I got married? My husband has left me in the *kohabar* and gone to the east. He has not looked for me or tried to get any message. He has not gotten any news from me. I didn't get any happiness. What kind of fate do I have?' Then the father says, 'Daughter, the *mela* will take place. I will take your karma there and change it. I will buy a new fate for my daughter.' The daughter says to her father, 'Oh Father, if any pots get broken, you can go and exchange them at the shop. But how can fate be changed?'"

Gangajali continued to describe the wedding traditions from the bride's side. "So the *barat* will go to the city of the girl, to the village, to the house with the musicians and the musical instruments. So the *barat* arrives in the girl's neighborhood with the singers, musicians, musical instruments, bright lights, enormous loudspeakers. People begin to say, 'The *barat* has arrived.' Now we have to go greet them. So from the side of the bride, ten people with her father go with a garland. From the other side, the bridegroom's people come. From here the bride's people go, and the bride's side people offer the garlands around the necks of the groom's side people. They meet them, and they offer the garlands around their necks. And the two fathers meet chest to chest. Then the *barat* moves from there ahead. Then, here at the door, the barber lady, similarly, she takes a plate as it was done in *parichhawan*. Now, the second time *parichhawan* will take place of the bridegroom. Then the barber lady has on the plate similarly rice, turmeric paste, and *roli* (turmeric paste and rice). She remains standing there. And the mother-in-law, *sali* (wife's younger sister), *sarahaj* (wife's brother's wife), and the other women of the neighborhood come and stay there. And they are singing. The *barat* is coming, so they sing the first song."

### SONG 78

Oh Father Anurudha, sweep your own lane.
The bridegroom *damad* is coming. (After marriage, he becomes *damad* to the *sasur.*)
The bridegroom *damad* is coming.
The bridegroom *damad* is coming.
Oh Father Anurudha, sweep your own lane.
The bridegroom *damad* is coming.
The bridegroom *damad* is coming.
Oh brother, sweep your own lane.
The bridegroom *damad* is coming.
The bridegroom *damad* is coming.

Like many of the other songs, each line here begins on a high pitch, or leaps there, followed by a gently descending line. This basic form is common in singing all around the world. I was delighted and surprised to hear Gangajali sing this song as it matched, in its melody and in its text, as a corresponding song sung by Hindu women living half a world away in Trinidad in the West Indies. Having been brought to this outpost through the indentured labor system, they managed to retain, without a written record, without any recording, the songs of their motherland. "Sweep the way" for the barat is a very important greeting for the party of the groomsmen as they arrive in the bride's village.

"After the *barat* arrives at the door, then the women sing," Gangajali explained. "The *barat* was asked to arrive early, so the door was decorated in the evening. But they arrived at midnight, and it is so dark that we have to light the lamp to see. They came in the dark. 'Oh, when we see with the lamp that some of them are one-eyed, some have a crooked mouth, and some have no legs. And some of the beards are hanging down, and somebody has shaved their head bald. Some are naked. What kind of *barat* arrived here?' This is a kind of *gali* for the *barati* people."

## SONG 79

### *Gali*

I asked for the *barat* to arrive early.
I asked for the *barat* to arrive early.
Oh, they arrived late.
We asked for a big electric light.
They appeared with an earthen lamp.
I hit on your sister.
She is laughing around Ballia.
I hit on your sister.
I hit on your sister.
I asked them to bring young people.
Oh, they brought the old men.
I hit on your sister.
She is laughing all over Ballia.
I hit on your sister.
She is laughing all over Ballia.
I asked for them to bring the people who chew pan.
They brought the ones with black teeth.
I hit on your sister.
She is laughing all over Ballia.
I hit on your sister.
She is laughing all over Ballia.
We asked them to bring an elephant and horse.
They came riding on the donkeys.
I hit on your sister.
She is laughing all over Ballia.
I hit on your sister.
She is laughing all over Ballia.

This mild and gentle *gali* is sung to a lilting melody, with an upbeat section that explains that "I hit on your sister. She is laughing all over Ballia." The purpose here is not to offend the bridegroom's party but to amuse them with a silly song.

And then the next *gali*, making fun of the bridegroom, who has just arrived with his *barat*.

## SONG 80

### *Gali*

Bridegroom, I see there is no *kajal* around your eyes.
Bridegroom, I see there is no *kajal* around your eyes.

Your mother is fucked by the oil presser.
Why didn't she come along?
Oh bridegroom, why didn't she come with you tonight?
She kept coming, and she kept fucking.
Mother-in-law keeps adorning her basket.
She was having one after another.
She kept coming, and she kept fucking.
Mother-in-law keeps adorning her basket.
Mother-in-law was having one after another.
Bridegroom, I saw your mouth. There is no betel in there.
Oh, your sister is fucked by the betel seller.
Why didn't he come with you tonight?
Why didn't he come with you tonight?
She kept coming, and she kept fucking.
Mother-in-law keeps adorning her basket.
Mother-in-law was having one after another.
She kept coming, and she kept fucking.
She kept adorning her door.
Mother-in-law was having one after another.
Bridegroom, I see you there are no clothes on your body.
Oh, your *bhauji* is fucked by the tailor.
Why didn't he come with the bridegroom tonight?
Oh, your *bhauji* is fucked by the tailor.
Why didn't he come with the bridegroom tonight?
She kept coming, and she kept fucking.
She had her house poked.
Mother-in-law was having one after another.
She kept coming, and she kept fucking.
She had her house poked.
Mother-in-law was having one after another.

"This *gali* is before *parichhawan*," Gangajali said. "The women ask, 'Oh stupid bridegroom, there is no *kajal* around your eyes. How is your mother? She kept the oil presser man for a day. He kept giving oil and making the *kajal* in the *kajarauta* (metal container in which *kajal* is kept). She could put it around your eyes.' She says it again, 'Oh bridegroom, you don't have betel leaf in your mouth. Your sister kept the betel-leaf seller. She would have given you the betel. So you could have chewed it while coming here.' 'Oh bridegroom, you don't even have your wedding garments. Your sister went to a tailor for one night. Even then he could give you a pair of clothes. Yes. You don't even have shoes on your feet. Your younger sister goes to the leather worker. The leather worker would have kept your sister for one night and would have fixed your shoes so you could have put them on and gotten ready.' This *gali* is for the bridegroom. He already has *kajal* around his eyes, he is also chewing pan. He is adorned. But even then, we will sing a *gali* like this."

"Then they do the *parichhawan* blessing," Gangajali said. "The bride's mother will do the *parichhawan* first."

### SONG 81

### *Parichhawan*

Great mother goes out after performing *parichhan*.
Oh, she has the ring and the *sindur* container in her hand.
Oh, she has the ring and the *sindur* container in her hand.
Whether I do *parichhan* of the crown on the head of the bridegroom,
Or the *tilak* on the forehead of the bridegroom,
Or the *tilak* on the forehead of the bridegroom,
The crown on the head falls on the ground.
Do *parichhan* of the forehead of the bridegroom.
Do *parichhan* of the forehead of the bridegroom.
The bridegroom's *sarahaji* (brother-in-law) goes out after performing *parichhan*.
He has the ring and the *sindur* container in his hand.
He has the ring and the *sindur* container in his hand.
Whether I do *parichhan* of the crown on the head of the bridegroom,
Or *tilak* on the forehead of the bridegroom,
Or *tilak* on the forehead of the bridegroom,
The crown of the head falls on the ground.
Do *parichhan* of the forehead of the bridegroom.
Do *parichhan* of the forehead of the bridegroom.
Married sister goes out after performing *parichhan*.
She has the ring and the *sindur* container in her hand.
She has the ring and the *sindur* container in her hand.
Whether I do *parichhan* of the crown on the head of the bridegroom,
Or the *tilak* on the forehead of the bridegroom,
Or the *tilak* on the forehead of the bridegroom,
The crown of the head falls on the ground.
Do *parichhan* of the forehead of the bridegroom.
Do *parichhan* of the forehead of the bridegroom.
Bridegroom's *bua* goes out after *parichhan*.
She has the ring and the *sindur* container in her hand.
She has the ring and the *sindur* container in her hand.
Whether I do *parichhan* of the crown on the head of the bridegroom,
Or the *tilak* on the forehead of the bridegroom,
Or the *tilak* on the forehead of the bridegroom,
The crown on the head falls on the ground.

Do *parichhan* of the forehead of the bridegroom.
Do *parichhan* of the forehead of the bridegroom.

"This song is for *parichhan*," Gangajali said. "The bridegroom has gone to his *sasural*. So the *sas*, *sarahaj*, his *sali*, and the bride's *bua*, *dadi*, whoever of the neighbor ladies are there, they do *parichhan*. But first of all, at the bridegroom's home was the mother, and here at the bride's home it is the *sas* (mother-in-law). She says, 'To whom are you performing *parichhan*?' Then she replies, 'The crown of the head is my heart. I am doing *parichhan* of my son.' So here the *sas* is asked what is she performing *parichhan* of. The *sas* replies, 'The crown of the head falls on the ground. I do *parichhan* of the bridegroom's forehead.' The meaning of this is the bride's people—mother or father, brother—accept the bridegroom. They do not think of any other wealth. He is everything for them—more than their house, animals, or wealth. The bridegroom is suitable for the bride. If he will be good, then my daughter will be happy. 'Oh, the wealth is the dirt of hands. Money is nothing. It comes and goes. I don't have attachment to any other thing.' So the *sas* says, 'I am doing *parichhan* of the bridegroom and not anyone else. I am doing *parichhan* of my *damad*.'"

"This song is to welcome the bridegroom," Umesh explained. "*Parichhan* is a blessing ceremony to protect the bridegroom from the evil eye. It is performed to greet the groom and also for saying farewell. When the mother sends her son away, she does *parichhan* so he will not get any evil eye (*nazar*). He is so handsome, and he is therefore so tender, fully garmented, fully beautified. Anyone who was looking at him had never seen him in such a beautiful form. So whenever he sees the same man in a different costume, he can give *nazar*, the evil eye. The mother has already done *parichhan* so her child will not get the *nazar*. Also, when the mother-in-law welcomes him, she also does *parichhan*. If he has gotten some evil eye, when he is there he will not be affected by the *nazar*. She has a ring and a *sindur* container in her hand. She is thinking, 'Do I have to bless the crown or the tilak on his forehead? The crown falls on the ground. This means the pride. So, I do *parichhan* of his forehead.' The crown itself has pride. Things are used to show pride. For example, a policeman when he is in uniform has pride, he has power, he is something. When he takes off his uniform, he is a simple man."

"At the bride's house, similarly she also takes a bath," Sashi said. "The *barat* arrives, and the girl does *nacchu nahawan*."

"As the *nacchu nahawan* took place in the bridegroom's house, the same ritual will take place in the bride's house," said Gangajali. "Now the *barat* has arrived. The door is shut. The *parichhawan* blessing is performed. And I was telling you, the bridegroom's water goes in one pot. The girl is given a bath with the same water. The bridegroom's side barber takes the water to the bride's house, where he meets with the bride's side barber. And he gives the pitcher full of water to the bride's barber to take inside. Now the bridegroom is seated in the *janmassa* (the place where the *barat* resides) after the *parichhan* blessing.

"Now the *barat* is having snacks. They are eating. Similarly, as people took snacks at the door. And the bath water reached the courtyard of the bride. Now the women are taking the bride to give her a bath. The bride will have *haldi* rubbed on, and the same song will begin in the bride's home once again."

### SONG 82

*Nacchu Nahawan (bride's side)*

Who has had the pond dug and has had the *ghat* made?
Oh, for whom are the water-pulling people filling it?
Who is taking a bath?
Oh, for whom are the water-pulling people filling it?
Who is taking a bath?
King Himanchal has had the pond dug and had the *ghat* made.
And the water-pulling people of Sunayananji pull the water.
The bride takes a bath.
And the water-pulling people of Sunayananji pull the water.
The bride takes a bath.
The bride takes a bath.
The bride asks her mother secretly,
She requests of her mother.
The bride asks her mother secretly,
She requests of her mother.
Mother, what is the meaning of this bath?
Explain it to me.
Mother, what is the meaning of this bath?
Explain it to me.
Mother explains with much love,
And has Gaura (the bride) listen.
Mother explains with much love,
And she explains to Gaura.
Gaura, after taking this bath, the sin will wash off.
They will flow away with the water.
Gaura, the sin will vanish.
And will flow away with the water.

"This is sung at the bride's home when the bride is taking a bath," Sashi said.

"Himanchal is Gaura's father," Gangajali said. "Here it is said for Gaura that he had the pond dug. The Sunanyanan *ghat* was made. Her water-pulling servant arranged water for her. As we have a servant or midwife at home, so they had the water brought by the *kahar*s (caste of water pullers) for any purpose. His or her *kahar* brings the water and gives it to her or him. And they take a bath. So Gaura asks her mother, 'What is the meaning of this bath?' And mother explains, 'Due to this bath, whatever defect is there in your bones, it is a penance for your sin. It flows away with the water. The body becomes holy.'

"So in a similar way, she is given fire in a clay dish, and everyone, her mother, *bhabi*, sister, *dadi*, whoever is there, they take the evil eye off her. That this bride becomes as tender and beautiful as Gaura. She has on a yellow sari. She looks as beautiful as a goddess. In case somebody has given her the evil eye, it is taken off with a blessing of caraway seed. It is sprinkled on the fire after blessing her."

FIFTY-TWO

# MONA'S *NACCHU NAHAWAN* IN RASALPUR

*Umesh and I attend Mona's wedding in Rasalpur, 2007*

I witnessed the ritual of *nacchu nahawan* in Village Rasalpur, Rameshwar, District Varanasi. We were invited to participate in the girl's side. The women of this household were extremely kind and did not deny me access to any part of their house, to any of their most private rituals, to any of their singing and dancing, to any of their musings and thoughts about the wedding that they were performing. With such a spirit of kindliness and friendship, I witnessed the bathing of the bride in April of 2007, sharing with them a most private moment that I did not photograph or record.

Our friend Narayan drove us out there early in the morning in his three-wheeler motor rickshaw. The bumpy ride on rural roads took over an hour. We carried with us three small children of the family in which the wedding was taking place. I was extremely nervous for their safety, for getting tossed from a rickshaw is daily business on India's dangerously crowded roads. There are no children's car seats. And there is no particular awareness of the danger a child is in when they are in a car or on a scooter or motorcycle, even on the handlebars of a bicycle. Finding the house was not difficult, for men were gathered outside, erecting a large canopy and stringing wires for twinkling lights and loudspeakers.

In many regards, the whole scene was typical of an Indian village. The dusty dry soil, the scrub grass, the fields—struggling to yield forth a new crop after thousands of years of human cultivation. The house was situated on a small hill. Its aspect was lonely, for it was somewhat separate from the other little houses of the colony. On the left was a government hand pump, and on the right, viewed from the front door, you could see the Varuna River. There were electrical poles, but the houses had no electricity.

One immense pipal tree dominated the picture and provided shade for the family and other visitors who had arrived early for the wedding. Water buffalo grazed to one side, taking some of the shade. We, too, took rest there and were fed delicious, sticky, freshly prepared sweets. We shared the cool shade of the tree, for better or worse, with crows, parrots, pigeons, and *gulguliya*—simple sweet birds. So we found relief from the morning sunlight but were left with sticky sticky fingers and were soon covered with bird droppings.

Viewed from the outside, the house had the appearance of a windowless brick fortress with small gun turrets. These turrets were in fact breeze openings in each tiny room. It was necessary to climb a small incline to enter the front door. Immediately, one reached the verandah, a covered porchlike space on all four sides, surrounding the dark inner courtyard. The verandah was cluttered with baskets, tins, lanterns, large burlap bags of food, electrical batteries brought especially for the wedding, and other paraphernalia. Clothes hung from pegs on the walls and bedding from the rafters. Inside, the courtyard was gloomy, too small to offer light for any of the little rooms that opened out onto it. For a young bride to be contained in this enclosure in *purdah* during her early married years seemed indeed like imprisonment.

The rooms themselves were dark, cramped, and stiflingly hot, without a single whisper of a breeze. But inside this gloomy shell of a house were the bright, kind, friendly women of Mona's family. How warmly they welcomed us. As Umesh hung out with the men and boys outside, I was invited inside. The women were inquiring about everything about me, my family, my country, and my reasons for attending an Indian village wedding. There was a flutter of activity as they busily moved from room to room, attending to daily business and the affairs of the wedding—preparing food, dressing children, making tea, and seeing to the bride's special wedding garments to be worn that evening for the arrival of the *barat*. It was an occasion when all women would adorn themselves in their best and finest saris and all their wedding ornaments, so there was much to do on this day of days.

The young bride was Mona Yadev, barely more than a teenager. As is common with Indian brides on their wedding day, she was not particularly dressed up this morning and was helping out with the chores of the day. She was happy to meet with me and a bit surprised that a white lady had suddenly appeared to attend her wedding. She asked me to take photographs of her with her sisters and her girlfriends and also kneeling at the feet of her mother (with her mother's hand resting on her head to bless her). They were very excited to have me there.

In the evening, inside the house, excitement mounted as we heard the sounds of the *barat* in the distance. The sounds grew louder as the procession of the groomsmen advanced. Mona became particularly tense as the sounds grew louder and more distinct, and the moment of her marriage moved inexorably toward its frightening conclusion.

After some time, the barber lady for Mona's family came in with a sealed clay pitcher. This was the bath water from the groom for Mona's *nacchu nahawan* ritual. The barber lady scraped the dough away from the lid and unsealed the jar. Mona was escorted out into the courtyard, where she was perched for her ritual bath on a very low sandalwood stool. The sounds of the *barat* could be heard as all this was happening. Mona unfastened her long black hair, and the groom's bath water was poured over it and rubbed in by her mother and sisters. Not a drop was wasted. They found the rupees inside the pot and kept them. The family women scrubbed hard at Mona's hair. Then her proper bath began, from top to toe, with fresh water. They modestly covered each part of her body as they moved on down to wash the next part. She was never left naked in any way. Many women helped to protect her modesty. Soon they slipped the crisply starched, brand-new yellow petticoat over her head and fastened it around her waist. Then she was helped into a very tight-fitting yellow blouse. There was no need for her to wear a bra. The ritual bath and the actual bath having finished, the ladies escorted Mona into a side room and began to put on her new pure yellow sari and started making up her face. Mona asked me to go outside and see her bridegroom and bring a report back to her. When I got outside, I found the men in the midst of *dwar puja*, the formal greeting of the bridegroom at the door, performed by the father of the family and the priests from both families. The groom wore a great golden tinsel crown tied tight on his head with a turban. Tassels hung down over his face, so I could not see him clearly. Nevertheless, I took several photos of him seated there at *dwar puja*—for Mona to see. I paused for a while to record the *gali*s sung by the family women aimed at the men of the *barat*.

When I returned inside to sit with Mona, she was so eager to see the photos of her bridegroom. So there I sat, showing his photo on the tiny screen of my camera. She was satisfied. And the role of the ethnomusicologist seemed absurd.

In the middle of the night, after the *barat* had departed, Mona and her betrothed were married, and the *kanyadan* ceremony was performed in the deep hours of midnight. For Mona's father, the work of a lifetime had been completed.

In the morning, without sleep, Umesh and I went back to our apartment with Narayan, in a state of total exhaustion.

FIFTY-THREE

# PROTECTING THE BRIDE FROM THE EVIL EYE

*Again we still are at the Hotel Sarang, Ballia, July 1989*

After performing the ritual bath of the bride, *parichhawan* is performed. Gangajali sang,

SONG 83

*Parichhawan*

Mother blesses her with caraway seeds and mustard.
Look, nobody should give her the evil eye.
Nobody should give the evil eye to Gaura Devi.
*Bhabi* blesses her with mustard and caraway seeds.
Look, nobody should give her the evil eye.
Nobody should give the evil eye to Gaura Dei.
Her sister blesses her with mustard and caraway seeds.
Look, nobody should give her the evil eye.
Nobody should give the evil eye to Gaura Dei.

Gangajali said, "Similarly, all women of the bride's house sprinkle caraway seeds in the fire. And, similarly, they break the *diya* that holds the fire. That clay pot has to be crushed in a go. For him and also for the girl once—not a second time.

"They just quickly stamp on it and lift up their foot," Gangajali said. "After breaking it, she goes ahead. She does not go back. She goes forward. It is a kind of trial by fire. It is for both the bride and the groom. She goes into the *kohabar*. Women adorn her, and she is adorned by many ornaments. According to our old tradition, she is dressed only in yellow cloth. She will have a nose ornament. Either there should be a golden pin or a nose ring. Parents donate to the daughter gold and yellow clothes. But nowadays people begin to adorn the bride with all sixteen *sringar* (traditional ornaments)."

"Those who offer the *jaymala* traditions," Sashi explained.

Gangajali said, "The bride and bridegroom do the *jaymala* in the same adornment they get married in. But in olden times this was not the tradition. The pure entire wedding was performed in yellow clothes."

"What did she have on in this area?" Umesh asked.

Sashi said, "She had a sari and petticoat as we have. Yellow sari, yellow blouse, everything yellow."

### SONG 84

*Gali*

Oh barber, cut the nails,
Oh, cut the nails.
Do not cut the toes.
Oh barber, cut the nails, cut the nails.
Do not cut the toes.
I'll give you the bridegroom's mother.
She will sleep to the side of your back.
I'll give you the bridegroom's *bhauji*.
She will clean your small bowl.
I'll give you the bridegroom's sister.
She will put the turmeric paste on you.
She will put the turmeric paste and clean the skin.
And she will sleep with you.
And she will sleep with you.
Oh barber, cut the nails, cut the nails.
Do not cut the toes.

"So this is the song for nail cutting," Gangajali explained.

"This song is sung at the time when the barber cuts the nails," Umesh explained. "It is a special ceremony. This song is a *gali*. The barber is asked to cut the nails and paint the fingers or toes. This is a *gali* to the bride's mother. In return for cutting the nails, the women say you will be given the mother of the bride to sleep beside you. You will be given the *bhauji* of the bride. She will clean your bowl. You will be given the sister of the bride. She will put the turmeric paste on your body. And she will take off the dry skin, and she will sleep you. This is the *gali*, a funny song that embarrasses the barber."

"Well, now the bride has dressed up," said Umesh. "What is next?"

"Now the bride's mother is waiting for her brother," said Gangajali. "This is the song for that."

### SONG 85

*Evil Eye*

Sita is staring down the road toward her *naihar.*
My brother has not arrived.
Sita is staring down the road toward her *naihar.*
My brother has not arrived.
The brother brings the empty pitcher.
He will charm my *yagya.*
The potters of the village are making clay dishes.
That is why the pitcher got expensive.
My brother washes the clothes of my sister-in-law.
She charms the *yagya.*
He will bring the birds for the wedding tent.
He will charm my *yagya.*
Brother will bring the empty basket.
And he will bring the birds for the wedding tent.
He will charm my *yagya.*

"Then the sister is waiting there," Gangajali said, "the sister is waiting for her brother. 'If my brother does not have a pitcher filled with *gur* and *ghee*, then bring the empty pitcher and place it. I want him here. I am arranging the wedding of my oldest son. I am doing my first *yagya*. I want him here.' Then brother replies, 'Sister, what do I do? The village potter has run away from the village. So pitchers got expensive. How can I bring that?' The sister says, 'Bring *bhauji* to wash my clothes and bring the yellow sari. This is my first big *yagya*.' Then he replies, 'Sister, your *bhauji's* clothes are torn off. How can I bring her?' It means do not bring fruit and sweets. 'When you come bring an empty basket. But surely come. This is my first big *yagya*. This is the wedding of my first son. Then bring everything from him or don't bring anything.'"

Umesh explained, "When there is a wedding in some house, the girl's house or boy's house, the girl expects something from her *maica*, from her brother. Whatever is offered by the brother to his sister, she gets respect or disrespect from that donation. She can show off what has been given by her brother or by her father. She can be proud of these things. Whenever the wedding takes place in the woman's house, whether it is her own children or her family, she looks forward to seeing her *naihar* people who will come to the wedding. She does not take anything away from her *maica* from the property of her parents. So from time to time, when she needs something, she should be served with this. It has become a custom, so even these people who don't have money, they also do something for their sisters. And we feel good to give something to our sisters if we have something to give. We must keep her dignity in her *sasural.* Here it is saying that Sita is looking forward to seeing to her brother. 'The brother will bring the empty pitcher. He will charm my *yagya.*' This song tells the love of the sister to her brother, and she wants his presence at the time of her son's wedding. That is very important to her. Never mind if he can bring anything or not for her. This is what she is saying.

"The brother is giving so many excuses. He says, 'Oh sister, the potter of my village is making clay dishes. That is why the pitcher has gotten expensive.' And so on. But the sister still wants to see him and for him to participate in the family wedding."

INTERLUDE ELEVEN

# LIZZIE AND HER LOVER

"DURING THE REMAINDER OF THAT MONDAY AND ALL THE TUESDAY, *Lizzie's mind was, upon the whole, averse to matrimony. She had told Miss Macnulty of her prospects, with some amount of exultation; and the poor dependent, though she knew that she must be turned out into the street, had congratulated her patroness. 'The Vulturess will take you in again, when she knows you've nowhere else to go to,' Lizzie had said—displaying, indeed, some accurate discernment of her aunt's character. But after Lady Fawn's visit she spoke of the marriage in a different tone. 'Of course, my dear, I shall have to look very close after the settlement.'*"

Miss Macnulty suggested that lawyers might assist her.

*"Yes;—lawyers! That's all very well. I know what lawyers are . . . Of course we shall live at Portray, because his place is in Ireland;—and nothing shall take me to Ireland. I told him that from the very first. But I don't mean to give up my own income."*

Lizzie boasted that Lord Fawn was in the Cabinet, astonishing Miss Macnulty, who "did not comprehend the depth of the ignorance of her patroness."

Lizzie had no notion what the difference was between an Under-Secretary and a member of the Cabinet. In any case, they agreed that she would stick to her plans for a visit to Fawn Court. "And as for bringing those dowdy girls to London, it's the last thing I shall think of doing."

*"And in truth, Lizzie almost had made up her mind to break if off. . . . But on Wednesday morning she received a note which threw her back violently upon the Fawn interest."*

The note was from Messrs Camperdown, asking for the address of her attorney. "She was frightened about the diamonds, and was, nevertheless, almost determined not to surrender them."

In either case, she would need a friend and confidante, and the thought of the relationship with Lord Fawn and the Fawn establishment gave her strength. She was certain that, being so poor, Lord Fawn would favor keeping the necklace.

In due course Frederic arrived, and Lizzie received him graciously, as a lover might. They sat side by side, the widow and the Under-Secretary of State from the India Office. Fawn felt he held the upper hand as he had told no lies. Then he asked Lizzie for the name of her lawyers, mentioning that they had better see his lawyer, Mr. Camperdown.

"'Mr. Camperdown!' almost shrieked Lizzie."

Lizzie showed Lord Fawn the letter she had just received from Camperdown, pulling it out from under her Bible.

*"Lord Fawn read it very attentively, and as he read there came upon him a great doubt. What sort of woman was this to whom he had engaged himself because she was possessed of an income. That Mr. Camperdown should be in the wrong in such a matter was an idea which never occurred to Lord Fawn. There is no form of belief stronger than that which the ordinary English gentleman had in the discretion and honesty of his own family lawyer."*

In a low voice, Lord Fawn asked about the diamonds. Lizzie claimed that her late husband had given them to her.

"When he put them into my hands, he said they were to be mine own for ever and ever."

Lord Fawn inquired as to their value, imagining that they might be just some trinket, and Lizzie offered to bring them down from her bedroom. Knowing nothing about jewels, Lord Fawn could see at an instant that they were genuine diamonds and not a sentimental trinket. Lizzie said they were worth about £10,000.

"'You don't keep them in the house do you?'"

Because he was slow in thinking, Lord Fawn did not realize that every word she spoke was a lie. He was in a state of dismay. "An action for the recovery of jewels brought against the lady whom he was engaged to marry, on behalf of the family of her late husband, would not suit him at all."

After some reflection, Fawn suggested that Lizzie return them to Camperdown. "To have his hands quite clean, to be above all evil report, to be respectable, as it were all round, was Lord Fawn's special ambition."

"'They're my property,' said Lizzie. . . . 'There's nothing he wouldn't do to get them.' . . . 'He wants to rob me.'"

Their parting was not as pleasant as their greeting.

Lizzie determined that Fawn should not escape her grasp. He would marry her. And she would keep the diamonds. She set out to announce her engagement to her family, writing a letter to her aunt Linlithgow, to Mrs. Eustace of Bobsborough, to her uncle, to the dean, and finally to Frank. Her mind drifted, and she thought of some sort of special relationship with Frank, "a secret understanding." And she had, in her letter to him, begged him to come and visit her during her upcoming stay at Fawn Court.

Umesh was really getting into the story. "I don't recall if we had such kind of people like trustworthy jewelers and lawyers who were helping, and people could trust them to keep things safe. We never had them. We got lawyers in India after the British arrived. We had no lawyers. This system was begun by the British in India. Before the British, justice was made by the king or by *panchayat*. In society, we have very trustworthy *panch* (five people make justice), and the *panchayat* was called to solve the problems. Bright and powerful people of the village (it doesn't mean they come by birth, not by caste), but people who are born bright. So they were called from different parts of the area if there was a big *panchayat* to get the justice. But for keeping things with the help of lawyers, we don't have this system. When banks began in India, then people began keeping their ornaments in bank lockers.

"When the British got here, we got this lawyer system. Ordinary people who didn't, these people could call a *panchayat* if they didn't have enough food or property. It belonged to *zamidar*s. These lawyers were helping the *zamidar*, and the poor people were quarreling with each. Justice was done by the *panchayat*, or if it was serious, the police came and put them in jail. And then a court case followed.

"We have two types of courts: one is the civil court, and the other is the criminal court. The civil court deals with the property and wealth—things. The other court deals with killing, beating, hitting, stealing.

"Lizzie is thinking that she is not going to give Lord Fawn money at all, none of the £4,000 that she gets out of the Scotch property. And she is telling Miss Macnulty, who asks her if Fawn was in the Cabinet. And Lizzie replies, 'Yes, he is in the Cabinet. But they won't come for tea. I won't serve them. And as for the Richmond people, I'll go there once or twice but not again. So must Lord Fawn live in Mount Street or on the Irish property!'

"Then Frederic arrives, and they sat down, and they had lovely talk. Lizzie flirts and makes nice talk. And then she brings her problem before Frederic. She is talking, and slowly slowly it comes up, and suddenly Frederic says that Camperdown will arrange the papers for their wedding. As soon as she learns about Camperdown, Lizzie jumps up and begins to shriek. Fawn doesn't know why she is talking that way. Certainly, she told that Camperdown caused her trouble, and she reaches for her Bible and under it is the note sent to her by Camperdown. She shows this to Frederic, and Frederic reads it. He thinks it could be a small thing like earrings or some small ornament, which shouldn't be so much trouble for her. And Frederic asks, 'Where is this ornament?' When she says she has it, he says he wants to see it. And she goes to get the ornament while he has so many thoughts in his mind about the ornaments. And as he saw the beautiful necklace, he asks, 'What is the worth of it?' She says, 'Oh, £10,000.' And Fawn's throat stops, and he says, '*Ten . . . thousand . . . pounds*—for the necklace—and keeping it at home.' And he begins to think that Camperdown is not such a person who would go for a small thing and make anyone in trouble. Camperdown is a very fair person, and Fawn believes in justice. Frederic tells her, 'He is my lawyer as well; he is not that kind of person. He has a great reputation all over London.' So Fawn has so many thoughts, and he begins to think about getting away from Lizzie. He begins to think that she could be very dangerous, because he lives for honesty. So he leaves the place. And Lizzie begins to think, 'I won't let him slip away from me.'

"Lizzie begins to think over the problems, and she writes four letters. The first one she writes is to Lady Linlithgow, to whom she used to call vulturess. She writes a very tough letter to her aunt. She writes nicely to other family people, announcing her engagement. But she writes a very beautiful letter to her cousin Frank, mentioning 'Dear Cuz' and that she would like to see him very soon. And she starts to think that perhaps there could be something. So she is thinking at the same time to marry someone and to have an affair with another one. She is thinking that she could criticize the Fawns to Frank—that they were such owls and oafs, and this would be very pleasing."

FIFTY-FOUR

# ARRIVAL AT THE *JANMASSA*

*A discussion in Karimganj, March 2014*

"In India, in Uttar Pradesh, *dwar puja* takes place as soon as the *barat* arrives," Umesh said. "In olden days the *barat* used to stay at the border, and gentlemen from the girl's side used to go and welcome them at the border of the village. One rupee as a *nazar* (offering) was offered to them, and food used to be given at the border (*paunchhak*). It means one fourth of the *puri* was given to them so they could have a snack. It is to welcome them to the village. Nowadays, when the *barat* arrives at the *janmassa*, then the girl's side men go there with one rupee, ten rupees, one hundred rupees (pennies to over a dollar). They offer this cash to the bridegroom's side, either to the oldest man of the village or the grandfather of the groom or the father of the groom—the older person from the girl's side will go and offer the *nazar* to the groom's side to welcome them in the village. At the same time, they will send snacks. From there they go to the *janmassa*.

"Oh, yes, at the *janmassa*. Then thereafter the girl's side barber is sent to the *barat*, and he says, 'Send the *barauna* pot.' Then the *barati* barber comes with the *barauna*. He has some music with him like a drum. This is a treat for the barber. Sometimes he is marked with turmeric and oil on his back. He brings a pot full of something, a clay pot—a *barauna*—and people joke with him. Women give him yogurt to drink with a lot of salt and pepper. In fact, he doesn't want to drink it. He knows there won't be any good thing in there. They just play. People push it against his mouth, and it gets all over his face. It is fun.

"When the *barat* used to stay for three days, the barber went to bring the bridegroom for *dwar puja*. This was the first day function. They were fed in the *janmassa*. They were not fed at home the very first day. Then in the morning they were given breakfast, at noon they were given lunch, and at three o'clock the *nimantri* used to take place in olden days. *Nimantri* means invitation, so from the girl's side, ten or twenty people used to go with so many things—sweets, dried fruits, fruits, so many things with them at the *janmassa* to offer them and to invite them for the real feast. It was called *barhar*. It was the invitation. At that time from both sides, the priests used to give their speeches. And also those people who knew poems, they used to sing wedding poems, how to live nicely, only *man* to *man* (heart to heart)—the women were not there. This was man-to-man talk in the *janmassa*. They were given very good talks, very good songs.

"On the third day, the wedding used to take place in the morning, and the *vida*—departure—was also on the third day.

"Now these days the *nimantri* custom has entirely died out. The wedding takes place altogether within thirteen to fourteen hours. So this kind of speech is not anymore in my village."

FIFTY-FIVE

# *GALI* FOR *BARATI* PEOPLE AND BRIDEGROOM

*Banaras, Sarang Hotel, July 2007*

Gangajali continued singing through the songs for the girl's side and the actual wedding. The songs came one after another, one after another. Here we have another version of the *imali*-biting as was also performed earlier by the bridegroom and his mother.

SONG 86

*Imali*

Oh, brother Sanjin is wearing golden sandals.
Oh, brother Sanjin is wearing golden sandals.
Where is older sister Saroj, so I can perform the *imali*?
Where is older sister Saroj, so I can perform the *imali*?
She keeps the yellow sari on her head.
She keeps the yellow sari on her head.
There are five golden coins in her hand.
Oh, so perform the *imali*.
There are five golden coins in her hand.
Oh, so perform the *imali*.

There are elephants and horses at the door.
And the cow is tied up there.
Where is older sister Saroj, so I can perform the *imali*?

"So this is an *imali*-biting song," Gangajali said. "So the brother is at his mother's home. Brother goes there under the wedding tent, putting on golden sandals. And the sister, the bride, is very happy. And the brother says, 'Sister, I have brought a yellow sari for you. And I have brought golden coins to give in your hand. I have brought everything—cow, buffalo, elephant, horse. I have brought a yellow sari, and you take it, cover yourself, and perform the *imali*. You are thirsty. Drink water.' So the brother gives her water to drink.

Then the bride is blessed with the rice and *dub* grass.

### SONG 87

#### *Chumawan*

With the *sathi* rice and tender *dub* grass,
Mother goes to kiss Sapan Dei.
Mother goes to kiss sweetheart Sapan.
As she kisses her, she blesses her.
My bride and bridegroom, live one hundred thousand years.
My bride and bridegroom, live one hundred thousand years.
With the *sathi* rice and tender *dub* grass,
The bride's *bhauji* goes to kiss.
The bride's *bhauji* goes to kiss.
As she kisses, she blesses,
My bridegroom and bride, live for one hundred thousand years.
My bridegroom and bride, live for one hundred thousand years.
Daughter's sister comes out to kiss.
Daughter's sister comes out to kiss.
With *sathi* rice and tender *dub* grass,
Daughter's sister comes out to kiss.
Daughter's sister comes out to kiss.
As she kisses, she blesses.
My bridegroom and bride, live for one hundred thousand years.
My bridegroom and bride, live for one hundred thousand years.

A similar song can be song for the bridegroom before the *barat* leaves for the bride's home.

## SONG 88

### *Chumawan*

Oh, kiss the bridegroom slowly slowly.
Oh, kiss the bridegroom slowly slowly.
Married mother comes out to kiss.
Married mother comes out to kiss.
Showing her the yellow sari slowly slowly.
Oh, jingling her golden bangles slowly slowly.
Oh, kiss the bridegroom slowly slowly.
Oh, kiss the bridegroom slowly slowly.
The bride's *bhabi* comes out to kiss.
The bride's *bhabi* comes out to kiss.
Oh, lavish her youth slowly slowly.
Oh, lavish her youth slowly slowly.
Oh, kiss the bridegroom slowly slowly.
Oh, kiss the bridegroom slowly slowly.
The bride's sister comes out to kiss.
The bride's sister comes out to kiss.
Oh, jingling her golden bangles slowly slowly.
Oh, jingling her toe rings slowly slowly.
Oh, kiss the bridegroom slowly slowly.
Oh, kiss the bridegroom slowly slowly.

Following these *chumawan* songs, which are performed from time to time during the wedding, the bride or the groom is escorted into the *kohabar*, the sacred wedding chamber. The home of the bride has set aside a room decorated to be the *kohabar*. Likewise, at the home of the bridegroom, a similar room has been prepared.

## SONG 89

### *Kohabar*

This new *kohabar* is made of bronze and brass.
The door is made of rubies.
The door is made of rubies.
Bridegroom Vijay sleeps in the same *kohabar*.
Oh, when sweetheart Sapan is together with him,
Oh, when he is against the thigh of sweetheart Queen Sapan,
Mother-in-law goes in and wakes them up.
Oh, Saroj's mother goes in and wakes them up.
Daughter, get up, it is dawn.
Daughter, get up, it is dawn.

Oh, such mother should be sold in the hands of the *samdhi*.
Oh, give her away in the hands of the *barat* people.
She shouts early in the morning at midnight.
She shouts early in the morning at midnight.

### *At the Hotel Sarang, Ballia, July 1989*

While the bride is being dressed, the men are outside performing the *dwar* puja to the accompaniment of *gali* singing.

"Then men come inside the house under the wedding tent for the *gurahatthi* ritual," Gangajali said. "The bridegroom, the groom's father, the groom's older brother, the *bhashhur*, and two or four or ten elders—those people who are oldest from the *barat*. They all come into the courtyard and sit under the wedding tent for *gurahatthi*. The barber's wife accompanies the bride and seats her at the altar. Then this song is sung."

### SONG 90

### *Gurahatthi*

All the gentlemen are seated under the eave.
Oh, the bridegroom is seated under the eave.
Oh, the bridegroom is seated under the eave.
Father Anrudhu shows anger in his eyes.
Father Bharathu shows anger in his eyes.
Brother Syaam Jibahu shows anger in his eyes.
Seeing all this, the gentlemen fell down unconscious.
Seeing all this, the gentlemen fell down unconscious.
Gentlemen, why have you fallen down unconscious?
Gentlemen, why have you fallen down unconscious?
My daughter Sapana is the pupil of my eye.
My daughter Sapana is the pupil of my eye.
Daughter, I could not eat or drink all day.
Daughter, I could not eat or drink all day.
Daughter, I could not sleep all night.
Daughter, I could not sleep all night.

Gangajali explained, "This song is sung in the courtyard when the *barati* people come and sit there. And as the girl is brought into the courtyard, the people from the girl's side and the *barati* people from the other side see her with much wonder. How beautiful the girl is. How beautiful is the virgin. People look at her there. The bride's father, brother, uncle, they wonder, they fall unconscious. How beautiful she is.

"Then the bride's people say, 'Why have you people fallen unconscious? My daughter is the pupil of my eyes. My daughter is such that out of worry for her I don't feel hungry or thirsty. And at night I cannot sleep.' The *gurahatthi* begins from here. There are so many *gurahatthi* songs.

"So the bride's brother and the bridegroom come, and both are seated at the altar. *Gurahatthi* takes place as the *bhashhur* comes forward, and these songs are directed at him, the older brother of the groom."

### SONG 91

#### *Gurahatthi gali*

I will break the leg of the *bhashhurawa*.
With these legs he made my wedding tent unholy.
Made unholy with these legs.
This *bhashhurawa* is winking his eye.
With the same eyes, he has seen my Gaura.
With the same eyes, he has seen my Gaura.
He has seen her with the same eyes.
I pulled the mustache of this *bhashhurawa*.
He licked my yogurt out of his mustache.
He licked my yogurt out of his mustache.
Oh, I'll squeeze the stomach of the *bhashhurawa*.
He has eaten my *puri*s in his stomach.
He has eaten my *puri*s in his stomach.
I'll break the teacup of this *bhashhurawa*.
He laughs with his teeth in my wedding tent.
He laughs with his teeth in my wedding tent.

"So the *bhashhur* comes," Gangajali said, "the older brother of the groom, and the virgin is seated there. All the ornaments, sari, clothes, and everything is given to her after worshiping Ganesh and Laxmiji. Everything is given into the hands of the virgin. This is also a part of *gurahatthi*. Whatever is brought from the groom's side—ornaments, saris, fruits, whatever they bring—they offer everything.

"So they are seated there. This song is sung for them. As the bridegroom's older brother comes in the wedding tent, more *gali*s are sung from the bride's side. After *gurahatthi*, *kanyadan* will take place, and the *lawa* will be mixed."

### SONG 92

#### *Gurahatthi gali*

You are showing the borrowed *tika* under the wedding tent.
You adulterous *bhashhur*, are you not embarrassed?
You adulterous *bhashhur*, are you not embarrassed?
You adulterous *bhashhur*.

You are showing the borrowed garments under the wedding tent.
You adulterous *bhashhur*, are you not embarrassed?
You adulterous *bhashhur*.
You are showing the borrowed droplet earrings under the wedding tent.
You adulterous *bhashhur*, are you not embarrassed?
You adulterous *bhashhur*.
You are showing the borrowed nose ring under the wedding tent.
You adulterous *bhashhur*, are you not embarrassed?
You adulterous *bhashhur*.
You are showing the borrowed necklace under the wedding tent.
You adulterous *bhashhur*, are you not embarrassed?
You adulterous *bhashhur*, are you not embarrassed?
You are showing the borrowed golden bangles under the wedding tent.
You adulterous *bhashhur*, are you not embarrassed?
You adulterous *bhashhur*, are you not embarrassed?
You are showing the borrowed ornamental belt under the wedding tent.
You adulterous *bhashhur*, are you not embarrassed?
You are showing the borrowed anklets under the wedding tent.
You adulterous *bhashhur*, are you not embarrassed?
You adulterous *bhashhur*, are you not embarrassed?
You are showing the borrowed toe rings under the wedding tent.
You adulterous *bhashhur*, are you not embarrassed?
You are showing the borrowed dress under the wedding tent.
You adulterous *bhashhur*, are you not embarrassed?
You adulterous *bhashhur*, are you not embarrassed?
You are showing the borrowed *badani* (obscure) under the wedding tent.
You are showing the borrowed sheet under the wedding tent.
You adulterous *bhashhur*, are you not embarrassed?
You adulterous *bhashhur*, are you not embarrassed?
I poke out the eye of this *bhashhur*.
He has stared at our Gauri.
He has stared at our Gauri.
I will break the teeth of this *bhashhur*.
He has torn off our wood with his teeth.
He has torn with his teeth.
Squeeze the stomach of this *bhashhur*.
He destroyed the wedding tent with his stomach.
He destroyed with his stomach.
I break the legs of this *bhashhur*.
With his leg he destroyed our courtyard.
With his leg he destroyed our courtyard.

"This is a *gurahatthi*," Gangajali said. "These are important *gurahatthi* songs."
"So the *bhashhurji* comes," Sashi said. "This *gali* is to welcome him."

"Now the *gali* is for the *bhashhurji*," Gangajali said. "Now that the bride is seated at the altar for *gurahatthi*, and the *tika* is brought for her. Whatever is offered is offered first to the gods Gauri–Ganesh. Thereafter it will be touched to the bride, offering it to her. Then it is placed. There is a designated person to place things. The barber of the other side gives it into the hands of the groom. The father gives it to the oldest son, to the *bhashhur*, who is the oldest brother of the groom. (He is *bhashhur* to the bride.) So he performs the *gurahatthi*. He will touch these things to his forehead and then give them to the bride's side. So the bride's side will keep them and write down how many things there are.

"Hundreds of people are standing there to see *gurahatthi*, what things are brought to the bride—how many ornaments and how many clothes are brought. This is called *charaw*. Women sing *gali* while playing the *dholak* and singing. 'Oh, I break the leg of the *bhashhurawa*. He destroyed the wedding tent with his legs. In his stomach he has eaten.' It means he has eaten *puri*s (fried bread) in his stomach. 'He is staring at my daughter with his eyes. Yes, I poke his eyes out. He is looking at my Gauri with his eyes.' Then 'borrowed,' it means it is not brought by earnings from their house. Oh, to show off the family name they borrowed things from elsewhere. All this is called *charawa*. He is trying to show off. Showing off the *tika* in the wedding tent. 'Yes, you adulterous man, oh *bhashhur*, don't you feel embarrassed?'

"So the people are seated in the wedding tent," Gangajali said. "All the women together sing *gali*s to these men."

### SONG 93

*Gurahatthi gali*

Have him listen to the welcoming *gali*s.
My girlfriends, have him listen.
Have him listen to the welcoming *gali*s.
My loving girlfriends, have him listen.
Have him listen to the welcoming *gali*s.
This *bhashhur* does not have a cap.
This *bhashhur* does not have a cap.
Put the ribbon or braid on him.
Dear girlfriends, put them on him.
Make a hair tail and a hair bun.
Oh dear girlfriends, make them.
Have him listen to the welcoming *gali*s.
Dear girlfriends, have him listen.
Have him listen to the welcoming *gali*s.
This *bhashhur* does not have glasses.
This *bhashhur* does not have glasses.
Put *kajal* around his eyes.

Dear girlfriends, put it on him.
Put the *kajal* around his eyes.
Dear girlfriends, put it on him.
Have him listen to the welcoming *gali*s.
This *bhashhur* does not chew betel leaf.
This *bhashhur* does not chew betel leaf.
Put lipstick on his lips.
Dear girlfriends, put it on him.
Put lipstick on his lips.
Dear girlfriends, put it on him.
Have him listen to the welcoming *gali*s.
Dear girlfriends, have him listen.
Have him listen to the welcoming *gali*s.
This *bhashhur* does not have a *kurta* on.
This *bhashhur* does not have a *kurta* on.
Dress him in a bra and bodice.
Dear girlfriends, dress him.
Dress him in a bra and bodice.
Dear girlfriends, dress him.
Dear girlfriends, have him listen.
Have him listen to the welcoming *gali*s.
This *bhashhur* does not have a *dhoti* on.
This *bhashhur* does not have a *dhoti* on.
Dress him in a skirt and scarf.
Dress him, dear girlfriends.
Dress him in a *lehanga* and scarf.
Dress him, dear girlfriends.
Have him listen to the welcoming *gali*s.
Dear girlfriends, have him listen.
This *bhashhur* does not have shoes on.
This *bhashhur* does not have shoes on.
Dress him with sandals.
Dress him with the anklets and toe rings.
Dress him, dear girlfriends.
Dress him with the anklets and toe rings.
Have him listen to the welcoming *gali*s.

As she would during an actual wedding, again Gangajali continued on to the next *gali* without pause.

## SONG 94

### *Gali*

Brother, Patna,
Brother, Patna city is pleasant and beautiful.
Brother, Patna.
Brother, Patna city is pleasant and beautiful.
Brother, Patna. I ask you, stupid *bhashhur*,
I ask you, stupid *bhashhur.*
Oh stupid, what kind of business do you do?
Pimp, what business do you do?
Brother, Patna,
Brother, Patna city is pleasant and beautiful.
Brother, Patna,
Brother, Patna city is pleasant and beautiful.
You live on the earnings of your mother.
And the earnings of your sister.
You live on the earnings of your mother.
And the earnings of your sister.
He gets fucked in his asshole.
Oh, he gets fucked in his asshole.
Brother, Patna,
Brother, Patna city is pleasant and beautiful.
Brother, Patna.
Oh, he asks a rupee for fucking his asshole.
He asks a rupee for fucking his asshole.
I have even a fifty percent share in it.
Stupid, I have even a fifty percent share in it.
Brother, Patna,
Brother, Patna city is pleasant and beautiful.
Brother, Patna.

"Finished," Sashi said.

"This *gali* could be longer, but you made it smaller," Umesh said.

Gangajali burst into laughter and said nothing. Then she said, "This *gali* is of this place. It is not made up."

"She is losing her voice. Don't lose your voice." I was concerned.

"Don't hurt your throat," Umesh said.

"Yes," I said. "We still haven't finished the wedding."

"By sitting and standing, the wedding is performed," Gangajali said. "It takes time. This is a religious wedding."

"How many more songs are there?" Umesh asked.

"There are many. I will give you the main songs. What comes first. I won't give you extra."

"People think this is an easy job," Umesh said.

"It is hard work," Gangajali said. "Here the Indian wedding is very hard. That is why the bridegroom's side and the bride's side people go through hardship."

FIFTY-SIX

# WHAT ABOUT CLOTHES AND ORNAMENTS?

*A short discussion in Umesh's home, Karimganj, 2014*

Umesh explained the customs of gifts from the bridegroom to the bride. "Most of the clothes and ornaments come from the groom's side with the *barat*. Five—seven—eleven saris or twenty-one, it depends, when the *barat* arrives. Thereafter also what kind of saris are they? They should be good saris. It depends what kind of wedding it is and how much the girl's side is spending. Also, what does the groom do—if he is employed, doing good business, or just walking on the street? Sometimes the girl's side doesn't like the saris. Perhaps none of us like them. Suppose they were cheap. And they claimed what clothes they wanted from us and demanded named brand names."

"Do you think the girl's side is always disappointed?"

"If worthwhile things come, they won't be disappointed. The only thing for me that if we find the good bridegroom. I don't care about saris. I don't care about ornaments. For my daughter, I just want a nice bridegroom. You can buy ornaments, you can lose ornaments. They can be stolen. But a knowledgeable, nice bridegroom is what is important. He can fulfill all the requirements of my daughter.

"The boy's side brings all kind of ornaments—whatever they can afford. Sometimes they borrow ornaments to show off. They are always gold ornaments. Sometimes people trick and make the fake ornaments in golden color. But then there will be a big fuss.

"In my area, the *piari* (yellow sari) comes from the *mama*. And also, one *dhoti* comes for the bride's mother. The bride puts the *piari* on at the time of the wedding.

"The girl's family also has to buy clothes for their daughter. Not very many, but it depends. Maybe three or four saris. It depends how well off the family is—if they give earrings, anklets, maybe bracelets. Whatever they can afford. It is important for the bride's family to give at least one ornament. It could be earrings. It could be anklets. It could be a necklace. One woman gave her daughter a $2,000 ornament! And ten *lakh* rupees—$25,000 wedding expense. The main thing is that the boy is good."

FIFTY-SEVEN

# BHAJAN INTERLUDE

*A new day, the fourth day, at the Hotel Sarang, Ballia, July 1989*

It was a new day and time for a new session with Gangajali. We began each day with a *bhajan*, finding that settled us down into a proper contemplative mood for work. Today she chose to sing about Mohan (Krishna).

SONG 95

*Bhajan*

*(Noisy start from the street)*

Mohan, your form is troubling me.
Mohan, your form in troubling me.
It is stuck in my heart in such a way that I cannot forget it.
It is stuck in my heart in such a way that I cannot forget it.
Mohan, your form is troubling me.
It is stuck in my heart in such a way that I cannot forget it.
It is stuck in my heart in such a way that I cannot forget it.
Kanhaiya, come now.
My eyes are calling you.
Kanhaiya, come now.
My eyes are calling you.

By crying, make a string of tears.
By crying, make a string of tears.
Mohan, your form is troubling me.
It is stuck in my heart,
Kanhaiya, come now,
Oh, poor eyes.
Kanhaiya, come now.
Oh, poor eyes.
They are saying by crying,
Listen to their sorrow.
By crying themselves to you,
Telling their own pain.
Why have you come to me now?
Why don't you come to see me now?
To poor me.
Why don't you come to see me now?
To poor me.
Will you also not come?
Will you also not come,
To listen to the pain of the poor?
Will you also not come,
To listen to the pain of the poor?
I will tell you later,
This story of fate.
(Umesh said here that Gangajali was remembering her late husband as well as God.)
Now Mohan, having come here,
Now Mohan, having come here,
Give me *darshan*.
Now Mohan, having come here,
Give me *darshan*.

"This *bhajan* makes our mind peaceful," Umesh said.

"Yes. I am beloved to God, and God is beloved to me," Gangajali said. "I am thirsty for him. I am waiting for him. When I am sad, I call him.

"All the world has forgotten me. Will you also forget me? I am dependent on you. You only are the help. You only are the hope. Will you also not come to give me *darshan*? Will you not hear my pain? Then who will hear it? Now come. I'll tell you the story of my fate later while moving ahead (after death). But now you satisfy me after giving me *darshan*."

Gangajali pours her heart out during this emotional *bhajan*. It is very real to her, worship through song, calling out to her Lord through song. She began this especially passionate singing style yesterday, and I could see that today it was to continue. She was relaxed with us. She was happy to sing for us her intimate inner thoughts expressed in her own compositions.

INTERLUDE TWELVE

# LORD FAWN AT HIS OFFICE

*THE NEWS WAS SOON ALL ABOUT LONDON—AS LIZZIE HAD INTENDED. She had made a sudden resolve that Lord Fawn should not escape her, and she had gone to work after the fashion we have seen. Frank Greystock had told John Eustace, and John Eustace had told Mr. Camperdown before Lord Fawn himself, in the slow prosecution of his purpose, had consulted the lawyer about the necklace. "God bless my soul;—Lord Fawn! the old lawyer had said when the news was communicated to him. 'Well—yes;—he wants money. I don't envy him; that's all. We shall get the diamonds now, John. Lord Fawn isn't the man to let his wife keep what doesn't belong to her."*

When Lord Fawn mustered the pluck to go see Camperdown, he was heartily congratulated by the old lawyer, who told Fawn the details of Lizzie's settlement with the Eustace estate and Sir Florian's will. The necklace, Camperdown explained, was Eustace property and must be returned. And he warned Lord Fawn about the disreputable firm of Mowbray and Mopus that Lizzie had hired as her lawyers.

As Fawn was meeting with Camperdown as an engaged lover, the old lawyer couldn't offer his frank advice about Lizzie. Under the circumstances, that was not possible. This conversation had made Lord Fawn very unhappy. The property in Scotland was hers only for her life, and certainly those damn diamonds belonged to the Eustace estate. *He could not unravel truth quickly, but he could grasp it when it came to him. She was certainly greedy, false, and dishonest. And—worse than all this—she had dared to tell him to his face that he was a poor creature because he would not support her in her greed, and falsehoods, and dishonesty! Nevertheless, he was engaged to marry her!*

He made off to his fine office, overlooking St. James's Park, resigned that his happy days, in future, would be spent there. *The House of Lords out of which nobody could turn him, and official life—as long as he could hold to it—must be all in all to him. . . . Then he wiped away a tear as he sat down to sign the huge batch of letters.*

A messenger arrived, announcing that Mrs. Hittaway was there to see him. She had come to speak her mind to Frederic about this dreadful engagement. To start with, she did not congratulate her brother and went on to say that she had heard many evil things about Lizzie.

She asked about the jewels, referring to other jewels that she recovered by borrowing money from Harter and Benjamin. Lord Fawn had assumed she was referring to the necklace and admitted that he knew of it and had spoken to Camperdown about it. Then Mrs. Hittaway brought up the topic of Lizzie's mistreatment of her aunt, Mrs. Linlithgow.

*"Dear Frederic," she said. "I only wish to put you on your guard. Of course this is very unpleasant, and I shouldn't do it if I didn't think it my duty. I believe she is artful and very false. She certainly deceived Sir Florian Eustace about her debts;—and he never held up his head after he found out what she was. If she has told you falsehoods, of course you can break it off."*

Lord Fawn was miserable, for he had that morning received letters of congratulations from the dean and the bishop.

*Lord Fawn was, therefore well aware that Lady Eustace had published the engagement. It was known to everybody, and could not be broken off without public scandal.*

Umesh had his own ideas about this situation. "And it seems that British high-class society found a nice way to keep the family property with the family—by hiring a good lawyer, saving those ornaments with a goldsmith, and another way so the family property will not get away from the family. If a family lady goes elsewhere or marries someone else after widowing, so at least if she remains married or unmarried, she could keep the earning of the property as was mentioned by the husband before he died.

"In India there was no such tradition. When a woman became a widow, she couldn't get married ever. It was considered disrespect for the family to have her married again. Even the ornaments she could keep but not the property, not the land. Is a kind of relation in two ways not to let go the property. In the British way, they hire people not to let the property go. I think it was similar in India with *sati.* If she was pregnant she could not—the mother, she could not be burned with the husband. But a widow could not remarry. But in India it is changing now.

"Before Lord Fawn reaches Camperdown, Camperdown already had the message of Fawn's engagement with Lizzie. As he gets inside the chamber, Camperdown saw him and congratulated him, and the talk begins between Camperdown and Fawn. Mr. Camperdown does not explain to him clearly about the situation out of the respect of long long relations with this family. As Fawn is also a client of Mr. Camperdown, Camperdown does not want to disrespect Lord Fawn by telling him all about Lizzie.

"When Fawn leaves, Camperdown is thinking how to get the necklace out of this woman without hurting Fawn. Fawn gets out of the office, and he finds his sister as soon as he opens his office door. She doesn't congratulate Fawn. All of the sudden, he realizes something is very strange. She has been searching Fawn in several places. She didn't go into the male club, but she had been hunting him down. Clara even called Lizzie a prostitute lady, and she is very upset. She is the sister, and she has the right to tell him the truth about Lizzie. Brother and sister were talking to each other, and Clara talks about the small small stones that Lizzie had had on her head, and she also tells that later, Sir Florian got so many debt bills that they caused his death. What kind of woman had he married? Lord Fawn thought that his sister, Clara, who had mentioned some stones, was talking about the necklace. This is quite a misunderstanding between them. Before departing, Clara is saying to Fawn that this talk isn't pleasant, and he says no, it is not pleasant. Clara is expecting a brotherly hug before departure that she doesn't receive, showing how upset Fawn is.

"That morning the dean and the bishop had sent their congratulations to Lord Fawn about his engagement. That was Lord Fawn's day. Poor Lord Fawn."

## FIFTY-EIGHT

# UMESH RECALLS HIS WEDDING

*Umesh tells of being in the* barat, *Karimganj, March 2014*

"Yes, those who are very close, family, also village, join the *barat*. There is so much trouble being in the *barat*. You sit in the bus, you don't know where to go to the bathroom, where to find a sleeping place, where to get food. In olden days, there was a barber or *kahar* who would carry your bed and lay a bed for you. He would press your legs. But not anymore. The social system has changed.

"Fifteen days before the *barat* departs, the father of the bridegroom goes house to house with the *supari* (areca nut). He gives *supari* to ask a man to participate in the wedding. Will you participate or not? Who accepts this challenge of the battle of the *barat*, he takes the *supari*. And he will participate in the wedding. That takes one or two days. Everybody knows that the wedding is going to take place, and people are waiting for the invitation. If he says no to the *supari*, there is deep anger in him. He will tell his family people that the person has refused to take the *supari*. They might all go to the person to please him. In a son's wedding, people expect that they should be requested to participate. So we make him agree to accept the *supari*. If he insists too much, then never mind then. He doesn't want to participate. But the main thing is that when one person refuses, he tries to stop other people from going to make his group against participation big. It is a kind of politics. We expect the person who has a son's wedding must come to bow. He needs the *barat*.

"This case is not with the girl's wedding. Only make the preparations and call the people, because we do not expect to eat at the girl's wedding. We don't feed the village people. Only the boy's side people will eat. Although these days it has become a custom to feed the girl's side people too because they have helped the wedding—physical help—and they may be relatives.

"In olden times people needed the *barat*, and it went by bullock carts, and people needed help who had no bullocks and carts. The son was to get married, so the father used to keep good relations with everyone so he could use those people who have bullocks and bullock carts for his son's wedding. So people have good relations with each other in this way. Those people who had nothing were always under pressure to keep good relations. Similarly, was also with big people. Because one cart and one pair of bullocks cannot do the work of the wedding. These days, it is very simple—go and get a bus. So this dependency is over. So people go to participate in the wedding. If they consider they were not treated well, they will not participate in another wedding of the family.

"Customs are changing very much, very much. I can say that when my *barat* went one day, they stayed until the third day, when they came back. Now the *barat* leaves in the evening and comes back that very night, and the bride comes the next day around seven to eight to nine o'clock in the morning. They have tea and breakfast at the girl's home, and then they are sent to the boy's home.

"My *barat* went by the train, and I was carried by the palanquin with six palanquin bearers, six *kahar*s (the caste for this job). Four carrying at a time. Two in front, two in the back, and two spare for changing shoulders. It was for two or three kilometers. I was in the palanquin. I felt very strange. I was afraid I would fall off. A big fear! Because I was leaning to one side. I don't know how they managed it. It did not have a cover. I was not a bride. The covering is only when the bride is inside. It is like a cot made out of strings. It is comfortable. Maybe some nice rug and sheet is laid on it. No horse, no elephant, no pearls. It was rice."

## FIFTY-NINE

# FEEDING THE WEDDING PARTY

*Karimganj, March 2014*

"Regarding the feeding of the *barat* people," Umesh explained, "previously people were seated on the ground to eat. The leaf dish was served to them and a *kullar* (cup) made out of clay. And there were many boys who were ready to help to serve. The cook used to be from the village. So we had to hire a cook and people to serve. We didn't need a tent to show off—and no throne system as is popular nowadays.

"So ever since the new custom arrived, so much work has been increased instead of decreased. Also the time of the wedding got shortened. The work has gone more, as well as the expenses, which is really unnecessary. People do this to gain respect among the relatives as well as among their own society people—for they have also sons to get married, other daughters to get married. If they don't do it properly to show off, the family is in trouble to arrange weddings for their other sons and daughters.

"To prepare food, three or four women will come for chopping vegetables, and also there will be making-dough women, and they will be making *puris*. We will hire women who come with the cook. They make the *puris*, and they cut the vegetables. Whatever other job that is there, they do it. Hiring the cook can cost ₹1,500 ($22.00). The cleaner also comes. Altogether its cost is more than that. Then there are the expenses of the food and the sweets.

"Sweets are not so important at the wedding these days. People have only one or two sweets these days. Usually what happens these days, when the *barat* arrives in the *janmassa*, the older man of the family tribe goes with the family people and the village people to greet *samdhi* to *samdhi* (father-in-law to father-in-law). At the same time, they pitch small small tents in which they have food, like *chat*, chow mein, maybe ice cream, maybe tea, coffee, so whatever people want to eat, they can eat there before they come for *dwar puja*. Thereafter *dwar puja* takes place. Gas stoves are used to cook the food. A furnace is only used if they want some *roti tandoori*."

"When the boy's side asks for *tandoori* or for buffer system, is it really important for them?" I asked.

"I think it is important to them—that is why they ask. On the other hand, it was not necessary before—then why do they ask? I think the bridegroom's family wants to show that they have not arranged a wedding out of some people who have nothing. They want to show off to their relatives that they have this and this and this.

"So the cost of feeding the *barat* comes out of the dowry. And the boy's side has to agree with that. One thousand, one hundred fifty, two hundred people come in the *barat*. But those people leave in the night, so it is only a one-time feast. And also family people's people, village people. It is also a burden on the groom's side. They have to have so many people to bring. On the other hand, suppose the *barat* comes on the same date from the same village, and people are very little in the *barat*. People make a search. 'Please, please come in the *barat*.' So people try to arrange for the *barat*, even for a small *barat*. Suppose I invite someone to my son's wedding, and he does not participate in my son's wedding, then I shall not participate in his son's wedding. So to get a *barat* for your son, you need to participate in weddings.

"The boy's side job is to bring the fireworks and the band and the people who play the music. They are called brass bands. They have clarinet, drums, *jhanj* (large cymbals), *manjira* (tiny cymbals), sunflower (sousaphone), *shahnai* (oboe), trumpets, baritone horns. The type of music varies. First of all there is filmi music. Sometimes they play *languriya* because some people dance to this. One singer sings these *languriya* with a loudspeaker and mike, and people dance there. This was not done before. This is recent.

"Where do they dance? When the *barat* moves from one place, from the *janmassa* (resting place for the *barat*) to the girl's house, the people dance. It is a very new custom. It was not before. Mostly it is boys and young men dancing. Sometimes the old father also dances. As soon as they reach the house for the *dwar puja* (worship at the door)—when they reach the gate, the *barat* begins to go to eat their meal for the feast, and then *dwar puja* begins.

"So, the *barat* arrives like an attacking army with loud music and fireworks and bright fluorescent lights—anything to make a big show. Finally, when the groom comes out of the decorated car, he is greeted—he gets another *tika* on his forehead. For *dwar puja*, two sets of pots are piled high with a lit *diya* on top. The pandit comes, the barber's wife draws an altar with flour on the ground, and the groom will seat himself on a small wooden stool at the altar."

SIXTY

# *DWAR PUJA*—THE NEW SYSTEM

*Back at the Sarang Hotel, Ballia, July 1989, another scorching day*

So we began our work afresh. Gangajali continued explaining the wedding rites. "*Dwar puja*, what is its meaning? This is the time for the lower-caste *chamar*s to perform on their musical instruments: the *dhapali* (single-headed frame drum) together with the *manar* (metal gong)."

Umesh explained, "*Dwar puja* is a custom that is carried out in Uttar Pradesh and Bihar as well as in western Uttar Pradesh, where I live. As these people call it *dwar puja,* we in western UP call it *darwaja*—for the dowry, money, and things are provided for the groom and his family. Among the things are pots to be given to the groom's family. *Dwar puja* is the main time when these large pots called *gagara* are given, usually a set in graded sizes, often stacked on one another in a decorative fashion. These *gagara* are used for water. These days the custom is to give stainless-steel pots and not the brass pots of olden times. All the *barat* people arrive at the door of the bride at the time of *dwar puja*. The barber's wife of the bride's side draws an altar in front of the door, and the groom is invited there, and *dwar puja* takes place. This is a time when women sing *gali*s and some other songs as well. So this is the first invitation for the *barat* and the bridegroom up to the bride's door.

"Thereafter there is a new custom—the *jaymala* wedding. The groom is carried to the place where the thrones are, and he is seated. And thereafter the bride is getting ready in the home for the occasion. She appears with some relatives and family girls, and they support her up to her throne beside the groom. At the same time when *dwar puja* takes place, the bride comes from the back, from where the women are standing, and she throws pearls on the groom to greet him. Nobody can see her, but she sees the groom. And pearls mean rice. We call it '*achhat*.' These are rice. So when people are eating, the bride and bridegroom are seated on large red thrones decorated with gilt. First the girl's side goes to bless the couple. The video camera is moving around, and people come in back of the thrones and sprinkle flower petals over the couple. This creates a kind of memory that this many people participated in the wedding. I don't think it is really blessings. But it shows that these many people—you can see the face of those people who participated in the wedding."

SIXTY-ONE

# THE ANIMAL PARTY

*At Umesh's home, Karimganj, 2014*

"So what do the men actually do during the wedding?" I asked.

"They have to do everything!" Umesh replied.

"Every job is done by the family people. Making all kinds of arrangements. These days it has become easier that we have a tent, so you go and hire a tent. The person who will give you the tent, his people will come and pitch the tent. Before we had to pitch the tent ourselves. Today you can hire a tent that you can pitch yourself, but you have to pitch in on your own, bring it from there to the house on your own, and return it on your own. If you are late—even one day late—it is very expensive. After the *vida* (departure), people get just totally exhausted, and it automatically becomes late. So it is better to hire the tent so they will come and pitch the tent and come and take it away. There is no problem with hiring a tractor to bring it home and take it back. So a big burden is over, the biggest burden of these days. My concept is not to get a fancy tent. Get a simple tent and feed guests on the leaf tray. It is inexpensive, clean, and so many people like to eat this way. They will be seated on the ground.

"But all the situation depends on the boy's side—what they ask for. The girl's side has to arrange that accordingly. Buffet—if they want buffet style, then we have to do that to avoid conflict. We usually call it "buffer" system. Conflict shouldn't begin for small matters like that. The only problem comes for serving people. We have to have so many people serving from the family or from the village. For the buffer system, people take for themselves from those pots. Those people who cook fill the pots. For buffer style we use crockery plates. In winter it is hard to clean the grease off. Even though there is hot water, the oil still remains on the plates—it is so greasy. I don't mind eating grease. But I certainly don't want to lick grease out of another's plate! God! In the buffer system, you cannot hold the leaf plate because it does not have much strength. You can use it on the table or on the ground only. We use metal spoons and plastic use-and-throw glasses instead of *kullar*. The use-and-throw are inexpensive and easy to handle, to put in one place. You need a lot of room to put the clay ones, and there are so many problems with them, so many broken ones. If I could make it, if there is enough room for people to sit down and make a nice place on the ground to sit them, and long tables like this, only one feet high, and sit down and eat from it, that could be very nice. Long long tables only this high, not touching the feet and safe. That would be nice. But I have never seen it.

"The buffer system is the most popular these days. It started recently. In the villages people still use the ground. Some villagers use buffer. Some lower-caste people who have money, they use buffer. Buffer is considered more fancy, more respectable, but for me it is the most ugly thing. If I am invited in the buffer and I reach on time, I can grab a fresh plate, not the second time cleaned, then I take food. Otherwise I chose a small paper plate, and I take only salad, and I eat. Sometimes I eat from plastic bowls, and I eat *chat* (salty snacks). I won't eat food—*puris*, vegetables, *roti*. I can only eat *chat*. I won't touch the food because of the dirty plates and because so many people have used it. They don't know how to serve themselves. They are eating food with their right hand and serving with the right hand. So the handle of the serving spoon gets dirty, it gets polluted.

"So several people in my village—he explained that if he reaches first he eats, otherwise he never eats anything. And I accepted that. We are passing germs on the serving spoons, and it is disgusting because people are not so civilized to use the buffer. It is upper class—I can say it because I've seen five-star hotels, and they have the buffet system there. It is a good thing. But the people have to be educated for that—how to use the buffet system. And also it is common sense, if people are eating on the right-hand side, they can use the left hand for the serving spoon. But people don't have an understanding of it, and their left hand does not work. They cannot serve themselves with the left hand. For one girl's wedding, I saw the pots *so* greasy, and I was thinking that we should also have another stove to heat up the water to clean the plates. There is a boy who was serving, and he came holding a plate toward me, and he was following me. He wanted money from me. He wanted a tip. I shouted at him. I had not hired him, and he wanted a tip from me.

"Village people call it an 'animal party'—the buffer system. Some rich people hire hot water to clean the plates.

"Cooking the food is also a problem. We hire a cook who cooks the food, as well as a sweets maker who makes sweets. If they want *tandoori*, we have a person who makes *tandoori*. And we make a *tandoor*—a furnace for that. Coal is used in it. It all depends on what the boy's side wants. They also may demand the *jaymala* thing. I agreed to it, but I was not agreed for the show—like the coming and taking photographs on the thrones. And the boy's side insisted. Since they insisted, we had to do it. All the burden falls on the girl's parents.

"Arranging a separate tent, lay the flowers, get these chairs, three or four, unnecessary time taking photos and video of each blessing, and so forth."

SIXTY-TWO

# DEPARTURE OF THE *BARAT*

*Again we are in Umesh's home in Karimganj, March 2014, while drinking tea*

"The time is mentioned according to the astrologer what is the best time for the wedding," he said. "The time is always given between three, four, five, six o'clock in the night. So sometimes people can't make it on that time, so it is almost always late. But the time is mentioned. So it takes time for the wedding to take place—in three or four hours. And most of the *barat* leaves at the same time after the feast at night. They bring their bus, and they go back by bus. This is not the girl's side problem, how they will go. They are not really coming to see the wedding, they come to dance—they come to eat. Only some important people of the village who are very close to the family—own relatives from the wife's side and the sister's side and family people like brothers, uncles—remain for the ceremony. Maybe twenty, thirty, forty people remain. The rest go back. Who are left at home in the morning, we give them tea or whatever they ask for and breakfast—some *puri*s, sweets—and thereafter the *vida*, the departure of the bride and groom."

INTERLUDE THIRTEEN

# I ONLY THOUGHT OF IT

"ACTUALLY LIZZIE HAS ARRIVED AT FAWN COURT TO MAKE TROUBLE," Umesh said. "She immediately discovered that she doesn't like Lady Fawn and the family girls. She picks one girl, Augusta, to be her special friend. Poor Augusta. She takes Augusta to Mount Street. Secretly she leaves Augusta downstairs and creeps upstairs to check the necklace—if it is still there.

"One morning Lizzie receives a letter from Lord Fawn, the owl. She doesn't show it to anybody. She coos and sighs and clutches her breast as if it were a wonderful love letter to show off in front of the Fawn women. In fact, the letter is short and cold. It only explains that he will be arriving later on Saturday. Nothing more. She feels annoyed and curses him to herself.

"On that Saturday afternoon, Frank arrives at Fawn Court to visit his cousin Lizzie, who had invited him. She has shown in so many ways to greet Frank to show her love in front of the sisters. She even cried. Tears are always out for Lizzie. Looks like she has a lake of tears behind her eyes.

"So Lizzie decided to have some fun and sent off Frank with Lucy to walk the grounds. This was her idea of attacking Lady Fawn from the back. They talk on the way, and this is the time when Frank claimed that he was in love with Lucy. He tells her that she is the princess of his castles in the air. Lucy says very few words. She did not want to say that she loved him, but her tone expressed the feelings of love in her heart. Before Lady Fawn returns home, Frank escapes."

SIXTY-THREE

# THE BRIDEGROOM ENTERS THE COURTYARD

*We continue at the Hotel Sarang, Ballia, July 1989*

Gangajali said, "So after *gurahatthi*, we have performed *nacchu nahawan* bath of the bride. This is done similarly as was done for the groom. Then the groom will come into the courtyard. Then the women sit in the courtyard and sing songs. Whatever the first main song is, I will sing it now. Thereafter, the wedding will take place. So this song is before the wedding."

## SONG 96

*Tune no. 1: In Whose River Is the Sparkling Water?*

Father's river has sparkling water.
Brother's river has moss.
Brother's river has moss.
Mother's river has the swimming fish.
What bridegroom spreads the great fishing net?
What bridegroom spreads the great fishing net?
Oh, Father's river has sparkling water.
Oh, Brother's river has moss.
Oh, Brother's river has moss.
Oh, Mother's river has the swimming fish.

Oh, bridegroom Vijay spreads the great fishing net.
Oh, bridegroom Vijay spreads the great fishing net.
Brother Sanjin speaks from the high bank of the river.
What *sarawa* (sister's husband, term of abuse in this context) is spreading the great fishing net?
What *sarawa* is spreading the great fishing net?
Bridegroom Vijay speaks from the high bank of the river.
Oh *sarawa*, I am spreading the great fishing net.
Oh *sarawa*, I am spreading the great fishing net.
Oh, *sarau*, do not trample the lotus leaves in the lake.
Oh, my fish is tender.
Oh, my fish is tender.
*Sarau*, I will meet my mate in the lake,
So the lotus leaves are being trampled.
Oh, I will trap the fish.
Oh, I will trap the fish and take her away.

"We call to father that he has water in his river," Gangajali said. "A girl lives as a fish in the water. And the fisherman comes and catches her and takes her away. Similarly, there is water in the river of father. And in the river of brother, there is moss on his side. The fish swim in it. And someone comes and traps her and takes her away. So, similarly, moss is in the river of brother. In the river of mother, similarly, in the lap of mother the boy and girl are born and raised. The girl in the mother's river is like a fish. And the groom comes in that river and spreads the fishing net. Then the bride's brother says, 'Oh *sarau*, who are you? Who is spreading the fishing net in my river? My fish is very beautiful. My fish is lovely. She is very tender and soft. Do not spread your fishing net.' Then he replies that '*Sarau*, I will spread the fishing net, and I will trample your lotus and lotus leaves. And by trapping them, I will take your fish away. Early in the morning, I will take her away. And you will be left crying, keeping the hankie at your mouth, wiping your tears.' It means you will be embarrassed. 'I will go taking her away. Nobody can disturb me.' The father is like a river. Out of his water the fish takes birth in the river of mother. And her brother is the moss. So she is trapped in the moss. As the fish is born in the river, similarly the girl takes birth out of her mother's womb. Whether it is a boy or a girl. In a way she is just like a river."

"It contains a deep meaning," Umesh said. "You have explained it very well."

"The bridegroom comes at night and gets married," Gangajali said. "The wedding tent is like the lake. The wedding tent is trampled, and a little bit remains. So the bridegroom comes similarly. And the trampling takes place in the wedding tent. Now the people of this place, the bride's side, see how the wedding tent becomes. Early in the morning he takes away the bride after the *vida*. This song is composed for that occasion."

Umesh was eager to talk about this song. "The deep meaning says that the composer puts the question mark first and asks to people, in whose river is the sparkling water? And in whose river is the moss? And in whose river is the swimming fish? And she answers herself in the next line that in the river of father there is sparkling water. Here the composer wants to explain the physical symptoms of the body, that the father is the river that carries the sparkling sperms. And mother's river—when he leaves the sperms in the mother—it is a river. The womb is the river of mother. When the child grows in the womb of mother, he or she moves around, a moving fish in the river. And then the moss is in the brother's river where the fish hides herself. In a sense moss is the brother to a fish as the moss protects the fish from danger of the fisherman. The young brother is responsible to take care of his sister or guard his sister and protect her.

"All this song in sung in *chhayabaad.* And several olden Hindi poets have composed their poems in this *chhayabaad.* It shows something different and means something different. Kabir and others, for example Jayasi, another poet, do this. I will give you one line of Kabir.

*Dulahini gavau mangal char*
*Hamghar yaehaim raja Ram bhartar*

"Actually Kabir did not believe in Ram. He believed in God, real God. This is my belief. Its meaning is that the poet is telling how he is saying to married women sitting around him, 'His disciples sing four auspicious songs. My husband Ram has arrived.' That is all. This is the meaning of it. But its meaning is, 'Oh people, sing *bhajan* about the Lord, my Lord has arrived.' It is not the husband. Nothing to do with the husband, nothing to do with the wives (married women). *Dulahani* is worldly people. The husband Ram is the Lord.

"I believe that in olden days those people who created this *chhayabaad* were the folk people. The sophisticated form was given by the composer of the period, but it was always there. What comes first, language or grammar? Language came first. Grammar is composed later. People on the Earth express their feelings. There are two types of people on this Earth. Some people say straight, and some people turn their tone. So the turning tone is the *chhayabaad.* Some people express their feelings through a hidden way. That is called *chhayabaad.*

"In one sense the people are sophisticated, and it is hard to face the reality, so they speak out in a hidden way. And some people are just plain talkers. There are hundreds, thousands of songs in *chhayabaad.* Most of Kabir's poems are in *chhayabaad.* It is very important for folk songs too.

"The mother and father are the biological system. But this song shows how the brother is a real part of the social system. In other cultures, the brother gets separated. But in India, after the father, all the responsibility falls on the brother. If something goes wrong to his sister, he is disgraced in his society—not for one day or two days but for years and years, from one generation to another."

Umesh then asked Gangajali, "After this sweet song, what comes next?"

And immediately she began to sing another wedding song.

## SONG 97

### *Ram Baithaki*

When the *barat* arrived at the door to confront,
Oh, Janak stands joining hands.
Oh, Janak stands joining hands.
I am unable to give anything.
I am unable to give anything.
I could not even serve you.
When the *barat* arrived at the door to confront,
Oh, Janak stands joining hands.
Oh, Janak stands joining hands.
I am unable to give you anything.
I could not even serve you.
I am unable to give you anything.
I could not even serve you.
I give you a dish, I give a jug.
I give you uncountable goblets.
I give you uncountable goblets.
I am unable to give anything.
I could not even serve you.
When the *barat* arrives in the middle of the courtyard,
Oh, Janak stands joining hands.
Oh, Janak stands joining hands.
I am unable to give anything.
I could not even serve you.
I give you a dish, I give you a jug.
I give you uncountable goblets.
I give you uncountable goblets.
I give you a daughter like Sita.
I offer her at your feet with humility.
I give you a daughter like Sita.
I offer her at your feet with humility.
When the *barat* comes in the middle of the wedding tent,
Oh, Janak stands joining hands.
Oh, Janak stands joining hands.
I am unable to give anything.
I could not even serve you.
I am unable to give anything.
I could not even serve you.
I give a dish, I give a jug.
I give uncountable goblets.
I give uncountable goblets.

I give a daughter like Sita.
I give a daughter like Sita.
I offer her at your feet with humility.
I give a daughter like Sita.
I offer her at your feet with humility.
When the *barat* arrived near the altar,
Oh, Janak stands joining hands.
Oh, Janak stands joining hands.
I am unable to give anything.
I could not even serve you.
I am unable to give anything.
I could not even serve you.
I give a dish, I give a jug.
I give uncountable goblets.
I give uncountable goblets.
Like Janak, like Sita,
I give the daughter like Sapana.
I humbly request you, take her under your protection.
I give the daughter like Sapana.
I humbly request you, take her under your protection.
Early in the morning the *barat* departed.
The crowd is standing in the wedding tent.
Janak is standing holding the pillar.
Mother Sunayanan is crying, holding the pillar of the wedding tent,
Taking the daughter in her arms.
Mother Sunayanan is crying, holding the pillar of the wedding tent,
Taking the daughter in her arms.
King Janak begins to say,
Take my son in your arms.
Take my son in your arms.
Janki will not be yours anymore.
Ram will take care of Ajudhya.
Janki will not be yours anymore.
Ram will take care of Ajudhya.

"When the *barat* arrives at the door," Gangajali said, "then Janak requests by joining hands in front of his chest, as in prayer. Any person who arranges the wedding of his daughter indicates by joining hands that I am not equal to you, the father of the groom. I have nothing to offer. And I am also not able to serve you. I am not able to do anything. We are offering our daughter at your feet. And when the girl goes after getting married, mother cries, holding one pillar of the wedding tent. She tells her husband, 'help me so I can meet my daughter. My heart is breaking.' Then he replies, 'you hold your son into your arms and be patient because your daughter is not yours anymore. Now Ram has taken her away to Ajudhya, and there he will establish his kingdom. From now on, she will not come from Ayodhya to you. Now you hold your son in your arms.'"

Then followed the next wedding song. Gangajali was feeling enthusiastic.

### SONG 98

*Baithaki*

Where have you made the sword?
To go to get married.
Oh mother, of what beloved?
The knife of the bridegroom.
Then, where has he won?
Oh mother, what knife is of the bridegroom, and where has he won?
The knife is made in Ballia.
To go to get married.
Oh mother, the knife is of the bridegroom Vijay.
Then he won in Ballia.
Oh mother, the knife is of bridegroom Vijay.
Then he won in Ballia.
Oh Sanjin brother, get the bow and arrow ready.
Oh Sanjin brother, get the bow and arrow ready.
Oh brother, your older brother-in-law has come.
Go and have battle with them in the field.
Oh brother, your older brother-in-law has come.
Go and have battle with them in the field.
Brother fought all the day.
He lost the war in the evening.
Brother fought all the day.
He lost the war in the evening.
Oh brother, you have lost the sister like Sapan.
Oh, bridegroom Vijay won.
Oh brother, you have lost the sister like Sapan.
Oh, bridegroom Vijay won.
Oh brother, brother Sanjin brother.
You have lost your wisdom.
Oh brother, you could lose a cow or a buffalo.
Why have you lost your sister?
Oh brother, you could lose all the elephants and horses.
Why have you lost your sister?
Oh brother, you could have even lost your loving wife.
Why have you lost your sister?
Oh Sapan, sister,
You have lost your knowledge.

Oh sister, the cow and the buffalo is the beauty of the door.
My sister belongs to others.
Oh sister, the cow and buffalo are my Laxmi.
My sister belongs to others.
Oh Sapan, sister,
You have lost your knowledge.
Oh sister, elephant and horses are our wealth.
Sister, you belong to another house.
Oh sister, the loving wife is the Laxmi of my house.
Sister, you belong to others.
Oh sister, the loving wife is the Laxmi of my house.
Sister, you belong to another house.

"You have sung two songs now," Umesh said. "Which was the last one? What will you call it?"

Gangajali said, "The same which I sang before. This is also sung at the time of the wedding. It is the *baithaki* of the wedding."

Umesh asked, "Both?"

"Yes, both," Gangajali replied. "The bridegroom goes from his village as someone is going for battle, and the battle takes place from both sides. So the bridegroom is coming from the other side with the *barat*. The sister says, 'The bridegroom is coming. You get ready with your bow and arrow and have battle with him. And if he is defeated, he will go back. I, your sister, will remain here. Look, do not get defeated.'

"Then the brother fights all the day with the bridegroom and is defeated in the evening. And in the evening, she gets married. Then the sister says to her brother, 'Brother, you got crazy. Have you lost your wisdom? You have lost your sister like Sapana. If you had to lose, you could lose a cow, bullock, buffalo, and even your wife. And you could lose elephants and horses. Why have you lost me?'

The brother explains, 'Oh sister, elephant and horse are the beauty of my door. And you belong to others. You have to go someday in someone's house. And my wife is the Laxmi of my house. She will not go anywhere. But girl, daughter and sister, they have to go someday to someone's house. Therefore, I lost you. You are of others. You have to establish yourself in someone else's house.'

"Now then, wedding rituals are performed under the wedding tent. The Brahman pandit comes and sits beside the altar. And for the other side, the bridegroom sits with his people. Then Gauri–Ganesh is worshiped there."

SIXTY-FOUR

# THE BRIDE ENTERS THE COURTYARD

*Day 4, we continue in the Hotel Sarang, Ballia, 1989*

"Now I will sing a song for Ganeshji," Gangajali said. "He is the first of all the gods, and he is worshiped before every other god. This is a *bhajan* for Ganesh."

### SONG 99

*Ganesh bhajan*

You are worshiped before any other.
Oh, first worshiped.
Oh supreme of all the gods, your worship is first.
You are the son of Gauri.
Oh supreme of all the gods,
You are the son of Gauri.
Oh supreme of all the gods,
You have elephant's teeth,
Oh, elephant trunk.
Oh supreme of all the gods,
Elephant trunk.
Oh supreme of all the gods,
You are the son of Gauri.

Oh supreme of all the gods,
You are the son of Gauri.
Oh supreme of all the gods,
You are offered garlands, flowers, and *laddu* (sweets).
Oh supreme of all the gods,
You are offered betel and flowers.
And offered a garland.
Oh supreme of all the gods,
*Sindur* beautifies your forehead,
With the garland as a necklace.
Oh supreme of all the gods,
You are the son of Gauri.
Oh supreme of all the gods (two lines repeated three times).
You are offered garlands and flowers,
And offered dry fruits.
Oh supreme of all the gods,
You are offered *laddu*.
Devotees serve you.

PAUSE

*The tape ran out here. The remaining lines are offered below.*

Oh supreme of all the gods,
Devotees serve you.
Oh supreme of all the gods,
You are the son of Gaura.
Oh supreme of all the gods,
You are the son of Gaura.
Oh supreme of all the gods,
You give eyes to the blind.
You restore health to the lepers.
Oh supreme of all the gods.
You restore health to the lepers,
Oh supreme of all the gods,
You are the son of Gauri.
Oh supreme of all the gods,
You are the son of Gauri.
Oh supreme of all the gods,
Barren lady.
You give wealth to the poor,
And sons to the barren ladies.
Oh supreme of all the gods,
And sons to the barren ladies.
Oh supreme of all the gods,

You are the son of Gauri.
Oh supreme of all the gods,
You are the son of Gauri.
Oh supreme of all the gods.

"So the groom and bride arrive at the altar, and I sang a *bhajan* for Ganeshji," Gangajali said. "The priest has them worship Ganeshji. Having seen his *patra*, I sing the Ganesh *bhajan* according to the situation. I can collect mantras out of his religious book. I have also explained everything in the *bhajan*. The bride's side people come, and the bridegroom is called from outside. And the bride is called to the altar. And the bride's brother is called there. What does the pandit do then? To our side here there is a metal dish and also a metal *lota*. And water is in this *lota*. At the movement, brother Brahman pandit and bride and groom, all their hands are piled up one after another. First is the hand of the Brahman, second is the hand of the groom, third is the hand of the bride, and the brother drops water on the hands from the jug. The water must fall in a continuous stream. It must not break. It keeps flowing. So the song is sung for this."

### SONG 100

*Daria*

Oh, oh brother Sanjin, brother.
Let the stream of water flow.
Oh, oh brother Sanjin, brother.
Brother, do not let the stream break.
Brother, do not let the stream break.
If the stream of water breaks,
Then the sister will be stolen.
If the stream of water breaks,
Then the sister will be stolen.
Oh, oh *chacha*,
Oh, oh *chacha* Bharath *chacha*.
Oh, oh brother Sanjiv, brother.
Let the stream of water flow.
Let the stream of water flow.
Oh, oh brother Sanjin, brother.
Do not let the stream break.
Do not let the stream break.
If the stream of water breaks,
Then the sister will be stolen.
If the stream of water breaks,
The sister will be stolen.
*Tape runs out here abruptly.*

Women do not expound on the musical intricacies of their songs. When asked what is important about a certain song, a woman would never answer with an exposition on the importance of leading tones or undulating rhythms. They would not say that their song, for example, illustrates the conquest of the bride, as does this song. Almost always, she will tell about the ritual for which it is performed. She will rarely even expound on the emotional content of the song itself. When this song telling about a *daria*—for the pouring of the water in a continuous stream—is sung, for instance, singers will not talk about how the brother of the bride is nervous or how the family is upset. The explanation will be simply, "This is the song for when the bride's brother pours the water. The stream must not break, or he will lose his sister."

"So the stream of water is poured on the palm," Gangajali said. "Then the women sing this song, 'Oh brother, the stream of water that you are pouring, do not let it break. If you break the stream of water, then you will lose your sister.' Therefore, he does not break the stream. He pours it continuously. Even then, by dropping the water, finally it breaks. When the water is finished, he loses. Then the water is not poured again. After this, *kanyadan* songs will be sung."

SIXTY-FIVE

# DONATION OF THE VIRGIN DAUGHTER

*We continue our session at the Hotel Sarang, Ballia, July 1989*

"The bride's father is called," Gangajali said. "And the bride arrives with the barber lady, and the bride is seated on the thigh of father. The priest has him do *kanyadan* of the girl according to the religious thoughts in the Vedas and Shastras. The bridegroom is there. The *kanya* (virgin) sits on the thigh of the father. And if the girl is mature, she is seated on a simple leaf tray in front of him. We call it *kanyadan*. Here the priest does the worship of Gauri and Ganesh, and father's hand remains under the hand of the groom. The groom's hand is below the hand of the bride, and the father keeps holding his hand like this. The father is giving his daughter in your hand. He is having him hold the hand of his daughter. This song is sung here."

SONG 101

*Kanyadan*

Oh father, what eclipse begins in the day?
And oh, what eclipse begins at midnight?
And oh, what eclipse begins at midnight?
What eclipse affected you, Father?
Oh, when will this eclipse be over?

Father, the solar eclipse causes trouble in the day.
Oh, the lunar eclipse causes trouble at midnight.
Oh, the lunar eclipse causes trouble at midnight.
Daughter, the eclipse of the father had influence in the morning.
When will these both end?
When will these both end?
Daughter, the solar eclipse will end.
The lunar eclipse will rise.
The lunar eclipse will rise.
Daughter, the eclipse of the father is very troublesome.
When will both end?
When will both end?
The *dhoti* is trembling.
The book is trembling.
Oh, the hand of the priest is trembling.
The hand of the priest is trembling.
Oh, Father, the eclipse began early in the morning.
It will end after the wedding.
Oh Father, after the *sindur*,
I will belong to my husband.
Oh, your eclipse will end.
Oh, your eclipse will end.
Oh Father, after the *sindur*,
I will belong to my husband.
Oh, your eclipse will end.

The slow and stately tempo of this song gives the listener a hint that the highest drama of the wedding has been reached. All precautions have been taken, but at the moment when the father donates his daughter, there is a solar eclipse and a lunar eclipse. Eclipses are very much feared in modern India, and many people choose to remain inside when they occur. But here, this powerful double eclipse causes the Earth to tremble, the universe to tremble, all the items assembled for the wedding to tremble, and also the hand of the priest to tremble. It is a time of terror. There is no going back. The trembling will only stop after *kanyadan* has been given and the father puts his daughter's hand into the hand of the groom.

"When eclipse comes to the sun and to the moon, and this way the sun and moon both got hurt by the eclipse," Umesh explained. "The sweeper used to use their broom and shouting and hitting the Earth so they could take over the pain of the sun or the moon. We believe that these eclipses hurt, give pain, to the human. From long ago in India, we have not come out during an eclipse. We have known it, but we didn't know how people got hurt. Some people got blind. We certainly believe that pregnant women get hurt by the eclipse. So to reduce the effect of it, we put some red soil from the market called *geru*. We put it in the water and make ink out of that. We put it on the back of the animals so they won't get hurt. Also, we tell our children, 'Don't go out. The eclipse is coming. Sleep inside.' These days it is broadcast on the television to not look at the sun during the solar eclipse."

"As the eclipse of the sun begins," Gangajali said, "then all the people on the Earth say, 'Alas, alas, the eclipse has come today. Don't do this, don't do that.' Look, man is simply a man, but even God is influenced by an eclipse.

"The lunar eclipse comes at night. Then the solar eclipse ends. Its influence comes, and it goes. Similarly, the lunar eclipse ends in the day.

"Until the daughter gets married, her body is in trouble and will be crying inside. The hope is that nothing unusual will occur, as any problem during the wedding of the girl will destroy the wedding. The *barat* might go back. Oh Lord! My daughter must get married. And thereby I will get over the debt of my life.

"So the daughter says, 'Oh, Father, the effect of the eclipse on you will end when my husband puts *sindur* in my parting. I will belong to him in every sense, and you will be released.' So this song is for the *kanyadan* ritual, when the father gives his daughter's hand into the hand of the bridegroom. The priest chants some mantras out of his book, and after chanting the mantras, the program here gets serious. He gives her hand in the hand of the bridegroom. And there is no need for the father thereafter in the daughter's life.

"In the olden days very young girls used to get married. They did not let them mature to get married. Oh, even they were married just after they were weaned. I have seen such a young girl's wedding with my own eyes. A girl was married in my neighborhood in the olden days. Milk was sent for her in her *sasural* in a bottle.

"'The *lota* is trembling, the pandit is trembling.' This is the effect of the eclipse on the father's planet," Gangajali said. "The effect of the planet is so heavy that he trembles as he gives the girl into the hands of others. The book of the priest, the *lota*, and his hand are all trembling at the time of offering."

"In a sense, the poet is trying to explain the pain and trouble of the father while losing his daughter," Umesh said, "giving away his wealth and beloved daughter at the same time. 'I can feel all the sudden I am in the shadow of it.' And he began to cry. There is no politics played at the girl's wedding, but surely for a boy's wedding there is politics," Umesh explained. "For a boy's wedding, anyone can say, 'No, I won't participate.' But nobody will say that he won't participate in a girl's wedding. Refusing not to help at a girl's wedding is a kind of sin because the donation of a daughter is a big thing. Even other caste people who cannot get inside of the house, they can send a small amount of money for *kanyadan*. The money that goes in *kanyadan* is never considered refundable. The five, ten, twenty rupees that is given in *kanyadan* is not like giving and taking. Because this money—he is donating this money for his sake—for own, not to help the family, and the money goes straight to the boy's family. Because donation means you donate something by your heart, you will be rewarded from God for that. No person can reward you for that. People give as much as they feel, as much as they can afford, under ₹50 ($.74) usually. Suppose a person wants to give something for *kanyadan,* and he cannot get inside the house. So he hands the money to someone, and the person will go to the priest inside of the house where the bride and groom are seated under the wedding tent at the altar. The money will be given to the priest, and they will say this is *kanyadan* for that person.

"And the pundit will chant the name of the person who has given this money. The parents do the *kanyadan*. *Kanyadan* is only from parents. It is their duty to do. But other people also get involved in this. He also wants to do something for *kanyadan*, so he can give a little money for that. Those people who don't have daughters, they surely give *kanyadan* because daughter is essential to have in a family. It is unspoken, but when you take someone's girl in your house, you have to give your daughter too. That is my deep understanding. That is why the people consider that the person who does not have a daughter, he is a sinner. A person must have a daughter to run the nature. If a family only has sons, they wish for a daughter. If you don't have any relatives from the daughter's side, the family is always lonely without a daughter. When so many relatives come to you on any occasion, when no daughters or sisters visit you, how a person will feel? If we live in a group in a village, a society—very linked to each other—we want to have relatives from the daughter's side. It is always good when the number of sons and daughters is even. We can't plan it, but we expect it."

SIXTY-SIX

# CEREMONY OF THE PUFFED RICE

*We continue our session at the Hotel Sarang, Ballia, July 1989*

"The *lawa* ritual comes after *kanyadan*," Gangajali said. "Puffed rice (*lawa*) is there from the side of the bridegroom. And here is puffed rice from the girl's side. Both *lawa* are mixed in one, and there is a bamboo basket like this—a small auspicious basket. And the bridegroom's side has a new *gamchha* (shawl) for the *sala* (wife's brother). The brother mixes the *lawa* that was brought from both sides. And if the family is rich, the groom's side people bring a full suit of clothes for the wife's brother. But poor people buy only a *gamchha*. A pouch is fashioned out of the *gamchha*. They put the puffed rice in the pouch, and brother ties it around his neck and hangs the pouch in front of him. And the bridegroom and bride hold it. The bridegroom's *lawa* is mixed with the bride's *lawa*. The bridegroom drops it from one side. And from the other side, the brother of the bride drops *lawa* on the same place. Then this song goes here."

SONG 102

*Lawa gali*

Your *lawa* and my *lawa*,  
Mix to become one.  
This adulterous bridegroom,  
He does not stop.

This adulterous bridegroom.
Your *lawa* and my *lawa*,
Mix to become one.
This adulterous bridegroom,
He does not stop.
This adulterous bridegroom.
Your barber and my barber lady,
Put them to sleep together.
This adulterous bridegroom,
He does not stop.
This adulterous bridegroom.
My grandfather and your grandmother,
Put them to sleep together.
This adulterous bridegroom,
He does not stop.
This adulterous bridegroom.
Your mother and my father,
Put them to sleep together.
This adulterous bridegroom,
He does not stop.
This adulterous bridegroom.
Your *lawa* and my *lawa*,
Mix to become one.
This adulterous bridegroom,
He does not stop.
My brother and your *bhauji*,
Put them to sleep together.
This adulterous bridegroom,
He does not stop.
This adulterous bridegroom.
Your *bua* and my *phupha*,
Put them to sleep together.
This adulterous bridegroom,
He does not stop.
This adulterous bridegroom.
Your *lawa* and my *lawa*,
Mix to become one.
This adulterous bridegroom,
He does not stop.
This adulterous bridegroom.
My priest and your priest's wife,
Put them to sleep together.
This adulterous bridegroom,
He does not stop.
This adulterous bridegroom.

My water-pulling man and your water-pulling lady,
Put them to sleep together.
This adulterous bridegroom,
He does not stop.
This adulterous bridegroom.

"This is the main *lawa* song," Gangajali said. "At the time of *lawa*, both *lawa* are mixed. Then women sing this *gali* for the bridegroom: 'Your mother and the father of the bride, put them in one bed to sleep. My barber and the wife of your barber, put them in one bed to sleep, and then my priest and the wife of your priest, put them in one bed to sleep. Oh, adulterous bridegroom, don't you feel embarrassed? And my brother and your sister, put them in one bed to sleep. Oh, adulterous bridegroom, don't you feel embarrassed? My *phupha* and your *bua*, put them in one bed to sleep. Bring all them in one place. And my *lawa* mixed with your *lawa* together. Oh, adulterous bridegroom, don't you feel embarrassed?'

"This is a *gali* type song. Whenever the wedding takes place, this main song will be sung at this point.

"So the *lawa* ritual is done," Gangajali said. "Now the *feri* will take place. So the groom and bride take seven *feri*s (turns) around the fire. The bridegroom's *gamchha* and the bride's *chaddar* (veil) are tied in a knot. The barber lady puts a coin in it and ties a knot around that. A small fire is lit under the wedding tent. Seven turns are taken around it. And women sing."

### SONG 103

### *Bhamar*

Oh, they take the first turn.
The sister is yours.
The sister is yours.
Oh, when the second turn is taken,
Then the bride will be yours.
Oh, when the second turn is taken,
Oh, when the third turn is taken,
Then the sister is yours.
Then the sister is yours.
Oh, when the fourth turn is taken,
Then she becomes your wife.
Oh, when the fourth turn is taken,
Then she becomes your wife.
Oh, when the fifth turn is taken,
Then the sister is mine.
Oh, the sister is mine.
Oh, when the sixth turn is taken,
Then the wife will be yours.

Oh, when the seventh turn is taken,
Then the sister is mine.
Oh, then the sister is mine.
Oh, when the seventh turn is taken,
The wife became yours.
Oh, when the seventh turn is taken,
The wife became yours.

"This song is sung when the *bhamar* (turns around the fire) take place," Gangajali said. "The groom and bride take seven *bhamar*s around the fire. Women sing for all seven turns. When the seventh *bhamar* is done, then the bride will be yours. Before that she is my sister.

"Then the priest explains the meaning of the seven *bhamar*s. On the seventh turn, the priest makes the bride and bridegroom resolve to keep their promises. Before the wedding, the priest is asking the bride and bridegroom, 'When I will be your wife, if you go to a foreign country, do I have to beautify myself with all sixteen *sringar*? And I shouldn't go anywhere. I should have no behavior against my husband. I shouldn't do anything against the will of my husband.' And the bride says, 'If I go in any *satsangh*, don't stop me. And you fulfill my needs. And you join me in my happiness. Fulfill my happiness. Do not stop me if I want to give away anything to any beggars. Don't stop me if I go to the houses of other women in the neighborhood. You accept all these happy things regarding me. Only then will I be your wife.'

"Then the bridegroom says, 'Okay, I also have questions for you. What are they? If I am not at home, don't go out of the home with anyone without asking me. Whatever you want to do, do it according to my thoughts. When I am with you, if I say "do," then do it. If I am not at home, don't go to the home of others. If I am not at home, don't go without me in sixteen ornaments. It is my advice.' Then she replies, 'It is all right. I shall carry out your wishes.' When they have pledged their acceptance of these vows, then the wedding takes place."

"Mix your *lawa* with my *lawa*." After having listened to over one hundred of Gangajali's songs, you might well be wondering, where did this tradition come from? How long have Indian women been sitting in groups singing? And why are there so many dirty songs?

It may come as a surprise that the earliest record we have of women's group singing comes from the Rig Veda (1700–1100 BCE), the earliest Sanskrit literature of the Hindu people. The translation and interpretation of this particular portion of the Rig Veda was accomplished quite recently by Sanskritist Stephanie Jamison. The topic was too laced with bestiality for earlier British scholars, it would seem. Jamison reports, "Eggeling, for example, resorts to suspension dots or inserts the untranslated Sanskrit. . . . Keith simply omits TS VII.4.19 d–k in his translation, with the comment 'the next verses are hardly translatable'; while Griffith 1899, omitting VS XXIII.21–31, saying rather huffily: 'the . . . stanzas are not reproducible even in the semiobscurity of a learned European language.' Even Caland opts for Latin when he encounters the root √yabh 'fuck.'"

What were these obscure passages that so offended Victorian scholars? These verses describe the great Horse Sacrifice performed by the king. In this enactment the queen is accompanied by her other queens, who encircle her, singing and slapping their thighs. As they perform, the main queen lies next to the dead horse and both are covered. Then, as the Veda says,

> Put the penis up between the two thighs
> Drive the sleek one, adorned at the end, along (the thighs)
> Which is the living pleasure-maker for women,
> Which is their hole runner/cleaner,
> The dear secret of women,
> Which has hit their *sardigrdi* [vulva or clitoris—only used in this
> hymn] in the black mark.

Jamison makes clear that this act is not a symbolic copulation, but in fact the act itself. I suppose the important point here is that the horse is dead. So we can picture women, queens, singing to their sister queen, the lines of the Rig Veda to accompany her performance.

I don't know of a single ethnomusicologist, myself included, who would harbor the notion that these bawdy songs, that women dancing in circles, slapping their thighs, that these actions so carefully documented in the oldest literary work of India were the forebears of women's village song in 2019. But this notion has its appeal as we recall the eternal question—as humans always do—"Where did I come from?" I would, however, hazard a few connections between hymns from 1500 BCE to 2019 CE. Number one: women sang then, women sing now; women sang in groups then, women sing in groups now; women sang bawdy songs then, women sing bawdy songs now—in fact, bawdy songs are, for women, their favorite songs. During the Hindu wedding in the area around Banaras, women joke and laugh as they sing very dirty songs about the family of a new groom—who his mother sleeps with, and so on. Now that amplification is popular in villages, the men will give these singing groups, often seated on the flat rooftops, a microphone or a bullhorn. These *gali* songs—as they are called—are hits and are blasted all around the village. I don't recall ever visiting a village where they were not sung for me.

SIXTY-SEVEN

# THE *SINDUR* RITUAL

*And the session is still going at the Sarang Hotel, Ballia, 1989*

"Then the priest worships Ganesh–Gauri by the bride's hand," Gangajali said. "With the hands of the bride, so the figures of Gauri and Ganesh, made of cow dung, these Gauri–Ganesh figures are stuck to the *kalas* with cow dung. Then they are offered rice, flowers, betel leaf, betel nut, water, turmeric paste, and *sindur.* Coins are also offered through the hands of the bride and bridegroom and the *kakkan* made out of the mango leaf tied up with yellow cotton thread. And the priest chants mantras and ties it on his hand. Two *kakkan* have been tied on both the bride and bridegroom before the wedding ceremony. Both are tied there, each with the handmade thread.

"When the time for the *sindur* (vermillion) ritual comes, the barber lady brings the bride covered with the veil. And the groom comes. And none of the mother's side people stay there under the *mandap.* Now only the barber lady remains there with the bride. But girlfriends and women who are there retire from the wedding tent, also the mother, father, brother, uncle—none of them stay under the *mandap.* Those *barati* people who come with the bridegroom also do not stay there. Only the bridegroom, bride, the barber lady, and the pandit are present for the *sindur* ritual.

"There is a red *sindur* container called *sinhara* in which the *sindur* is kept. The *sinhara* is brought. Then the bridegroom picks up the *sinhara* in his hand. The area is covered with a sheet on one side, and the barber lady keeps the bride inside, covered with the sheet and her head covered with her veil. The bridegroom does not see her face. I am telling you what takes place in the olden type of wedding. Then she opens the hair carefully like this, but she keeps her face covered and keeps the parting open. And the bridegroom, who has the *sinhara*, he pinches up some *sindur* and puts it in her parting. Here this wedding song is sung."

### SONG 104

*Sindur*

She cries, "Father, Father."
Father does not reply.
The father does not reply.
Because of the authority of the father,
The bridegroom marries me.
Because of the authority of the father,
The bridegroom puts the *sindur*.
She cries, "Uncle, Uncle."
The uncle does not reply.
The uncle does not reply.
Because of the authority of the uncle,
The bridegroom puts the *sindur*.
Because of the authority of the uncle,
The bridegroom puts the *sindur*.
She cries, "Brother, Brother."
The brother does not reply.
The brother does not come.
Because of the authority of the brother,
The groom puts the *sindur*.
Because of the authority of the brother,
The groom puts the *sindur*.
She cries, "*Phupha, Phupha*."
Nobody replies.
Nobody comes.
Because of the authority of everyone,
The bridegroom puts the *sindur*.
Because of the authority of everyone,
The bridegroom puts the *sindur*.

"The *sindur* is put in her parting, and she got married," Gangajali said. "It is a very happy thing. Then the bridegroom is going to put *sindur*, placing a pinch of it on the forehead of the bride. Then the bride calls there for her father. She shouts and calls, 'Oh Father, where are you people? Brother or Uncle, *Phupha*, where are you people? Nobody is here from my *maica*. And he is putting the *sindur* in my parting against my wish. Uncle, where are you? Look. He is putting *sindur* in my parting. Brother, where are you? He comes to put the *sindur* in my parting. You people come here. He is putting the *sindur* in my parting by force. You people come to me.' But nobody comes. And the bridegroom puts *sindur* in her parting. She says, 'I have called everyone, but no one came. Because of the force of everyone, the bridegroom has put the *sindur*.' So nobody came. 'He put the *sindur* on my parting.'"

Of all the wedding songs in the Bhojpuri repertory, this *sindur* song has the fewest variations. In India, it appears to be sung word for word in exactly the same manner from village to village, likewise in the diaspora with the exception of Mauritius, where the family women also mention appeasing the gods by grinding clove and cardamom. This uniformity of performance tradition is notably unique in this worldwide diasporic song repertory. Why do all the other songs take so many forms, while this one item is identical throughout Bhojpur and the diaspora? I don't know.

"Then after this song, all women sing happy *gali* for the bridegroom," Gangajali said. "This is a *gali* type."

### SONG 105

#### *Gali*

Put the *sindur*.
Oh bridegroom, put the *sindur*.
Put *sindur* in the parting of your mother.
Put the *sindur*.
Oh bridegroom, put the *sindur*.
Oh, put the *sindur* in the parting of your sister.
Put the *sindur*.
Oh bridegroom, put the *sindur*.
Oh, put the *sindur* in the parting of your *phua*.
Put the *sindur*.
Oh bridegroom, put the *sindur*.
Oh bridegroom, put the *sindur* on the neighbor lady.
Oh bridegroom, put the *sindur* on the neighbor lady.
Put the *sindur*.
Oh bridegroom, put the *sindur*.
Put the *sindur* on your *bua*, sister, close family ladies.
Oh bridegroom, put the *sindur*.
Oh, put the *sindur*.
Oh, put the *sindur* on your neighbors.
Oh, put the *sindur* on your neighbors.

"After that, this is the main *gali*," Gangajali said. "This *gali* is for the bridegroom, that you have put *sindur* on my girlfriend. You put *sindur* on your mother. As we are fighting. Why did you put it? You put this on your mother and on your sister. Your close relatives and on your neighbors, whoever is there. So the *sindur* is on everyone.

"Now the *sindur* has been put, all the people will gather. There the *chumawan* will take place similarly. This is the last *chumawan*.

"There are hundreds of *chumawan* songs," she continued. "To perform *chumawan* there are many other songs, but I am giving you the main old songs. This is the oldest, and until today, the most important."

### SONG 106

#### *Chumawan*

Oh, *sathi* rice and tender *dub* grass.
*Suhagin* (happily married) mother goes to kiss.
Oh, *sathi* rice and tender *dub* grass.
*Suhagin* mother goes to kiss.
Oh, as she kisses, similarly she blesses.
Oh, my bridegroom and bride, live for one hundred thousand years.
Oh, my bridegroom and bride, live for one hundred thousand years.
With *sathi* rice and tender *dub* grass,
The *suhagin bhauji* goes to kiss.
As she kisses, similarly she blesses.
The *suhagin bhauji* goes to kiss.
As she kisses, similarly she blesses.
My bridegroom and bride, live for one hundred thousand years.
My bridegroom and bride, live for one hundred thousand years.
Oh, *sathi* rice and tender *dub* grass.
*Suhagin* sister comes out to kiss.
*Suhagin* sister comes out to kiss.
With *sathi* rice and tender *dub* grass,
Daughter's sister comes out to kiss.
Daughter's sister comes out to kiss.
As she kisses, similarly she blesses.
My bridegroom and bride, live for one hundred thousand years.
My bridegroom and bride, live for one hundred thousand years.
The son is without milk.
The son is without milk.
The son is blooming.
All creatures enjoy,
The kingdom of Ayodhya.
All creatures enjoy,
The kingdom of Ayodhya.

"People will take the bride and bridegroom into the *kohabar* after *chumawan*. The same song will be sung as before, when after each ritual they were taken into the *kohabar*: 'This new *kohabar* is made of brass and bronze.'

"After that a *jog* will be sung and then one or two *sohar*," Gangajali said. "Singing the *sohar* for the birth of a son is auspicious for the bride and bridegroom. After that *khilauna*, songs of childhood, playing, and toys are sung."

The ritual songs contained in these last few chapters are sung deep into the night as the solemn rituals of the marriage proper are performed. At this point, the bride and groom are very sleepy, as are other participants. Nevertheless, the songs of *sindur* mark, for many Indians, the actual moment of the union. At this point the bride feels totally helpless as she calls out to the members of her family to save her from this fate.

Edward O. Henry, an early student of Bhojpuri song, concludes that the wedding song repertory expresses three main themes: the plight of the bride, the conquest of the bride by the bridegroom and his groomsmen, and the joking insults of the *gali*. The plight of the bride is clearly expressed in the touching words of Song 104: She cries, "Father, Father." Perhaps this particular item, word for word, tune for tune, has been preserved throughout the Bhojpuri region of India and in the island diaspora because this is one central theme of the wedding. In comparing Gangajali's repertory, as she chose to present it to us, and the wedding songs collected by Henry, it would seem that he heard more obscene *galis* than we did. However, Gangajali sang many more songs directly linked to the wedding rituals and the acts thereof than were sung for Henry. Umesh always said of Gangajali, "She kept the limit." Just a few words. But very meaningful for Umesh. Although Umesh didn't criticize Henry's collection in any way, he did feel that they went beyond the limit that Gangajali had set for herself. In considering this, we must bring to mind the context in which these recordings were made. For Henry, he was a male trying to learn about the world of village women. For Umesh and me, we presented as a couple, which, for Gangajali, reminded her to keep to her limit. She emphasized the important ritual items that kept the world and the wedding moving forward. She sang those songs that she regarded as essential for the marriage to be fulfilled. It was serious business. *Gali*? She sang a few funny ones, many involving silly metaphors. Mostly, however, for us, she said that these were "useless" songs.

Thus, Gangajali carefully controlled the songs that were to go out into the world. Some scholars have expressed a wish to be a "fly on the wall," a curious notion indeed. I would never want to intrude in that manner, and I totally accept Gangajali's mediation in her presentation of self.

SIXTY-EIGHT

# THE *KOHABAR* RITUAL

*Session 4, at the Hotel Sarang, July 1989, continues*

"After this, the bridegroom and bride go into the *kohabar*, and they are seated there, and all women are singing *jog* there. *Jog* of *kohabar*."

SONG 107

*Jog of kohabar*

*(The fan is on.)*

Oh, bridegroom Vijay,
Take the shovel on your shoulder.
Oh, bridegroom Vijay,
Take the shovel on your shoulder.
Bridegroom, go to the forest.
Dig out the root.
Bridegroom, go to the forest.
Dig out the root.
Where is the grinding stone from?
Where is the grinder from?
Where is the grinding stone from?

Where is the grinder from?
Oh, where is the daughter from,
Who grinds the *gari* root of Ballia?
Oh, where is the daughter from,
Who grinds the *gari* root of Ballia?
The grinding stone is from Ballia.
The grinding stone is from Deoria.
The grinder is from Deoria.
The grinding stone is from Deoria.
The grinder is from Deoria.
Oh, the daughter is from Ballia,
Who grinds the *gari* root.
Oh, the daughter is from Ballia,
Who grinds the *gari* root.
She grinds the root forcefully and lifts it up.
She grinds the root forcefully and lifts it up.
Oh, bridegroom Vijay,
Drink the root of *suhhag* (married happiness).
Oh, bridegroom Vijay,
Drink the root of *suhhag*.
The bridegroom feels very nice after drinking the root.
While drinking, the bridegroom got dizzy.
While drinking, the bridegroom got dizzy.
Oh father, where is the ascetic from,
Who was brought inside the house?
Oh father, where is the ascetic from,
Who was brought inside the house?
Father, I have been given the root of *suhhag* to drink.
Father, after drinking it I got dizzy.
Oh son, don't call my daughter-in-law an ascetic.
Oh son, don't call my daughter-in-law an ascetic.
My son, you will sleep with the ascetic in her bed.
My son, this ascetic will work in the kitchen.
Oh son, don't call my daughter-in-law an ascetic.
Son, this ascetic is the Laxmi of the house.

"And this is the *jog* of *kohabar*," said Gangajali.

This song is in the form of a dialogue between the bridegroom, the bridegroom's father, and the flock of women singers, who ask the important questions. Here the objects of everyday life, the shovel and the grinder, become *mangal*, auspicious, in the liminal space of the wedding. The "root of *suhag*" is the joy of married life. The term *suhagin* refers to a happily married woman, who expresses her happiness by wearing the sixteen traditional ornaments of the wife whose husband is living. At the death of her husband, the widow beats her arms against the brick wall, in grief, to break her brightly colored glass bangles. She will never wear them again. She washes the sindur from her hair and removes other jewelry. From that hour onward, she will give up wearing brightly colored saris and choose rather a pure white sari or ones with flowery prints in subdued colors. She is no longer the *suhagin*, the happily married woman. She feels abandoned, alone, unprotected, as she loses much of the meaning of her life. At this critical point, it is essential for her brothers to once again assume the important support role that is her birthright.

"Here is another *jog* of *kohabar*."

### SONG 108

*Jog of kohabar*

Where is the *sinduara* from?
The *sinduara* is full of *sindur*.
The *sinduara* is full of *sindur*.
My son, oh, where is the yellow sari from?
The jingle bells are stitched to the yellow sari.
Oh, the jingle bells are stitched to the yellow sari.
My son, oh, where is the yellow sari from?
The jingle bells are stitched to the yellow sari.
The jingle bells are stitched to the yellow sari.
Oh, the *sinduara* is brought from her *sasural*.
The *sinduara* is full of *sindur*.
Oh, the *sinduara* is full of *sindur*.
Oh my son, the yellow sari comes from her *naihar*.
The jingle bells are stitched to the yellow sari.
Oh, the jingle bells are stitched to the yellow sari.
*Nanad* plasters the courtyard,
Then appeases the gods.
Oh, appeases the sun.
My *dewar*.
Oh *bhauji*, if you had arranged the marriage of my son,
Oh, I would have brought the yellow sari.
Oh, I would have brought the yellow sari.
Oh, before she could appease the gods, the son was born.
Oh, the son was born.
My son.
Oh, the joyous childbirth songs were being played,
And *sohar* were sung in the palace.
Oh, and *sohar* were sung in the palace.
Mother is seated on the cot.
She is very wise.
Oh, she is very wise.

My mother.
I will take the yellow sari of *bhauji*.
The jingle bells are attached to the yellow sari.
Oh, the jingle bells are attached to the yellow sari.
Mother-in-law asks politely,
Listen to me my sweet *bahu*.
Oh, listen to me my sweet *bahu*.
Oh *bahu*, give away your yellow sari.
The daughter is our guest.
Oh, the daughter is our guest.
Well, mother-in-law. . . . (obscure).
Oh, I will go to my *naihar*,
Oh, mother-in-law.
I will play with my son myself.
Oh, I will not give away my yellow sari.
Oh, I will not give away my yellow sari.
Father Vijay comes in from outside.
Oh, he shouts with anger.
My sister.
Oh, I will have another marriage.
I will get you a yellow sari to put on.
Oh, I will get you a yellow sari to put on.
Oh, when Sapan daughter heard these words.
Oh, my *bahu* snatches out the yellow sari.
Oh, she throws it in the courtyard.
She throws it in the courtyard.
Oh, my adulterous *nanad*, take this yellow sari.
Leave my courtyard.
Leave my courtyard.
Oh *nanad*, take this yellow sari, you brother fucker.
Leave my courtyard.
Oh, become my rival wife.
Oh, leave my courtyard.
Oh, become my rival wife.

"The *sinduara* full of *sindur* is brought from the *bahu*'s *sasural*," Gangajali said. "And from her *naihar*, *puri*s and a beautiful yellow sari with silver jingle bells attached to it.

"But the sister of the groom, the *nanad*, loves the yellow sari. She plasters the courtyard and thinks, 'Oh Lord, if my *bhauji* gives birth to a son, then I will ask for this yellow sari as a reward.' So she appeases the Lord.

"Then the *bahu* becomes pregnant and gives birth to a son. Then the *nanad* says to her mother, 'Out of happiness over the birth, I will take the yellow sari of *bhauji* on which the jingle bells are attached.'

"The *bahu* replies, 'Oh Lord, I won't give away the yellow sari from my *naihar.* I will take care of my child myself. I will not live here. I'll go to my mother's home. But I will not give away my yellow sari.'

"Then her husband comes from outside. As he arrives, his sister complains that the *bhauji* is not giving her the yellow sari. The *nanad* cries to her brother, and he says, 'Oh sister, why do you cry? I will not keep her at home. I will have another wedding. And that new wife will have a son, and I will get you a yellow sari better than that of *bhauji*.' Then the *bhauji*, the wife, hears that he will have a second marriage. Then she quickly opens her box and throws the yellow sari in the courtyard with anger. And she throws the jingle bells. 'Take it, you adulterous lady' (she swears like this). 'You adulterous woman, take it and get married to your brother and become my rival wife. Or go away from my house quickly. Or take the yellow sari and be my rival wife.' Then the mother says to the *bahu*, 'Oh daughter, you gave away your yellow sari. My daughter is a guest in my house. She is about to go to her *sasural.* You give away the yellow sari?'

"And the *bahu* says, 'No, no, I will not give away my yellow sari. This is from my parents' home. I will go to my parents' home. I will take care of my child myself, but I will not give away my yellow sari.'"

This wonderful song explains the relationship of a man, his wife (*bhauji*), and his sister (*nanad*). Both the wife and the sister want the yellow sari with the jingling bells, which has been sent by the wife's parents from her natal home. In an olden village setting, where the women had but few possessions, a bright yellow sari with jingling bells would be a prize.

However, the sister performs ritual work at the time when the wife gives birth to a son. The sister expects her due for being back home for performing important ritual duties. She wants the jingle bells. But so does the wife, as it has been given to her by her kinfolk. This conflict of a man's wife and his sister is a common theme in traditional life, village or city, and is often the topic of important songs.

### SONG 109

*Khilauna*

Nobody should put a spell on the boy.
Nobody should put a spell on the boy.
Spell on the boy.
Spell on the boy.
Nobody should put,
Spell on the boy.
Nobody should put.
The black curly locks of our son.
The black curly locks of our son.
Nobody should put a spell on the curly locks.
Nobody should put a spell on the curly locks.

Nobody should put a spell on the boy.
The big eyes of our son.
The big eyes of our son.
Nobody should put the spell on the beautiful glance.
Spell on the beautiful glance.
Ah, nobody should put the spell on the *kajal*.
Nobody should put a spell on the boy.
Our son has thin thin lips.
Our son has thin thin lips.
Ah, the spell on the smile,
Nobody should put the spell on his smile.
Spell on the boy.
Spell on the boy.
Nobody should put a spell on the boy.
Nobody should put a spell on the boy.
My son has a broad chest.
My son has a broad chest.
The spell on the shirt,
Ah, the spell on the shirt,
Nobody should put the spell on the *kurta*.
Spell on the boy.
Spell on the boy.
Nobody should put,
My son has tiny tiny hands.
My son has tiny tiny hands.
The spell on the jingle bells toy,
Ah, nobody should put a spell on the toy.
Spell on the boy.
Spell on the boy.
Nobody should put.
Oh, my son has small small feet.
To our son.
To our son.
Little little feet.
The spell on walking,
Nobody should put a spell on the patter of his little feet.
Spell on the boy,
Nobody should put the spell on the boy.

"Some lady has a newborn son, so she says no one should bring a spell on my child. And then she says, 'My child has black hair, black curly hair. Nobody should put a spell on his curly hair. My son has big eyes. Nobody should put a spell on his glance. Oh, nobody should put a spell on his *kajal*. My son has thin lips. Nobody should put a spell on his smile. My son has a high, good chest.

Nobody should put a spell on his shirt (*kurta*). My child has small small hands. Nobody should put a spell on his jingle bells. My son has small small feet. Nobody should put a spell on the patter of his little feet.' This is a song here. This is called *khilauna*, and the singer is trying to bring out all kinds of features of the child's body. And she deeply feels that nobody should bring a spell on any part of his that looks beautiful. Or on his actions, his walking, his twinkling eyes, his jingling bells when he laughs and plays.

"'The *khilauna* I sang last,' Gangajali said. "So then the boy is born in the courtyard. So he is ornamented with the *kajal*, *tika*, and *tilak*. After dressing him up, he is placed in the courtyard. Then his mother says, 'Nobody should give *nazar* to the boy. Nobody should give a magic spell to the boy. I mean my son is playing in the courtyard. His hair lock looks very beautiful. He has beautiful black curly hair. Nobody should give him *nazar*. He has big eyes. How he stares with his glasses. He is beautiful looking. So he should not get the unusual *nazar* from others so he will fall ill. And how his face is beautiful. What thin lips he has. How his dress looks beautiful on his body.'"

If you chance to visit an Indian family who has a newborn child, don't rush in and stare at the babe and declare how beautiful he or she is. As soon as you leave, the family will immediately perform the necessary rituals to lift off the evil eye that you cast on their child. Typically, mothers place a black smudge of *kajal* on the face of the baby, or on the soles of their feet, so that the first glimpse is of something ugly. In this way women protect their children from harm. So don't stare at and compliment the baby! It goes against the grain of Western folk to refrain from this, but resist the temptation and follow the Hindu rules.

"That is the complete *kohabar* ritual, including the auspicious *sohar* and *khilauna*. Then the bridegroom and bride stay there, and girlfriends of the bride may also remain with them in the *kohabar*. Any songs may be sung now—filmi, Hindustani, Pakistani. Talk also begins for the first time between the bride and bridegroom."

SIXTY-NINE

# CEREMONY AT THE GANGES

*Continuing the session at the Hotel Sarang, Ballia, July 1989*

"After that," Gangajali said, "on the same day in the early morning, there will be *puja* of the *kakkan*, the sacred thread and small bundle worn on the wrists of both bride and bridegroom. Here in the Bhojpuri area, we call this sacred item '*kakkan*.' The *kakkan* of both the bride and bridegroom are worshiped, and songs are sung for this. After the *kakkan* ritual, the groom and bride are free. Whenever they want to meet, they can meet. Whatever they want to do, they can do.

"First of all, the women go to the Ganges to perform rituals before untying the *kakkan*. Along the way, we sing three important songs to Mother Ganges.

"There are three *kakkan* songs. This song is sung on the way to the riverbank."

### SONG 110, PART 1

*Kakkan*

The high bank of the Ganges.
Oh, having seen it, she gets frightened.
Oh, Mother Ganga, one of you,
One lady is crying for your protection.
Oh Mother Ganga, a lady is crying and wailing to you.
Oh lady, either your parents' home is far away, or there is trouble for you
in your *sasural*.

Oh lady, what trouble has fallen on you,
So you are crying to me?
Oh lady, is your husband in a foreign country?
What sadness are you crying for?
Oh Gangaji, neither my parents' home is far away,
Nor is there sadness in my *sasural.*
Oh Mother, my husband is also not in a foreign country.
I am crying for my womb.
Mother, I got seven sons.
They were stillborn.
The Lord gives us seven sons.
Then the eighth one.
Oh, there is no hope for the eighth one.
Oh, Mother Ganga.
The eighth in the womb is an incarnation.
So there is no hope for that one.
Oh lady, be quiet.
Oh, be quiet, do not die from crying.
Oh lady, I give you my child.
Oh lady, I give you my child.
Gangaji offers the salty sesame seed, and the seed is salty.
Oh, mother Ganga, what is the borrowing of the womb?
Oh, then you offer me that.

*(continued without pause)*

### SONG 110, PART 2

*Kakkan*

Tell me, how far is the Ganges?
Tell me, how far is the Ganges?
I'll offer the yellow sari to my Gangaji.
I'll offer the yellow sari to my Gangaji.
It is important to fill up the pocket.
Tell me, how far is the Ganges?
Tell me, how far is the Ganges?
I will offer a *puriya* to my Ganges (*puriya* is a leaf pouch with *dub* grass, incense, *sindur*, sweets, flowers, and cloves).
I will offer *sindur* to our Ganges.
It is necessary to offer flowers.
It is necessary to offer a garland.
Tell me, how far is the Ganges?

*(continued without pause)*

*Kakkan*

Oh Mother Ganges, give me your blessing. Oh, grant me.
Oh Mother Ganges, the bride remains *suhagin* for ages and ages.
Take her under your protection.
Bhiruga Baba, give me your blessing. Oh grant me.
Oh Bhirugaji, grant your blessings to me.
Oh, so the bride and groom will remain *suhagin*.

Here, the three songs are sung without any silence between them. This is a common practice in the Bhojpuri region—songs are often sung in groups with "this" following "that" and so on. These three songs are about worship of the holy Ganges River and can be distinguished one from the other by a change in the melody.

"When we arrive," Gangajali said, "we take a special bamboo basket in which we have placed the crown of the bridegroom, the yellow sari, the *sindur* container, the wedding necklace, garlands, flowers, incense sticks, rice, turmeric, turmeric paste, and sweets for the bride. Before we begin to hand the sweets out, first we take out some for the gods. We also have prepared roasted rice flower mixed with sugar and chickpeas. This mixture, which is used for our ritual purposes on the bank of the Ganges, is called *kukadaur*. Another mixture consists of ground barley flour, ground turmeric in oil, and a sweet-smelling spice mixture called *bugwa*. These two mixtures are brought from the bridegroom's side to the bride's home. We take out a little bit of these to serve to the gods.

"We begin to move from the house early in the morning, around five o'clock, for the Ganges. The girl's people take this crown (if the girl goes to her *sasural* after the wedding, then the crown will remain at the house of the bride). Taking this crown, the mother of the bride goes with her female friends, somebody who has enthusiasm to do it. They go with the music and musical instruments. Otherwise one or two women go. And having reached the bank, having sung songs of Gangaji on the way, the yellow sari and the *kukadaur*, *bugwa*, and sweets are offered to Gangaji. *Arti* is performed using the necklace, garlands, flowers, and incense sticks. As another part of the ritual, the women make round balls out of dough and push a coin and betel nut in them, then make marks of *sindur* on them. Two of these are offered to the Ganges. And after offering this, the bridegroom takes a bath in the Ganges. His wedding dress is taken off, and he puts on other clothes. Then worship will be done of other gods like Bhraguji and Baleshwarji. All the people go to their temples. At each place the *kukadaur* is offered, as the gods are asked to bless the couple so the bride will be *suhagin* for ages and ages and so the couple will be fruitful and can live a wealthy life. All these blessings are requested from the gods. They all go to each temple at the place of the devi, at the place of the Lord, and at the place of Gangaji. Then they come back to home. Then the bride and groom are seated at the altar.

"The *kakkan* are untied. For the bride that does not go to the *sasural*, when the bride's *vida* is not done in the wedding, her *kakkan* will be untied in her parents' home. Her mother helps her to untie the *kakkan*. So the ceremony is performed at either the bride's altar or the bridegroom's altar. The same ritual will be carried out in both places, whether the bride remains in her *sasural* with the bridegroom or not.

"If both *kakkan* will be untied in the bride's *sasural*, this ceremony is performed. Both are seated together at the altar. There is the worship of Gauri–Ganesh. The water from the sacred pitcher will be poured down, and the pitcher is filled with fresh water. The lamp is lit. All the garlands and flowers are offered to Gauri–Ganesh. And also the *kukadaur* and *bugwa* are offered then.

"On the day of untying the *kakkan*, a basket full of *puri*s are fried and *khir* (rice pudding) is made out of rice either with sugar or *gur* without milk. We consider *khir* cooked with milk inauspicious. We consider *khir* without milk auspicious. So the *khir* is cooked without milk and with *gur*. The *khir* is cooked in much *gur*, and we place the *khir* in each corner of the wedding tent on a *puri*. And two *puri*s are placed in front of the *kalas*.

"The priest unties the *kakkan* from the hands of the bride and groom after chanting mantras and worshiping Gauri–Ganesh. The untied *kakkan* is placed around the neck of the mother. So the mother will keep it tied around her neck for one-and-a-quarter years. Each mother does this. So both mothers will tie the *kakkan* of their son and daughter around their neck. So the rule is to save it for one-and-one-quarter years. If they cannot keep it for one-and-one-quarter years, they must keep it for one-and-one-quarter months. Anyhow they keep it tied around their neck. And after they take it off, they keep it in a safe place where it cannot be burnt by fire.

"And after one year, it is put in the Ganges. And whatever things that were there in the wedding tent that were used for worship, those all are put in the Ganges after one year.

"Then the wedding is finished. The wife can live with her husband with all comforts. There is no obstruction."

INTERLUDE FOURTEEN

# SHOWING WHAT FRANK GREYSTOCK DID

"FRANK DID NOT WANT TO SEE LADY FAWN," UMESH SAID, "BECAUSE HE did not want to have his feelings ruined by her. She certainly would have attacked, and he knew the character of Lady Fawn. She, Lady Fawn, also knows that Lucy loves Frank. Frank has very important court work to do to face a jury. However, he can only think about Lucy. He goes to his chambers in Temple Court, and he sat down there and begins to classify his life. There are two paths. One is to stay with these upper-class people, keep his seat in Parliament, go to his club, and live in a fashionable neighborhood. Or chose Lucy and go on the second lane, where he will have to live north of Oxford Street, quit his club, quit Parliament, cut down on his expenses, and work hard. He's imagining these types of path for his future—to choose one of these. Marrying Lucy, he has only one path to go on.

"If he does not marry Lucy, he might have a chance to marry another woman and remain in high society, in a fashionable neighborhood, in his club, and in Parliament. He is already living the third option.

"He feels that he is making the main decision of his whole life. People might say that he was doing well, but for love he destroyed his financial future.

"After having so many thoughts in his mind, Lucy does not go out of his mind. And she takes complete control of love. And he begins to write a letter to Lucy. He says that I didn't come to Fawn Court intending to declare his love for Lucy. However, the moment made him claim it since he is already in love with her. He says he hopes Lucy loves him and will have him as his wife since Lucy has not said anything to claim her love for Frank. He also writes his feelings of love for Lucy, and he concludes his letter 'yours ever and always—if you will have me.'"

SEVENTY

# ARRIVAL OF THE BRIDE IN HER *SASURAL*, THE *GAUNA*

*We are chatting in Umesh's home, Karimganj, 2014*

"Before the *vida*, we decide when the girl will come back to her parents' home," Umesh explained. "It is called *chauti*—means fourth. She has to be back on the fourth day—also it can be eight days or fourteen days—but it is called *chauti*. But it does not happen these days. Usually the bride remains with her husband's family for from seven to ten days. If the younger sister is at home, she goes along with the bride, or if she has a younger brother, he stays with her until she comes back so she does not feel lonely. She is not all the time alone with the women. The family also have relatives to take care of. So they are busy with that. She does not do any work at this time. She will not even touch a spoon to do anything.

"She will eat food. If there is someone in the family, that woman will clean her pots, or if no one is there, she will clean her pot only in which she eats. As long as she stays there at this time, no work. When she goes in *gauna*, she doesn't do any work too. Then there is small ritual called touching the pan, 'the pan-touching ceremony.' The bride will touch the *karahi*. It means she cooks that day for everyone, and she serves food to family people, mother-in-law, father-in-law, anyone older in the family, and they give her presents for that. Then she begins to work for the family."

SEVENTY-ONE

# LOVE MARRIAGES

***Our chat at Umesh's home continues, and I ask questions, Karimganj, 2014***

*Do the boy's side ever say thank you?*

"Thank you!?" Umesh was astonished at this question. "I believe that the 'thank you' word is not in the dictionary in the villages of North India. I don't mean to upset the city people. Certainly these words are used in big cities. They can show their appreciation with their face. They can say *bahut accaha*."

*Can you ever really please the boy's side?*

"Hard to say. There is always something wrong. Whatever they are given—suppose they ask for things, and they get everything—they are still upset because they think, *I could have asked for more and got more.* He got everything. If he is not given what he asks, he feels cheated and also swears. He does not speak good."

*So after the wedding, do both sides really feel cheated?*

"No. If the girl's family gets a good groom—although he spends money—never mind, because his daughter will be in a good position. So for the welfare of his daughter or sister, they don't feel cheated because what they have done is great. Certainly, they get upset if they are doing everything and it is not appreciated. The girl's family gets upset. It is my belief that every father, every brother does his best to arrange their daughter's or sister's wedding. With his financial strength, with his physical strength. It is my belief. Satisfaction is the greatest thing. If the boy's side are really good people, then there is no problem. Sometimes we find really good people."

*Suddenly you discover what kind of family they are. Does that happen?*

"It can be shocking, but now nothing is changeable. Sometimes it happens, and people send the *barat* back. They don't care about money. They send the *barat* back. Then they try to find a girl in the same area and arrange another wedding. They come back empty handed, and it destroys their respect. What happened?"

*What do you think about young people meeting each other before marriage?*

"Well, it is a real tough question for me. Because if you ask me what I am going to accept for my daughter, I will never let her meet to a man to talk about marriage herself. Simple thing. I can be considered backward too. If she knows somehow through some link, then I can make an investigation if it is good for her and for the family reputation."

*So you don't believe in love marriages?*

"In other words, if according to current Indian society, if girls get married to whom she loves with the agreement of the parents of both sides and in same caste, it would be great. I would be willing to do it. But I know one thing for sure. If a girl gets married from a high caste to a low caste, she will never get respect in the family where she will reach because in her mind she will always remain Brahman. For the lower caste family, she will always be the *bahu* of the family. And in deep, she will think herself high caste, but the husband's family will assume that she is as simple as they are. And culturally we see that all the castes look the same, but they are not. Culturally they are different. For food, for thinking, for worshiping, and living they are different, although living together in the same village."

*Will the wedding be successful?*

"Only when the priest is under the wedding tent, he gives a speech to the bride and groom both about how to carry out married life. And that is not a good thing because both are so sleepy at this point in the middle of the night. There is a song from Gangajali that when Shivaji and Parvati were under the wedding tent, Shivaji got tired and dozy. And with a toe, Gaura pushed him to wake him up. We have this in song. So Shivaji got annoyed. This is in our songs."

*Is all this done for respect? What I'm asking is, is all this for show?*

"The reason we follow these customs is for respect. The girl's side shows respect for boy's side. The boy's side feels that he is getting respect. And the girl's side is feeling that they are spending too much money to do this all. On the other hand, this show is only for rich people, not simple village people. But people are carrying it now, so if people don't do it, they cannot send their daughter in a better family. And they want to see their children happy. It can be also a show from the girl's side. Because he can invite some of the important people that he knows to show that he is an important person too—by spending money. Show comes by spending money. You have to show something to be known. In any way, in any sense."

*There is no such thing as a quiet, simple wedding?*

"It always depends on the boy's side. The girl's side would be really very happy if such a quiet wedding they could make. It always depends on what kind of family it is. Suppose a rich family is there, they can say to the boy's side this is not your burden. I am spending money. Then they have to accept how they are doing. Both sides must agree. But it is all for show from both sides. At the conclusion, it is from both sides. But the girl's side has to do what the boy's side has asked them to do."

SEVENTY-TWO

# FIVE DAYS

*We are still at the Hotel Sarang, Ballia, July 1989*

"It took us five days to record these wedding songs," Gangajali said. "That is appropriate. We like to perform the wedding in five days. It is called *pach mangara*. The *pach mangara* wedding is considered very good. Five days. But these days we do all things quickly, sometimes in just one day or in three days. But we consider that the five-day *pach mangara* wedding is the best.

"Out of happiness for finishing up these wedding songs, I will drink tea and eat some sweets surely. It is important to sweeten the mouth. People eat their stomach full of sweets, but I will surely sweeten my mouth.

"Well, it has been auspicious work. Until the work was not finished, we were always saying 'tomorrow, tomorrow.' I am getting very sad to be leaving your company. I have deep pain inside. As if we are lovers to whom we love a little, oh the love gives much pain. I get pain inside my heart. There is much pain to leave, much pain now after so many days together.

"Now there are one hundred thousand talents in me," Gangajali said. "If I had not given it to anyone, kept it to myself, in case I die it would also go with me. It would not remain in the world. That is a very happy thing. Whatever was in me it, will remain in the world whether I live or not. All this of mine is very old, and until now is still in practice and will continue in India.

"The people who make money can do anything. But I have not been doing like that from the beginning. What is the value of earning by doing bad deeds?

Well, one day I have to leave this world. But the bad thing will give the reputation. People will say she was like that. But at least one of them will say, 'But she was a good person. Oh, she is dead. How nice she was.' And nobody arrives on this Earth with wealth, and nobody will take it with them when they die. But we must keep our path of life very clear. Whether we make money or do not, we have to leave the world."

SEVENTY-THREE

# JUST ONE MORE SONG

*A new day, day 5, our last day, at the Hotel Sarang, Ballia, July 1989*

"Ram is coming from Ayodhya to get married in Janakpur," Gangajali said. "So people look at him. As they see, they ask where the *barat* is coming from. And where is it going? Who is the bridegroom, and who is the bride? Where are these people coming from?

"Then they reply that the *barat* is coming from Ayodhya. The *barat* is coming from Ayodhya. And the bride is from the palace in Janakpur. Who is the bride? She is the daughter of a king. Then how is Ram coming? He is coming seated in the chariot to get married. And how does the bride come? The palanquin bearers, four on each side, are carrying the palanquin. The red-colored palanquin cover is attached to it, and the bride is seated inside. The bride is coming from the palace in the palanquin. Then how did they get married? Then Ram has *sindur* in his hand, and the bride slowly lifts up her veil. And Ram gives her the *sindur*. And she becomes his bride. So he is taking her."

SONG III

*Wedding Bhajan*

From where comes Ram, who bears the bow?
From where comes Ram, who bears the bow?

## SPOKEN

Should I sing
Good.

From where comes Ram, who bears the bow?
From where comes Ram, who bears the bow?
It is drizzling.
It is drizzling.
Where does the bride come from?
It is drizzling.
Drizzling.
Where do those who bear the bow come from?
It is drizzling.
Ram who bears the bow comes from Aawadh.
Ram who bears the bow comes from Aawadh.
The bride comes from the palace.
It is drizzling.
The bride comes from the palace.
It is drizzling.
Those who bear the bow come from Aawadh.
It is drizzling.
From where comes?
Where do those who bear the bow come from?
It is drizzling.
Drizzling.
Drizzling.
Drizzling.
Where do those who bear the bow come from?
It is drizzling.
Ram who bears the bow comes from Aawadh.
Ram who bears the bow comes from Aawadh.
The bride comes from Janakpur.
It is drizzling.
The bride comes from the palace.
It is drizzling.
Where do those who bear the bow come from?
It is drizzling.
Drizzling.
Drizzling.
Drizzling.
Where do those who keep the bow come from?
It is drizzling.
On what does Ram who bears the bow ride?
On what does Ram who bears the bow ride?

On what does the bride ride?
It is drizzling.
On what does the bride ride?
It is drizzling.
Where do those who bear the bow come from?
It is drizzling.
Drizzling.
Drizzling.
Drizzling.
Where do those who bear the bow come from?
It is drizzling.
Ram who bears the bow rides on the chariot.
Ram who bears the bow rides on the chariot.
Ram who bears the bow rides on the chariot.
Ram who bears the bow rides on the chariot.
The bride rides in the palanquin.
It is drizzling.
The bride rides in the palanquin.
It is drizzling.
Where do those who bear the bow come from?
It is drizzling.
Drizzling.
Drizzling.
Drizzling.
Where do those who bear the bow come from?
It is drizzling.
Where does he come from who lifts up the *sindur*?
Ram who bears the bow lifts up the *sindur*.
Ram who bears the bow lifts up the *sindur*.
Ram who bears the bow lifts up the *sindur*.
Ram who bears the bow lifts up the *sindur*.
Ram who bears the bow lifts up the *sindur*.
Lifts up the veil,
The bride slowly lifts up the veil.
It is drizzling.
The bride lifts up the veil.
It is drizzling.
Where do those who bear the bow come from?
It is drizzling.

Gangajali said, "It means the gods sprinkle the drizzling with the happiness in this wedding as if they are sprinkling flowers. We call it drizzling. When they got married, in the happiness of the wedding, all the gods sprinkle flowers on them. So, small small droplets. This is a wedding *bhajan*, a *bhajan* in God's name."

Through this book, Gangajali has sung songs based on the life of Ram. From childhood, Indians learn his story, of the prince and hero, who is believed to be the seventh incarnation (avatar) of Lord Vishnu, the "preserver." Everywhere there are reminders of the presence of Ram as a central theme of cultural life—statues and pictures in temples and at family altars, comic books illustrating his life, and Hindi films dramatizing the legendary events of his career. The story of Ram is as old as the Homeric epics of the Western world, and, like Homer's *Iliad*, is the tale of a ravished bride and her rescue. There are two well-known written versions of the Ramayana. As far as is known, the earliest was written in Sanskrit some two thousand years ago by the sage Valmiki, a foundational figure in Indian literary history. This ancient epic has some 24,000 verses and is one of the longest of the ancient epics of the world. It is the later version, the Ramcharitmanas ("Wonderful Lake of the Life of Ram") of Goswami Tulsidas (1552–1623), written in the northern Indian Awadhi vernacular (spoken immediately west of Bhojpur) that is known and loved by Hindus throughout North India.

Ram Naumi, the commemoration of Ram's birth, is observed on the ninth day of the second half of the month Cet (around March). During the ten-day Ramlila festival (in the month of Kuar, around September–October) Brahman children reenact each event of his life—his birth; his breaking the great bow of Shiva as a demonstration of his superhuman strength; his betrothal and marriage to Sita; the jealousy of his stepmother Kaikeyi; exile in the forest; the loyalty of his three brothers; the abduction of Sita by the demon Rawan and their flight to Lanka; the loyalty of Hanuman, king of the monkey army; the rescue of Sita; the slaying of the great ten-mouthed Rawan; Ram's rejection of the faithful Sita and her trial by fire; Ram's triumphal return to the kingdom of Ayodhya; his noble and righteous ruling of his subjects; Sita's final return to the lap of Mother Earth; and Ram's ascension to the kingdom of the Gods.

Umesh explained, "We have Ramayan readings several times a year—house to house. Sometimes a person will decide—if they succeed in whatever they are doing, for example, in business or curing illness—they will do *akhand* ("unbreakable") Ramayan. First the singer sings the *doha* (two-line couplet) exactly as it is from the Ramayan, and then he explains it in simple spoken Hindi. He picks several good *chaupai* (four-line verses) related to the incident out of the same chapter of the Ramayan to sing. Several singers take turns to complete reading of the Ramayan from beginning to end.

"It is a ritual. Villagers make a stage, beautify it with saris, and the Ramayan book is there and also one diya (clay lamp). People come to listen. It begins in the morning around eight or ten o'clock and continues unbreakable nonstop singing for twenty-four hours. As another person comes to sing, he picks up before the first singer ends. Always there are seven or eight singers—people keep coming and going. After each *doha*, to give a rest to the leading singer, all the other singers chant a *chaupai*.

"When I was dying from that heart attack, I vowed that I would hold an *akhand* Ramayan at my home. And I have done that.

"And people kept watching this Ramayan on television. Throughout India, they never wanted to miss it. But people had not many televisions that day in the village. It kept going for a serial for one year in the late 1980s. So the serial was really very helpful to let people learn small details and the concepts as well. Farmers left their plows, shepherds left their cows, office people left their offices, women left their kitchens, whoever was there, everyone wanted to watch TV for one hour on Sunday. People stopped walking on the streets and gathered in front of any shop where there was a TV! You remember when you were ill with typhoid in Banaras your doctor said it was too dangerous to broadcast once in a week for India because Pakistan might attack! And he said his house had been robbed during this hour and he couldn't get the police to come! In Mainpuri, near my village, there was a shortage of power and the power-cut time was the same as the Ramayan broadcast. For the first two weeks people tolerated that. On the third week, people assembled and marched toward the power house. Ever since then there was no power cut for the Ramayan period.

"This is what Tulsidas did at the time of Akbar. He combined several versions and composed the Ramcharitmanas, and this brought East, West, North, South together. This was very helpful for India at that time. And today again, to keep united through one story—Ramayan—taking out and joining things together once again through the TV serial, as in a beautiful mala of so many perfect pearls, East, West, North, South will be together again on the basis of religion. India will never break. Now it is 2019, but the Ramayan is an evergreen epic."

SEVENTY-FOUR

# GANGAJALI'S STORY

*Continuing our last session at Hotel Sarang, Ballia, July 1989*

The electricity went out as Gangajali was finishing this song. We took the chance to have tea and talk—sitting there in the dark—about Gangajali's life.

"My birthplace is here, Ballia," she said. "My parents passed away. I have a brother. He works in a bank as a peon in Gorakhpur. In his family I have two or four nephews—two, four, or five. And I have a *bhabi.*

"My *naihar* is at Mahaviir Ghat. It is very close to here. My father's name was Munna Ram. By caste he was a *kahar*, a water-pulling person. My mother's name was Vidhya Devi. My brother's name is Baijanaath Singh. I don't have any sisters. One was born, but she is no more. After doing her wedding, the *gauna* had to be done. At that time she passed away. I don't know what happened to her because I was in my *sasural.* Surely she was sick. She was my younger sister.

"When I was little, I was in school. When I became older—not. In olden times, people did not think to educate their girls. They used to say, 'Come on, the girl has enough education to write a letter. We don't want to get my daughter a job.'

"I was born after the death of so many children of my parents. That is why they loved me the most. People used to say, 'Oh, she got feverish. My daughter will not go to study. She is getting sunstroke.' They loved me and protected me very much. So I was stopped after a little education. I can write a letter a little bit. I can read *bhajans*, the Bhagwat Gita, and the Ramayan. I understand too. I had the same education—Hindi like '*a*,' '*b*,' '*c*,' and '1,' '2,' '3.' I did not study math. So I can add and subtract. But I did not pay attention to all these lessons.

"My parents taught me at home too. They taught the 'matras' (alphabet) so I could learn how to write a letter.

"From deep inside, I am fond of *bhajan*s. In my heart, there was delight when I heard them. I used to dance and sing. I used to sing *bhajan*s with passion. And whenever there used to be songs for the Lord, even though I was very little, I remained seated until it was performed. I listened. I loved it very much—the songs for worship and the Lord's *bhajan*s. I liked these. And I used to learn. In childhood being seated, I used to hear the *dholak* drum being played. And while seeing, I learned a little bit how to play. So I began to play the *dholak*.

"As I listened, I used to memorize. I used to go to see movies. So as many songs as there were—ten or twelve—I came to know them. Those tunes would hit my heart. Those tunes were also made inside me—that is, I remembered the tune—the tempo, high pitches, low pitches, subtraction, addition. But now I am a little bit older. So I cannot sing in the same way. Back then I could imitate just like it was sung in the movie. People used to make fun of me that I was Lata Mangeshkar. People used to tease a lot about my throat and voice. 'Be seated, be seated, Lata Mangeshkar, be seated, be seated.'

"My mother was not a singer. She couldn't even hum. And my father sang the Ramayan in the temple or where men assembled. He sang the Ramayan like this, playing *jhal* cymbals. My father used to sing when there was a man's program.

"I used to sing among women when I was a child. Children sing, dance, and play with each other. Not those older people. If I couldn't find anything to play, I searched for a tin container, and I would play with that, and we people would sing.

"I don't sing because I feel it is important. I love it. My mind and heart love to do it. It is like an addiction. And what I see and hear, I also sing that. And at the time when my mind sinks in deep sadness, then I begin to sing a sad song. And for happiness, a happy song, especially while I am working.

"For me the songs construct themselves. When one song is composed, the troubles of my mind lift up. I keep singing that one, and one song is composed.

"My talent for singing came by itself. Oh, we all sing in childhood, and see and hear, so in this way we learn how the song is sung. But practicing, it grew in me—and also a fondness and passion for singing. It grew in me itself. And I don't take money for my singing. Look, I am in trouble. The first *bhajan* I sang today, this was composed by me. When I get very sad from my sorrows, and in one day I was crying, tears were flowing out of my eyes. And I was working. I was helpless. Then to whom could I complain? There is no one of mine to take care of me. But I have much attachment to Him. So I complain to Him. It comes from inside me. I become sad. Then I complain to the Lord. Oh, will you not take over my pain or sadness or, come on, at least grant me patience? The pain is growing in my heart. My tears are flowing. I am crying aloud. I compose about these feelings.

"I consider singing a necessity because after singing, my body feels lightened up. I cannot tell anyone my sorrow or happiness. And I also do not consider if it is good, this complaining of mine by singing.

"Oh brother, I sing in a loud pitch. Listeners enjoy it. I sing of my pain, of loneliness. I sing for me. I sing for God. And I sing while working. At the place in the song of sadness, I begin to cry, and at the place of happiness I begin to laugh. There are songs that give happiness to the mind. Some songs are also there which give pain. As I sang in the first *bhajan*, 'Come Mohan, my eyes are calling you.' Flowing tears by crying—so it is a song of pain. I had much pain in my heart. So I sang this. As the feeling was passing over me, I sang the *bhajan*. By singing that, my pain was removed. The pain got out through the tears of my eyes—the pain flowed out.

"At the time of extreme pain and death, *nirgun* is sung. The sad songs are sung. The songs of pain. *Vilap* (wailing) is also a kind of song. The pain is in there. In the Ramayan, Bharat did *vilap* when he met Lord Ram because he delayed arriving. So Bharat was crying *vilap*. He was crying so much that his life was going. He was ready to give up his body. By then Hanuman had arrived with the message of Ram. Otherwise he was going to leave his life during *vilap*. And when Rawan was stealing Sita, that was also *vilap*. It was the *vilap* of Sita, that now I am separating from Ram. Whether my Ram will meet me or not. This *raxas* is taking me away.

"*Rona*, *vilap*, they are the same, the crying, the pain—this is all one. People do *vilap* in pain and sadness to whom he or she wants to meet and couldn't meet. For crying, people can cry anywhere. People also cry in happiness. And people also cry in sadness. *Vilap* takes place when there is waiting for someone, and he is not appearing—as was the case for Bharat. You did not come and could not meet him, therefore my heart is weeping. We call it *vilap*—when there is no hope left. *Rona* is just like when I do the *vida* of my daughter. When she is going to her *sasural*, she is separating from her mother. So I will be doing *rona*. Will there be laughing when you send your daughter away? So that is not *vilap*. In your country, you don't know the meaning of *rona* and *vilap*? Then how will you know what thing this is?

"Men do not cry openly as women do. But inside, their heart cries. They cannot have their tears flow. Their tears dry out inside. They also cry in their heart. But their tears do not drip out. There is more pain in that. We cry with the sound. And tears flow out. So a person gets lighter. The sadness flows away. But the pain of the man does not flow away. He suffers a lot inside.

"I also cry in happiness. Due to happiness, the eyes get full of tears. For example, suddenly my beloved, to whom I cannot meet ever—suddenly he meets me. Then my heart begins to feel like how I would embrace him to my chest. And with this same, happiness tears spill out of the eyes.

"What was the most happy day of my childhood? I can't say which was my happiest day. When I was little, there was only happiness. I used to get very much love from my parents and everyone, and relatives loved me very much because six or seven children before me had passed away. Wherever I used to go, people loved me. As long as I was in my parents' home and I was not married, I was loved. Until then I was happy, only happy. I never felt sad.

"Once I got married, I became sad. I had trouble living in my *sasural*. I did not get any happiness. I always ran into trouble. Trouble, trouble. Everybody does not get happiness in their *sasural*. This is the game of our own fate. I fell in trouble after getting married, and due to the sadness, I also did not tell it to anyone. My *sas* was tough. Then I began to go to temple to worship. I began to go to *sat-sangh*. I began to sing *bhajan* there. My mind became lightened from the sadness.

"My wedding took place with the usual customs. It was olden times. Today there is such inflation. In those days the value of milk was six *ser* for one rupee. These days it is one kilo. In those days the *ser* was used to measure weight. Rice cost was one rupee for five *ser*. One *ser* of oil was for five or six rupees, and ghee cost nine rupees per kilo, and cloth was bought with the help of a ration card. When I got married it was hard to find clothes in the market. The ration card was used to buy clothes. All the clothes were brought from there for me—my saris, blouses, and petticoats, *chadar*s—all the clothes of cotton. Gandhiji was living in those days."

"Was Gandhi alive at the time of your wedding?" Umesh asked.

"I was ten years old at that time. I am now almost fifty."

"Were you married in your own caste?"

"Yes."

"What kind of people are you?"

"We are *kharawar*. *Kharawar* is a caste as *kurmi*, *rawani*, *kharawar*, *rajpat*. In this manner. There are seven *kumris*. So I am *kaharwa*. We will get married only to another *kaharwa*. If somebody is *rawani*, the wedding will take place to another *rawani*. If somebody is *kurmi*, the wedding will take place to another *kurmi*. People do not marry into another *kul* (tribe, group).

"In olden days, the main work for *kaharwa* people was to carry the palanquin. And nowadays the caste system is breaking down. All people, small or bigger, become rich (and they may even keep servants). And rich people became poor. So they do service, jobs, work for others. These days, people who are rich are called *bhai sahib*. They keep servants, and the poor do their jobs such as pulling water and cleaning pots."

"The water-pulling job was the main job," Umesh said. "And these people used to be very close to the higher castes."

Gangajali said, "It was also in the period of Ram as I sang in the *baithaki*. 'Dasarath had the pond dug and had the ghat made. And the *kahar* pulls water for Queen Kausilla.' Then Ram is given a bath. So this is my caste. That in the olden period we people also worked in the house of them. And we gave a supply of water to them. Then they drank it. This is my *jati*."

"Do you remember your wedding day?" Umesh asked.

"Yes," she said. "I was just a little child, and children don't know anything. It was like we were watching a drama that was going on. I was about eight years old. We were little fools, and the fools of the old time did not understand anything.

Nowadays, little children know what marriage is. We knew only what was going on. We were seated, and we saw. I went to sleep at the time of *kanyadan*. My father was seated having me in his lap. And the groom was also a very little one. In this period children were married very young.

"I was not sad at all at my wedding. What did I know about sadness and happiness? Yes, I felt sad when I was seated in the palanquin taking me out of the house. I did not know that I had to go to live in the house of others. I saw that people were taking me into the palanquin, and my mother, *nani*, *mausi*, everybody was crying loudly, and my father was also crying. Having seen all this, I began to think—where was I was going? Where were the people sending me? All of the sudden, I was startled and began to cry very hard. And after my departure, my *nani*, my mother's mother, she became almost crazy. She began to ask, 'Where is my granddaughter? Has she gone to the market? Go and have a look. Where has she gone?'

"I was loved so much that they went mad after sending me away so young. And as many days as I was there, I used to cry loudly. I did not eat or drink anything. I was only crying for my mother. 'I'll go to my mother. I'll go to my *nani*. I'll go to my father. Send me. Take me there.' Saying such words day and night, I cried and cried. Then, after the third day, my father went along with the *chauthari* (food, sweets, etc.), and said, 'I don't want anything. Just send my daughter home.'

"In my *sasural*, I was not treated the way I should be. I was little. I was dressed up in a sari. I tied up my *anchal* so I could play. And village girls came in a flock. We went on the cots, jumping from this one to another. As many days as I was there, they called me *kanya*—daughter. Older people cooked dal and rice. I used to play in the same courtyard. People said, 'Be seated like this.' I uncovered my arms and pulled the veil over my face.

"My *gauna* was five years later when I was almost mature. My first child was born five or six years after my *gauna*. By then I was mature. So after this daughter, who is now a widow, this oldest daughter came to my womb. Oh, hardly when I was fifteen or sixteen years old, this girl was born to me. Thereafter I got three who only survived for less than a year each. And thereafter my younger girl was born. I have daughters, not sons.

"I lived with my husband for twenty years. He didn't like me to go out singing. He did refuse. And then he fell very ill. My father-in-law and mother-in-law separated from us because my husband was not earning. We had to live on our own. They said that, 'Since your husband is not earning, how will you eat? You do your own work.' So I got out of the home. As before, I was living inside in purdah. I got out of the purdah, and I began to work.

"So he fell very ill. He was an operator in the movie hall. At that time, he used to feel bad that I was going out to sing with other women. He used to feel bad because singing women have a bad reputation and they also develop bad habits like drinking and smoking, and they did—what? What they did and what they didn't do. He would not trust me. So when he fell ill and we stopped buying medicine for him, then I began to do singing to run the family. It was not enough to live on. So I talked to a singer lady and asked her to take me with her. I worked in the day and at night—on wedding nights at midnight, one a.m.—I used to sing. So many people want singers at wedding time. I used to be in much trouble because of all this. Work during the day and singing at night, and my voice was very good. I was young, and my voice was sweet. I knew how to sing well. I also knew how to dance nicely because I was young. People liked it. So only I was told to do the singing and dancing. 'You sing your own songs and you dance.' People didn't ask other ladies to do this. That was the biggest problem for me, but I had to do it for the money. Although I didn't want to, I had to do this. And I got tired. Then I explained to my husband, I don't have to do any undignified work. Whatever these singers like to eat—bad things—or they do an undignified job, but my eyes were only on my earnings for his medicine and for the children for expenses. 'Do not be suspicious of me. I am only doing such work for you.'

"When he was sick and he was in bed, then he was helpless. Not all the singing women were bad. There were many who had religious thoughts. They eat pure food. They don't smoke. They don't drink. They don't use ganja, betel, tobacco, and so forth. And the other women singers, some are like this. They drink, they smoke marijuana, chew pan, eat meat, fish, everything, and some people are like this. They leave their path, and they take another path. Everybody knows it. That is why good people hate singing. If the good people go along, they will also turn like them. Though people don't do anything, but because of living with other people, they begin to learn it. So many people remain good living with bad people, and they save themselves although they are living among bad people.

"While he was healthy, he did not let me work outside. Because he fell ill—it was due to the helplessness. Ever since, I began to do my job. For two or four years, he was ill all the time. He was taken by a bad illness. He began to have a fever and a bad cough, and so many times he had medicine. After all, he was a machine operator. He did not pay attention to me and kept drinking a lot of liquor. Yes, he used to drink, and his liver got damaged.

"After my husband died, I educated both girls. When he died, my oldest daughter was studying in seventh grade. She passed high school. I made her do high school with the help of my job. And the youngest one was in my lap. Later she too was sent to high school.

"I arranged the marriage of both my daughters. Her wedding was done, and she got a son. I became a *nani*. It felt good. For the *chatti* of the child, I gave money and presents happily. As much it pleased me. It was according to my wish. Either by borrowing money or with cash, by working, I just gave with an open heart. I have him play day and night. He is a small child. He loves me the most. If I don't see him for two days, he will fall ill.

"When I became a *nani*, sure, I certainly sang. The child was born in her *sasural*, so those people invited me. They said, '*Nani*, you sing.' I said, 'Surely I will sing. A grandson has come to me. Surely I will sing.' And with *dholak* I sang a lot. I sang five nice *sohar* and *khilauna* in the *chatti* (celebration six days after the birth of a son).

"Now I have come to know as long as I live, problems will remain with me. Because the granddaughter of the oldest daughter, she is older now. I am worried day and night for her marriage. How to arrange her marriage."

"Which are your favorite songs?" we asked.

"I like the songs for God more than any other songs. Otherwise I sing any song for money. But my favorite songs are *bhajan*s. I like all other kinds of songs, *jhumar*, *baithaki*, *sahana*. I have given you all those names to write down. Four we have not done—*kajari*, devi songs, *nirgun*, and *biraha*. Village women sing *biraha*, and I can sing them. When I have the work of singing, then I have to sing a little bit of everything. For village *biraha* singing, they make two groups, and they compete with each other, singing from each side. They do not play any instruments with these."

"For *biraha*, do the women play the *dantal*, a long iron rod beaten with a second piece of iron?" I asked.

She said, "I don't know the name of it, but until now there is an instrument played with a piece of iron. When there are men's songs, then there is an iron bar and also something that gives a sound like tin-tin-tin-tin-tin-tin. It is quite long, and they rest it on the floor. It is played with something like a stick, quite a long stick. There is also one *kartal*. A round thing is stuck to it (sistrum rattle). And they play the *dholak*. Also there is a *jhal* made out of brass or white metal. The *jhal* is played. There is also the *dapla* or *nagara*, which is played with two sticks. It is also called *dapli*. The *nagara* is round round. It is covered with skin, the same kind of skin used for the *dholki*. I play the *dholak* and a pair of *jhal* also. Whoever sings a song in the same tune, I can play that *tal* on either the *dholak* or *jhal*. I don't play the *thali*.

"In the village, we often sing in two groups. But we people in the city sing together. And in the village the song may take the form of a question and answer. One group will pose the question, and the other group will give the answer. We also have a kind of leader–chorus form. But sometimes, when I am singing alone, I have to sing continuously. The question-and-answer form is sometimes used when we perform dramas. When I sing at weddings, the women who live with me join in with great enthusiasm.

"If a son is born in someone's house, those people may arrange to have *sohar* sung. From the day he is born until the *chatti* is performed, we people sing songs. There are three kinds of songs sung at this time—*sohar*, *khilauna*, and *jhumar*. Those families who have money have the songs sung for their son. So only the person who wants songs will have singing in his house. I'm not sure how many *chatti* I sing every year—not so many. In the month of Bhadon (around August), after Sawan, there is the celebration of the birth of Krishna. It is believed that he was born on the eighth day of this month. For eight days the *sohar* and *khilauna* of 'Janam Ashhtimi' are sung for his birth. I sing in the homes of other people who have a *dholak* and who have made a little altar for the baby Krishna. I am called to sing, and I am paid for it. We have to sing for six days and are paid whatever they decide to give us, as we cannot negotiate for songs sung in honor of the Lord. Whatever they will give happily, we will take, for isn't this for the Lord? He is also something to me too, and I also have to do something for Him. He is also my Lord. The women in the family sit down and hear the songs. They listen, and they look, and if the song pleases their mind and heart, women of the house fill up a winnowing basket with grain or rice or flour. They give when we people get up to dance. They give us rupees, circling the money around the head of a child or new *bahu*. This custom is called *nichhawr*. It takes away any bad omen from the child or the bride. It is a kind of blessing. Some women give five rupees, some give eleven—whatever pleases their mind, they give us. And they watch and listen in happiness.

"At the time of *lagan*, I sing at twenty or twenty-five weddings a year. When people called me to sing at wedding time—from the beginning to the end until the wedding is not completed and the *kakkan* is not untied—then I have to sing in their home. For that, whatever money I ask for, he will agree to pay me or not. Who agrees, I'll go there. If he will not agree, I will not go. And for the entire wedding, from the *tilak* and *lagan* until the *kakkan* is untied, I have to sing in his house whether it takes ten days or less. We ask for money according to that—how many days they need us for. If we have to sing for that many days, he has to pay that much. When there are very many weddings, then singers get very busy. So one singer in a day may visit five, six, or seven houses. In every house, when we have many houses to sing in, we won't be able to sing many songs. We will sing the main songs of the *lagun* like *baithaki*, *sahana*, songs for the Lord, and songs for man, plus three or four *jhumar* in every house. We will do all the work in his house, and we will finish the auspicious work of *lagan*. The auspicious hour must not be missed. We will sing songs in every house. We will give that much time that the job will be completed in that many houses. If there are not many weddings, then we will happily sing in one house.

"Songs were sung at my wedding. These songs were also sung in those days. As all the women were singing with the *dholak*, sometimes I also used to beat the drum. In those days all these songs were sung. The same *jhumar* were sung—and all these wedding songs. These are very old songs. Nowadays, artificial songs are making a change.

"Those who follow the old tradition sing the old songs. And nowadays, people of modern times can sing any song in any way. As with the filmi tunes, never mind whether the person can sing. For those people who arrange weddings according to the Vedas and Shastras, these old traditional songs are necessary. And those people who do not believe in it, they may arrange a wedding in a club, hotel, in the court, in the temple. What is the importance of the song then? There is no importance of anything there. Nowadays, the new tradition of *jaymala* is becoming popular. Friends are fed at a party, and the wedding is done.

"But people will always remember the old wedding songs. This is a custom, so it will not stop. Those people who will follow the religion and Shastras, for them this will continue. It will never stop."

"Are younger people learning these songs?" Umesh asked.

"No. They sing any songs on filmi tunes. They take a small piece out of any song and compose it to a filmi tune. I don't like them. There is no originality in them, but those songs are good for those people.

"I have sung so many songs and *bhajans* in my life," Gangajali said. "But I never had explained the meaning of it to anyone because nobody wanted it. And I saw that you wanted this, so by churning myself, I gave you the meaning. I feel trouble by explaining the song instead of singing it. But I am also happy that you love it. That you know its importance and are gaining knowledge of it. So I give you the meaning of every word. I never had told this to anyone until today. I just sang.

"I will miss you when you leave. You are like my daughter. Whenever you come to Ballia, meet me surely if I live. My heart doesn't want to leave you. I feel troubled inside leaving you. I'm getting hurt leaving you."

"Then let's meet tomorrow and sing some *kajali*," I said. "And also we didn't hear any *nirgun* or any *biraha*. We have lots of work still to do, don't you think?"

These words solaced Gangajali, who lived for the love of music.

## INTERLUDE FIFTEEN

# "DOAN'T THOU MARRY FOR MUNNY"

BY NOW, UMESH WAS COMPLETELY ENGROSSED IN LIZZIE'S STORY. "LADY Fawn returns to Fawn Court to discover that Lucy and Frank were in the shrubberies, and she gets upset," he said. "Lizzie suggests that Lucy made some sort of a trick to get alone with Frank. And Lady Fawn can't believe it. Lady Fawn goes to Lucy and asks her what happened. Lucy tells everything, that he was here, that they walked in the shrubberies, that they had nice talk. And he told her that he loved her, but she did not reply. Frank did not say that he would marry Lucy. Lady Fawn says this is not the way to know if he wants to marry her because he didn't propose. Lady Fawn said it is not a dignified way to accept love and live as a mistress. So in a way she is correct. On the other hand, she doesn't let Lucy get away from her and her children. This kind of feeling she wants to fit into Lucy's heart and mind. But Lucy is very happy, even though he did not propose, but she claims that she loves him. And love is God. When Lady Fawn arrived, Lizzie tried to poison her by telling that she called her cousin Frank because she is very close and does not have anyone else. He is her cousin—what else? And then Lizzie tells about Lucy—what went along with Frank. Somehow she is playing a conspiracy, and Lady Fawn says, 'No, it can't be.' She doesn't believe what Lizzie says of Lucy.

"Lord Fawn arrived late. Lizzie is playing very clever, facing her cheek toward him a little, so nobody will recognize that she is asking him to kiss her. If he doesn't, she will not be embarrassed, but as she shows the side of her cheek, Lord Fawn kisses it. So Lizzie managed for herself that they met as lovers.

"Lord Fawn asked to talk to her in the morning ten minutes before church. And they do talk. He says straight to her to give away the necklace, and how could she wear the necklace of another husband, being his wife? Lizzie says, 'I never meant to wear it.' They go back and forth over this topic, and finally Lizzie declares that she will not go to church. She goes up to her room. And Lord Fawn goes, leaving her a note demanding that she restore the necklace but claiming that he is not quitting their engagement."

SEVENTY-FIVE

# ONE LAST SONG

*Our last session at the Hotel Sarang, Ballia, July 1989*

"First I will sing the *kajali* of the devi," Gangajali said.

*Kajali*

*(not included on the recording)*

Oh *devi*, when will you appear to me?
The month of Sawan has already begun.
Kali, when will you appear to me?
The month of Sawan has already begun.
The *tika* looks beautiful on the forehead of Kali.
The *tika* looks beautiful on the forehead of *devi*.

"In the month of Sawan, there are days for the devi. In the month of Sawan, we go everywhere for *devi darshan*. It means these are the days for *devi* and Lord Shiva, and when we go for *darshan* (holy vision), we sing this. That 'Mother, the month of Sawan has already begun. When will I get your *darshan*?' It means, 'Mother, when will you give *darshan* now that the month of Sawan has begun?' And whatever clothes and ornaments she has covering her body, we praise them all. That the *tika* looks beautiful on the forehead of Mother. The ornaments are beautiful. How beautiful Mother is. Mother gives *darshan* in the month of Sawan. We go everyplace, here and there, from country to country, for example, to Mahiar, to Vaishhnuu Devi, as people are going these days. We go to Baijuudhaam for the *darshan* of Bhola (Shiva) in the month of Sawan. We are singing there. This is the first *kajari* for *deviji*. In the beginning, we people sing songs for *deviji* or for God. After this we sing any song.

"You did come on the last day of last month, and the next day was the very day that Sawan began. It was the Purnima day (full moon)—aah, it was not Purnima. It was the first day of the new moon. Sawan began on the next day, and I said to you, 'Sawan has begun today, and you should put on green bangles and a green sari.' So this *kajali* song will be sung for the entire month of Sawan. We sing anywhere. Anywhere where there is singing. If two or three women are singing in someone's house, we go to join them and form a group. And when somebody swings, they also sing *kajali*. Or if we go to worship *devi*, we sing *kajali* on the entire way. We sing this song in this month. And in the other eleven months, we do not sing *kajali*. Another example is *chaiti*, which are sung only in the month of Chait. The songs of Phagun will be sung during the month of Phagun. Not in any other month."

## INTERLUDE SIXTEEN

# I'LL GIVE YOU A HUNDRED-GUINEA BROACH

UMESH EXPLAINED, "THE PROBLEM IS THAT LADY FAWN KEEPS TROUBLING Lucy, while Frank's letter, posted on Saturday, remains in the red letter box until Monday morning.

"I love this story," he said. "I need to go through it two or three times so I will get the real essence of this story. This story is quite like an Indian story. Although the traditions are shown in a British olden country, we had arranged marriages. And it was almost an arranged marriage in the British country. The girl could choose her husband, and the boy could choose the girl. Nevertheless, the parents had the power to not let their children get in the wrong hands. And then they couldn't do the wedding without Fate. Parents arrange the marriages of their sons and daughters. They work hard to search for good families so their daughter and son both get good respect in the society as well as in the two families.

"In India, the custom was by spending money, also having a reputated family. They got married according to their status in India. It is still carried out. Now the demands have increased and are different. The demand is different from each side. No father wants to arrange his literate, well-qualified daughter's wedding with a simple man. They try to see the equal match so there won't be suffering in their life. The same comes from the boy's side. If the girl is tall, the family does not want to arrange a wedding if the boy is shorter. The pair looks unusual. If the girl is fair, people want to give their daughters to a fair groom. And the social status should be similar, even within a caste.

"So, at breakfast on Monday, Lucy gets the letter. She opens it and reads the first sentence and the last sentence and puts it away. 'Yours ever and always, if you will have me, F. G.' These words give her great hope, and she blushes until her face is crimson to the roots of her hair. Lady Fawn notices and sends her out to read her letter. Soon everybody in Fawn Court knows the happy news.

"Meanwhile, Lizzie sent down a note to Lucy inviting her to visit her in her room. Lizzie asks Lucy if she can give this family's news to her on a daily basis in a short letter. If Lucy does this, she will be given one hundred guineas! Having heard this, Lucy gets furious, and she absolutely refuses to be a spy on the family she loves. Some who are weak in their heart and character could accept that kind of offer. But no dignified person could do it.

"Likewise, everywhere in the villages of India, people always keep an eye on what other people are doing. I don't see this in the big cities. But in the villages, it is always like that: What is he eating? How much is he earning? How are they spending? What kind of social life are they creating for themselves? Eyes are everywhere. Spies are everywhere. Until they don't learn the weaknesses of other people, they cannot hurt each other. Lizzie wanted to leave by making a big show in the family, but the arrival of Lucy's letter from Frank destroys all her plans of destruction.

"Helen, all people have some weaknesses, I believe. We are not God. But the actions of some people hurt other people so much—so much that it is hard for their targets to live. And this author points out carefully through Lizzie (and others) their flaws. Our author, Trollope, puts it nicely by just throwing flakes of humor. Altogether, it creates the comedy of life. And although these appear to be simple love stores, they are sharper than a poisoned arrow."

SEVENTY-SIX

# PREPARING FOR CHINA

*Final days at our Banaras apartment, 2007*

As the nine months in our Banaras apartment drew to a close, we still kept up with our work—at a fast pace. With over three thousand pages transcribed and translated, we could see the goal in sight.

Our daily routine remained the same. Tea and toast in the morning. The power cut still left us without electricity from ten o'clock to two o'clock. But that didn't really matter. The weather was chilly, we had heavy clothes on and wrapped up in our quilts, even while we were working during the day.

We continued reading our Trollope. So the colonial white other stormed into Umesh's life each and every day. But he loved the story and loved Lizzie. It even seemed that he loved the British. But I could see it was a love mixed with the power of resentment. Mostly, he thought that Lizzie wanted ornaments and that that was not a bad thing. But only God could save her from herself, he said.

Our translations improved as the weeks passed. By the end of each day, the dictionaries were spread out all over my bed. We had Hindi–English dictionaries, English–Hindi dictionaries, English–English dictionaries, Hindi–Hindi dictionaries, a selection of old dictionaries, many brand-new dictionaries. The Bhojpuri–Hindi dictionary was the one that Umesh liked the most. We shared a love of dictionaries, and we looked up many many words. From time to time, but not every day, there was a word or a phrase that just eluded our efforts, even with our battery of dictionaries. So, after exploring every possibility, we marked these—reluctantly—as "obscure."

We worked together with ease. After nearly thirty years, that was not to be wondered at. While we were working, we each had fond thoughts of Gangajali. I was so hoping that these songs could be published, that the tapes could be preserved and archived—first in Delhi and later at the Indiana Archive. In 1989, those were the days of analog recording. So it came as a delight when Indiana digitized these special reels for me many years later. And plans for this book began to materialize.

In November, we celebrated Diwali, the Indian festival of lights. We bought *diya*s, tiny primitive earthenware cups, into which Umesh placed the handmade wick. At sunset, he set the *diya*s along our wall and around the door. And we lit them. Then we wandered down the streets of our neighborhood, enjoying the lights everywhere. Everybody else was out too, enjoying the light displays. The *diya*s were the most beautiful, but many families had set out long strings of colorful Christmas lights to great effect. Everywhere we went, the whole scene glowed.

Umesh arranged a special Diwali *puja* for us. He had us both take baths and put on absolutely clean clothes. Then he arranged an altar with special things on it. There were *diya*s, of course. And a dictionary. But I especially recall how he asked me to bring out one of my father's books for this unique altar. Umesh chanted prayers in Sanskrit and then spoke in Hindi and then in English. It was a lovely time that I will never forget. We had learned together how to carve out a piece of space and time that contained only—us.

The next celebration, a month later, was Christmas. We made it a special day. Out to dinner at the Bread of Life bakery. Afterward, Indian sweets. And Umesh surprised me with a beautiful pair of pure gold earrings. We put the headphone splitter on my iPod and listened to Christmas carols together. It was a peaceful day.

In fact, all the days were peaceful. We didn't argue. No, we never argued. We tried to enjoy simple pleasures. The treats. Cadbury Dairy Milk chocolate bars. Taking time to arrange three packs of differently colored potato chips on our large *thali* (plate) and then having them with tea. Since it was winter, Umesh was flavoring the *deshi chai* with ginger, and it was very warming. He always brought my tea in the ₹150 stainless-steel cup that he had bought especially for me. We read stories to each other from books, and we told family stories to each other.

I wasn't really keen to leave India. I was enjoying the steady translation work and also our ventures out into the countryside to attend village weddings. We had made friendships in our neighborhood. Banaras Hindu University and all that it offered were just down the road. And it was a special experience living in Banaras. Most important, we had settled into a steady routine that we both enjoyed. Quiet and productive.

There was the problem of my packing. It would be bitter cold in Beijing. And burning hot in Bali. The other stops were Hong Kong, Jakarta, Perth, Sydney, Uluru, Melbourne, Auckland—and then home. I could only carry one bag weighing no more than 50 lbs.

So I left most of my clothes in Banaras. I left all the expensive mics and recorders with Shubha at ARCE. Umesh would take the mic stands, windscreens, battery chargers, and so forth home to Karimganj. I had shipped so many books out to India, and Umesh would take those. And we had bought so many household items—from beds and the air conditioner to forks and spoons, and the many God posters posted all around our apartment. There were lovely sheets, mattresses, and handmade quilts. A stove. There were two clocks, a folding table, and four plastic chairs. The list went on and on. And I was heaping it all on the head of Umesh.

SEVENTY-SEVEN

# LEAVING BANARAS IN 2008

*In Karimganj, March 2014*

"So Helen left," Umesh recalled. "I made tea for you up to the end. We took the train second class AC sleeper two tier. I always took the upper berth because it offered a kind of privacy. They offer sheets and blankets and also a pillow. The white sheets are very clean, and the train compartment is absolutely clean. It is cool and comfortable and in summer warm and comfortable. From time to time they offer tea or coffee from the kitchen of the train. These are not great, but they are good enough.

"Also whoever wants can buy lunch and dinner. One person comes to take orders, notes the seat number, and arranges the meal. We ask how long it will take, and the answer can be half an hour or one hour or two hours. Maybe around 6:00 or 7:00 p.m., according to the weather. They serve rice, four chapattis, mango pickle, water in a sealed plastic glass, and a couple of vegetables. They give plastic forks and spoons with the food. I don't think they have knives. And there was yogurt, pepper and salt in small packets, also packs of sugar. And they always served some sweets for after the meal. It is called *thali* (plate). Mostly they served only vegetarian. They did not serve meat on the train because I think people might throw bowls here and there and make everything dirty. On the other hand, there are so many vegetarians. If a vegetarian learns that veg and non-veg are being served from the same kitchen, perhaps from the same pots, a vegetarian will not take any food at all. The whole business cost only about ₹25, but now the price has gone up. They also sold mineral water called Railwater. It is clean, just like other bottled waters that are sold in the market.

"From the train, you can see so many small villages, towns, farmland, roads around the train tracks, tube wells, animals grazing in the field, and people plowing their fields using tractors. From time to time you can see farmers are plowing their field with a team of bullocks. But mostly these bullocks are out of a job these days. From time to time we saw schools, primary and secondary, with children sitting on the ground studying. And we saw many beautiful mango groves and in summer the dense shade under the mango trees.

"We got to Delhi and went to Hotel Blue in Connaught. I don't recall how many days we stayed there, but you flew soon."

"Yes," I said. "From there I took a Cathay Pacific flight to Hong Kong."

"I was surprised that you left so many things behind," Umesh said. "You gave your microphones and important electronic equipment to Shubha to be stored in their climate-controlled archive at ARCE. And so many important things were left behind with me, like three mic stands, so many handmade mic cables, and I didn't know the names of these things. The only thing was to save them. But I didn't know for how long.

"After you left for China, I returned from Delhi to Banaras by train. So I returned to Banaras and went to the apartment and lay down there in Helen's room because I had the entire possession of the house. I was the boss. I was so so lonely it is hard to explain now. I arrived in the day, and I needed rest. I slept. It was the very beginning of the new potatoes time, maybe in January.

"Finally, I called Narayan, the rickshaw wallah, and talked to him. He really was our friend. And he offered his support to pack up all those things and help me out. He came down to see me, and I told him to help me to take the fans down first, and I began to pack the books. It was a big job for me. I had already collected so many Bislari cartons, hidden under one of the *chauki*s. You had drunk so many Bislari bottles, so the cartons remained. We had many of them. I took the curtains down from Helen's room first. I did most of those things that I could do without help. We had already saved the box of the AC. We had known from the beginning that we would need it. We had already decided to give away one ceiling fan to Narayan. Ramwati, our cook, wanted a mattress, and she wanted a *chauki* because she had been sleeping on the ground. I called Ramwati and offered the *chauki* and sheet, and she requested for the mattress. And I gave her a mattress."

"I, Helen, had encouraged Umesh to share these things with his family. But mostly Umesh had the concept that I would come back and need these things."

"Narayan got a ceiling fan. He wanted your ceiling fan, but it was the best, so I gave him a different one from the front room. Also, I gave Narayan the cooking stove and gas cylinder. We had this idea right from the beginning.

"Narayan had been very helpful throughout the nine months. We had used his three-wheeler just like our own car. I could send you alone with him. Once he took you alone to the Banaras airport.

"Then I had one big *chauki* of yours to bring to Karimganj. Anyhow, I had to bring so many things from Banaras that I had to hire a small truck.

"I stayed two more days because I was afraid the owner would charge another month's rent. He was nice and said, 'No, no.' But he was very careful with his property. I cleaned the apartment. I didn't want to leave anything, any paper, in the dump. I carefully checked each paper. I gave all the newspapers to Narayan, and he could sell them. And I asked Narayan to make a search of trucks that I could take to Mainpuri. Narayan made a two- or three-day search, and he found a good truck that was going to buy new potatoes near Bewar. Narayan brought the driver of the truck to meet me, and we bargained for a price. He asked for ₹10,000 and I got it for ₹8,000. If I would have known at the same time that the truck was going to buy potatoes, I could have gotten him down a little bit more. At that time I didn't know it. Narayan arranged it for a certain date, and he brought it near our house on the lane.

"I began to fill up all those things together, files, books, clothes tied in some rope in bundles, and laid your cotton mattress first on the floor of the truck. We also had two small wipers to clean the bathrooms, and one was bigger. But I left the smaller one there in the bathroom as well as the bigger one.

"The day we were leaving, I asked Narayan to bring someone to take down the AC. And he made it possible. And I took out all those CFL light bulbs. Slowly, I packed your paperwork, cassettes, Gangajali notebooks, dictionaries, seven or so suitcases, mattresses, quilts, sheets, the battery, the charger. I had to buy a special lid to close the battery, or the acid would leak out and spoil everything. I still today (2014) get back ten minutes of light from this battery. It is helpful during power cuts so we can at least find our flashlight! We had these electric mosquito killers. I even brought the bamboo bookshelves we bought. These already had begun to rot because dust came every day out of them from some bamboo-eating bugs. I had an idea I must have some model so I could have made several of these at my home. And I did it, and these new bookcases are very helpful for the family.

"I showed the house to the owner, and all of a sudden he didn't go anywhere. He went into the bathroom first. He saw only two bathrooms first, and he was pleased. He didn't look at the rest of the house. I had cleaned everything perfectly, and he didn't find a single paper.

"When we left, Narayan sat in the front beside the driver, and I went in the back of the truck, lying down on the mattress. I had a fear that somehow the truck could get slow and somebody could get inside and could take things that they would throw out because they thought there was no use for them. It happens. It took a long time to get to Karimganj. We moved from Banaras in the morning and got to Karimganj in the night, and the truck needed to be back to Bewar, to fill the truck up with the potatoes by that very night. Two men, who had been sitting in the front with Narayan and the driver, had been dropped off in Bewar to buy the potatoes. So we took down all the things from the truck in Karimganj and just stuffed them in my home everywhere. Also, I didn't know what was where, and one thing breaks down the entire system. Suppose a child came and picked up a small thing. I would never know until you don't use it. And people keep coming in this house. Also, the courtyard was so far away from the truck at my house. It was better to bring them inside. Suppose it rained. And the truck left, but Narayan stayed. In the evening, I fed him food—we ate all together inside the room. At nine o'clock in the night, I put him in a bus for Delhi because he wanted to go there to see some relatives.

"Slowly slowly we thought what to do, and slowly we shifted many things to the back room under the big *chauki* and on top of the *chauki*. And then slowly, I had the shelves made for the bedroom as you can see right now. One of them is full of cassettes, more than one hundred cassette boxes, and a bookcase entirely full of dictionaries, and one more for files."

SEVENTY-EIGHT

# CONCLUSION

*At Karimganj, 2014, when Umesh offers twenty reasons why people have music in the wedding*

Number 1. Music helps to perform the wedding according to the religious way.
Number 2. Singing songs takes off the pain of the bride's mother and is a kind of psychological treatment.
Number 3. Music is essential for amusement at the time of wedding.
Number 4. Music shows off your station in society.
Number 5. Music appeases the gods and goddesses by inviting them to help perform the wedding.
Number 6. Music causes people to feel joy.
Number 7. Music keeps the old traditions alive.
Number 8. Music provides spiritual, mental, and physical exercise (by Alka, Umesh's daughter).
Number 9. Singing and playing competitions from both the bridegroom and bride's side prove superiority.
Number 10. Songs give the deep history of India through the wedding of Lord Shiva.
Number 11. Songs offer the use of antibiotic root medicines out of the Vedic Age.
Number 12. Songs teach throughout the wedding how the couple can lead their life happily.

Number 13. Songs express heart-touching feelings from the bride's side. They give relief to get rid of the pain of the girl's parents.

Number 14. *Gali* songs provide fun, teasing, and joking while there is so much tension. In *gali*, women use physical words that they don't utter in daily life at all.

Number 15. Songs tell the pain of the bride, who, with fear, is losing her parents and her family. Although she cries for help, her parents can't help but remain silent, crying themselves. Only music can express these heartbreaking feelings.

Number 16. Songs broadcast to the whole village that a wedding is taking place in my house.

Number 17. Music and songs express the whole Hindu tradition like the pain, the joy, the happiness, the tenderness, the heartbreaking feelings as two families join together for the rest of their lives.

Number 18. Songs connect the life of simple people to the lives of kings and queens, gods and goddesses. Simple people sing about pearls, but in fact it is only rice.

Number 19. Songs are auspicious.

Number 20. Songs are the charm of the wedding.

## INTERLUDE SEVENTEEN

# *THE EUSTACE DIAMONDS*

"LIZZIE'S COUSIN FRANK TAKES LIZZIE TO SCOTLAND BY TRAIN," UMESH said as we thumbed our way through the rest of the book. "On the way, they are mostly silent. And she is flirting along the way in so many ways. But Frank is annoyed with all this flirting because he knows this is just Lizzie. At one point, he felt like turning back and leaving Lizzie to get home herself. By the end of the journey, the lock of hair that she flirted with looked like such a mess, and he was thinking she should have tied it up for the journey. Her face was dirty. Her hands were dirty. Whatever she had on which made her beautiful looked very ugly to Frank. It shows that he is seeing Lizzie—everything is ugly, nothing is good at all, so he sees no charm whatsoever in Lizzie.

"If you love someone, whether the locks goes somewhere or their hands are dirty, all these look beautiful to you. When time passes slowly slowly, you learn a lot, and at the same time if you are loving someone else, it may also create a kind of dislike for someone. Being apart from Lucy, he recalls Lucy the most, knowing her character, talking, behaving, very gently, and better than any royal person. However, Lizzie seems more beautiful than Lucy, but her character makes her ugly. But she is painted as the heroine of this story. This is what Trollope does.

"No one really cares what happens to Lucy, but we are all interested in what happens to Lizzie. We are looking forward to seeing her—that she is not defeated. Even then, at the last, Trollope says, 'find out who is the heroine.' It depends on the reader to whom he likes to be a heroine. The writer does not want to heap over the reader his idea to make a heroine of somebody. But at the very end he slips up and confesses that he meant her, Lizzie, to be the heroine, flawed though she is.

"Frank returns up to London early the following morning. He goes straight to see Lucy at Fawn Court, even though he passed six months without even writing to her. Lucy gets the news that somebody is calling for her outside, and she knows who that somebody must be. As she goes out, she finds Frank coming toward the door, and he runs and hugs her and kisses her over and over again. And then the Fawn daughters and Lady Fawn appear, and they pay their respects to the happy couple and treat them like family. Then Frank takes her away to his mother, and after some months the Fawn family arranges the wedding, accepting Lucy as the daughter of their family. Trollope concludes his story about Lucy and Frank there.

"The case of the diamond necklace is on trial. Mr. Benjamin and Mr. Smiley are accused of the theft. So many witnesses, including burglars from other countries, are called to London to appear in the court. And a notice is also sent for Lizzie to appear in the court. Now, this time she has sent a letter saying that she is very ill and unable to move from Portray—and *absolutely* cannot appear in the court. She arranged for a medical certificate stating all this. The court sent a doctor to Scotland, but she said she was too sick to see even him. Then Camperdown did not want to go there but claimed that she should be dragged out of there to London by 'cart ropes.' He had used up all of his legal weapons against her, and undefeated Camperdown couldn't defeat Lady Eustace. The court cannot wait for her because all the witnesses and burglars from different parts of the world have already appeared. So they had to keep the court running without Lizzie.

"It had not to be over, because Lizzie got in trouble at the end by a man who showed himself a clergyman but has several wives hither and thither. And I feel sorry for her. This is also human nature—that people want things, and from the very beginning she had the charm of having stones in her hair. And she had much attachment to have those kinds of gems. When she received the diamond necklace, she couldn't give it away because from childhood she loved those sorts of things. I feel this is human nature. For that, she was living in the kind of society, the kind of life, which made her to be that way. The role Lizzie plays almost all of the time makes people hate her. But finally, when she falls into the wrong hands, I really really feel sorry for her. Maybe because she was the heroine of the play, her character had to be like this. She had to change into a nice person to live a happy life at the end. This is what I would have liked."

"But who could change her?" I asked.

"The Lord."

"The Lord could have changed her?"

"Of course, if we believe that everything is done by the Lord—creation, destruction—then he could have also done this too. Doing something wrong, we must not kill a person. We must work hard to change their thoughts and actions."

"How do you feel now that the book is finished?" I asked.

"I want to reread it. I don't know how many times I will do it. For me it just looked like rereading and never ending. Like the ocean, just dipping in the ocean."

"You want the novel to be everlasting."

"It is, it is very well done. Grief leaves a mark on the heart high. Happiness does not remain on a person forever, but the spark of grief remains on the heart forever and ever."

"You said to me that I didn't come to India to read novels. But can you understand how I didn't want to put down such a book? I was lonely for my mother."

"You were lonely, and nobody was there to fulfill your thoughts and feelings. No one was there to console your feelings. Umesh was there, but you needed a continuous company who couldn't leave you, and books were the only way to keep you company, not a person. I was also thinking at that time that you were reading one after another. Also I was thinking that you were reading those books searching for what kind of shape you could give to our book."

"That is exactly why I was reading. For solace and for a never-ending story to inspire me to live on," I said.

"The person who can read such books can find these characters are alive for them forever, until they finish it."

"When we read the end, I felt terribly sad because Trollope left us. I didn't miss the characters. I missed the author."

"I will read this book over and over. Like the Ramayan, when we finish it, we begin it again. It is never ending."

SEVENTY-NINE

# UMESH TELLS A STORY FROM KARIMGANJ

*Defence Colony, New Delhi, March 30, 2014*

We were in our apartment in Delhi for a couple of days before my flight back to New York. We kept working on our book, right up to the hour to leave for the airport. But Umesh grew restless because he was bursting to tell me a story. On the morning of my flight, he told this tale.

"This is a story from my village, Karimganj," he said. "In this tale, first Nal married to Motini, and later he married to Damianti. Here is the story.

"In the beginning, Nal took a boat *manjusa* like they make themselves, like we see on the Discovery Channel. And he saw flowing, in a leaf bowl, the golden hair of some girl. She combed her hair, put it in the leaf bowl, and dropped it in the river. And Nal was there far away at the bank of the river, and this bowl was coming toward him. By the way, it blew toward Nal, and he saw this bowl of leaves of golden hair. And he was fascinated with it. And he decided to follow the bowl by the shore.

"It was hard to move because there were so many forests along the river, so he made a *manjusa*. And then he sailed backward up the river. It was hard. And he went up the river by boat. He saw a big castle beside the river and got off there. He had all the weapons of those days—sword, shield, and bow and arrow. And he went around the castle, and there was no gate to get in. And he hid himself somewhere, and the demon came in the evening—and he was sniffing, and he was feeling that some animal or man was there. But Nal hid himself in the bushes far away. On the one side, he pushed a heavy stone inside the fort and made a way to get into it.

"In the morning, the demon came out for hunting for something to eat. The demons are considered cannibals (*danaw*). (If somebody eats too much food, people say, 'Are you *danaw*?') On the other hand, the *dani* is a nice person who donates to a poor person. So the demon went out, and Nal came at the same place where the stone was that the demon had pushed inside, and he tried to push it open. But it was so heavy that he couldn't do at all. Then he appealed to the goddess. Because she was very kind to Nal, the mother goddess helped him to push the stone inside, and he closed it from the back, so he was inside.

"There he found a beautiful lady. She had golden hair. And she liked to see him. And they had a talk. This girl belonged to some goddess. This *dani* had stolen her, and he raised her as his own daughter. Now she was young. Nal stayed there. They played games (*chausar* and *sar panse*) inside the castle, and they got to know each other. In the evening, the demon began to move toward the castle, and the air began to blow fast, and she learned that her father was coming. So she was the daughter of the goddess, and she was full of magic. So she turned King Nal into a spider and put him somewhere on the wall.

"And the demon is just sniffing, and he said, 'I am having a human smell around.' And the girl said, 'You have eaten four humans, hung around four humans, and blood is around your mouth, and your nose is full of human blood. And you are wondering why you are smelling a human!' And he was silent and went to sleep.

"This was happening day by day. Finally, they agreed to get married, Nal and Motini. They are the main hero and heroine of this drama. The story is quite long. I'm just giving a glimpse of it.

"So Motini had her father killed by Nal because he was living as a demon. But his life was in a bird, a pigeon far away somewhere, and until the bird was killed, the demon would not die. She found out this secret from her father and had Nal kill the bird by twisting its neck.

"This is an epic, and there is so much to tell. Before they got married, Motini had already announced to Nal that she was the daughter of a goddess, and she won't be able to give birth to any child. If Nal got remarried, she would quit him and fly away. But she still promised him that she would help him three times to save his life.

"Nal broke his promise and got remarried. He got married with Damianti. Before Motini left, she made this promise, and she left. And she gave her word that she would help him three times to save his life. The mother goddess was already helping him in so many ways, time to time."

"In this, I was thinking—well—how could Nal do it when the lady had arranged to kill her father to get married to Nal, and her soul saved his life three times after her death? This episode hurt and affected my heart so much. I was at a tender age. How could he, Nal, do it? And I felt to write something, and I began it and never finished. I didn't know how to begin it. Oh, I felt deeply depressed, sad, so unhappy, deeply in my heart. The story was played by the village artist, Ram Sarup, so well that it affected my heart and mind to put me in grief.

"And writers of scholarly books should remember that they are just storytellers. They come to see, and they see what they see—it is just their story. It may be true, or it may not be true. Anyhow it should be a story. All we can do is tell the stories of our experience. We are not the Lord. But by combining several stories together, the reader can be amused, entertained, satisfied, and learn that East or West, there are ties that bind us together as human beings through art."

EIGHTY

# A PASSAGE TO INDIA

*November 26, 2015, New Delhi*

I had not seen Umesh since we parted at the airport on March 31, 2014. More than a year had passed. We kept in constant touch through the Facebook messenger app. From what he said, he was spending all of his time and effort to arrange the marriage of his daughter Alka. Every week, he searched through the "matrimonial" section of the newspaper. When he found a suitable Brahman boy living in Uttar Pradesh State, he immediately began making phone calls.

But all his attempts failed. I felt I needed to see him to give him courage. I felt it keenly. I gave him the time of my arrival, and he was there, waiting outside Indira Gandhi International Airport. It was so great to see him. He spotted me before I saw him. He snuck up behind me and whispered, "Are you looking for someone?" And that took me by shock.

I was deeply concerned when I saw that Umesh was limping badly. Apparently, he had had an incident on his motorbike. I had never before seen him like this.

We quickly hired a prepaid taxi and drove to Defence Colony in New Delhi. Several years prior, I had found a wonderful apartment there advertised by Airbnb. Umesh loved it. It was quiet and peaceful. There was no noise from the street. There were no family quarrels.

The apartment had a very large living room with several modern sofas for lounging. There were lovely paintings on the walls and interesting sculptures placed here and there. There were two large bedrooms, each with its own bath and Western-style toilet. Umesh's bathroom even had a Jacuzzi, but I don't think he ever used it.

The apartment was on the third floor. At the gate to the building there was a twenty-four-hour guard. At the apartment, Reena was our cook. We would pay her money for food—flour, bread and butter, vegetables, rice, dal, and so forth. She made lovely Indian vegetarian meals for us.

We stayed there for two days. Then the plan was that my son Ian Woolford would be arriving on the third day. As we both needed to visit India around the same time, we arranged to spend a few days together in Delhi before we both ended heading out in different directions. Me to Karimganj to the south, he to the east to Patna.

The three of us had a wonderful time. First, we went to the Amrit Book Company on Connaught Place. Ian chose a bunch of short story books and poetry books in Hindi for Umesh. He also found him a Hindi copy of Stephen Hawking's *A Short History of Time*. He helped me pick out the best new Indian books, novels, scholarship in English. And he chose a huge pile of Hindi books for himself that he intended to use in his classroom teaching in Melbourne.

Then we three set out to visit the famous Hindi novelist Ramdarash Mishra at his home. He is in his nineties. Ian has maintained this special friendship for several years. He had gone out to Mishra's elder brother (in a rather remote village) the year previous, and the brother had sung songs for Ian. Then, in the meantime, the elder brother had died. Ian brought to Mishra the video of his now-deceased elder brother singing. It was a moving experience.

The next day, Ian invited the amazing Daisy Rockwell (granddaughter of the famous painter) to our Delhi apartment. Daisy brought her daughter Sarafina. And this was so much fun too. I couldn't believe how warm and loving (and talented) Daisy is.

Much too soon, the day came when Ian had to catch his plane to Patna. Umesh and I decided to stay in the apartment a couple more days to rest up. Then he arranged for a taxi to drive us down to his home in Karimganj.

While we were loafing around at the apartment, Umesh took the chance to tell me more about *The Eustace Diamonds*. I was a bit surprised that he was still interested in talking about it.

He said, "This kind of story of England fit in the social system at Victorian times when this novel of Lizzie was written. So in India, it is still carried out the same in the present time, because greed of ornaments, greed of clothes, greed of money and wealth, and trickiness of people at the time of arranging the wedding. Greed is seen on both sides—both for Lizzie and for the Indian bride, but the only connection we can say is that the ornaments the girl takes in India belong to the joint family, but Lizzie is taking the family heirloom jewelry. In India, if the bride takes money from her parents' home, it is considered stealing—if it is not donated by the family. Also, similarly, if she is in her *sasural*, her father-in-law or mother-in-law owns the jewelry, and if she takes it secretly, that is like stealing. So Lizzie was stealing the Eustace diamonds. And in the end, they were stolen from her.

"The thief steals from the thief everywhere on this Earth. So the story of the Eustace diamonds belongs with the story of the Indian wedding. They are a good match. Sometimes, by telling stories from different cultures, we can learn more about our own culture.

"I like the story, very charming. It gives nonstop reading. You keep turning the pages one after another to see what happens next, what happens next. Also Lizzie, in the beginning, she is a very charming girl. Although the situation is quite different, and she is a young girl, but her aunt just didn't let her be as a young girl should be. That is why Lizzie hates her aunt. Lizzie wanted to live well off and lead her life nicely. Later she was looking for a high position in society, a title as well as money. Your purpose was to just enjoy reading. I did not know that it would be so charming. It helped me improve my English. But the story sucked me in."

"So would you have liked to have married Lizzie?"

"Well, I don't know what to say. I am sixty-five years old now. My duties to my family have pulled me so deep, hardly I can think of anything else. But Lizzie was not made to be a *bahu* (village bride)! Even so, she was not good for a royal family either. The royal family doesn't need jewelry to show off. Their duty is just to take care of their subjects. But Lizzie is—in every sense she fails. Because she is full of greed—a mentally disturbed lady—and not raised well. So she couldn't belong to a family at all. Royal family members must know the rules and regulations, how to carry it out. The king's daughter is married to some other king's son. Money is nothing for them. But if a king marries a poor girl, she can get greedy for money. She can disturb the family for money.

"So we made this book so that people can read it and compare the stories about human nature in two different cultures. Did you like it? Human nature is according to the culture, but good and bad people live in every age and in every culture. But this point only gets interesting when we look afar and see it play out in Victorian England or in Ballia. This becomes quite a big story. This is a book about ethnomusicology. And it is a book about how to move ahead in a story."

"But why did you tell me the story of Nal and Motini?" I asked.

"We were talking about sadness," Umesh replied. "All of the sudden, this jumped into it because of the sadness of Motini's death. The sadness pulled me back many many years until I was twelve or thirteen years old—toward the grief of Motini's death. Motini loved Nal so deeply, she helped him to kill her demon father, even though Nal couldn't ever face him in a fight. Motini asked that Nal would not get remarried, and he accepted it. If he would remarry, she would go. And she, Motini, would never be able to give birth to any child. Motini helped Nal to win so many wars. She was the daughter of a goddess, stolen by this demon.

"Nal was helped by the mother goddess to win so many wars and get over so many troubles. Motini did not die, but she left. She went straight to heaven. She had come down to help Nal.

"Eventually at the end, Nal got remarried. Motini had already promised him that even though she was dead, she would help him three times more. Seeing the character of this woman, I had fallen deeply in love with this goddess. I cried for several days, and I planned to write a book to prove that Nal was nothing without Motini and the devi, the mother goddess.

"This was my first love with a female character."

EIGHTY-ONE

# BANGLES IN BALLIA

*December 20, 2015, at our apartment in New Delhi*

"No, Helen, it was *not* very bumpy to get there! Although the route we had chosen was long, it was also good. Since we were very tired before reaching Banaras, and we did not know the exact road to get to Ballia, we had to go straight through the city of Banaras, and it was very crowded. In fact, it was gridlock. This discouraged us. As we got through and got out of Banaras, the road was good. And until Ballia, the road was very long, but it was good enough."

We had decided to set out from Karimganj to try to find Gangajali and Sashi in Ballia. It was a long and difficult journey, even by private car. There were new toll highways that helped us to speed along. And then there were the congested streets of Banaras that took two hours to pass. Two hours for only a few kilometers. Then we proceeded on back roads to Ballia.

"But the driver was not behaving well," Umesh continued. "He was sitting in the driver's seat doing his all *asanas* (yoga poses) to drive. It looked like he was a real great disciple of some great sanyasi teacher of yoga. All of the sudden, we realized that he was falling asleep, and he stopped for at least five or ten minutes, washed his face, rinsed his mouth, and spit out his tobacco. And he was just comforting himself. And before moving from there, he tore out one pouch of tobacco and stuffed it into his mouth. And we saw that the driver was driving the vehicle very slowly—say 15 km per hour—and we saw a car was backing up (nobody else was there). It was dark night. And I warned him, 'Look—the car is backing up!' I don't know where from the energy filled in him, and he began to drive fast. I said, 'What happened to you?' And he replied, 'Well, I can do anything if we are dying.'

"Although he began to drive fast, we had a big fear that he might fall asleep while driving the car. Helen warned me, 'Keep him awake, no matter what you do.' When we began our journey from Karimganj, we refused to permit him to play loud music in the car. But this time we happily wanted him to play music as he liked. Well, he was too discouraged until now that he couldn't play music. He said it, and he had no one to talk to because he accused us of talking to each other and understanding each other, but he couldn't. So he said he became lonely.

"I decided to moo myself like a cow to keep the driver awake. First I recited a play out of the Radheshyam Ramayan when Rawan's sister goes for help from her brother Rawan, and her nose got cut. As much as I had memorized, I recited. I then thought to do a prayer to Lord Shiva in Sanskrit. And I mooed one line, and I stopped. I realized that he did not know Sanskrit. Also I found the best shouting singing was the Hanuman Chalisa—to save our lives. And I went through the entire Hanuman Chalisa. And slowly we were also reaching to Ballia that night, although it is quite a long way to get to Ballia from Banaras. It was scary all the way.

"We got to Ballia around 11:15 p.m. and began to search for the twenty-six-year-old place, Hotel Sarang, where we stayed in 1989. It seemed that all the people knew this hotel, but nobody was trying to tell where it was situated. Ballia was already changed. Our driver took us to so many places to find this hotel, and we failed.

"It took almost one hour and fifteen minutes to get to a hotel at the railway station. And we found a hotel there to stay. Helen was so tired, she wanted to sleep anywhere. And we checked into the hotel. We started from Karimganj at half past ten in the morning and got to Etwah via Mainpuri. Helen asked me if the driver liked to drink tea. He claimed that he didn't like tea. Helen said, 'Never mind, we would like to have tea, so stop place to place to drink tea.' The message was in it—so that we could rest, also we could use the restroom. I am confirmed that he didn't like my words. I kept asking him to stop somewhere so we could have tea, time to time, over and again. But he was too stubborn to stop. After three or four times, Helen told me, 'Ask the driver to stop at some gas station' so she could use the restroom. Then the driver could only think people need to go to the bathroom. And he stopped. He also awarded us the privilege of having tea and using the restrooms.

"While we were on the way, Helen alerted me. 'Umesh, when we reach Ballia, we will find Sashi, Gangajali, or maybe we will not find them.' I agreed to it, but we may find them too. And we also began to talk about Sashi to whom we considered a clown from long long ago—twenty-six years ago. She used to come with Gangajali. In fact, Gangajali brought Sashi with her because she, Gangajali, had never been in any hotel to sing. And this was the only big hotel in Ballia at that time. While Gangajali was singing, Sashi began to interrupt, and Helen asked me to tell her not to interrupt while Gangajali was singing.

"Sashi was a schoolteacher, and she had had a one-year-old baby girl to take care of. She had to go back quick to her home to feed her daughter. As well, she wanted to join Gangajali so she could have some extra earning besides her teaching job. After each song, she used to talk something that was not related to the song but unusual like, 'Oh, what was the price of this microphone?' 'How did you get here?' 'Why are you recording these songs?' 'How much did your sari cost? It looks very nice on you.' 'Oh, your bangles are beautiful. Do you wear bangles in your country?' And certainly, we began to be annoyed when she made a time limit to stay for singing. There was so much work to do, and Sashi had no time to offer. So anyhow she had to stop talking about the time limit. At least five hours. Because meanwhile we had to take tea and turn on the fan to cool down after each song. She was also annoying because Gangajali was being so careful to sing each song in its proper place, while Sashi was rushing her and saying, 'Just sing anything. The reel is running.' Gangajali had promised to sing all the wedding songs, from the beginning to the end, of each and every ritual, and she insisted she would not sing any dirty songs. And up to the end she carried it out, even though she did mention the word 'asshole' and also calculated the depth of Helen's pounding pot.

"The next day staying in Ballia, I decided to go to find out Hotel Sarang. By then, we had learned that it had shut down. And also I went to find out about Gangajali and Sashi. I talked to the hotel receptionist about Hotel Sarang, and he called a rickshaw puller, and I went to Hotel Sarang. I reached there and found the owner seated in a chair and doing accounts. He was running Britannia's company's food products. This business he was running since we saw him running the hotel. And I told the owner that we had stayed in his hotel twenty-six years ago twice. And I had an American lady with me. And she was recording women's wedding songs. He did not recall this because he had had so many guests over the years. And in fact, we had never met him back then.

"I asked the owner, 'Oh, your hotel was running well. What happened? Why did you shut it down?' He was upset and said, 'Because powerful people did not pay their bills staying and having meals for a long time.' But when I was talking to the receptionist of the hotel where we were staying this time, I said, 'Oh, it is very bad that the hotel was shut down.' The receptionist replied, 'The hotel is still the best building in Ballia, but it shut down because of a family quarrel among brothers.'

"In the afternoon, I went in search of Gangajali. I had the only clue to go to the movie hall VJ Talkies. I had already learned that the VJ Talkies had shut down. But the building was still there. When I got there, in front of the Talkies, I found a big cloth shop. I had taken a rickshaw to get there because I had forgotten the location of this Talkies over twenty-six years. I talked to these people who were selling cloth, and I found them very professional. They listened to my talk for two or three minutes. I was asking the address of Vijay, the grandson of Gangajali who worked in the Talkies. They didn't say anything, and then one of them replied that they don't know of such a guy. They sell cloth here and far away. I got a bit discouraged. One person directed me toward a small shop on the other side of the road in front of the Talkies. This was the old man selling betel leaves. How to begin to talk to this person? I gave it a thought and decided to use Helen's technique. Buy a betel leaf, spend some money to make myself close to the shopkeeper. I asked for a plain betel leaf without tobacco. And he made it very nice. Without asking its price, I handed him a ten-rupee note. He returned me a one-rupee coin. And I began to chew pan. I then asked him the name of Gangajali's grandson Vijay. I also told him that we were here twenty-six years ago and how she sang beautiful wedding songs for an American lady. And we want to meet her. Now she (the American lady) is here. Well, he began to see toward the sky, and two people came to his mind named Vijay. None of them ever worked in the Talkies. But one Vijay was not there, and another sells eggs. And I could find him in the evening. And I returned to the hotel to see Helen and give her all this news.

"Helen leapt up and shouted, 'Let's go!' So we got our car and headed out. We reached the Talkies. We left our car behind as there was no place to park it, and we kept moving ahead and asked for the lane where Gangajali lived. As we got inside of the lane, we found so many people working and sitting around. Helen told me to ask these people about Gangajali. I talked to these people, and they were not aware, but at the same time a tall person appeared and listened to us. He knew all the people of the neighborhood. He told us that Gangajali was no more there but that she lived here long ago. But that she had died. All of a sudden we were stunned and cried, '*Oh, no!*' It was shocking to learn that she was no more. This began a deep depression that is still with us now and ever.

"This lawyer took us to the home of Sashi. Although she had been the clown of the show, we were glad to learn that she lived. The lawyer called her from her doorstep, but there was no answer for a long time. As we decided to return to our hotel, her son appeared from the outside. He learned that we were looking for his mother to whom we knew since the last twenty-six years. He phoned her and said that she will arrive right away. As she saw us, she could not recognize us, and we couldn't recognize her. We had all changed with the years. We reminded her of the story of singing twenty-six years back in Hotel Sarang. And suddenly she remembered it all and embraced Helen. All of the sudden, she was overwhelmed and wasn't sure what to do next. She opened the front room of her house and invited us to come in and take a seat. She promised tea, and they brought coffee, and it was great. Never mind tea or coffee, we were overjoyed to see her. She also brought snacks. And we began to talk and talk, and we felt she had not changed at all, despite her missing teeth. But at the same time, we learned that her husband had passed away one year back. It was painful to learn this, that now she was a widow not wearing fancy clothes as she used to dress. Half an hour later one *bahu* appeared, and she was very nice woman with two daughters. Thereafter, another *bahu* appeared with a one-month-old baby girl. We took so many photographs of all of them plus us too.

"At the same time, Helen invited the entire family to visit us in the hotel where we were staying and that we would collect Sashi's life story and then have a big party with a big chocolate birthday cake and five candles.

"Then Helen announced to all that she had come to buy 'Bangles in Ballia.' It was a joke, but she wanted them anyhow. So Sashi took us to a very good bangle shop and helped Helen to choose a set of red and golden glass bangles, fit for any bride.

"Just as we were moving along the way, we met her youngest daughter. Boy, had she changed! She herself had a three-year-old daughter with her.

"So when we reached our hotel, we ordered a feast to be prepared for nine people along with the three of us—me and Helen and driver sahib. So many mixed vegetables, dal, rice, chapatti, et cetera, and a nice big chocolate cake with chocolate icing and five candles.

We had made a program to move back to Delhi the next day, but since we had seen Sashi, we decided to postpone our departure so we could have this big party.

"The next morning, we woke up, bathed, put on our best clothes, and then started nervously to wait. I had already warned the hotel guys to prepare the food on time—two o'clock sharp.

"Sashi had promised to arrive at one o'clock so we would have an hour to record her life story. One o'clock came and went. And Helen said, 'Oh, Indian Standard Time!' But as the time ticked away, we were just on edge. But then we remembered that Sashi was Sashi. Finally, she appeared at half past two, together with a family girl. We ordered tea for them, and then we got down to work on her life story. Actually, as it turned out, it wasn't much of a story, so we won't repeat it here so as not to bore our reader.

"Helen discreetly slipped ₹10,100 into her hand. Sashi refused this money at first, and in the end she accepted it.

"Then Sashi began to receive phone calls. She replied to the first phone call that she would be at home soon. And we kept talking for a long time, but it was just small talk. Then at three o'clock, she had to go back. And she promised to come back straight away. There were some *sasural* people waiting for her at home. And they were due to go by train at four o'clock. And she left our hotel.

"Our party was messed up. We were very concerned because we had ordered food for nine people and a very nice, big chocolate birthday cake with five candles. But we had hope that Sashi would return with her family, but as she left we knew that she had no intention of returning. We were very discouraged at the cost of the food. Putting so much money, and there were only three people left to eat it, and one was our damn driver. We wondered whether we should eat the cake or take it to Delhi. And we really didn't feel like lighting five candles.

"We waited until six o'clock and decided to go and make our hotel reservation for the following night in New Delhi. The market was full of people running hither and thither, and the traffic was just too much. It was even very difficult for me to move around. People were not able to tell us where the Internet café was. Finally, we found it on our way back to the hotel.

"While we were on the way back to the hotel, I got a phone call from Sashi. And she wanted to come to the hotel with her family right away. We were totally exhausted and said, 'Not today.'

"But we had a fear that she would certainly show up in the morning and that it would be very difficult to get out of the hotel in time.

"So we got back to the hotel, and I informed the receptionist, with a heavy heart, that we were sorry we caused you so much trouble to prepare so much food and to arrange for the chocolate birthday cake with five candles. I said, 'I'm sorry it was such a big financial loss.' And he said, 'Never mind. I haven't cooked anything till now. We can cook this in fifteen minutes. As for the cake, we never got it, so don't worry.'

"For sure, if I had not ordered them to buy five candles, it would be my duty to buy them, and we would have had to carry them to Delhi.

"So we ordered dinner following the same foods we had asked for the party. Except the cake. Then I said, 'Excuse me for a moment.' And I went out, and then I returned to the hotel with two big pieces of chocolate cake. Perhaps that was actually meant to be part of our cake with five candles. Anyhow, it was really tasty.

"The next morning, I had two phone calls, and I didn't want to pick up. I had a fear that she will ask us to come visit and perhaps insist on having that damn party with the cake and five candles. Since we were getting ready for a long and difficult journey to New Delhi, we actually didn't have time to see her. I didn't want to be rude to her by saying it, refusing, so I placed my phone in my room.

"Ten or fifteen minutes later, she burst into Helen's room with her youngest married daughter. She had a complaint that I was not picking up the phone. She came, and we greeted her warmly. And then she called Helen 'sister.' And her daughter called you *mausi*. And Sashi came out with the real story of her life. And it was sad.

"Her daughter's husband's side people, altogether eight people, had arrived to decide whether she, Sashi's daughter, and their son should be divorced. It took a long time to decide this. She had had a real reason not to enjoy the party while they were negotiating a divorce. So how could we blame her? The girl said that her husband was beating her every day and throwing her on the ground. He was a chain drinker. The daughter explained how her mother-in-law used to teach her son how to beat her—for no reason. The daughter also said they are illiterate people in the village. And she presented Helen with two fantastically beautiful silver-colored *kada*, which Helen managed to put them on together with her rather sizable set of red wedding bangles.

"She is wearing them now, and these silver ones make quite a nice sound as she types this ending chapter.

"After they left, I found that I was suffering from a deep grief. Even though we had met Sashi, we were badly hurt that we had missed Gangajali.

"The trip back to Delhi was really tough, and we only reached there, exhausted, at 6:30 a.m. That morning, while you slept until noon, I said that I hadn't slept since Ballia. Two thoughts disturbed the peace of my mind.

"No matter what happened, that Gangajali was pushed out from where she had her home, as we had discovered, what else could be there where Gangajali resided except the temple of Lord Shiva? She was Gangajali, and the Gangaji resides on the head of Lord Shiva.

"Also while we met Gangajali in the Sarang Hotel and from the beginning when you promised her that you would make her songs immortal, she said that she would sing songs for you from the beginning to the end for each ritual of the wedding. Those that are the real songs. Nothing ugly. And she kept her promise. She never broke the limit (*maryada*) in singing her songs. Similarly, as Tulsidasji never broke the limit while composing the Ramayana. He composed the Ramayana within the limits, so people can enjoy their lives and get social benefit and spiritual benefit. So Gangajali also did the same. With such thoughts that run to the heart of my religion, I am in deep grief.

"Helen said, 'Umesh, now that we have lost her, you can finally understand the difference between anthropology and ethnomusicology. Music strikes us at the depth of our being. Music creates in us feelings that are so special and unusual that nothing can match them. And no words can explain them.'

"Helen continued, 'You spent hundreds of hours transcribing Gangajali's songs, and you can't escape the effect of that music on your soul. As happy as you were to hear her sing, you are equally as grieved at her passing. As happy, as sad. Human life runs according to this equation. It is just. So, Umesh, this pain will remain with you for a long time, I'm afraid. But life is a story, and this story should have a happy ending. So I believe that in the end, for you, her songs will overcome the melancholy of her death.'"

"And I hoped that Helen's words were true."

"What is the difference between anthropology and ethnomusicology?" I asked Umesh.

Umesh said, "There is no difference. No one likes to be studied. Anthropological studies investigate the social system of the rural areas. How do you think? How do you work? What kind of religion do you follow? How do you learn? What do you eat in one day? At each meal? Also about the social life, about relations between husband and wife, between parents and children. They want to learn everything, how the people live and work together. They also learn a little ethnomusicology as they do need to study songs of the rural area, what kind of songs they have and what time they are sung. How the songs affect on the human nature? How these songs pull in life from one place to another in life? Now we see new—first we are born, we think for childbirth songs, thereafter so many ritual songs are sung, and the wedding songs, so many types of wedding, from childbirth to thereafter. So many other songs before marriage, and then at childbirth, so many *bhajan*s are sung, so many other songs. And then the time comes for wedding songs, each is sung—different songs for different wedding rituals. So these songs allow the wedding to move farther ahead. Thereafter we have sad songs for when somebody dies. When women cry while we are in sadness, the wife may also curse her husband in death—why did he leave her?—she curses him in song.

"Actually, these rural people are studied very much by anthropologists and ethnomusicologists. So *my* question is—when I go to the United States to some very high-ranking people, will they let me study either anthropology or ethnomusicology? For example, I learned about the chastity belt. I would like to study that. So it was the husband held her and locked her body parts so she would remain pure and nobody will reach there.

"Oh, in olden times anthropologists measured our height and weight. So we are offering information, but the informant can't learn what is written about themselves. But sometimes, while transcribing and translating works for anthropologists, I learned some ugly, painful things. And I don't like to talk about that ever.

"When I reach the United States, I want to write a chapter about parking. So if I ask some American professor, 'Do you enjoying parking?' and so many questions will arrive: How many times do you go parking? How many different women have there been? Are they married or not? If I go and talk to people, will they let *me* do it?"

## EIGHTY-TWO

# ACROSS THE SEVEN SEAS

*At our apartment in New Delhi, December 20, 2015*

"Helen, since you have been reading to me this story about Lizzie and her diamonds, gems, pearls, and the necklace, I would like to end our book with a story from my village. It is about such ladies and such gems, told by Ram Sarup, a famous *Dhola* epic singer. He was a well-known singer and storyteller of our area. He was illiterate, but he was educated more than any professor. He studied and taught *Dhola* and had so many gurus in his life, beginning in his childhood. And he had many disciples that helped his *Dhola* company onstage to put on a show. He offered social teachings in his art, also warnings against bad ideas, and also told so many omens in which North Indian people believe. And he could use a few words to tell the very meaning of our lives. He would have loved Lizzie's story and listened to it night after night—from the very start until the very finish.

"So hear his story about Indian gems and jealousy now. Shortly before he died, I went to him with my cassette recorder. And the words he spoke are given here."

***Sat Samundar Par, "Across the Seven Seas," by singer and storyteller Ram Sarup***

*Prologue*

*"Oh, the sweet smell from the belay flower and the sweet smell of the flower of the chameleon."*

*And the story moves from here.*

*During the story repeat "hum, hum," as during the military march, they play the nagara drums. Surely these must happen. If you are interested in hearing a story, the noise must stop.*

*The Story*

There were four friends. One of them was a prince. They decided that now we all four should go from here in our own country or to a foreign country for a few days, earning a little and living. Our parents are annoyed with this. So all those four friends moved from there. After moving for two days, what did they see? So they decided to tell each other their skills. "Now tell me your skills." One fellow asked another fellow, "Do you have any skill?" He replied, "I don't have anything, but I have one skill. If any one of us four is missing or lost, I can find him by his footprints within one year. I can find him in one year."

Some of them said, "Friend, you have quite a great skill! It is hard to search for someone by their footprints after only three hours. And you are telling us that you can find him after one year!? The footprints vanish."

He replied, "Whether they remain or have vanished."

"Oh, can you do it?"

"YES!"

And the next fellow said, "And if I have somebody's grandfather and have not seen his father, then I can tell whose child is this."

"Oh friend, you have told of a skill greater than the first one."

Then they asked the prince, the son of the king. Ask the son of the king, "Have you got any skill?" He replied, "I don't have any skill. But this five-kilo sword is hanging from my shoulder. Even if death comes before me, I will keep fighting him. I will keep fighting him as long as this sword is hanging from my shoulder. Until then, nobody can defeat me."

"Oh, sir, you are greater than the last one!"

After having this conversation, they asked the son of the *khatii*, "Have you got any skill?"

"Yes, I also have a little gift," he replied. "If I am given wood, nails, and tools, I can make a beautiful flying machine vehicle within twelve hours. So, within this time and without oil, push a button and enjoy the United Kingdom!"

"Oh, you are even greater than the previous ones."

When it was asked of the son of the Brahman, they asked the Maharaja, "What kind of talent do you have?" He replied, "I can do this. If the other guy can make a search within two years, but if I can get the bones of a dead person, I can bring him back to life."

They said, "Brother, you are the second god. Now dude, let's go."

They moved, and then what occurred? All of the sudden a big dusty and rainy storm came from the west. What occurred was because of that storm. Three guys were blown away in one direction in that storm. And the prince was separated from them. Then the prince began to search for these three guys, and all those three were searching for the prince. None of them were inferior to the others in talent. When these poor four guys got caught up in this situation, so many days passed. Then the prince thought, "I don't know whether my three friends have lived or died. Now I am left alone. Let me do something so I can earn something for my food." So he went to the king for a job.

He said, "I am the son of another king, but now I am in trouble." Then the king replied, "Never mind, son. There is no work for you here. Be seated in a chair in our court and watch out. And there is not any work for you. Eat food, put on clothes, and you will be paid."

He accepted it happily. So the prince was employed by the king. While he was employed, he had a day off on Sunday. He thought on the day off, "Today I have the day off." Where he was working in the court, there was a betel leaf shop. When he used to sit at the shop because of the king's courtesy, he also got a betel leaf to chew. Whether he went to the shop four or five times a day, the shopkeeper offered him a betel each time free of cost. He kept taking this betel leaf from him.

It was Sunday. He planned for the day. A river was flowing there, and he decided to go and take a bath in it. There was also a washerman's stone at the bank of the river. "I shall also wash my clothes there and take a proper bath." The prince reached the river, washed his clothes, and took a bath. It took him two hours. By then his clothes were dry. Now, putting on those clothes, now make a search for those guys.

As he got ready to move, he saw a gem floating toward him in the river. The prince said, "Brother, it looks like a gem." The water was flowing up to his thigh. So he waded into the river and picked up the gem. So he picked up the gem and put it in his pocket. He returned to the place of the betel leaf seller and sat down in a chair. The betel leaf seller prepared a betel leaf and handed it to him. By then, the wife of the betel leaf seller arrived there. The prince handed the gem to the wife. The king's palace was above, and the betel leaf seller's home was below. And she got the gem. Slowly, she put it on her nose ring.

Having uncovered her face, she began to sweep the courtyard. The queen of the palace was looking down and saw her.

"Oh! I am married to a king, and she is the wife of the betel leaf seller. And she has put the gem on. And my king does not even have a golden coin."

So upset, she went to her cot.

*Listener*: "Oh, lie down on it."

The king got the message. The message came that "your queen is upset today." So the king thought to have a look.

The king arrived. "What's the matter?"

Now, the king arrived and said, "Queen, get up and have some food. If somebody has winked at you, I can have his eye cut out. If anyone has spoken against you, I can have his tongue cut out. If anyone has raised a hand to you, I can have his hand cut off. If any wall has touched you, I can have it broken down."

She replied, "These are not the problems. But do this. *Are* you the king?"

He replied, "Oh, yes! I *am* the king."

She said, "Oh, *are* you the king? Look! The wife of the betel leaf seller has a nose ring with a gem! And I am wandering around without it as if I were a widow. Only the king should have the right to have the gem, not the betel leaf seller's wife. The king has the right to have gems. These are the rights of the king! Not for the people who sell the betel leaf for two paisa."

And all the day she kept wandering in her courtyard with pride, and her nose remained unadorned.

So the king told the betel leaf seller, "Look, brother, your wife has a gem. Give it to me."

The betel leaf seller went to his wife and demanded that she give him the gem. "The king wants it."

She replied, "If you had it made for me, then take it to the king. If the king had it made for me, then give it to the king. It never belonged to you or the king."

Then the king asked, "Who gave it to you?"

She replied, "I got it from your servant."

"Oh, my servant gave it to you?"

The queen called the prince who was serving him. The queen said, "I arranged for you to take a bath and wash your clothes. I had the bed laid for you. I had all the conveniences prepared for you. And the valuable thing you brought, you gave it to her? Was *I* not a woman?"

The prince replied, "Oh queen, I was thinking what would the king do with it? Since I have given it to her, I will also bring one for you. What else? Oh, where I got it, I will search one out for you."

She said, "Go!"

He left there for six months, taking from the queen money for his expenses. The prince moved from there with all these things. Now he began to walk beside the river, walking against the current.

"Oh," he said, "bloody nothing came from the east side. It makes sense to go to the west so I can find it. I will go where it came from."

So he hung his sword on his shoulder. Where the evening falls, in the dense forest, with so many big dangerous bushes having resulted from the soil erosion, the prince moved ahead alone. Whenever he felt sleepy, he went to sleep.

As dawn appeared, he began to walk. While he was walking ahead, fifteen or twenty days passed. He saw a gem was floating with the current. He thought to let it flow on. He said, "I will not take it out. Somewhere there is a garden with a tree of gems. If I need another one, let me find its source."

He left the gem and walked ahead. He continued walking for five or six days more. There he saw two gems floating in the river, one after another. This meant that the tree of the gems was very near. And he walked farther ahead. Then, when he saw one or two gems after another, he thought that the tree of gems was near. In same day he kept moving ahead, and ten or fifteen days passed.

Then he saw in the valley the river was flowing on one side, and a fort was built there. And the water was flowing under the fort. He saw there a daughter of a demon was hanging with half of her neck cut and her body lying on a wooden screen. Whenever one drop of her blood dripped into the river, that drop was turned into one gem. And they were floating in the river. Then he proclaimed, "The main garden! The origin! This is it!"

Then he tried to get inside the fort. When he got inside, the demon of the fort was not there. But he found the daughter. Her neck was half cut. He saw two wooden bars, one under the girl and one over her. He asked himself, "Why are these wooden bars here?" So he switched the two bars so the bottom one was on top and vice versa. And as he switched the bars, the girl came to life and got up. She thought, "It is not the time for my father to come back? But who is he?" She asked, "Who are you?" Then he replied that I am such and such a person. She said, "Okay." Then the girl said, "What will we do, and what is going to happen? If my father comes, he will kill you." He replied, "Whether he kills me or not, I have to stay here. First of all I have the magic sword with me that was given as a boon—he will not be able to kill me. He won't be able to kill me easily." The daughter said, "Here I am in the hold of the demons *rakshas*. This boy is also the son of some king. If I get married to him . . . I believe that the Lord has sent him for me."

The girl began to love him. And they began to live together. The boy said, "Being here like this, how can we live? This is no way to live life." So he asked her, "Find out where the soul of your father is. Until I kill him, we cannot live happily." She said, "I didn't know these people had a life elsewhere. Since you have told me this, then I will try to get him to spit it out."

The next day when the demon returned, she asked her father, "Father, you leave me behind and half cut my neck every day. I remain lying here on the screen alone, and so many flies and mosquitoes piss and shit in my mouth. My mouth is mucky! And due to this I always feel I have a fever. If you leave me alive here so that I can sweep here, I can do some other things for the home. And tell me what is the secret of your essence (*kal*)? Where is your soul? So I will be able to keep an eye on your *kal* if you leave me alive. So I will know that you are alive all the time. If you leave me here dead every day, I will never know whether you are dead or alive."

"Oh," the demon thought, "this is an impossible thing she is asking. This girl never talked like this before. Today she is talking like this. She is asking the secret of my death." He said, "Listen, daughter. I am telling you the secret of my death. Across the seven seas there is an *akaibar* tree on an island. On each branch, there is a snake, and on each leaf there is a scorpion. And demons are guarding this tree. And there is a cage hanging on this tree. Inside is a small female ibis."

Umesh paused while telling the story. He said, "Message there is that these gems don't come easily until you suck the blood of people. Trump is using the blood of the people of the United States. What did they get in return? He gave great insult, took their dignity, and he took their blood. Oh, he is the president of the United States. This will be the freedom of sex for men of the United States. For women, pain, blood, mentally disturbed—she loses everything. This is the way these kind of girls begin to hate. Their life cannot be normal ever. All men and women on this Earth act like animals. Trump has done this."

And Umesh continued with the story.

The demon explained, "My life is in that female ibis. If somebody breaks her leg, my leg will break. And if somebody breaks her hand, my hand will break.

If somebody twists her neck, then I am dead." The daughter said, "Oh, Father, this is the thing I wanted to know. Well, I will not be able to get to the island *sat sumandar par*. At least I will live with hope." The demon told the secret, and then he left to hunt for food. The daughter said to her boyfriend, "Sweetheart, now you leave." The boyfriend said, "For what reason?" She said, "You will not be able to do this job because you don't have the power to cross the seven seas (*sat samundar par*). Neither will you be able to reach *sat sumandar par*, nor will you be able to fight the demons there."

He replied, "Never mind if I reach there or not. Never mind if I cannot reach there and I cannot fight with the demons. When you fell in love and you told the secret of your father's essence, I can give my life. But I cannot go back. If I find the life of the demon in the ibis, then I will bring it, or I will die there."

"Oh, sweetheart," she said. "Then now you go for your mission." Now, alas, the prince did not have a vehicle to go from there. He hung his sword and began to move ahead along the side of the river. So he hung his sword, and he was moving like a crazy man—moving ahead along the bank of the river. In the evening, he got tired and went to sleep. And in the morning he got up and moved ahead.

While moving, when he reached the dense forest, it was noon, and he was very thirsty. He was dying of thirst. He was so hot, and he said, "Oh, I am dying. The sweat is also hurting my eyes like there are chilies in my eyes. Oh, there is a banyan tree, and its shadow is very cool. So let me lie down here so I can rest and I can sleep." He laid his cloth there and lay down to sleep. On the banyan tree, there was a nest of the male and female swans and their young ones. The female swan laid her eggs six or seven times in the tree. Every time, something went wrong with the swan's nest so that some creature began to eat their young ones or their eggs. So they couldn't raise their young ones up to adults.

The prince, he was trying to sleep. One cobra was trying to climb up the banyan tree. And the baby swans began to cry loudly. When the young ones began to cry, he thought, "Oh, some bird's young ones are in the tree." Then all of the sudden he saw that a cobra was climbing the tree, showing his hood. And the cow's hoof mark was on this hood. The prince held his sword out and cut the cobra into three pieces. After cutting the snake, he covered the snake with his shield. After performing these tasks, he slept.

Meanwhile, the male swan and female swan arrived. They found the prince sleeping there. When they found him lying there, the male swan got into a hot anger. He said, "Whatever young ones we lost, the thief is caught. Today, I caught the enemy! Today I will kill him!" He told the female swan, "You go and feed our young ones. I am going, and I will pick a stone or two or three *man* (a great weight) and will drop them on him. Two hundred and fifty to three hundred *mans* will drop on him. So I will turn his body into sauce."

The young ones saw the situation, and said, "Oh Lord, this prince is our Lord. Another father who saved us. If this prince dies, it is better that we die. Because his life is going because he saved us. It is better that we die." When the female swan tried to feed their young ones, they turned their butts toward their mother. When she went to the other side, they turned their butts again. Both did not take food. And the babies said, "Oh lord, help us speak, or take my life back." All of a sudden, the young ones began to talk. The mother swan asked, "My kid, why don't you eat?" They replied, "Oh, it is not my religion. You are doing an ugly job (literally, 'putting your tooth on pus'). He is the savior of us. My Lord is lying on the ground. Lift up that shield. This Lord has killed our enemy."

Now the male swan regretted his words. "By mistake I could have killed this man!" The young ones said, "Throw your food that you brought for us. We won't eat for today. We won't eat the food until the decision in favor of this person is taken." The female swan quickly flew toward the male swan, and from far away she shouted, "Oh, sweetheart, throw this stone away. Don't take it with you anymore. He is a well-wisher of us. Who used to hurt our eggs and kids, this enemy snake, it has already been killed. He has killed it." And the male swan felt sorry, and he threw the stone away. After throwing the stone and returning to his young ones, he told the female swan, "I can see this son, this prince, is sweating. Oh, blow some wind on him with your wings." The female swan sat down at the head side of the prince and began to flap her wings, flapping and flapping so he slept so comfortably. The male swan said, "Look, I am going to some town to get a dish of sweets, and you go where you can get water. Bring a pitcher or a bucket full of water." Both of them went on their way. He brought sweets, and she filled up a pitcher with water. She brought water from the well and thus arranged for food and water for the guest. Then the prince got up and thought to move ahead. And both those swans were busy serving him. They asked, "Who are you?" He replied that he was a foreigner. He lifted up the shield and saw the dead cobra with the great hood.

The male swan said, "You have put me in great debt." The female swan said, "I laid eggs seven times and also had young ones. And all the time this snake ate my young ones and my eggs. We got rid of this enemy today." The male swan said, "You wash your face and mouth. Take this food, and drink cold water. And clean your face and feet, and drink cold water." The friend began to eat food. When he had had his meal, then the male swan asked, "Friend, tell me why are you roaming in this dense forest where there are so many wild animals? Also your face is getting withered. You are getting so tired."

He replied, "Oh, this is my condition because of the difficult way I am going to get the essence of life of that demon. And it is across the seven seas. I feel very tired. It is hard to move. How can I reach there?" The male swan said, "Oh, don't worry. But you cannot reach there by yourself. You won't be able to cross the seven seas. You have fulfilled my necessities, and I will fulfill yours in return."

The prince was happy, and he said, "Oh, this is great news." Then the swan made the prince rest there for the night. Early in the morning, the male swan said, "Now you sit down on my back. Now we will move." The male swan began to fly fast, and they went. Mr. Swan flew fast.

In a little while they reached the border of the island of the banyan tree. The male swan was a sky flyer. When they reached their destination, the swan said, "Listen, son, there are too many guards. It will also be difficult for me to save my life here. I am going easily, but you don't get disturbed. While I am flying by, you grab the cage. Thereafter it is my responsibility. Nobody will be able to do anything to us. I'll take you away in the blink of an eye."

The swan flew through, but the prince couldn't catch the cage. The swan was flying fast, and the prince reached out with his hand quickly, but he couldn't hold the ibis. When they passed the tree, the prince became discouraged and said, "Oh, Lord, what will we do now?" "Son, I tried my best." The male swan said, "The next time I will be more careful. The next time I can stop for one minute." Then they took a turn for a long time to trick the demons and came back to the banyan tree once again, and the swan stopped flapping his wings and hovered. Meanwhile, the prince cut the branch on which the cage was hanging and grabbed it and said, "Let's go!" So the male swan brought the prince up to the banyan tree in which the ibis lived and in which there was the essence of the demon.

And then the swan asked, "Son, what will you do now?" He replied, "I have to go to such and such a place." And the swan said, "It will take a long time for you to get there. I don't know how long it will take you to reach the place, how much trouble you will have getting there. Now I will take you there to the fort of the demon." The prince said, "Okay, I am ready to go." So the swan began to fly to the fort of the demon where the daughter of the demon was. At the same place, the swan landed on the attic where she was. And the swan took out a quill with his beak and gave it to the prince. "So whenever you get in big trouble and feel that you need my help, take this quill to the fire and warm it up a little. Wherever I am, it is just like a wi-fi for me. You will find me there." The prince said, "Oh, Lord, this is also a great help." So he stayed there at the fort and began to live happily with his sweetheart.

One evening the prince said, "Let us resume the work on our plan." Day broke, and the demon went out in the forest to hunt. The prince took the ibis out of the cage, and he began to squeeze the ibis. All of the sudden the demon got a big big fever. When the demon began to move toward his home, the trees were falling down. The Earth began to shake just like an earthquake. The prince said, "Oh, daughter of the demon, now you tell me this. It seems that the Earth is swallowing this fort." She replied, "The fort is not sinking inside the Earth. My father is still twenty-five miles from here. The Earth shakes like this when my father walks. He even eats birds from the trees as he moves along the way."

By then they realized that the demon was coming. He had eaten four birds, and four were hanging on him on both sides. All of the sudden, the daughter broke one of the ibis's leg. As she broke the ibis's leg, the demon became lame. Now the demon tried to run faster. She said, "It looks like he is going to kill us." When the demon approached, she broke the ibis's other leg. When he approached even closer, she broke the ibis's right arm. And before the demon arrived at the door of the fort, the girl broke the ibis's left arm. All of a sudden, the demon fell on the ground just like a hollow pipal tree. Then the demon said to his daughter, "Dear, what did you do? I assumed you that you were a necklace to adorn my neck. You turned into a cobra to bite me. Daughter, I did not know this. Otherwise why would I have told you the essence of my time, my death?

Now I am helpless. What can I do? Now you kill me, now you make my boat of life cross to the other side. Now you do whatever you like."

She said, "Okay." She said, "Father, now you have to perform *kanyadan.* You will also be pardoned in the court of God. The demon said, "The *kanyadan* has happened, it is already done. I don't have my hands or feet. Shall I take the *kanyadan* out of my mouth?" (Audience laughs). The daughter said, "Now you make a resolution of performing *kanyadan.*" He made a resolution of *kanyadan*, and at the same time she twisted the neck of the ibis, and she killed the demon. When she twisted its neck and when the demon died, then the daughter said, "Now we can marry. Don't go anywhere. Oh, uncountable wealth is in this fort. And the fort is to live in. We can easily carry on our life."

So the prince began to live there very comfortably, living there for a few days. Then the new queen, the demon's daughter, gave birth to a beautiful son. When the son cried, pearls fell. They got such a son. And this queen had all the golden golden hair. They lived there happily.

One day the prince went for a hunt in the forest. The queen came out of the fort, sat down on a stone at the bank of the river, opened her hair, and began to take a bath. After taking a bath, as she combed her hair, so many broken hairs came out in the comb, and she took it in her hand. She thought, "Oh, this is my golden hair. If I throw them, it will turn them to dust. If I make a leaf bowl and put these hairs in that and put it in the river, if any poor person gets it, it will be helpful for them." So she floated the bowl with the golden hair in the river. The bowl kept moving ahead slowly slowly. It took a long time.

On the way there was a town at the bank of the river. Girls have girlfriends, boys have boyfriends. So the boys of the village decided to play a game in the water called "red bahu." The boys decided to swim and take a bath in the water. So they were taking a bath, and they wondered, "What is in that leaf bowl?" Oh, here is also a son of a king who is playing with these boys in the water. The son of the king was a bloody one-eyed boy. His one eye was just shining just like Venus. Well, he told his friends, "Go and get this leaf bowl from the water." The boys swam and brought the leaf bowl to the one-eyed prince. The prince saw the ball and the golden hair, and the broken golden hair was very long. Then they began to think, did this hair belong to some boy or some girl? The prince's friends said, "You are the son of a king. Now you test them. See them. Check them if these are hairs of a man or a woman."

"These look like a woman's hair," the boys said. The one-eyed prince thought, "My wife must be like this—the same one." The friends said, "Your eye is shining just like Venus, you are closing your one market." (Umesh can't stop laughing.) "And you want to marry such kind of beautiful girl! How can you do it?" Oh, the one-eyed prince said, "The one eye won't work there (in her pussy)."

So the one-eyed prince came into his own palace of sorrows and disappointment. And he lay down there. The queen sent a message to the king that your son is lying in the palace of sorrow and disappointment. The king thinks, "Oh, you are already one-eyed. Give me a break! What more trouble have you gotten into? What kind of person are you?" Then the king thought, "Okay, never mind. He is my son. Let me go to see him." The king arrived and said to his son, "Come, get up and have your food. If somebody has used their hand to insult you, I will have his hand cut off. If somebody has moved his tongue, I will have his tongue cut out. If somebody has winked his eye, I will have his eye poked out. If the wall has hit your head, I will have the fort torn down."

The one-eyed prince said, "Oh, nothing like that, Father. Hold this leaf bowl." When the king saw the golden hair, the prince said, "I would like to marry this girl." The king thought, "Oh! Such a kind of girl won't permit him to polish her shoes. This one is one-eyed, and the girl is made of gold." The king said, "Son, how will this dal and rice get mixed? How can you marry her?" The prince said, "Oh, Father, if it does not happen, I will surrender my life." The king thought, "Never mind that my son is one eyed. At least I have a son who will sit on the throne. At least he will carry my name onward." He said, "Never mind. Wait. I will try."

Then the king called four female secret agents that lived in his palace. He asked the first woman, "What can you do? In what are you a specialist?" She said, "I can slice a cloud." He shouted, "Hey, no! You have come here. Have I called you to slice some cloud?" He asked the second one, "What can you do?" She said, "If she will slice the cloud, I can patch it." And the king said, "Neither will the cloud be sliced, nor will you patch it. You just go." The king asked the third one, "In what are you a specialist?" She said, "I can separate people who are very close." And the king said, "Aah, I am not asking you to separate people. I am asking for some different job. You are worthless!" He questioned the fourth one, and the fourth one said, "My job is to put those people that are separate together. Never mind how big enemies they are. I can put them together so they can have a meal together." The king said, "That's good. You are the only one that is suitable for my job." And the king handed those golden hairs to the fourth secret agent. "I don't know where they came from, but these were at the bank of the river." The fourth secret agent asked the king to grant her one year and for four young boys to help and a harmonium. "Grant me a drum player, and I will take all these people for one year because I won't come back until I find her. If the time will be up, there will be expenses for food and living."

The king had a small boat made and handed it over to her. And he filled up the boat with whatever things she asked for and gave her the four boys she asked for. One of the four boys could sail the boat. And three were extra. The king said, "Now you go." The agent brought her box with her things and got ready.

The ship moved day and night, and when they felt sleepy, they slept, and when the day came, they saw everything. They kept going continuously for two months, and they reached the fort. When they saw the fort, she thought that it could be that the magic of the golden hair was to be found there. She stopped her boat a little bit away from the fort. And then she took her quilt and some dried fruit, and oranges and apples, some sweet fruits. Carrying many fruits, she reached the gate of the fort. There was a maid of the queen. The secret agent told the maid, "Tell your queen that the mother's sister of your husband has arrived." The maid servant told the queen that such and such and that a lady is standing at the door, and she had a lot of luggage with her, and she looked like a dignified person. "But she said that 'I am the aunt of your husband.'" The queen said, "How can I believe this? My husband never told me this. He kept telling me about his family, parents, everyone, but he never told me about this aunt. He also told me about the condition of the village and the condition of his friends. He never told me about this aunt. How did she get here?" She replied, "Oh, you should know that." The maid replied, "I have also not eaten her *chatti* (talking, joking), so how can I know it? If she is yours, I will call her. Otherwise, I will refuse." The queen said, "If she has come from so far, maybe she is younger, and my husband doesn't know her. So go and bring her here." As the maidservant reached the woman, she unloaded everything and put everything down.

The queen thought that, "This aunt to my husband, she is also a mother-in-law of mine." The queen touched the feet of the aunt, and the aunt offered five golden coins to the queen. When she offered her five golden coins, the queen thought, "If she is not the aunt, why has she given golden coins? She could have given a few rupees."

So the aunt rested there. The queen told her husband that in such and such a way your aunt has arrived. The prince said, "I haven't seen her ever. If she is my aunt, she must be my aunt. But never mind. There is plenty of food for her." So the secret agent lived there very nicely, and the son of that couple was so beautiful, as his tear came, it turned into pearls. When he smiled, flowers fell out.

The agent felt regret. "Oh, what am I going to do here? How handsome is this husband, and how beautiful is this child. And how is the wife? All are so beautiful, so nice. And this bloody one-eyed prince wants her. How will they live without the queen?"

Then, she thought, "I shouldn't be thinking this. Do I have to see to my well-being or to their well-being? I don't have to worry about them. My job is to kill." Now the agent relaxed, and she ate. Oh, happily she lay down. She orders work for the queen to do.

One day the secret agent lady began to ask the prince, "You always have your five-kilo sword hanging on your shoulder. It is so rusty. Hang the sword on the peg, otherwise you will get tetanus." He replied, "Aunt, I wouldn't do it. While I am sleeping, it is always with me because as this sword does not hang from my shoulder—will be away from me—I will die."

Then the queen said, "Aunt, you can talk about anything, but do not talk about this sword because this sword is a boon for him." She thought in her mind, "I'll see this boon of a sword one day. Someday it will come into my possession." The agent, she ate food, she swept the house, and she told the queen, "You play with the son." And she took an axe and began to cut the thorny thorny bush and fill the moat with the thorny branches. When she filled up the moat in three or four months with the thorny bush, then once again she tried to trick the prince and said to the prince, "At least you could take off this sword at least once. Your shoulder is just like that of a male buffalo. At least for one day hang this sword." The aunt says, "I am so worried, I can't sleep all the night." She kept saying this over and again, "Just hang it on the peg and see if you are comfortable or not."

And the queen said, "This aunt keeps saying this every day. Please do it at least once." And he hung his sword on the peg, and the prince took another sword and went in the forest.

What did this agent do? She swept and completed her duty and said to the queen, "Have this meal, and I shall also eat." And after finishing her meal, she told the queen, "Have the child play, and I am going to sit out in the air." All of the sudden, the agent took the sword off the peg, and quickly she went where she had piled the thorny bushes and pushed the sword inside there. And soon she set those dry bushes alight. The fire burned, and the heavy wood burned, and the boy was caught by the fever. The sword melted. And the prince arrived at the fort and died. The queen began to cry. The secret agent also shed crocodile tears. The agent said, "Daughter, don't cry. If the head will remain, so much hair will grow up again. You are not old yet. You will remain. You will get so many men, so many husbands." Then the agent said, "Either cremate him or slip his body into the river." The prince had already told his wife, "If I am deceived somehow and I die, neither cremate my body nor slip my body in the river. Just bury my body very deep in this room."

Then the agent said, "Either bury the body or slip it in the river." The queen said, "Neither will I slip this body in the water, nor will I cremate him. I will bury this body in this room. I will remain seated on it and pass my life because I am wingless. My child is small. Until my son grows up, until then I will not leave this place." The agent said, "Dear, the prince is not here anymore. Now you come with me and stay for a few days with me, and then we will come back here for a few days."

The queen said, "Mother, I will not leave this place. I will not go anywhere." Then the agent said, "Never mind, it is all right. Let's go and take a bath in the river. Let's take the son with us. You take a bath. I will remain standing. Thereafter I will take a bath." So the agent went with the queen to take a bath in the river. There was a boat there. The agent said, "This looks nice, so we will go inside and then take a bath there." The agent took a bucket to take a bath. As they climbed into the boat, she also put the bucket there with the soap. The queen took the bucket, and as she sat down to take a bath, the agent pushed a lever so that the boat was just covered from all sides.

The prince remained buried there, and the queen was locked inside the boat. And the agent moved from there with the queen and her son. When she moved and passed the way, the agent brought the queen and her son to the palace. The agent brought her and presented her in the court of the king and said, "Take this. This is the golden-bodied girl." The one-eyed prince said, "Perform my marriage." The queen said, "The lady is like the vine of the *lauki* and the *torai* (two squashes). When it grows, it needs space. If it does not get space, it grows on other things." The queen said, "I must get married because I cannot live alone like this. But I was told of one year of fast. When my fast will be fulfilled in a year, thereafter I shall marry you." The one-eyed prince said, "Never mind. Don't get married for four years. Now you came to my home. Where will you go now? Where will you go? The wedding will take place." The queen said, "Have a separate house built for me so we will live together in that house." And the house was built, and the top room of the house was a well-carved attic. And the queen was assigned four soldiers so she wouldn't get down out of the house. There were four soldiers in the morning and four in the evening. There were eight soldiers to guard her, and the queen was living in the carved attic with her son.

When one year passed, then it will be seen. Well, whatever time is passing is passing.

On the other hand, the prince had had those three friends. They were continuously making a search for this prince. "I am still finding the footprints of our friend," said one. "We will find him." They were coming, searching for him, and on the other side this queen was looking around from the roof at the carved attic, having her son in her arms. These three fellows were passing through and saw the girl. One of them was *chaudri*. He shouted, "Look at that woman who is holding that child. That is our friend's son." One of them swore to him, "We don't know where our friend has gone or if he has died. You are telling that this girl who is holding the boy, he is the son of our friend?"

Oh, look. When an *ahir* talks, he talks loud. One of them said, "Shut up, you stupid idiot. Somebody will beat you up so badly that they won't leave a single hair on your head.

Your friend has died somewhere, and you are saying that this is our friend's son." The other friend said, "I promise you. This is the son of our friend. I am telling you the truth. If I fail to find our friend, you can chop off my head."

The queen heard this talk that the son belongs to his friend. She called for a soldier and ordered him to arrest all those three and bring them to her. The soldier went to the three friends and said, "The queen wants to see you." One of the friends said, "I have already told you, you have died before your time. You are searching for someone else. Now we are being searched by other people. What will we do now?" The friend said, "Let us go there. If this is our fate, it will be seen. If this is our fate, then we cannot be saved. We are now in the hands of the soldier." As he brought these three friends to the queen, she set out three chairs for them and ordered the soldier, "Go attend to your duty. What are you doing here? (What right does the servant have to stay when the master is ordering?)" Those soldiers left the queen. Then the queen questioned the three friends. "What did you say when you were on the road? That this son belongs to your friend? How can it be?" One of the friends replied, "Whatever I said at that time, I am saying the same thing now. That this boy belongs to my friend."

And the queen said, "Now you, you explain all this to me."

"We four friends left our house together. Due to the storm and rain, we got separated. One got blown to one side, and three went to the other side. So we got separated. A hundred years has passed in search of our friend the prince. And today we found out about him."

Then the queen replied, "For sure he was your friend. Whatever he used to tell me, I am seeing it now. I see these are three." Then she said, "How can I get out of this place? Tell me the way. Tell me how can we get together and be free." Then the friend who was a pundit said to the carpenter boy, "This is your turn now." Two people have already displayed their talents. So one of them said to the queen, "You ask your king to arrange some wooden boards, hammer and chisel, and some thin strips of metal. Get me all these things and lock me in a room, and don't tell anybody. Within the twelve hours of the night, I will make such a *pushpak viman* (airplane). Push the lever, and you see England!"

The queen sent a servant, saying, "Tell my father-in-law to get ready for my wedding. Also make a good bed and grant some very good wood, and also arrange for ghee." The king and his son were happy that now the queen was ready to be married. One year had passed. The king quickly had very good wooden boards brought to the queen, and those boards were given to the carpenter, who was locked in a room. "You three or four people remain outside with the son and lock the room."

The carpenter was busy making the airplane. He kept working all night, and he completely made it by eight o'clock in the morning. And the carpenter said, "Unlock me now and let me out." And he was released, and he showed them "This is the plane." And he took the plane outside and said, "Why are you folks delaying now? Let's go!"

The queen said, "Such kind of bad behavior has been committed against me. I want to punish them. Help me to take action against them."

The friends said, "We will help you with that. Please do not leave this secret agent behind. We will take her with us. Also, we will take the one-eyed prince." The queen agreed. "Also, put this one-eyed prince in this plane, make him enjoy the air. He has given me a lot of trouble." They replied, "All right, the queen is going to enjoy the air, so why don't we join her?"

So the one-eyed prince was blinking his eye just like Venus. He was already ready to go because she was his wife. "It is important for me to be with her," he said. So they all three also sat down. The queen sat down and the one-eyed prince sat down in the plane. So the son of the carpenter pushed the lever, and the plane flew "Quick! Fast!" When they went up one hundred *yogan*, then the carpenter's son said to the *ahir*, "Is he the *damad* of ours (daughter's husband)? Either he is the *damad* of ours or the *saru* (wife's sister husband). Throw this bloody guy out of the plane." The one-eyed prince was thrown down, and he died. "Ram naam satya ho gayee. Rest in peace." One of them said, "Oh, now serve *mausi*, the secret agent, very well." "She helped a lot," she said. "My husband wouldn't have died. She killed him."

First her bun was cut off. Then her neck was half cut. The queen said, "Now I shall throw her." And she was thrown out, and she also died. "So now we can go without worry," she said. "Now where should we go—home?"

"No," they replied. "We have to find our friend first." After killing these two, they eventually landed. When they came out of the plane, they asked the queen, "Where is the dead body?" She unlocked the room.

All together they dug out the soil from the top of the body and took out the body from the grave, and they put his mortal remains in a basket and took it out of the room.

The punditji said, "Bring the basket to the bank of the river." Panditji washed all the bones in the river and dried them with a cloth and placed the bones according to the shape of a body. They placed the skull where it should be. Panditji cut his finger and let his blood drip on the skeleton. And he let one drop of his blood fall on the skull. And the body took shape.

And he became alive! He got up and said, "Oh, today I slept a lot." The panditji said, "We know that you were sleeping, or the Lord knows." Thereafter, they got ready to go to the king. Now the son, the queen, and all those four guys altogether became six. Now these people came to the king. The king said, "Oh, my servant has returned after a long time. He must have brought the gem." He asked about the gem, but the prince had the gem. The prince said, "These are the gems, so now you choose out of these." So the king thought, "Now I can get all of these gems." The king's wife took one gem and fixed it on her nose ring. The wife of the betel seller had one gem, and now the king's wife had one. The king said to the prince, "The betel seller's wife has one. At least give two to my wife because she is my wife." The prince gave the king another gem. When two gems were fit on the nose of this queen, then the king asked his subjects, "How beautiful are we?" Somebody said, "It does not look good." The king asked, "How can it be fixed?"

"The person who brought the gems, your daughter has to marry him," they said. "Then it will be holy. Otherwise the beauty is useless. This prince is priceless. We have not seen such a person." The queen said to the king, "He is a servant, but he is not like a servant. We have to marry our daughter to him." The prince said, "When we are equal, then we will go."

All four guys got married. And they got a lot of wealth from the king. He brought the mine of the gems with him.

So all four friends returned to their homes after twenty years. They all took their queens. So the prince became the king, and his wives became queens. And his friends went to their homes with their wives.

*Postlude*

*And the storyteller says, "And I returned to my home. What else could I do there? There was nothing for me there."*

EIGHTY-THREE

# UMESH ARRANGES FOR THE SWAN'S QUILL

"SO, UMESH, WHAT DO YOU THINK OF THIS STORY FROM YOUR OWN village?" I asked.

He replied, "The story is not really finished because the quill of the swan was forgotten. I can fix this. So, suppose from the very beginning there was one princess of the king and the queen who wanted the gem for her nose ring. Her daughter already had fallen in love with this prince. They had agreed to marry. Then he left in search of the gems at the bank of the river. Now he had already reached the fort from which the gems were coming drip by drip from the blood. So, the messenger lady, the secret agent, who was sent by the father of the one-eyed prince, when she arrived there, the girl, daughter of the demon, and the prince were living together. This secret agent kept forcing the prince with tricks—to force him to take off his sword and hang it someplace. Eventually he agreed when the daughter of the demons persuaded him to get relaxed and hang the sword on the peg. While he hung his sword on the peg, he also pushed the quill between, in the gap between the two stones of the fort walls. When his friends arrived there where his dead body was found and he came to life, he went to search for the quill, and he found it there. And this prince kept the quill safe. After killing the messenger and the one-eyed prince by throwing them on the ground, they reached back to the king whose queen wanted the gem for herself. This king became very greedy, and he wanted all the gems.

"So the prince said, 'You can have all those gems, but I want your daughter to marry.' The king got furious and ordered the prince to be hung to death, just here in his court. And he was asked if he had a last wish. The prince asked to smoke the hookah. And he was permitted. As the hookah was given to him to smoke, he checked the fire and just began to smoke. As the fire grew, he took out the quill and put it on the fire, and it began to smoke. And the quill got warm. All of a sudden, the husband and wife swans arrived there and flew hard around and around the palace, just like a dust storm came. They flapped so hard with their giant wings that a heavy dust storm came. Everybody just ran hither and thither. The four guys and the princess of the king, along with prince and the daughter of the demon and three more princesses of this king, sat down in the *puspak viman* and flew from there to their kingdom. Three of the friends married the three princesses, and our hero got two wives. So they became kings and queens. And all these people lived happily ever after."

EIGHTY-FOUR

# THE RELIGION OF HUMANITY

"FOR ME, GEMS ARE NOT SIMPLE," UMESH SAID. "THEY ARE VERY VALUable—they are jewels. People cannot get these valuable things working hard in their fields or doing physical work. People flow their sweat and blood by working hard, and other people collect this flow from their bodies, and other people collect from them their earnings for one rich man or a king. And that rich man is able to buy by spending a lot of money. This is also the sense of it. Gems don't come easily. They come out of the blood. This is the message. As we read and hear about Mr. Donald J. Trump, he can have these things. We read newspapers, we hear from other people he is very very rich. This is not one person's hard work. This is the hard work of hundreds of other poor people.

"By believing the religion of humanity, humanity can bring the equality. And great teachings just like we have in the Bible, also in the Qu'ran, also in the Vedas, the teachings of Lord Buddha all together, the religion of humanity has to be made of all the good things for humanity. The question is how to bring equality. The only thing is that until satisfaction appears in a person, he keeps busy accumulating wealth. And until the deep teaching of satisfaction, through religion, through the words, through the books, only these can be helpful, I believe. Because so many poets and writers have also given their thoughts. Even religious books have a great role for how people can live comfortably. Each man and woman, child or old person deserves care, disabled or able-bodied deserve care, freedom, food, clean water, clean air, shelter, *roti, kapra, and makan*, bread, clothes, and home, medical care, and a clean atmosphere. There must also be teaching to help the poor. Not to hurt old people. Not to hurt disabled people, to help them to work as able-bodied people do. We must worship nature and respect nature.

"We must know the problems people have so we can name them. As in the story, we met the one-eyed prince. This is kind of disgusting. But in India, some people like this fun and laugh at it. That is why the storyteller is saying it. Actually, people must not laugh at the one-eyed man. Such kind of sentences and thoughts must not be raised up in writing or in talking. People don't actually hate blind people, but we call them Surdass. 'Oh, come on, Surdassji.' There is no disgrace for them. Sometimes people make fun of the lame people. Also bald people.

"Actually people begin to think of a topic. For example, how can we keep our atmosphere clean? People get suggestions from other people. Then it becomes easier to understand the essence of the truth. It can also be called *research*. We think and think. One idea comes. For this idea, people read books of top people, of different kinds of people. And then they put these ideas together, and they give their own thoughts to it to make a powerful conclusion. It is easier to determine the result of it. I always have a big concern for nature because nature gives us life—she makes us survive. We cannot live without nature. If plants lose their life, any other creature will not survive on the Earth.

"If the entire world will accept the religion of humanity, there won't be any problem. This is how I believe. So we can have a fair world for all."

## EIGHTY-FIVE

# STORYTIME

"THIS IS THE DIFFERENCE BETWEEN ME AND YOU," UMESH SAID. "OF fairness. I believe in fairness. Life must go smooth. It must finish with a smooth feeling. Never mind whether it is good or bad, it must finish with a happy ending. Life or story. But this is not possible.

"In the Trollope, my feelings go to Lizzie. On the other hand, my feelings go to Motini. Because she took actions to help, having promised to remain forever with Nal. Even though she loved him the most, Nal agreed to remarry, and Motini gave him three more chances to live, even after her death. And in the story she did.

"On the other hand, Lizzie is playing the human nature. Easily you can find anywhere that greed makes people fools—for self-satisfaction. And finally she gets out of trouble, and she falls in the wrong hands at the last, trusting this clergyman. I am interested in the happiness of the lady.

"Don't ask why," Umesh said. "You are one of them.

"I hate this word 'clergyman' now because he betrayed my heroine. So the character of Lizzie shows to keep working hard at whatever you are doing. Success will follow. But people reap what they sow."

"So Ram Surup has died," I said. "What did he take with him?"

"Well, fame," Umesh said. "All the people in my village liked him, especially his singing. I heard him since I was in eighth grade. His voice was just like a *papiha*, a very small bird that sings so well."

"And who sings the *Dhola* now in your village?"

"No one is left. People are listening to his cassettes, but there is no charm. Charm came when so many people came into the village, and people knew it, and they assembled at one place where the *Dhola* was going to take place. One man played a lady's role, Motini, and one man Nal. Ram Sarup himself played the role of Nal. And the harmonium, *nagara*, and drum, these instruments were used for the music. Ram Sarup played his role, and other artists played the other roles. *Dhola* was sung by one person. So this was a one-person thing in the very beginning. It was Ram Sarup who gave a form of drama in my area, not just in my village. He sang in Etah, Mainpuri, Farukhabad, Etwah. I know these places. And he performed in competitions in so many places, and he claimed that he had won the competitions."

"But he was from Karimganj?"

"Originally his parents were from Karimganj. Later they moved to his mother's home in district Etah. Then they came back to Karimganj. The family is in Karimganj now. They are water-pulling people, *kahar.*

"Singers don't have a caste," Umesh said. "Musicians and singers don't have caste. It is deep inside them. Already the Lord filled them with music.

"I do miss him. He was always enthusiastic for singing. In his old age, he said, 'I am still young for singing.'

"Everyone likes music, but to get involved in singing and playing music is God gifted, it is already there. Nobody can neither destroy it or force it from the musician. It can't be done."

"And what about our heroine, Gangajali?"

"In the beginning, she did not know that her singing, collecting was important. I believe for her it was just a joke. She was also full of fear coming to the hotel. She brought another lady with her, Sashi, to get support. Within two days of her arrival for singing, she understood the meaning of this song collection, what we wanted, and she felt free sitting among one Western lady and some man from western Uttar Pradesh who she never met before. Within two days she was comfortable all of the sudden, seeing our behavior toward her. Singers sing for themselves but only not for their self, for the audience, to make people happy by their art. They get pleasure by being appreciated and making other people happy through their art. When she learned that we were not here just joking, she became serious, and suddenly Gangajali realized Sashi was an extra person, that she was annoying and interrupting and she did not have enough time for this job. She had to take care of her family and other jobs at home. So for Gangajali it was difficult for her to stay a long time with us. So the next time we returned to her in 1990, Gangajali came alone.

"She was so sweet. Very sweet, very gentle, very cooperative. What she said, she did. She kept her words. Trustworthy. And poor. I was hoping she could buy something big for her house with the money we offered her. When we were about to part, you said, 'Oh, we didn't sing *sohar*, *kajari*, *biraha*, and so many others.' So she came back to us the next day for one last opportunity to say goodbye. Actually, this just extended the pain for everybody. So we are missing her.

"We have put so many stories in this book. I believe this story begins before humans existed," Umesh said. "For example, now we read stories about the dinosaurs and different species that do not even exist now. A story itself has so many faces. It comes from the history. We make stories out of the past—history—it comes from the imagination. It comes from the current feelings as the songs come. Some people who cannot compose, they write their feelings. There are two types: write a text or write poetry. Sometimes we feel it is poetry.

"To me stories are just like music. They take time to read, as music takes time to listen. Both involve the consumption of time. Either you write it, compose it, sing it, read it, or play it, it is a consumption of time.

"Time is also of feeling. Feelings do not come out of thinking. Feelings grow. So similarly for art, for the painter it consumed time to make it. He takes it deep in his heart to paint something. It does not come by itself. And then he thinks, thinks how to draw it beautiful. The same is true of sculpture. Everything is. Art is art. All these things take energy, thoughts, feelings, creativity, and inspiration.

"Inspiration comes from deep in the heart and mind. And those people are already born for the job in the mind and the structure of the body to be great. It is already cultivated from the womb, I believe. Some people force themselves to do these jobs. They can be artists, musicians, composers, singers. But they are not the same as those who come from the womb. Art begins when the body is constructed in the womb.

"There are so many people who run to win the race. Several are faster, several are slower, but only one or two come on the top because physically and mentally they are born that way. Similarly, one person can listen once and memorize it, and some people can hear five or six times and they can memorize it, and some people can hear hundreds of times and they just can't memorize it. Lizzie was very quick to memorize poetry. She could do it in one reading. God had given her this art to be a winner in life. One the other hand, some people are born very enthusiastic, some are dull. Some people are born with negative thoughts, some with positive thoughts. All this occurs over the painters, sculptors, musicians, singers, and writers.

"Trollope was so full of imagination, but he did not have a real time to write because he was working for the post office. So, whatever he wrote, it appeals to people, it is great, but in the same age other writers were considered the greatest ones. Why was he not considered the best? While he was working in the post office, he was just thinking in his mind how to write a story. He could do two works at a time. And when he got the chance, he just took it down. He was a genius.

"When Trollope describes a person, he may mention the most tiny flaw that completely ruins the beauty he is describing. For example, Trollope said, 'Lizzy found Mr. Emilius's hooked nose very handsome.' In India, we call this parrot beak. Nobody likes it. People say jokingly, 'Parrot arrived, parrot arrived.' Trollope does this with each description of his characters with the single exception of Lucy Morris. Although he describes her as plain, we come to find her beautiful.

"He is writing three chapters a month for publication in magazines. It is a great pressure. But he had this gift of storytelling, laced with comedy. Trollope comes like Sashi in this book. It interrupts the main story of Gangajali. Even Gangajali got annoyed for this interruption. But Sashi had some great ideas, and she pushed the Gangajali story farther. So does Trollope. He too pushes the Gangajali story farther.

"What we are writing about here is not just about singing. It is not just about wedding songs in eastern Uttar Pradesh. We have woven a tapestry of stories to delight the reader and to remind the reader that all art is one, and it comes from the blessing of the Lord. Ram Surup is together with Gangajali, who is together with Trollope. All of them were with us in our apartment in Banaras in 2007. And they remain with us today."

If we shadows have offended,<br>
Think but this, and all is mended,<br>
That you have but slumber'd here<br>
While these visions did appear.<br>
And this weak and idle theme,<br>
No more yielding but a dream.<br>
—William Shakespeare<br>
*A Midsummer's Dream*, "Epilogue"

"This is it. *You* are the real dream that comes and goes. You *are* the dream."

—Umesh, March 29, 2017, 10:00 a.m., New Delhi

APPENDIX

# RITUALS OF THE HINDU WEDDING IN BALLIA

*Before the wedding day*

Tilak—The engagement ceremony. The bride's family men (but not the bride) visit the bridegroom's home bringing fruit, sweets, dried fruits, clothes, pots and pans, and a ring. The bridegroom's family serves them snacks. A small ritual is performed.

Sagun—Ceremony performed separately at the bride's and bridegroom's homes when women beg the augur to bring good omens. Often followed by five songs to Shiva.

Matikor—Procession of women to dig the clean soil, especially near a pond or river. The soil is used later to make a miniature oven and is placed under the wedding tent. During the digging, there is much merriment, joking, singing, and many beautiful dances.

Kalas and Harish—The kalas is a clay pitcher symbolizing the womb. It is decorated by family women. The harish is a plow shaft and fertility symbol. They both are placed in the center of the wedding tent.

Haldi Lagana—Applying turmeric paste in separate ceremonies to both the bride and bridegroom. It makes the skin shine and is also considered auspicious. This ritual, performed by girls or women, is carried out several times a day before the wedding.

Chumawan—Literally, "kissing." This small ritual is performed after the haldi ritual, several times a day. Women or girls take a pinch of rice and touch it to the feet, knees, shoulders, and head of the bride or bridegroom.

Kohabar—The bride or bridegroom is led into the sacred wedding chamber after chumawan.

Lori and Sil—The stone and grinder. Dal is ground with these by the mother and father of the bride or bridegroom together, covered with a sheet.

Trapping the gods and ancestors—In both homes, songs inviting all the gods and ancestors to the wedding so they will not feel insulted. "The rain, big ants, small ants, scorpions, snakes, winnowing baskets, strainers, mortar and pestle, big pans, fire. Now I am going to trap all these forces so that they don't interrupt the wedding."

Siri—Clay pot. A procession of women goes to the potter's home to collect this, singing sahana, jhumar, and gali along the way. Balbhaddar (a small man) and a small ladder are inside the siri. The siri is placed in the kohabar.

*Day of the wedding*

Nacchu nahawan—Ritual bathing of the bridegroom on the morning of the wedding.

Parichhawan—Blessing the bridegroom with mustard and caraway seeds that are then thrown into the fire. This ritual protects the bridegroom from the evil eye.

Bridegroom puts on his clothes.

Barber cuts bridegroom's nails.

Imali—The bride and bridegroom separately are given five leaves and must bite the ends off and spit them into the mother's hand.

Parichhawan—As above.

Barat—The "army" of the groomsmen proceed to the bride's home with many lights, firecrackers, and loud amplified music.

Jaluaa—After the barat leaves, at the bridegroom's home family women sing songs, play jokes, and act out silly dramas about marriage and childbirth.

Arrival of the barat—The groomsmen reach the bride's home and continue wild dancing, gunshots, loud amplified music, and fireworks.

Parichhawan—The mother of the bride blesses the bridegroom.

Nacchu Nahawan—Bride receives a clay pot containing bath water from the groom's bath. She bathes in this.

Parichhawan—Performed again to protect the bride from the evil eye.

Dwar puja—The bridegroom and his father are greeted at the gate by the bride's parents. A ritual is performed.

Gurahatthi—Bride is led to the altar and seated there. The groom's family offers clothes and ornaments. Gali are sung.

Worship of Gauri-Ganesh—The priest leads the couple in the worship of Gaura and her son Ganesh.

Daria—The bride's brother pours water into the cupped hands of the priest, the bride, and the groom. The stream of water must not break, or he will lose his sister. But the stream always breaks.

Kanyadan—Donation of the virgin bride as the universe trembles with the eclipse.

Lawa—Puffed rice from the bride's side is mixed with puffed rice from the bridegroom's side.

Bhamar—The bride and bridegroom walk around the fire seven times.

Sindur—The bridegroom places vermillion in the part of the bride's hair.
Chumawan—Literally, "kissing." Women or girls take a pinch of rice and touch it to the feet, knees, shoulders, and head of the bride or bridegroom.
Kohabar—The bride and bridegroom are led into the sacred wedding chamber after chumawan.
Gauna—Departure of the bride with the bridegroom for her sasural, his natal home.

*Next morning*

Kakkan—These are untied at the bank of a river.

# GLOSSARY

This glossary is intended to offer the English-speaking reader some idea of how the Hindi and Bhojpuri words included herein actually sound to an American ear. Every attempt has been made to follow the spoken or sung word as it was pronounced. Many of these words have been taken directly from sung texts and hence may be affected by the melody and rhythm of the music. For those who are particularly interested in the vast literature on the linguistic areas of eastern India, kindly consult G. A. Grierson, *Linguistic Survey of India*, Calcutta, 1928. Numerous more recent studies also abound.

*achhat (achchhat)* rice
*Agni* god of fire
*Ahilya* the wife of a rishi who was turned into stone and then saved by Ram
*akashvani* "sky sound," broadcast
*almyra* large closet
*anchal* end part of the sari to cover the breast and protect the baby
*angocha* men's cotton scarf, a very useful item
*antara* melody at a higher pitch
*arti* offering of light to the gods
*Aruyavedic* said in fun; "real good food"
*Ayodhya* kingdom of Lord Ram
*Badrinath* Lord Badrinath; also a place in the Himalayas
*bahnuiya* brother-in-law
*bahu* new wife
*bahut accha (achchha)* very good
*Baijuudhaam* religious site
*baithaki* devotional song genre
*baithaki (baitke)* women sitting to sing songs
*Baleshwarji* holy man of Ballia
*Baleshwarnath* rishi who resides in Ballia
*Baliram* older brother of Krishna
*banda-bandi* bridegroom and bride

***banigi*** bad
***Banshidhar*** Krishna, who plays the flute
***barat*** the bridegroom's army
***barati*** people of the barat
***barauna*** clay pot
***barhar*** wedding feast
***barmala*** in the wedding, exchange of flower garlands
***Basudev*** birth father of Krishna
***belan*** rolling pin
***beti*** daughter
***bhabi*** sister-in-law
***Bhadon*** month around July–August
***bhai*** brother
***Bhairowanath*** rishi, devotee to Kali; Ballia, where he resides, was named after this holy man
***Bhairug Baba*** baba who resides in Ballia
***bhajan*** Hindu hymn
***bhamar*** in the wedding, taking turns around the havan fire
***bharuaa*** pimp
***bhasur (bhashhur)*** brother-in-law
***bhauji*** sister-in-law
***Bholanathji*** Lord Shiva, easy to please
***Bhraguji*** Father of Ram
***bichhuaa*** toe ring for woman
***bindi*** beauty spot for the forehead
***biraha*** sung stories
***birny*** flesh
***Brahma*** the Lord, especially as creator
***brahman*** high caste
***Brahmaniji*** the wife of Lord Brahma
***bua*** aunt
***bugwa*** barley and rice mixture
***byah ke git*** wedding song
***chacha*** uncle
***chaddar (chadar)*** white veil or sheet
***chaiti*** song for the month of Chait, around March
***chakala*** wooden cutting board
***chaki*** small wooden stool
***chamain*** midwife
***chamar*** leatherworking caste
***chapatti*** thin wheat pancake

*charaw* clothing and ornaments brought by the groom
*chat* snacks
*chatti* celebration for the birth of a son
*chauk* altar
*chauki* wooden cot
*chausar* a game like chess
*chautal* Holi springtime songs
*chautara* platform
*chauthari* brother with gifts bringing his sister home
*chauti (chauthi)* fourth month, as in pregnancy
*chhayabaad* song with hidden meaning
*chhoti* small
*chin (mara)* round yellow rice
*choti* lock of hair on the back of the head
*chulha* clay oven
*chumawan* blessings to the bride or bridegroom
*churi* bangles
*dadi* grandmother
*dahej* dowry
*dahi* yogurt
*dal* bridegroom's army; olden word for king's army
*dal* lentils
*damad* son-in-law
*damaw (danav)* cannibal
*Damiantii (Damayanti)* second wife of Nal in the *Dhola* epic
*dani* a nice person
*dantal* long iron stick idiophone, in Fiji and Trinidad
*dapla* single-headed frame drum played with two sticks
*Dardar Muni* rishi; brother to Bhaironath and Bhairug Baba; Dardar Muni resides in Ballia
*darshan* holy vision
*darwaja* in the wedding, worship at the door
*Dashrath* Ram's father
*dehati jhumar* village dancing songs
*devi darshan* vision of the mother goddess
*devi git* goddess songs
*Deviki* birth mother of Krishna
*dewar* husband's younger brother
*dhapali (daple)* single-headed frame drum played with the fingers
*dharma* the Hindu religion, religious duty
*Dhola* sung epic of North India

*dholak* double-headed barrel drum
*dholki* small dholak
*dhoti* Indian-style trousers
*diljaniyan* "heart lady," loving lady
*dipchandi tal* rhythmic cycle of 14 beats
*diya* tiny earthenware lamp
*dub* a very useful kind of grass
*Dwarikanath* Krishna, who resides in Dwarika near Gujarat
*feri* during the wedding, taking turns around the havan fire
*gagara* large pot
*gali* funny songs of abuse
*gamchha* men's long cotton scarf
*garariya* caste of shepherds
*gari* same as gali
*gauna* final departure of the bride from her parents' home
*gaunra* gifts, goods given by the bridegroom's side to the bride's side
*Gaura* Lord Shiv's wife
*ghanta* time
*ghanti* bells
*ghat* steps down to the river, especially in Banaras
*ghee* clarified butter
*ghora* horse
*Girdhari* Krishna, who lifts the mountain on his pinky
*Girmit* contract
*Girmitiyas* Indian indentured laborers
*godna* tattoo
*Gokul* town where Krishna was raised
*Gopal* Krishna
*gopi* milkmaid, especially of Lord Krishna
*Gopinath* Krishna, who is the lord of the gopis
*Gorakhnath* rishi who resides in Gorakhpur
*gota* border of a sari or skirt
*Govindala* Krishna, when he is born
*gulguliya* simple, sweet bird
*gur* raw sugar
*gurahatthi* Ballia wedding ritual
*gwalas* cowherds
*Haisati* sister of Bhaironath
*haldi* turmeric
*halua* sweet pudding
*Hanumanji* the monkey god

*Haridar* the gateway to the Lord; in Uttra Khand
*harish* plowshaft
*Himanchal* Father of Ghora
*Holi* springtime festival of colors
*Indra* Lord of Rain
*jajmani* system used to run society, with each jati having its own work
*jaluaa* women's drama on the wedding night including dancing and singing
*Jamuna* great river of North India
*Janakpur* home of Sita
*Janam Ashhtimi* birth of Lord Krishna
*Janki* another name for Sita
*janmassa* resting place for the groomsmen
*Janmastami* religious holiday; the birth of Krishna
*jati* caste
*jaymala* marriage garland
*jethani* older brother's wife to younger brother's wife
*jhal* cymbals
*jhanj* cymbals
*jhanjhar* clay jug
*jhijhiri* amusing game
*jhumar* woman's dancing song
*jija* brother-in-law
*jiwain* caraway seeds
*kachcha* opposite of pukka; raw; low versus high, unholy versus holy
*kachha* raw, bad, unpaved (road)
*kachhi* farmer caste
*kachori* fried dough stuffed with lentils
*kahar* water-pulling caste
*kaharwa tal* rhythmic pattern of 8 beats
*kajal* black makeup
*kajari* monsoon songs
*kalapani* the forbidden black waters beyond India
*kalas* womblike holy vessel
*Kali* fearsome female goddess, especially in Bengal
*Kamdev* the lord of sex
*kangan* gold or silver bangle
*Kanhaiya* loving name of Krishna, especially in childhood
*kanji* human pupil of the eye, like that of a cat
*kankan (kakkan)* small bundle containing wool, a knife, and other ritual items tied on a string and tied on the wrist of the bride and bridegroom
*Kans* Uncle of Krishna who killed six children of his sister Devaki

***kanya*** virgin daughter
***kanyadan*** donation of the virgin daughter
***karabat*** side, as in sleeping on the left side
***karahi*** cooking pot
***karava chauth*** women's fast to protect their husbands
***karmi*** disgusting food
***kartal*** metal clappers
***Kartike*** Son of Shiva, brother of Ganesh
***Kausilya*** Mother of Ram
***kharawar*** Bhojpuri caste
***khariboli*** Hindi
***khilauna*** childbirth song
***khir*** rice pudding
***kohabar*** holy chamber of the wedding
***koirini*** lady turmeric grower
***kos*** an old measurement, approximately two miles
***kukadaur*** mixture of rice flour, sugar, and chickpeas
***kul*** tribe, group
***kullar*** clay cup
***kurmi*** farming caste
***kurta*** Indian man's shirt
***lachari*** gently teasing songs
***laddu*** sweets
***lagan*** in the wedding, the auspicious times
***lahanga*** long olden skirt, now popular in modern weddings
***lahar pator*** an antique skirt
***lakh*** one hundred thousand
***languriya*** devi git (to mother goddess)
***Laximan (Lakhan)*** younger brother of Ram
***Laxmi*** wife of Vishnu
***laya*** melody
***lila*** holy play, associated with Krishna
***lori*** grinder
***lota*** metal jug
***Madhuwan*** forest, now village, near Krishna's home
***Mahadev*** Lord Shiva
***Mahiar*** a goddess
***mahua*** disgusting food
***maica*** mother's home
***man to man*** chest to chest
***manar*** gong

*manara* "empty" day of the wedding
*mandap* wedding tent
*manjeera* tiny cymbals
*manjhya* middleman for the wedding
*manjusa* a boat
*marawa (mandap)* wedding tent
*markin* thick disgusting cloth
*masala dosa* large South Indian rice pancake with stuffing
*masan* ghost of a small child
*Mathura* kingdom of Krishna
*matikor* wedding ritual when women go to dig the soil
*mausi* mother's sister
*mehindi* henna, used to decorate hands and feet
*mem* government midwife
*monikyamy* joking name
*Mother Ganga* the holy river Ganges; also, sister of Gaura
*Mother Haisati* sister to Baleshwarnath; she resides in Ballia
*Mother Kali* goddess who resides in Kolkata
*Mother Saraju* a holy river; it passes by Ayodhya
*Motini* heroine of Dhola epic, wife of Nal
*muni* holy man
*munj* type of grass used for making cots
*Muralidar* Krishna, who plays the flute
*nachhu nahawan* ritual bathing of the bride or groom
*nachhabar* ritual of giving money to relations
*nagara* kettle drum
*Nagnath* Krishna, who has the bridle of the snake
*naihar* wife's parents' home
*naktaura* at the wedding, women's nighttime drama
*Nal* hero of the Dhola epic
*nanad* sister-in-law
*Nand Baba* stepfather of Krishna
*Nandalal* Krishna as a child, "son of Nand"
*Nandalala* Krishna, son of Nand
*nani* maternal grandmother
*nazar* the evil eye
*neem tree* special medicinal tree of India
*neg* in a ritual, the right to take money for doing a job
*nichhawr (nichhawar)* circulating money around a person to bless
*nimantri* wedding invitation

*nirgun bhajan* often composed by Saint Kabir; hymn to God who has no form; opposite of sagun, God with form such as Ram or Ganesh

*ojha* a person who takes off the evil eye

*orni* olden veil

*pach mangara* the fifth month of pregnancy, the five days of the wedding

*paisa* penny

*pakkah* cooked, good, paved (road)

*pakora* battered and fried vegetables

*panch* village judge

*panchayat* village council of five people

*papiha* sweet-sounding bird

*paratha* fried bread pancakes

*parichhan (parichhawan)* taking the evil eye away

*parvar* type of vegetable

*Parvati* wife of Lord Shiva

*patuk* lap

*Phagun* month around February

*Phagwa* Holi springtime festivals of colors

*phupha* aunt

*pipari* hot masala spice given to postpartum women

*pittar-nyota* invitation to the ancestors

*pradhan* headman of a village

*pralaya* the never-ending water world

*Purana* ancient holy book

*puri* fried bread pancake

*puriya* leaf pouch with dub grass, incense, sindur, sweets, flowers, and cloves

*purnima* full moon day

*Raghubar* Ram

*Raghuraiya* another name for Ram

*rajpat* caste of weavers

*raki* sacred thread bracelet from sister to brother

*Ram* king of Ayodhya; the Lord

*Ramayan* holy book of Tulsidas

*Rawan* villain of the Ramayan

*rawani* Bhojpuri caste

*raxas (raksha)* men with an evil spirit

*rishi* holy man

*rona* to cry

*rori* mixture of rice, yogurt, and turmeric used in the wedding

*sahana* a wedding song genre

*sakhi* girlfriends

*samadhi* bride's father to the bridegroom's father; they embrace chest to chest

*sar panse* a game

*sarahaj* aunt

*sarangiwala* player of the sarangi, a bowed lute

*Sarau* river near Ayodhya

*sarawa* abusive kinship term

*sas* mother-in-law

*sasur* father-in-law

*sasural* husband's home for a wife; wife's home for a husband

*sat samundar par* across the seven seas

*sathi* olden type of rice

*sati* widow burning

*satsangh* musical group

*Sawan* rainy month around July

*ser* olden measurement for weight

*shadi* wedding

*shahnai* oboe

*shamlya* blue-black, the skin color of Ram and Krishna

*Shankar (Shankarji)* Lord Shiva who resides in Kailas

*Shastras* ancient Hindu texts

*sheshhnag* snake in the sea of milk, on which Vishun resides; the Earth rests on the hood of the sheshhnag

*sil* grinding stone

*sinaura (atiya)* container for sindur

*sindur* vermillion, applied to the part of a married women's hair

*sindurdan* ritual when the bridegroom first applies sindur to the bride's part

*singar* sixteen traditional adornments for the bride

*siri* clay pot with lid with a small clay man and a clay ladder inside; essential for wedding in Ballia

*sohar* joyous song for childbirth

*sthayi* melody at a lower pitch

*suhag* the husband is a suhag (ornament) for the wife

*suhagin* happily married woman

*Sunaina* mother of Sita

*sup* winnowing basket

*swayamvar (syambar)* ceremony during which the bride chooses her princely husband

*taandur (tandur, tandoor)* clay oven

*tal* rhythm

*tandoori* food baked in a clay oven

*tante* a string made of a goatskin

*tapas* sacrificial worship

*Tarika* one of Rawan's gang; Ram killed her

*tasa* flat frying pan for cooking chapattis
*tassla* large mixing bowl
*tel* vegetable oil
*tel charana* in the wedding, application of holy oil
*thali* large metal plate played to accompany songs
*than* unstitched cloth
*thariya* metal plate, often played as a musical instrument
*tika* dot on the forehead
*tikh hai* good
*tikh hii hai* good enough (not really good)
*tilak* engagement ritual; also mark on bridegroom's forehead
*Tulsidas* composer of Ramcharitmanas
*ubtan* paste made of turmeric and oil
*urad dal* type of lentil
*Vaishhnuu Devi* goddess from the Himalayan mountains
*Vedas* the first Aryan texts
*vida* departure
*videshi* foreigner
*vilap* mourning
*Vishnu* the Lord, especially as sustainer
*Vishwamitra* rishi
*wallah* guy
*Yashoda* stepmother of Krishna

# BIBLIOGRAPHY


Abu-Lughod, Lisa. *Veiled Sentiments: Honor and Poetry in a Bedouin Society*. Berkeley: University of California Press, 1999.

———. *Writing Women's Worlds: Bedouin Stories*. Berkeley: University of California Press, 1993.

Agee, James, and Walker Evans. *Let Us Now Praise Famous Men: Three Tenant Families*. New York: Ballantine Books, 1960.

Archer, William George. *Songs for the Bride: Wedding Rites of Rural India*. Edited by Barbara Stoler Miller and Mildred Archer. New York: Columbia University Press, 1985.

Archer, William George, and Sankatha Prasad. "Bhojpuri Village Songs." *The Journal of Bihar and Orissa Research Society* (1948): 1–48.

Arya, Usharbudh. *Ritual Songs and Folksongs of the Hindus of Surinam*. Leiden: Brill, 1968.

Babiracki, Carol. "Musical and Cultural Interaction in Tribal India: The Karam Repertory of the Mundas of Chotanagpur." PhD diss., University of Illinois at Urbana-Champaign, 1991.

Barrington, Judith. *Writing the Memoir: From Truth to Art*. Portland: Eighth Mountain Press, 1997.

Barua, Hem. *Folksongs of India*. Delhi: Indian Council for Cultural Relations, 1963.

Beames, John. "Notes on the Bhojpuri Dialect of Hindi Spoken in Western Bihar." *Journal of the Royal Asiatic Society* 3 (1868): 483–508.

Beck, Brenda E. F. *The Three Twins: The Telling of a South Indian Folk Epic*. Bloomington: Indiana University Press, 1982.

Behar, Ruth. *The Vulnerable Observer: Anthropology That Breaks Your Heart*. Boston: Beacon Press, 1996.

Behar, Ruth, and Deborah A. Gordon, eds. *Women Writing Culture*. Berkeley: University of California Press, 1995.

Bender, Ernest. *The Nalaraya-Davadanticarita (Adentures of King Nala and Davandanti)*. New Series, vol. 40, pt. 4. Philadelphia: American Philosophical Society, 1951.

Biggar, Henry Percival. *The Voyages of Jacques Cartier*. Toronto: University of Toronto Press, 1993.

Blackburn, Stuart H. *Moral Fictions: Folktales from Oral Tradition*. Helsinki: Academica Scientiarum Fennica, 2001.

Blacking, John. *How Musical Is Man?* Seattle: University of Washington Press, 1973.

Bohlman, Philip. *The Study of Folk Music in the Modern World*. Bloomington: Indiana University Press, 1988.

Boodhoo, Sarita. *Kanya Dan: The Why's of Hindu Marriage Rituals*. Port-Louis, Mauritius: Mauritius Bhojpuri Institute, 1993.

Chaturvedi, Marmadeswar, ed. *Bhojpuri Lok Git* (Bhojpuri Folk Song). Lucknow: Uttar Pradesh Sangeet Akademi, 1989.

Cheney, Theodore A. Rees. *Writing Creative Nonfiction: Fiction Techniques for Crafting Great Nonfiction*. Berkeley: Ten Speed Press, 2001.

Chaudhuri, Shubha. "Sohar, Kajri, and Steel Bands: Helen Myers' Collection of Bhojpuri Songs from Felicity, Trinidad." *Samvadi, Newsletter of the Archive and Research Centre for Ethnomusicology*, New Delhi (Summer–Fall, 1989).

Clifford, James. *The Predicament of Culture: Twentieth-Century Ethnography, Literature, and Art*. Cambridge, MA: Harvard University Press, 1988.

Clifford, James, and George Marcus, eds. *Writing Culture: The Poetics and Politics of Ethnography*. Berkeley: University of California Press, 1986.

Collins, Peter, and Anselma Gallinat, eds. *The Ethnographic Self as Resource: Writing Memory and Experience into Ethnography*. New York: Berghahn Books, 2010.

Crang, Mike, and Ian Cook. *Doing Ethnographies*. Los Angeles: Sage, 2007.

Crystal, David. *The Stories of English*. New York: Overlook Press, 2004.

Davies, Charlotte Aull. *Reflexive Ethnography: A Guide to Research*. New York: Routledge, 2002.

Doniger, Wendy. *The Hindus: An Alternative History*. New Delhi: Speaking Tiger Publishers, 2015. First published in 2009 by The Penguin Press, USA.

Doniger, Wendy, ed. *Hindu Myths: A Sourcebook Translated from The Sanskrit*. London: Penguin, 1975.

Doron, Assa, and Robin Jeffrey. *The Great Indian Phone Book: How the Cheap Cell Phone Changes Business, Politics, and Daily Life*. Cambridge, MA: Harvard University Press, 2013.

Eck, Diana. *Banaras: City of Light*. New York: Columbia University Press, 1999. Originally published in 1982.

Eliot, T. S. *Four Quartets*. London: Faber and Faber, 1944.

Ellen, Roy, ed. *Ethnographic Research: A Guide to General Conduct*. London: Academic Press, 1984.

Emerson, Robert M., Rachel I. Fretz, and Linda L. Shaw. *Writing Ethnographic Fieldnotes*. Chicago: University of Chicago Press, 1995.

Faigen, Sandra. "Women's Music in Rituals in the Bhojpuri Region of North India." MA thesis, Monash University, 1982.

Faruqi, Ali Azhar. *Uttar Pradesh ke Lok Git* (Folk Songs of Uttar Pradesh). New Delhi: Bureau for Promotion of Urdu, 1981.

Flood, Gavin. *An Introduction to Hinduism*. New York: Cambridge University Press, 1996.

Flueckiger, Joyce Burkhalter. *Amma's Healing Room: Gender and Vernacular Islam in South India*. Bloomington: Indiana University Press, 2006.

Forché, Carolyn, and Philip Gerard, eds. *Writing Creative Nonfiction: Instruction and Insights from Teachers of the Associated Writing Programs*. Cincinnati: Chorus Press, 2001.

Forester, E. M. *Aspects of the Novel*. New York: Harcourt, Brace & Company, 1955. First published in 1927.

Fraser, H. "Folklore from Eastern Gorakhpur." *Journal of the Indian Society of Bengal* 52, pt. 1 (1883): 1–32.

Geertz, Clifford. *Works and Lives: The Anthropologist as Author.* Palo Alto: Stanford University Press, 1989.
Gell, Alfred. *Art and Agency: An Anthropological Theory.* Oxford: Clarendon Press, 1998.
Ghosh, Amitav. *In an Antique Land: History in the Guise of a Traveler's Tale.* London: Granta Books/Penguin, 1992.
——. *The Shadow Lines.* New York: Viking, 1989.
Gold, Ann Grodzins. *A Carnival of Parting: The Tales of King Bharthrai and King Gopi Chandas Sung as Told by Mathdu Natisar of Ghatiyalli, Rajasthan.* Berkeley: University of California Press, 1992.
——. "From Demon Aunt to Gorgeous Bride: Women Portray Female Power in a North Indian Festival Cycle." In *Invented Identities: The Interplay of Gender, Religion, and Politics in India.* Edited by J. Leslie and M. McGee, 203–230. Delhi: Oxford University Press, 2000.
——. "The 'Jungli Rani' and Other Troubled Wives in Rajasthani Oral Traditions." In *From the Margins of Hindu Marriage: Essays on Gender, Religion, and Marriage.* Edited by Lindsay Harlan and P. Courtright, 119–136. New York: Oxford University Press, 1995.
——. "Gender, Violence, and Power: Rajasthani Stories of Shkari." In *Women as Subjects: South Asian Histories.* Edited by Nita Kumar, 26–48. Charlottesville: University of Virginia Press, 1994.
Gold, Ann Grodzins, and Bhoju Ram Gujar. *In the Time of Trees and Sorrows: Nature, Power, and Memory in Rajasthan.* Durham, NC: Duke University Press, 2002.
Gornick, Vivian. *The Situation and the Story: The Art of Personal Narrative.* New York: Farrar, Straus and Giroux, 2001.
Grierson, George Abraham. *Bihar Peasant Life, Being a Discursive Catalogue of the Surroundings of the People of that Province. Primary Source Edition.* Calcutta: Bengal Secretariat Press; London: Turner & Co., 1885.
——. *Linguistic Survey of India.* 11 vols. Calcutta: Government Printing Office, 1903–27. 2nd ed. Bombay: Motilal Banarsidas.
——. *Report on Colonial Emigration from the Bengal Presidency.* Calcutta: Government of India, 1883.
——. *Seven Grammars of the Dialects and Subdialects of the Bihari Language: Spoken in the Province of Bihar, in the Eastern Portion of North-Western Provinces, and the Northern Portion of the Central Provinces. Part 3, Magadhi Dialect of South Patna and Gaya.* Calcutta: Bengal Secretariat Press, 1883.
——. "Some Bihari Folksongs." *Journal of the Royal Asiatic Society* 16 (1884), 196–246.
——. "Some Bhoj'puri Folksongs." *Journal of the Royal Asiatic Society* 18 (1886), 207–67.
Gutkind, Lee, ed. *In Fact: The Best of Creative Nonfiction.* New York: W. W. Norton, 2005.
Harlan, Lindsay. "Abandoning Shame: Mira and the Margins of Marriage." In *From the Margins of Hindu Marriage: Essays on Gender, Religion, and Culture.* Edited by Lindsay Harlan and P. Courtright, 204–227. New York: Oxford University Press, 1995.
——. "Battles, Brides, and Sacrifice: Rajput Kuldevis in Ranasthan." In *Is the Goddess a Feminist? The Politics of South Asian Goddesses.* Edited by A. Hiltebeitel and K. M. Erndl, 69–70. New York: New York University Press, 2000.
——. *The Goddesses' Henchmen: Reflections on Gender in Indian Hero Worship.* New York: Oxford University Press, 2003.

——. *Religion and Rajput Women: The Ethic of Protection in Contemporary Narratives.* Berkeley: University of California Press, 1992.

Hall, John N. *Trollope: A Biography.* Oxford: Clarendon Press, 1991.

Hart, Jack. *Storycraft: The Complete Guide to Writing Narrative Nonfiction.* Chicago: University of Chicago Press, 2011.

Henry, Edward O. *Chant the Names of God: Musical Culture in Bhojpuri-Speaking India.* San Diego: San Diego State University Press, 1988.

——. "Folk Song Genres and Their Melodies in India: Music Use and Genre Process." *Asian Music* 21, no. 2 (2000): 71–106.

——. "The Meanings of Music in a North Indian Village." PhD diss., Michigan State University, 1973.

——. "Melodic Structure of the Khari Birha of North India: A Simple Mode." *Asian Music* 33, no. 1 (2001–2002): 105–124.

——. "Music in the Thinking of North Indian Villagers." *Asian Music* 9, no. 1 (1977): 1–12.

——. "The Rationalization of Intensity in Indian Music." *Ethnomusicology* 46, no. 1 (2002): 1–56.

——. "The Variety of Music in a North Indian Village: Reassessing Cantometrics." *Ethnomusicology* 20 (January 1976): 49–66.

Hertig-Skalická, Jitka. "Fifty Bhojpuri Folksongs from Ballia District: Text, Translation, Commentary, Skeleton-Grammar and Index." PhD diss., University of Basle, 1974.

James, Allison, Jenny Hockey, and Andrew Dawson, eds. *After Writing Culture: Epistemology and Praxis in Contemporary Anthropology.* London: Routledge, 2003.

Jamison, Stephanie W. *Sacrificed Wife Sacrificer's Wife: Women, Ritual, and Hospitality in Ancient India.* New York: Oxford University Press, 1996.

Karr, Mary. *The Art of Memoir.* New York: HarperCollins, 2015.

Keay, John. *India: A History.* Revised and expanded edition. New York: Grove Press, 2010.

Kendall, Laural. *The Life and Hard Times of a Korean Shaman: Of Tales and the Telling of Tales.* Honolulu: University of Hawai'i Press, 2006.

Koskoff, Ellen. *A Feminist Ethnomusicology: Writings on Music and Gender.* Urbana: University of Illinois Press, 2014.

Kramer, Mark, and Wendy Call, eds. *Telling True Stories: A Nonfiction Writer's Guide from the Nieman Foundation at Harvard University.* New York: Plume, 2007.

Lewis, Oscar. *Village Life in Northern India: Studies in a Delhi Village.* Urbana: University of Illinois Press, 1958. Chap. 5, "The Marriage Cycle."

Lopate, Philip. "Writing Personal Essays: On the Necessity of Turning Oneself into a Character." In *Writing Creative Nonfiction: Instruction and Insights from Teachers of the Associated Writing Programs.* Edited by Carolyn Forché and Philip Gerard, 38–44. Cincinnati: Story Press, 2001.

Malinowski, Bronislaw. *Argonauts of the Western Pacific: An Account of Native Enterprise and Adventure in the Archipelagoes of Melanesian New Guinea.* London: George Routledge & Sons, 1961. First published in 1922.

Manuel, Peter. *Tales, Tunes, and Tassa Drums: Retention and Invention in Indo-Caribbean Music.* Urbana: University of Illinois Press, 2015.

——. "Transnational Chowtal: Bhojpuri Folksong from North India, to the Caribbean, Fiji, and Beyond." *Asian Music* 40, no. 2 (2009): 1–32.

McLean, Athena, and Annette Leibing, eds. *The Shadow Side of Fieldwork: Exploring the Blurred Borders between Ethnography and Life.* Malden, MA: Blackwell, 2007.
Marcus, Scott. "The Rise of a Folk Music Genre: Birha." In *Culture and Power in Banaras: Community, Performance, and Environment, 1800–1980*. Edited by Cynthia Frietag, 93–113. Berkeley: University of California Press, 1989.
Marriott, McKim. "The Feast of Love." *Krishna: Myths, Rites, and Attitudes*, edited by Milton B. Singer. Chicago: University of Chicago Press, 1966.
——. "Social Structure and Change in a U.P. Village." In *India's Villages*, edited by M. N. Srinivas, 106–121. London: Asia Publishing House, 1955. 2nd rev. ed., 1960.
McCarthy, Cormac. *The Crossing*. New York: Vintage, 1995.
Mead, Margaret. *Coming of Age in Samoa: A Psychological Study of Primitive Youth for Western Civilization*. New York: W. Morrow & Co., 1928.
Merriam, Alan P. *The Anthropology of Music*. Evanston: Northwestern University Press, 1964.
Myers, Helen. "Felicity, Trinidad: The Musical Portrait of a Hindu Village." PhD diss., University of Edinburgh, 1984.
——. "Folk Music," *The New Oxford Companion to Music*. Oxford: Oxford University Press, 1983.
——. "Indian, East India, and West Indian Music in Felicity, Trinidad." In *Ethnomusicology and Modern Music History*. Edited by Stephen Blum, Philip V. Bohlman, and Daniel M. Neuman, 231–241. Urbana: University of Illinois Press, 1991.
——. *The Music of Hindu Trinidad: Songs from the India Diaspora*. Chicago: University of Chicago Press, 1998.
——. "The Process of Change in Trinidad East Indian Music." *Journal of the Indian Musicological Society* 9, no. 3 (September 1978): 11–16.
Myers, Helen, ed. *Ethnomusicology: An Introduction*. New York: W. W. Norton, 1992.
——. *Ethnomusicology: Historical and Regional Studies*. New York: W. W. Norton, 1993.
Narayan, Kirin. *Alive in the Writing: Crafting Ethnography in the Company of Chekhov*. Chicago: University of Chicago Press, 2012.
——. "Birds on a Branch: Girl Friends and Wedding Songs in Kangra." *Ethos* 14 (1986): 47–75.
——. "Ethnography and Fiction: Mapping a Border." *Anthropology and Humanism* 24 (1999): 1–14.
——. *Mondays on the Dark Night of the Moon: Himalayan Foothill Folk-tales*. In collaboration with Urmila Devi Sood. New York: Oxford University Press, 1997.
——. *My Family and Other Saints*. Chicago: University of Chicago Press, 2007.
——. *Storytellers, Saints, and Scoundrels: Folk Narrative in Hindu Religious Teaching*. Philadelphia: University of Pennsylvania Press, 1997.
——. "Tools to Create Texts: What Creative Nonfiction Can Offer Ethnography." *Anthropology and Humanism* 32, no. 2 (2007): 13–44.
Narayan, Kirin, and Kenneth M. George. "Interviewing for Folk and Personal Narrative." In *Handbook of Interview Research*. Edited by Jay Gubrium and James Holdtein, 815–831. New York: Sage, 2000.
Nettl, Bruno. *The Study of Ethnomusicology: Thirty-Three Discussions*. 3rd ed. Urbana: University of Illinois Press, 2015.
Pande, T. "Bhojpuri Folklore and Folk Music." In *Folkmusic and Folklore: An Anthology*. Edited by Hemango Biswas. Vol. 1. Calcutta: Folkmusic and Folklore Research Institute, 1967.

Rabinow, Paul. *Reflections on Fieldwork in Morocco*. 30th Anniversary Issue. Berkeley: University of California Press, 2007. First published in 1977.
Raheja, Gloria Goodwin. "'Crying When She's Born, and Crying When She Goes Away': Marriage and the Idiom of the Gift in Pahansu." In *From the Margins of Hindu Marriage: Essays on Gender, Religion, and Culture*. Edited by Lindsey Harlan and Paul B. Courtright, 19–59. New York: Oxford University Press, 1995.
Raheja, Gloria Goodwin, and Ann Grodzins Gold. *Listen to the Heron's Words*. Berkeley: University of California Press, 1994.
Rao, Velcheru Narayana. "A Ramayana of Their Own: Women's Oral Tradition in Telegu." In *Many Ramayanas: The Diversity of a Narrative Tradition in South Asia*, edited by Paula Richman, 114–136. Berkeley: University of California Press, 1991.
Sacks, Oliver. *Musicophilia: Tales of Music and the Brain*. Rev. and exp. ed. New York: Vintage, 2007.
Sahai, Prem. *Hindu Marriage Samskara: Marriage Rites and Rituals of Hindus*. Allahabad: Wheeler Publishing, 1993.
Saha-Achuthan, Nisha. "Folk Songs of Uttar Pradesh." *Ethnomusicology* 31, no. 3 (1987): 395–406.
Said, Edward. *Orientalism*. New York: Pantheon, 1978.
Sharma, Russell Leigh, ed. "The Art of Ethnography: Narrative Style as a Research Method." Special issue. *Anthropology and Humanism* 32 (2007).
Singh, Chandramani. *Marriage Songs from the Bhojpuri Region*. Jaipur: Kitab Mahal, 1979.
Talese, Gay, and Barbara Lounsberry, eds. *Writing Creative Nonfiction: The Literature of Reality*. New York: HarperCollins College, 1996.
Tedlock, Barbara. *From Participant Observation to the Observation of Participation: The Emergence of Narrative Ethnography*. New York: Sage, 2015.
Tewari, Laxmi G. *Folk Music of Uttar Pradesh: India*. Compact Disc (Musicaphon BM 55802). International Institute for Comparative Music Studies, Traditional Music of the World 2, 1990.
——. *Music of the Indian Diaspora in Trinidad*. Coconut Creek, FL: Caribbean Studies Press, 2011.
Tiwari, Udai Narain. *The Origin and Development of Bhojpuri*. Calcutta: The Asiatic Society, 1960.
Trollope, Anthony. *An Autobiography*. New York: Oxford University Press, 1999. First published posthumously in 1883.
——. *The Eustace Diamonds*. London: Penguin, 2004. Revised Edition. First published in 1873.
Upadhyaya, Hari Shankar. *Bhojpuri Folksongs from Ballia*. Atlanta: Indian Enterprises, 1988.
——. "The Joint Family Structure and Familial Relationship Patterns in the Bhojpuri Folk-songs." PhD diss., Indiana University, 1967.
Upadhyaya, Krishna Deva. *Bhojpuri Lok-git* (Part 1). Allahabad: Hindi Sahitya Sammelan, 1954.
——. *Bhojpuri Lok Sahita ka Adhayan* ["A Critical Study, in Hindi, of Bhojpuri Folklore and Folk Literature"]. Banaras: Vishwavidyalaya Prakashan, 1960.
——. *Bhojpuri Lok-git* (Part 2). Allahabad: Hindi Sahitya Sammelan, 1966.
——. "An Introduction to Bhojpuri Folksongs and Ballads." *Midwest Folklore* 7 (1957): 85–94.

Wade, Bonnie C. "By Invitation Only: Field Work in Village India." *Asian Music* 3, no. 2 (1972): 3–7.
——. "Songs of Traditional Wedding Ceremonies in North India." *Yearbook of the International Folk Music Council* 4 (1972): 57–65.
Wadley, Susan S. "A Bhatki Rendition of Nala-Damayanti: Todar Mal's 'Nectar of the Life of Nal.'" *International Journal of Hindu Studies* 3 (1999): 1–29.
——. *Raja Nal and the Goddess: The North Indian Epic Dhola in Performance.* Bloomington: Indiana University Press, 2004.
——. *Struggling with Destiny in Karimpur, 1925–1984.* Berkeley: University of California Press, 1994.
Wiser, Charlotte. *Four Families of Karimpur.* Syracuse: Maxwell School of Citizenship and Public Affairs, 1978.
Wiser, William, and Charlotte Wiser. *Behind Mud Walls: Seventy-five Years in a North Indian Village.* Revised and expanded edition with new chapters by Susan S. Wadley. Berkeley: University of California Press, 2000. Originally published in 1930.
Wolpert, Stanley. *A New History of India.* 8th edition. New York: Oxford University Press, 2009.
——. *India.* 4th ed. Berkeley: University of California Press, 2009.

# INDEX

**HELEN PRISCILLA MYERS** has held numerous posts and published widely in the field of ethnomusicology. Currently she serves as Professor at Large at the American University of Ellis Hollow, founded in 1950 by Robert Frost, the poet, and her father, Henry Alonzo Myers, the philosopher, in the rolling hills of central New York State and beyond. There she enjoys total intellectual freedom. Might we all celebrate the motto of this noble institution, "Everything for the Head and Nothing for the Overhead."

**UMESH CHANDRA PANDEY** is an elder and a farmer from Karimganj, Western Uttar Pradesh, India. There he grows potatoes, wheat, barley, chickpeas, corn, mustard, garlic, sweet potatoes, lentils, and rice. A subject since birth of American anthropological research, he has now turned to writing as a career. As he states, "In this post-truth era, I am most concerned with the destruction of Planet Earth. As we say, *prathvi satya par tiki hai* (the Earth lies on the Truth)."

CPSIA information can be obtained
at www.ICGtesting.com
Printed in the USA
BVHW060932170619
551186BV00003B/30/P

9 780253 041630